Justin,

Congratulations on graduation. This book is an insight into officers and how they think — or don't — so enjoy the ride.

John M. Scanlan

SPEED IS LIFE, MORE IS BETTER

John M. Scanlan

Bookmasters, Inc.

Mansfield • Ohio

For information about permission to reproduce selections from this book,
write to Permissions, c/o John M. Scanlan Literary Services
5 Gumtree Road, #F20 Hilton Head, South Carolina, 29926

Visit our web site: www.speedislife.us

Library of Congress Control Number - 2004093517

ISBN 0-9755405-0-5

Printed in the United States of America

Book design by John M. Scanlan and Ryan Feasel

PHOTO CREDITS: front and back covers courtesy of Mr. Randy Jolly

To Mom and Dad, I love you.

To all the crazies that I flew with,
thanks for the fun.

To Patrick LoBrutto, who tolerated all of my mistakes as an
"FNG Writer",
thanks for the patience.

To Amy, who gave me a refrigerator magnet,
please know that I touched it every morning.

Contents

Acknowledgements

Randy Jolly, of Aero Graphics Inc., snapped the outstanding photographs
of the F-18D that adorn both the front and back covers,
in addition to my web site.

The professional wizardry of Rick Hogan, Rick Hogan Design, Inc.,
allowed me to design those covers, construct a web site,
and advertise in the appropriate periodicals.

Andrew Reilley III, from United Webworks
was the mastermind behind www.speedislife.us

Dave DeWitt, of Stuff with Names, provided the skilled graphics
which permitted me to design both business cards and a web site.

Scott Moody, portrait photographer from Pro Photo Inc.,
so perfectly captured the "older me" to convey the narrator's
reminiscing, as well as the passage of time from the "younger me".

Richard Cerretti, from Creative Photography,
provided the masterful shot Of Easy Eddie used on my web site.
It is actually a statue of Huck Finn in Hannibal, Missouri.

Ian Heffernan, graphic artist, constructed the business cards
for *Speed is Life, More is Better*.

The Hilton Head Island Writer's Network tolerated my picking their
brains on the first and third Mondays of every month.

David Josephson, Cameo Publications, Inc.,
was the genius behind my marketing plan.

Lastly, I couldn't have done it without the gang at Bookmasters, Inc.

Introduction

THE BOYS FROM EASY

Pilots	WSOs
Bama	Buick
Booger	Dago
Butt Munch	Fig
Chunks	Frap
FOD	Ninja
Ghost	One Nut
Ham Fist	Ping
Hick Boy	Pope
Hollywood	Shitscreen
Jock	Spine Ripper
Joisey	
Screech	
Tuna	
Yeti (Now a FAC)	

The below definitions are in accordance with Joint Pub 1-02, *DOD Dictionary of Military and Associated Terms*, and A1-F18AC-NFM-000, *Naval Air Training and Operating Procedures Standardization Flight Manual for Navy Model F/A-18A/B/C/D*

CAOC	Combined Air Operations Center	A jointly staffed facility established for planning, directing, and executing air operations.
CAS	Close Air Support	The delivery of air-to-ground ordnance within close proximity to friendly troops on the ground, and which requires detailed integration with those forces
FAC	Forward Air Controller	An aviator assigned to infantry units for the purpose of controlling CAS
HARM	Classified	A missile used for the SEAD mission
HUD	Head-up Display	The primary flight instruments, weapon status, and weapon delivery display in the F-18

ICS	Intercom System	Provides amplification and distribution of all voice communications, voice alerts, and tones to the pilot and WSO
ROE	Rules of Engagement	Directives issued by competent military authority which delineate the circumstances and limitations under which forces will initiate and/or continue combat engagement
SAM	Surface to Air Missile	A surface-launched, guided missile for use against air targets
SEAD	Suppression of Enemy Air Defenses	The neutralization, destruction, or temporary degradation of surface based enemy air defenses by destructive and/or disruptive means
WSO	Weapons and Sensors Officer	The aviator in the rear Cockpit of the F-18D

Monday

1537
Easy 51 and 52 in the Training Area south of the airfield
"Tape's on, fight's on."

"Easy 51 is heading two eight zero," said Bama, the flight leader.

"Easy 52, same," replied Ham Fist.

For poor Ham Fist in Easy 52, today's flight was a rite of passage. As one of the squadron's FNGs - fuckin' new guys - he had been scheduled for a one-versus-one against Bama, the best fighter pilot in the squadron. So far, Ham Fist was zero for three, having been shot on all three previous engagements. The fourth and final set-up of the day would be a "butterfly" start, the most demanding. In Ham Fist's back seat was a very experienced WSO, who went by the callsign of Buick; whereas, a brand new WSO, One Nut, was behind Bama in Easy 51.

At eighteen thousand feet and abeam each other with two miles of lateral separation, Bama initiated the fight.

"Easy 51, speed and angels on the left," he stated, meaning that his F-18D was currently at the proper airspeed and altitude briefed for the butterfly start.

"Easy 52, speed and angels on the right," echoed Ham Fist.

"Take a cut away," instructed Bama.

Both jets executed a thirty-degree turn away from each other, and both pilots simultaneously selected afterburner in anticipation of the fight. After a three second delay, the F-18Ds were approaching each pilot's visual limits, so Bama made the next radio call, stating, "Easy 51, tape's on, fight's on."

"Easy 52, tape's on, fight's on."

Both Hornets immediately turned in towards each other at approximately four hundred and fifty knots. Each pilot raced to position his F-18D's nose on the other and attempt a shot.

In Bama's backseat, One Nut had been unprepared for the g forces that Bama had suddenly snapped upon the jet; consequently, he experienced tunnel vision due to the lack of blood to his brain.

"I lost him," One Nut grunted over the ICS.

Fuckin' WSOs, thought Bama as he continued his pull towards Easy 52. *They're worthless.*

Bama had been flying single-seat F-18Cs for three years, and he didn't like flying with WSOs in the F-18D. Furthermore, he wasn't shy about making that fact known.

"Don't worry, I got 'im," replied Bama sarcastically.

Bama aggressively bled some airspeed with a harder pull to the right, intending to get to the inside of Ham Fist's turn. Then he rapidly reversed left while manipulating the numerous knobs and controls on both the stick and throttle.

Meanwhile, in Easy 52, Ham Fist was behind the power curve.

"Buick, I don't have him," he panicked over the ICS.

"Fuckin' new pilots," chuckled Buick, the team player. "They're great."

"Look sixty degrees left, thirty degrees high. He's the speck above the cloud."

"I got 'im. I got 'im. Thanks, Buick."

As a new pilot, Ham Fist liked flying with WSOs. He figured that he could use all the help he could get. Fortunately, he couldn't have had a better WSO behind him. Buick had years of experience in fighter aircraft, having come from the old F-4S before transferring to the newer F-18D.

"Left-to-left," said Bama with the mandatory training rules call over the radio.

"Left-to-left," repeated Ham Fist.

Bama had been here a million times before. Prior to even rolling wings level out of his reversal, he had obtained a radar lock and heard the proper indications in his helmet. Bama squeezed the trigger, simulating the firing of a heat-seeking Sidewinder missile into Ham Fist's face.

"Fox two", called Buick over the radio, declaring the proper training call to advise Ham Fist of his shot.

In Easy 52, without a radar lock and with the improper weapon selected, Ham Fist could only muster a weak acknowledgment, replying, "Roger."

However, in the back seat of Easy 52, Buick had been here a million times before. He reached down with his left thumb and gave three quick pumps to preemptively inflate his g-suit, in preparation for the impending g's. Simultaneously, his right thumb was dancing on the decoy expendables switch in the rear cockpit.

"Chaff, flares, chaff, flares," replied Buick over the radio, in an effort to save their lives, simulating the ejection of numerous missile decoys.

By that time in Easy 51, Bama had already changed his weapons select switch from Sidewinder to gun, and squeezed the trigger again, simulating sending two thousand rounds of twenty millimeter bullets into Ham Fist's face.

"Trigger's down," Bama calmly stated over the radio.

Easy 51 then broke off the gun attack slightly to the right in time to avoid a training rules violation. Bama was certainly aggressive, yet still safe and smart.

Immediately there after, both Hornets passed left-to-left in a blur with the required minimum of five hundred feet of lateral separation. Bama had managed his airspeed better since the fight's beginning, and was closer to the F-18's optimum turn parameters. Ham Fist had lost control of his airspeed, and was close to five hundred and fifty knots.

"Five fifty," pimped Buick over the ICS. They were too fast.

Immediately after passing, both jets turned across each other's tail, with Bama turning nose low to his left, and Ham Fist turning level to his left. The two F-18Ds were inscribing a figure eight in the sky, and the experience level was evident in each cockpit.

In Easy 51, Bama quickly brought his head into the cockpit to check his airspeed in the HUD, while simultaneously reselecting Sidewinder and jockeying the throttle. Then he looked back over his left shoulder to reacquire Easy 52 in his left turn. All Bama could hear over the ICS was One Nut grunting in an effort to stay ahead of the g's and not pass out, "Ugh…ugh…ugh."

"Fuckin' WSOs."

Meanwhile in Easy 52, Ham Fist struggled to keep sight of Easy 51 as he looked over his left shoulder and grunted under the g's. In accordance with his game plan, Ham Fist immediately yanked the stick back into his lap and shoved the throttle into full afterburner, beginning a zoom climb into the sun. However, his faster airspeed caused him to inscribe a huge arc in the sky as he ascended. Bama seized the opportunity and pulled harder to his left, simultaneously commencing a climb. In Easy 51's back seat, the hapless One Nut grayed out under the sudden application of g's, and lost sight of Ham Fist's aircraft again.

Bama was now inside of Ham Fist's larger turn, and selected the gun once more. Meanwhile, Ham Fist recognized Bama's nose coming up to bear in an offensive position, and tried to collapse the fight by pulling down into him.

"Make us skinny," instructed Buick over the ICS. He recognized Easy 51's impending gunshot, and wanted Ham Fist to place Easy 52's wingtip toward Bama's aircraft, thus presenting a smaller target.

It was too late, as Bama was now staring through a front windscreen full of Easy 52's planform at approximately fifteen hundred feet.

Trigger down," calmly stated Bama.

"Roger."

Ham Fist helplessly maneuvered his F-18D into a defensive, nose-low dive.

"Trigger still down."

"Roger."

"Guns kill on the F-18, nose low, passing through two-two thousand feet."

"Roger, copy, kill," returned Ham Fist.

"Easy 52, 51, knock it off, knock it off," commanded Bama.

"Easy 51, 52, copy knock it off."

"Steady up on a heading of three two zero," instructed Bama.

"Wilco. Coming to three two zero."

In the four different cockpits, there were four different reactions. In Easy 51, Bama coolly brought his F-18D to the appropriate heading, altitude, and airspeed like the disciplined flight lead that he was. Simultaneously, he scrawled notes from the fight on his kneeboard card for purposes of debriefing Ham Fist. Meanwhile, in the back seat, One Nut was just regaining consciousness. His kneeboard was blank.

"You ok?" Bama queried over the ICS, like he really gave a rat's ass.

"Yeah," mumbled One Nut, about to vomit.

In Easy 52's back seat, Buick was simultaneously taking notes while maintaining sight of Easy 51. The precarious moments immediately after the knock-it-off call were fraught with the most potential for a midair collision. In the front seat, Ham Fist was pounding his left fist on the throttles in frustration.

Damn it, he thought. *How the hell did I get killed on all four engagements?*

Then Ham Fist quickly checked the fuel gauges by his left knee.

Damn it, again, he thought. *Shit. Shit. Shit.*

"Easy 51, Easy 52 is bingo fuel," stated Ham Fist, telling Bama that his jet had reached the briefed amount of fuel to return back to the base.

"Roger, copy bingo fuel," replied Bama.

"Good call," Buick told Ham Fist over the ICS.

"That's it for today, Ham Fist," said Bama over the radio. "We're goin' home."

Damn. Bama was good. Real good.

1604 Monday
A five-member Marine Reconnaissance team
on a hill in Bosnia.
Location – classified SECRET
"Jesus, Mary, Joseph."

"Jesus, Mary, Joseph. I've been HIT!"

"Be cool, Sean."

"I'm bleeding. Oh, Jesus, Mary, Joseph."

"Relax, Sean. Help is coming. MEDIC!"

"Jesus, Mary, Joseph. I don't want to die. Jesus, Mary, Joseph."

"MEDIC! WE NEED A MEDIC!"

Ten meters to the east, a dazed Navy Petty Officer pushed himself to his knees, bleeding from his neck and shoulder. With no regard for himself, he grabbed his medical kit and sloshed through the mud to Lance Corporal Sean Patrick O'Connor.

Sklorsh, sklorsh, sklorsh, sklorsh, sklorsh.

"What's the matter?"

"It's Sean. He's taken a hit to the chest."

"Oh, God."

"Jesus, Mary, Joseph. I don't want to die."

"Tear off the rest of his t-shirt while I get him a shot of morphine."

"Jesus, Mary, Joseph. Stop the pain. Jesus, Mary, Joseph."

Riiiiiiiiiiiiiiip.

"Relax, Sean. You're going to be ok."

Twenty meters to the north, a young Marine Captain sat erect. Blood dripped from his forehead onto the gold wings that adorned his chest, designating him as a fighter pilot. He scrambled on all fours back to his radio and grabbed the handset.

"Viper 61, this is Gunner 14."

He heard nothing but the crackling frequency of a damaged radio.

"Viper 61, this is Gunner 14, Yeti."

"Gunner 14, this is Viper 61, go ahead," nonchalantly replied the flight lead of two Air Force F-16s as they climbed back to their altitude sanctuary.

"Viper 61, Yeti. YOU JUST DROPPED YOUR BOMBS ON OUR POSITION."

"Oh, fuck," replied Viper 61, noticeably shaken. "Is everyone ok?"

"Viper 61, Yeti, a couple Marines are wounded - we've got one hurt really bad."

"I don't want to die. Jesus, Mary, Joseph. I don't want to die."

"Viper 61, Yeti, who cleared you to drop on these coordinates?"

"Gunner 14, Viper 61, *you* did."

"I DID NOT," screamed Yeti.

"Gunner 14, Viper 61, well *somebody* on this frequency calling himself Gunner 14 gave me those coordinates and cleared me to drop."

Yeti silently squeezed the handset in anger.

Damn it, thought Yeti. *Damn it*.

"Jesus, Mary, Joseph. Those fuckin' fly boys. Jesus, Mary, Joseph."

"Viper 61, Gunner 14."

"Gunner 14, Viper 61, go ahead, but be advised you're coming in very weak."

"Viper 61, Gunner 14, roger, I copy weak, standby."

Yeti dropped the handset from his bleeding face and wheeled about.

"Sergeant."

Sklorsh, sklorsh, sklorsh, sklorsh, sklorsh.

"Yes, Sir?"

"There's been a breach of security and our position has been compromised."

"Yes, Sir."

"Get on the radio and call the Regiment. We need a medical evacuation *asap*."

"Yes, Sir."

Sklorsh, sklorsh, sklorsh, sklorsh, sklorsh.

"Viper 61, Gunner 14."

Only silence whispered into Yeti's ear.

"Viper 61, Gunner 14."

"Gunner 14, Viper 61, go ahead, but I can barely hear you."

"Viper 61, Gunner 14, I have some information for you to pass to AWACS."

"Gunner 14, Viper 61, repeat your last."

"Viper 61, Gunner 14, I say again, I have some important info for AWACS. Are you ready to copy?"

"Gunner 14, Viper 61, we can't hear you. Click the mike twice to acknowledge."

Yeti sighed and hung his head, clicking his microphone switch two times.

"Damn it."

Gunner 14, Viper 61, we copy your acknowledgement. We've got to go home. We're switching to AWACS."

Yeti felt abandoned and alone.

Sklorsh, sklorsh, sklorsh, sklorsh, sklorsh.

"Captain, Sir?"

"Yes, Sergeant."

"Regiment says the helos are on the way."

"Thanks."

"Sir, how did this happen?"

"I don't know, Sergeant," replied Yeti, shaking his head. "But more importantly, how did they get our frequency, and know that we were here?"

"Jesus, Mary, Joseph. I don't want to die."

* * *

Ten pounds of shit in a five pound bag

F-18D pilots and WSOs lived their lives by a white, eight and one half inch by eleven inch piece of paper called the flight schedule. The problem was, there was just too damn many strings on that schedule tugging on their flight suits. Flying, meetings, duties, formations, lectures, studying, inspections, and a desk job - it was overwhelming. Plus, a workout every now and then would've been just peachy keen. Oh yeah, it would've *also* been nice to eat and maybe catch four hours of sleep. Daily, it was like putting ten pounds of shit in a five pound bag.

1644 Monday
The Ready Room
SPEED IS LIFE, MORE IS BETTER.

God, tonight is going to be a total orgasm," Ping said aloud.

Standing at the Ready Room duty desk just twenty-four hours earlier on Sunday, he had held a fresh copy of Monday's flight schedule in his hands. He had double-checked and triple-checked and quadruple-checked the flimsy, white Duty Officer's copy, because he couldn't believe his eyes. His Monday night was completely free.

To be sure, he had first run his right index finger down the column containing all of the flights, and verified that he wasn't scheduled to fly on Monday night. All Marine F-18 aviators were pretty boys who hated to *not* fly, because it was the only orgasm of their deployed day. However, a day off every now and then was nice. Yep, it was true - Ping hadn't been scheduled to fly on the night vision goggles.

Yesterday he had run his right index finger down the list of names in the upper left corner of Monday's flight schedule to check the list of Duty Officers. Jackpot again. Ping had no Monday night stint at the Ready Room's duty desk as a glorified secretary, answering the phone, monitoring a radio, and jumping on sweat grenades. He didn't have to worry that the Ready Room coffee pot was full, that the Ready Room refrigerator had enough Gatorade, or that the Ready Room itself was clean. Aviators were pigs.

Thirdly, he had run his right index finger down the list of flight notes located at the bottom center. If there were any other demands to his time, then they would be listed there. Shit hot. There was no all-officer's-meeting. There were no aircrew training lectures. There was no urinalysis. There was no formation. There was no inspection. There were no static displays for visiting bigwigs, no flu shots, and no organized physical exercise. There was nothing in the flight notes for Ping to attend.

Lastly, he had run his right index finger down the Alert list in the bottom right corner. Whoo, hoo. Ping had no alerts to stand, fighting off sleep while waiting for the CAOC to cry wolf. He didn't have to spend the night in the Ready Room on the sixty-minute alert, briefed and ready to walk to the jet. He wasn't scheduled for a thirty-minute alert, where he would have to stand in Maintenance Control, fully dressed in his flight gear and awaiting the order to launch. He didn't have to stand the fifteen-minute alert, actually sitting in the F-18D, and all strapped in. There, two engine starts and a flight control system check were the only three things standing between himself and the wild blue yonder.

Now twenty-four hours later, all Ping had to do was repeat the process with Tuesday's flight schedule and have the same luck for Tuesday morning. Then he would be home free for some serious REM. So Ping double-checked and triple-checked and quadruple-checked Tuesday's flight schedule for the same commitments. In addition to being pigs, aviators were also creatures of habit.

First, Ping double-checked Tuesday's schedule for possible early morning flights. Bingo. He wasn't scheduled to get up at some ungodly, oh-dark-thirty hour on Tuesday morning and fly a goggle hop. Ping had one test down and three to go in his quest for some major league rest.

After that, Ping checked the duty portion of the flight schedule. Bingo again. That was two down with two to go - Ping was halfway there to some big-time sleep. He continued to the flight notes. Ping was good to go. Likewise, he had no alerts.

Ping stood at the Ready Room duty desk, totally dumbfounded. He had absolutely no commitments to Uncle Sam until 0730 on Tuesday morning, when he would walk the flight line. Ping had the next fifteen hours all to himself - fifteen grand and glorious hours. Thus, he had only one goal in life for at least the next twelve - to crawl into his sleeping bag, escape from Tent City, and catch some serious REM.

On his way out of the Ready Room, Ping stopped beneath SPEED IS LIFE, MORE IS BETTER., the huge motivational banner that hung above the white board at the front of the Ready Room. The boys in Easy lived by that banner; and they would touch it for good luck on their way out of the Ready Room to fly every mission. That is, everybody but Dago and Ping, for they were too short to reach it.

Ping scanned the massive white board for any possible changes or additions or notes that someone might've added. There was a note for all aircrew to pay their coffee mess bills by the close of business on Thursday, and another note reminding everyone that immediate action exams were due to the Safety Department Nazis by Friday. There was a scrambled note about a possible surprise inspection from some Marine General. There were two different messages for Buick to call his wife. Ooooo. . . could there be trouble in paradise? Lastly, someone didn't erase his blue and red arrows from debriefing a fight, probably because his blue arrows had gotten the better of the red, and he wanted everyone to see it. What kind of an ego would do such a thing? Anyway, there was nothing added onto the white board to concern Ping, so he bolted out of the Ready Room before anyone got any ideas. Ping's Monday night and Tuesday morning were completely free.

* * *

Which was more valuable - a second set of eyes or eight hundred pounds of gas?

One debate that will probably rage forever in the fighter community is the classic dilemma - one seat versus two. Which was better?

The F-18 Hornet was introduced in the early 1980's as a single-seat, fighter-attack aircraft. Then in 1990, the two-seat F-18D was introduced. In this new jet, the fuel capacity of tank number one was reduced by eight hundred pounds to allow the addition of a "mission-specialized" rear cockpit. Yep - mission specialized. What mission? Well, the F-18D was billed to excel at night attack, the rock-n-roll, grainy, green world that was flying on night vision goggles. The thought process was that the extra seat would greatly reduce the pilot's workload, which it did. The WSO's function was to concentrate solely on the F-18D's sensors and systems while the pilot flew the jet.

In any case, "mission-specialized" meant no stick or throttle in the back seat. Instead, the rear cockpit had right and left hand-controllers outboard of the WSOs thighs. These hand controllers had a myriad of wheels and buttons and switches and knobbies that this new back-seater would operate to employ the F-18D's various sensors.

Therein lied the rub. "Old corps" single-seat F-18 pilots would only relinquish control of their aircraft's radar if you pried their cold, dead fingers off of it. The single seat F-18 pilots could already operate the F-18's sensors using their own myriad of wheels and buttons and switches and knobbies that were on the stick and throttle in the front seat. So who needed a WSO in the back? Besides, because WSOs had no stick and throttle, most pilots thought that WSOs were crazy bastards anyway.

Some of the older pilots around the Marine Corps had flown the F-4S Phantom, so they were used to having someone four feet behind them. That classic flying cement truck was the epitome of crew coordination, because of the division of tasks inherent in the older technology. There was "pilot shit", and then there was "back seat shit" - and never the two shall meet. Those two tasks had to be flawlessly meshed to successfully survive in the Phantom. Not so in the F-18D. Even with a WSO seated in a mission-specialized rear cockpit, all tasks could still be accomplished alone from the front seat.

Once, an old Navy F-14 pilot told me that a good back-seater was worth his weight in gold. So it basically came down to one simple statement - the best F-18D pilots didn't *need* a WSO, but they knew how to *use* a WSO.

1941 Monday
In the Ready Room
"I refuse to coddle these young, wussy pilots."

In the front of the Ready Room, Bama cast a very imposing and intimidating figure next to the squadron mascot, "Easy Eddie". Standing four feet tall and carved out of teak, Easy Eddie was a "Mark Twainish" looking imp, strutting home with his cane pole over his right shoulder and a stringer of fish in his left hand. Buick had gotten him made when the squadron was in the Philippines the previous year. He had decided that such a figure would be perfect for a squadron with the callsign of "Easy". Such a carefree boy truly represented a time in life when things really were easy.

So in addition to aviators being pigs and creatures of habit, they were also superstitious. Besides reaching up and touching SPEED IS LIFE, MORE IS BETTER., the boys from Easy also stroked Easy Eddy's stringer of fish. It was a reminder that someday they too, like that little boy, would be going home.

But fish be damned, there was Bama. In his left hand, he held a wooden model of an F-18D that had been impaled on the end of a wooden stick. In his right hand, he clutched another airplane model on the end of a wooden rod, only that one was a Russian Mig-29. Behind him was a white board, upon which had been drawn the spaghetti of blue and red arrows from today's fights. To Bama's right, in a cabinet on the floor, was a massive conglomeration of tape players and video machines and cables and boxes and wiring, used to show over and over and over and over and over and over and over again how Easy 51 had killed Easy 52.

"Ok, that completes the butterfly start," said Bama. "Any questions?"

His captive audience of three tired aviators said nothing. They were all brain dead. Two hours was a long time for a flight debrief, especially for poor Ham Fist. He had been totally humiliated. Furthermore, the brain could only absorb what the butt could handle, and Buick was squirming in his seat, trying to get the blood flow back to his Gluteus Maximus.

"Well, then, that wraps it up," concluded Bama.

Ham Fist stood up, grabbed his nav bag, and began the long trek to the Ready Room door with his tail between his legs.

"Ham Fist," said Bama.

"Yes, Sir?" returned the vanquished pilot, stopping in his tracks.

"I'll catch you some time tomorrow," commanded Bama, "and then just you–n-me will talk pilot shit for a couple more hours."

"Yes, Sir," said Ham Fist, continuing his tired trek to the door, scuffling his boots.

"Sir, do you have anything for me?" inquired One Nut, as he stood up.

"No, One Nut, you did fine today," Bama returned quickly, obviously blowing off the young WSO's request for flight performance feedback. To Bama, WSOs weren't worth the effort. Buick made a mental note, but said nothing.

One Nut retrieved his nav bag from beneath his seat, and stepped off in a lively manner to catch up with Ham Fist, his FNG tent mate.

Meanwhile, Buick had already stood and stretched, in addition to getting a cup of tepid, muddy coffee from the machine next to the duty desk.

The only other Officer in the Ready Room was Booger. He was the last Duty Officer of the day; consequently, he was required to man the duty desk until Easy 51 and 52 had safely returned. He wiled away the empty hours with a small piece of rope that he always carried with him. Booger had been on the sailing team in college; thus, he could work magic tying and untying all kinds of knots.

"Booger, what are you still doing here?" asked Bama.

"Yeah," added Buick. "We landed over two hours ago."

"Yeah, yeah, I know," answered Booger, "but I had to put up the aircraft status board for tomorrow's flights."

"Good call," said Bama.

"Ghost, Pope, Dago, and Joisey will be here around midnight tonight to brief," continued Booger, "so I just wanted to have everything ready for them."

"You're a good Duty Officer," said Buick.

"Hey, Booger?"

"Yeah, Bama."

"Are you feeling ok?"

Momentarily taken aback, Booger cocked his head like a dog.

"Sure, why do you ask?"

"Oh, I don't know," Bama continued. "You just don't look too good, that's all."

"No, I feel fine," returned Booger.

"Hmmmm," said Buick. "You look terrible but you feel fine. According to my medical journals, that makes you a vagina."

After the laughter had died, Booger continued his defense, stating, "Seriously, I'm fine. It's just a typical Marine deployment - an exercise in sleep deprivation, that's all."

"Maybe you should see the Doc," advised Bama.

"I *am* seeing him tomorrow," said Booger. "I have my annual flight physical."

"Oooooo," said Buick. "That sucks. Good luck."

"Yep," agreed Bama, "I hope you get to fly for another year."

"Thanks, guys."

"Why don't you hurry up and finish that project," added Bama, "and get back to Tent City for a good night's sleep?"

"Roger that," returned Booger. "I'm done anyway."

"Bama," said Buick, "I can't believe that you used 'Tent City' and 'good night's sleep' in the same sentence."

"You're right," chuckled the former offensive tackle. "What an oxymoron."

"What did you call me?" asked Buick.

"Huh?"

"Did you just call me an oxen moron?"

"Buick," snickered Bama, "you just never quit, do you?"

"Good night, Bama," said Booger, leaving the Ready Room. "See ya, Buick."

"Good night."

"See ya, Booger."

The Ready Room was eerily silent as Bama turned to erase the spaghetti from the white board, and Buick flopped his fat butt down into a chair to enjoy his tepid mud.

"Hey there, Bama," began Buick. "I have a question."

"Yeah?" returned the muscular pilot, continuing to erase.

"Do you think that you might have been a little rough on Ham Fist today?"

Bama stopped erasing, but didn't immediately turn around. He squeezed the eraser, exhaled, and then slowly turned about to glare at Buick.

"What the hell are you talking about?" Bama asked between clenched teeth. "I am going to take *every* opportunity to shoot my adversary in a one-versus-one."

"I'm not talking about the flight," said Buick. "You can shoot the shit out of him - I don't care. It's the only way that he's going to learn."

"So then what *are* you talkin' about?"

"I'm talking about the debrief," returned Buick. "There's no need to put such an ego into the debrief and humiliate a young pilot."

Bama whirled about and angrily launched the eraser into the white board. Then he spun to face Buick once more.

"DAMN IT," he yelled. "I refuse to coddle these young, wussy pilots."

Buick arose from his chair to face the challenge, asking, "You refuse to coddle? How would that be coddling?"

"For one thing," returned Bama, "they're already learning to fly with a crutch in the back seat called a WSO."

"But this is a specialized, two-seat jet," countered Buick, "an F-18D pilot has to learn how to work with a WSO."

"Bullshit," said Bama. "An F-18 pilot is an F-18 pilot is an F-18 pilot."

"Not true."

"Yes, it *is* true. An F-18 pilot *has* to be able to do everything by himself."

"You just don't get it, Bama."

"If one of these young pilots ever faces a Mig-29, I want to be damn sure that he is able to kick its ass without any help from the rear. I know that *I* certainly can."

"Bama, all you ever talk about is shooting down Migs."

"Yeah? So? Is there any other reason to be a Marine fighter pilot?"

"You don't have the big picture, Bama," countered Buick. "Sure, we're over here enforcing a no-fly zone, but the *real* reason we're here is support that Marine Lance Corporal with an M-16 who's over there on the ground."

Suddenly, the door to the Ready Room opened, and Joisey entered with his nav bag. Bama and Buick each stepped back from each other.

"Hi, Bama. Hey, Buick."

"Hey there, Joisey," smiled the former football player from Alabama.

"What are you doing down here?" asked Buick.

"I've got the early brief in a couple of hours with Ghost, Pope, and that idiotic little Italian from Brooklyn," replied Joisey.

Bama and Buick looked at each other and chuckled.

"Do you think that you and Dago will *ever* see eye-to-eye?" laughed Buick.

"I pray to God that I *never* see eye-to-eye with that little, Italian shit."

"Good Lord," mused Buick, "the Operations Department didn't schedule you to be in the same jet with Dago, did they?"

"No," returned Dago. "They *know* better."

"Whew," proclaimed Buick, wiping a fake bead of sweat from his brow.

"I'm with Pope tonight. Dago is in Ghost's back seat."

"Well, that doesn't tell us why you're down here so early," said Buick.

"Oh, I wanted to put the finishing touches on my briefing board."

"Ok, well, Bama and I were just leaving, so we'll get out of your hair."

"Thanks," added Joisey, "but I shouldn't be long."

Bama and Buick headed for the Ready Room door, as Joisey searched his nav bag for the appropriate briefing cards and a Sharpie marker.

"Soon, we'll be back in the real world, and Christmas will be here before you know it," said Joisey.

"Yep," concurred Buick, momentarily halting at the door.

"I hope to get a nice sweater for Christmas," smiled Joisey.

Bama and Buick just looked at each.

"Yeah, I've already gotten a moaner and a screamer," continued Joisey, "so this year I thought I'd ask Santa Claus for a sweater."

Bama and Buick only shook their heads and laughed, as they exited the Ready Room for the walk to Tent City.

"Good night, Joisey," said Bama.

"Have a good flight with Ghost, Pope, and Dago," said Buick.

"Eat shit and die."

* * *

Green Slugs and Masterbatoriums

For all the billions of taxpayer dollars that Uncle Sam invested in the tools of war, no amount was better spent than the few measly dollars invested in the simple, green, Marine Corps sleeping bag. What a great piece of gear. Crawling into that sleeping bag at the end of the day was like returning to the womb.

Originally known as "the green slug", a more affectionate moniker later adopted was "the horizontal time accelerator". Yes, the sleeping bag helped the deployment's lonely hours to zip right by. The way F-18 aviators looked at it, if you were overseas for six months, but you slept twelve hours a day, then the deployment was only three months long. Right? Who could fault such logic?

During the warm nights of an Italian July, it was no different trying to sleep than in the California desert of Twenty-nine Palms where Marines trained. Hot, tired Marines unzipped the sleeping bag down its entire length, and spread the two sides open, forming what looked like a giant vagina. Then, they stripped completely down to their boxers, and crawled into the middle of the vagina, lying spread eagle as if they were crucified. Such a body position helped dissipate body heat, plus allowed valuable air to circulate around dirty bodies that missed the shower hours.

The next key to a good night's sleep was the successful construction of a "masterbatorium" around your horizontal time accelerator. Resembling something like the Queen of Sheba's tent, a well-built masterbatorium was vital. A Marine used an odd concoction of sheets, blankets, towels - whatever - along with lengths of rope swiped from the Air Force side of Tent City, to erect a canopy over his horizontal time accelerator. This masterbatorium would serve two purposes - provide much needed privacy, and block out any light that would be an obstacle to REM.

Living in a world where the only highlights were eating, showering, flying, and sleeping, Marine aviators desired to control as much of their lives as they possibly could. They had no power over the food that was served in the dining tent. They had no power over the shower hours that were mandated for Tent City. Likewise, they couldn't manage the events of flights in-country. But they could *damn well* control those precious hours spent in the horizontal time accelerator. If it was possible, one's best escape was to "eat until you're tired, and sleep until you're hungry."

1916 Monday
Tent City, Tent 07
"What the hell was THAT?"

Next, Ping commenced phase two of Operation REM, deciding to forsake the nightly social scene in the Officers' Club tent. Every day in there was ground hog day anyway, so it wouldn't matter. Buick would be sitting on his corner stool, drinking himself stupid. Hick Boy would be behind the bar serving up Jack Daniels with that towel draped over his shoulder. Dago would be right by his side serving up insults. Hollywood would be watching some type of movie from the front row couch with a bowl of popcorn, and four poor saps would be dodging the Queen of

Spades in a game of Hearts at the game table. It was all too predictable. No, Ping could live without one night in the Officers' Club.

Long hours of uninterrupted REM were indeed a rare and precious commodity for a deployed Marine aviator, and Ping wasn't about to miss this opportunity. He yearned for that good, deep, kind of REM sleep where you eventually wake up, and you're ready to take on the world. However, this same type of REM had *one* disadvantage. It inadvertently led to some totally bullshit, off-the-wall, out-of-left-field, absurd, and unexplainable dream. Then upon waking up in the morning, and barely remembering only bits and pieces, the dreamer invariably asked himself, "What the hell was THAT?"

Ping crawled into his horizontal time accelerator like he was on a mission from God. He completed his pre-REM checklist in meticulous detail. Masturbatorium curtain pulled tightly around the rack? Check. Alarm clock shut off? Check. Wristwatch alarm shut off? Check. Roommate's alarm clock shut off? Check. Foamy earplugs tightly rolled and inserted? Check. Empty Gatorade bottle stashed at bedside to use as a nighttime urinal? Check. Ping was all set.

After being up for twenty straight hours, and now having a full belly of food, Ping shifted in his horizontal time accelerator one last time to get comfortable. Ping was instantly asleep. He didn't even hear the grenades exploding fifty yards away on an Italian training range, or the Italian tanks that rumbled by one hundred yards to the south.

With eyes closed, Ping drifted off into a make-believe world - dreaming, dreaming, dreaming . . .

Holy Shit. It was a squadron party - a Halloween party. This was going to be great. Ping absolutely loved a Halloween party. It was the one night of the year when you could be anybody that you wanted, and nobody gave a rat's ass. However, the circumstances were eerie and spooky. Not because it was a Halloween party, but because of the out-of-body experience that Ping was having. It was like Ping was there, but he wasn't. He was walking around, and could hear what everyone was saying, but no one acknowledged his presence. They couldn't hear him talk, nor could they see him.

True to form, this party was just like any other ever held by a fighter squadron - a classic case of gender segregation. The women all clustered together and talked about whatever it is that women talk about. The squadron's pilots and WSOs, even though they saw each other sixteeen hours a day, five days a week, in the same stinky flight suits, also clustered together, talking with their hands as if they were airplanes, and shooting down their Rolexes.

Appropriately enough, the Commanding Officer was dressed as a king. The C.O. fit the regal mold quite well with his studded crown and golden scepter. He wore a royal blue robe, with fur around the collar that looked more like something Liberace' would wear. Beneath the robe was a plain white t-shirt with "fifty-one %" printed on the chest. It was the skipper's favorite joke - that he ultimately held fifty-one percent of the vote when it came to the decisions recommended by his staff. That was the C.O. He always had to be in charge, whether it was King or President or whatever.

Doc's costume was hilarious. All he did was wear his doctor's white lab coat, with a stethoscope around his neck and a latex glove on his right hand. However, he had rigged some kind of a monstrous, fake middle finger that protruded from the ripped glove, and it had some type of brown substance smeared up and down its length. Ping later learned that it was chocolate, after Dago and Joisey licked it off in a scripted move that brought the house down.

Jock walked in from the living room with a psychiatrist's couch strapped to his back. Dressed like some kind of an athlete - even though he wasn't - all kinds of medications for depression overflowed from the pockets of his gym shorts.

Frap yelled "FIRE IN THE HOLE," from inside the confines of the bathroom, and then the sound of a flushing toilet was heard from behind the closed door. Moments later, Frap emerged from the bathroom dressed as some type of a bird. He wasn't the San Diego Chicken, and he wasn't Sesame Street's Big Bird, but Frap still had the full body costume, with feathers and a beak and wings - even booties that resembled a bird's claws. He looked more like a seagull than anything else. Tuna and Hollywood occasionally threw rocks at him in an attempt to get him to fly.

Butt Munch was on the patio, dressed as a kid in high school. Rebellious, fun loving, and adamantly refusing to grow up, Butt Munch sported his old varsity jacket and the cheesy moustache of a pubescent boy who thought he was cool. Furthermore, he wore other relics from the late seventies - bell-bottom jeans, Converse sneakers, and a KISS t-shirt.

Further inspection of the patio revealed Screech as a United Airlines pilot. Could he have made a more obvious statement on his future intentions with the Marine Corps?

Hick Boy perpetuated the Tennessee stereotype, with a Jack Daniels baseball cap upon his tangled hair and a piece of straw in his mouth. He wore a tattered, plaid, sleeveless shirt, unbuttoned to the waist, and faded blue jeans that were cut-off at the knees and held up by suspenders. Hick Boy wore no shoes, and had somehow made the back of his neck look bright red. As if the costume wasn't classic hayseed enough, Hick Boy cradled a jug of moonshine in his left hand. Still, he exuded the air of a politician as he worked the crowd. His wife, Cathy, clung dutifully onto his arm in the same backwoods garb, to include a matching plaid shirt that revealed her massive cleavage.

Chunks and Fig strode in from the grill, carrying a fresh plate of burgers and dogs. Chunks was dressed as an angel, white from head to toe with a glowing halo affixed over his head and a very realistic set of wings rigged to his back. He was pushing a baby carriage for some reason. Fig was dressed as a stopwatch, with his second hand fixed at four tenths of a second.

Ping walked into the kitchen to see FOD and Ninja representing sunny California in their costumes. Both had wigs with sun-bleached hair down to their shoulders, black sunglasses, and white, sun-blocked noses. They sported tank tops and flowered shorts with sandals. FOD had an electric guitar slung over his shoulder, and Ninja held a surfboard under his arm. They were both in their own little rock-and-roll world, listening to some type of alternative music on their headphones. FOD and Ninja also had FNG stamped on their foreheads, but they were too cool for anyone to notice.

Ham Fist's costume was even more appropriate. He had the tail end of a heat-seeking missile protruding from his ass, with the missile's seeker head sticking out of his stomach. His humble costume brought loud guffaws from the squadron's more experienced pilots, who shot him on a daily basis. Lastly, like One Nut, poor Ham Fist also had FNG stamped on his forehead. But a line had been drawn through that acronym, and the letters C.O. scribbled above it.

After Frap exited the bathroom, One Nut slipped in behind him. In his costume, One Nut looked like some type of a geeky scientist or a nerdy engineer. Or was that even a costume? He wore the classic, black, horn-rimmed birth control glasses, and had his greasy hair parted down the middle like Our Gang's Alfalfa. A pocket protector holding numerous pens, and even a slide rule, protruded out of the breast pocket of the obligatory white shirt buttoned at the neck, which was tucked into black, high water pants. Lastly, Frap had FNG stamped on his forehead too.

Then Ping spied Tuna in the living room. God, he was such a pretty boy - like the kind of model in GQ ads for cardigans and cologne - and his costume looked as such. With every hair in place and a glistening smile, he was the man who always commandeered the mantle at the ski *lodge, and had beautiful women crawling all over him. Normal men like Ping hung out on the fringes of such pretty boys, hoping to simply make contact with the beautiful scraps that fell from their tables. Underneath the open jacket of an airlines pilot, Tuna sported a t-shirt from the Avis Rental Car Company, with a scripted "I try harder. I'm number two."*

Spine Ripper was uncharacteristically late to the party, entering through the front door in an executioner's costume. He presented a very intimidating figure in a black, hooded robe, and God only knew where he got the bloodied executioner's axe that was his costume's coup de grace. With that ugly purple vein popping out of his forehead, that dude was wound just a little too tight.

Hollywood entered the living room and began a conversation with Tuna. Of course, he was the only other pretty boy in the squadron who could do such a thing. Together, they looked like an ad for cotton Dockers. But just like his Tinsel Town namesake, Hollywood and his costume both had a façade. Were the strands of hair on his shoulders from a receding hairline? Was that a glasses case in his pocket? Was that shirt just a little too tight around the waist?

On the other side of the living room was a beautiful scrap that obviously didn't get discarded from Tuna's table - his wife, Lisa. She and Hollywood's girlfriend, Cindy, were two drop-dead gorgeous babes conversing on a topic that Ping felt pretty damn confident didn't involve nuclear physics, rocket science, or brain surgery. Appropriately enough, they were dressed as bimbos. Shortly thereafter, Spine Ripper's wife, Susan, joined Lisa and Cindy, only she was dressed as a 1920's Flapper.

Shitscreen came to the party dressed exactly like his callsign - a screen for shit. Strapped to his front was a classic screen door found on the summer homes in Anytown, U. S. A. Somehow, he had affixed all kinds of fake shit to the front of the screen. Thus, having successfully fended off the world's shit, Shitscreen was all smiles and laughter and fun as he carried a stack of children's books under his arms.

Holy shit. Joisey and Dago had rings in their noses like pigs and were arguing about something. Dago was wearing nothing but a sweater. No, wait a minute - that wasn't a sweater. It was Dago's hairy back. Dago was naked, save for the logo of some sports bar tattooed on his chest. He was heavily engaged in a heated conversation with Joisey, whose costume consisted of a flasher's raincoat. That pervert. However, every time that he flashed his coat, Ping noticed the striped shirt of a convict. Oinks and grunts frequently interrupted their animated dialog, yet they acted as if that was perfectly normal. They understood each other, nodded, and continued their conversation, still not really seeing eye-to-eye.

Entering through the front door was Ghost, dressed as some type of an athlete. He was in black, stretchy pants and a tank top, with a weightlifting belt loosely cinched around his waist, and weightlifting gloves adorning his hands. But why were General's stars on his tank top?

Pope walked into the party behind Ghost, and he was dressed as a Catholic Priest. That was a good call. He had a pillow stuffed under a classic, brown, floor length robe that was tied at the waist with a white rope. Somehow, he had obtained a wig that made him look bald on top with a ring of curly, fuzzy hair above his ears. He looked like a fat, pious version of the Three Stooges' Larry.

Bama walked in from the patio wearing a flight suit from the U. S. Navy's Fighter Weapons School, better known as "Top Gun". His offensive tackle body caused the seams of the flight suit to strain, as he strode to the keg like he owned the place. He wore dark wrap-around sunglasses and had mousse in his fighter pilot hair, while wearing a white scarf around his neck and a huge watch. Bama's wife, Linda, clung to the arm of her husband, dressed as a Top Gun Groupie. At the keg, Linda slipped away to the cheese tray, while Buick and Bama exchanged subtle whispers. If those two had been a cartoon, icicles would've formed from their word balloons.

Buick left in a huff to go over to the corner of the dining room. There, he was alone, having planted himself at the end of the buffet line as if it was his own personal feeding trough. Since the metal tub with the ice and the keg was on the other side of him, Buick had grown roots and wasn't about to surrender his position between the food and the beer. Buick's wife, Jenny, was trying in vain to uproot her husband from his throne and get him mingling, all the while growing more perturbed.

Booger was beyond the patio, actually out in the backyard next to the garden. He was dressed as a dogcatcher, the kind that was always after Huckleberry Hound or Scooby Doo. Booger sported a white overcoat, an official looking white ball cap, and an oversized butterfly net. A small piece of rope was draped over his left shoulder. Booger's two guests at the party were two very friendly dogs, which frolicked and played and rolled with Booger in the backyard. Sometimes Booger acted as if those two dogs were his only friends.

Lastly, Ping's costume was that of Charlie Chaplin. One quiet, little comic genius was dressed like another. Ping donned the perfect black derby, and his outfit matched Chaplin's oversized black suit, right down to the giant black shoes. Lastly, he had mastered the Chaplin waddle, twirling his cane and crinkling his nose, which caused his tiny black moustache to wiggle back and forth. The only noticeable difference was that a small red book protruded from the side pocket of Ping's jacket. It looked like some kind of a journal or diary.

Ping suddenly awoke, and bolted upright in his bed.

"What the hell was THAT?"

2021 Monday
Marine Aircraft Wing Headquarters,
Aide-de-Camp's Office,
On the computer
"But it's sometimes funny how the view is much better down here."

Dear Becky,

Hey there, girl. How are classes going at UCLA? Fine I hope. As for me, life is good. But I have to keep this letter short because I am typing on my boss' computer. He doesn't like young, female Lance Corporals getting nail polish on his keyboard.

But, Becky, don't feel sorry for me. I know that you tried sooooo hard to talk me out of enlisting in the Marine Corps. Remember the night of the prom, when you cried because I wasn't going to UCLA with you? Those were wasted tears. Seriously, girl, I have absolutely no regrets. There is no doubt in my mind that I am serving my country with the best people that America has to offer.

The General is an outstanding man, but he's never had a female driver before, so it creates some awkward situations. As for my boss, the General's Aide, I feel sorry for him. He has to sweat the smallest minutia of the General's every move, which must be a total pain in the butt.

Tomorrow night I have to drive the General and his Aide all the way down to some Air Force base so that he can do an unannounced inspection of an F-18D squadron there. Or at least, the General *thinks* that it is unannounced. But I can tell you for fact that every enlisted Marine in the squadron knows that he is coming. As a lowly Lance Corporal, I'm not very high on the Totem Pole, but it's sometimes funny how the view is much better down here.

As for the Marine Officers in F-18 squadrons, I've seen hot shots like them before. Frankly, I don't really think that they match their egos. All of the Air Force pilots think the Marine F-18 aviators are just a bunch of ne'er-do-wells and crazies, and I tend to agree. Becky, they can best be described as "grown up boys with expensive toys". Most of them are suffering from a severe case of testosterone poisoning, so that every conversation that doesn't involve flying is centered on their crotch or women.

Yet simultaneously, Becky, those very same F-18 aviators have an attitude about duty, loyalty, and honor that would make your momma cry. They always do the right thing. I feel sorry for them too. They are pawns on a chessboard enforcing a no-fly zone that I don't understand. I'm not sure that *anyone* does.

Lastly, F-18 guys are control freaks, so it kills them to not have a total grasp. Becky, it's so ironic. As a woman, I have more control over those cocky jet jocks than ANY man with stars on his shoulders.

So how's your sex life, Becky? I would imagine that you can pretty much have your pick of just about any frat boy with an earring and a backwards baseball cap that you want. You go, girl. On the other hand, I can't even tell you about my sex life. Maybe someday I will after I get out of the Marine Corps.

Becky, you take care. I'll write you again later.

Love,
Heather

Tuesday

0448
On the Dirt Trail from the Ready Room to Tent City
"My God, she's nineteen."

Ghost, Pope, Dago, and Joisey were walking under the fading, early morning moonlight from the Ready Room back to Tent City. Their in-country flight was over, and the post-flight debrief was complete. The four tired aviators cut across the dead grass towards perimeter road, striking up a conversation.

"Man, that KC-135 kicked my ass this morning," said Ghost. "God, I hate getting gas from that thing."

"From one pilot to another - ditto," agreed Joisey, nodding his head.

"Who was the sadistic asshole that invented that thing?" inquired Ghost.

"I don't know," said Joisey, "but aerial refueling shouldn't be that hard."

"So how about that SA-2 that was shot at us?" asked Pope, changing the subject. "Did anybody *else* see that thing besides me?"

"See it?" returned Joisey. "How could you *miss* it?"

"Yeah, no shit," said Ghost. "That thing looked like a smoking telephone pole as it came up at us."

"Can you imagine getting hit by one of those things?" asked Dago.

"No, thank God," said Pope, the consummate Catholic. "It wouldn't be pretty."

"Hey, speaking of the SA-2," said Joisey, "has Spine Ripper shot that one SA-2 site in the northwest corner yet?"

"Nope, not yet," laughed Pope, "and it is totally killing him."

"Man, Spine Ripper *hates* that SA-2," said Dago.

"You ought to try flying with him," said Ghost. "Spine Ripper is so intense in his effort to knock that thing out. It's hilarious."

"Spine Ripper? Intense?" returned Dago. "Shit, if you look up 'intense' in the dictionary, you see Spine Ripper's picture."

"It's funny, too," said Joisey, "because that ugly, purple vein in his forehead pops out every time that he just talks about that SA-2."

With aviators being masters of compartmentalization, it didn't take long for the four tired Marines to put the events of the flight behind them. Not surprisingly, the topic changed to women.

"Have you guys seen the latest *Playboy*?" asked Ghost. Evidently, the squadron's preacher of honesty and integrity was not above lusting after the female body.

"Nope," returned Dago. "Is it good?"

"Oh, man. You ought to see Miss July," said Ghost. "She is a definite *ten*."

"No way, Ghost," stated Pope. "I saw that issue and I figure that she's maybe a four or a five - max."

"What?" countered Joisey. "Pope, are you brain dead?"

"A four or a five?" returned Ghost. "How can you possibly say that?"

"Well, I use the 'Budweiser scale' when rating women," said Pope.

A puzzled look came over the other three faces, and they all glanced at each other.

"Ok, ok," said Ghost. "We give."

"When I say she's a four or a five," explained Pope, "I mean that's how many Clydesdales it would take to pull me off of her."

After the laughter had subsided, Ghost continued, stating, "In any case, Miss July is hot. I'd make soup out of her bath water."

"That's nothin'," said Joisey. "I'd eat the corn in her shit."

The other three aviators just shook their heads and chuckled at the latest pearl of wisdom to come from the squadron's pervert. Joisey was pure New Jersey through and through. Born in Bayonne and proud of it, he claimed to have lost his virginity at the age of twelve to the baby sitter. He even went so far as to get a personalized license plate that read NE1 4 A BJ?

"Joisey," said Dago, "you are just a sick, horny bastard."

"Oh, yeah, right," returned Joisey. "That's coming from a guy who calls himself 'the Italian Stallion'."

"Geez," stated Dago, tongue in cheek, "I can't *imagine* why your first wife ever left your ass."

"Hey, hey, hey," injected Ghost, "do you two *ever* get along?"

The horny pervert from New Jersey and the feisty Italian from Brooklyn merely glared at each other.

Then Pope, the oldest of the four aviators, suddenly got philosophical.

"Man, you talk about how things are all relative," he began. "Listen to how four words can change in the span of twenty-two years."

"Go ahead," said Ghost.

"I can remember hiding in the downstairs bedroom as a sixteen-year old kid with a *Playboy* stolen from my brother in college," explained Pope. "I opened up to the centerfold, and thought *My God, she's nineteen.*"

"Yeah, so?" inquired Joisey. "We've all been there, done that, got the t-shirt."

"Well, she seemed so worldly and mature and experienced in an Anne Bancroft kind of way," continued Pope. "Now, here I am, thirty-eight, and still single. I open up to the centerfold, and think *My God, she's nineteen.*"

The other three aviators laughed aloud.

"Now, those four words are said in a whole different context. That same nineteen seems so young and innocent - and I feel so old."

"Good call, Pope," said Dago. "That's a defining moment in a man's life when he first sees a playmate who is younger than he is."

"Well, if Miss July is like any other woman," stated Joisey, "she wouldn't piss on me if I was on fire."

The four stopped at perimeter road to look left, checking for traffic. It was more out of habit than anything else. Nobody was driving at 0500. As they stood there, moths flittered about the glowing bulb of a street lamp overhead, which eerily cast their shadows in all four directions. Their trek continued towards Tent City, actually walking on perimeter road's yellow stripe.

"Joisey," said Ghost, "I don't see how you could ever date a woman, and treat her with the dignity and respect that women deserve."

"*That's* my problem," said Joisey. "I'm a classic case of bitter irony."

"What do you mean?" asked Ghost.

"Well, I don't want to marry the kind of a girl who will have sex with me on the first date," explained Joisey, "but if she doesn't have sex with me on the first date, then there won't be a second."

They next stepped onto the sidewalk that led them into Tent City and turned right. The sound of flight boots scuffling on the concrete belied the amount of energy left in their tired bodies.

"You guys keep talking like this," said Ghost "and I'm going to have to take a cold shower before I hit the rack."

"Shit," added Joisey. "I've taken so many cold showers here, that now I get a hard-on every time it rains."

The foursome's laughter seemed to echo off of the canvas tents that lined both sides of the sidewalk. They were now in downtown Tent City, walking by the dining tent to the right, and the bathroom building to the left - an interesting set-up, to say the least. The standard joke said to flush twice because of the long distance to the chow tent. The four turned ninety degrees to the left and commenced the final twenty-five yards to their tents and racks. Ahead was the obligatory signpost with arrows pointing to various cities and hometowns around the world, ala "MASH".

By the time the laughter had died, they had reached their destination. The four tired aviators split in different directions to each one's individual tent and his personal masturbatorium.

"G'd night."

"See ya tomorrow."

"Sleep tight."

"Eat shit and die."

0554 Tuesday
Tent City, Tent 05
"Tower, Diamond 01, ready for take-off."

Bama parted the flap at the entrance to his tent, and hunched over to make a silent entry, being careful to not wake his tent mates. Half asleep, Bama was still cognizant enough to make his way through the darkness to his masturbatorium. Like all of the aircrew, he had memorized the steps from flap-to-rack, and had made that zombie-like trek a million times before. However, at step seven, he accidentally kicked someone's flight boots, muttering, "Damn it."

Bama froze in his tracks and listened. No one stirred. He slowly continued, but with exaggerated high steps like a college majorette to avoid any further disturbances. At step twelve, he turned right, and resumed his normal steps for a count of four. He was back on *his* turf now. There would be no more flight boots lying on the floor to trip over.

He parted the curtains of his masturbatorium, and sat on the edge of his rack, shaking his head. Bama exhaled. God, what a night it had been. Having just been relieved from the all night, sixty-minute alert, he was going to catch a catnap before today's first commitment. However, that would be the hardest part of the whole evolution - just trying to simply get wound down and then to sleep.

Bama sighed as he buried his forehead into his palms. Slowly, he reached down and untied the knot of his right boot. After jiggling the laces, he kicked off the first of what felt like leg weights.

"Oh, man," Bama said, bolting upright and scrunching his nose. "Is that my socks? Man, I've got to do some laundry."

Then Bama chuckled to himself.

"Yeah, right," he whispered. "During my spare time, I'll get right on it."

He held his breath, and bent over again to untie the left knot. He kicked off his second flight boot, and then allowed his body to collapse backwards onto his horizontal time accelerator. Bama's intention was to simply rest his eyes for a second, and then actually crawl into his green slug - stinky flight suit and all.

God, it has to be close to dawn, he thought, drifting off to sleep.

Three hundred yards away, four humongous Air Force F-15Es had just taxied into the hold short area.

"Tower, Diamond 01, take-off four."

"Roger, Diamond 01, taxi into position and hold."

The lead Strike Eagle goosed his throttles and led the second and third members of his flight onto the runway while the fourth repositioned his jet in the hold short area just to the side of the runway. The three F-15Es on the runway formed a perfect forty-five degree echelon to the right on the available two hundred foot width as the first red hint of dawn pierced the clouds to the east. When a gloved thumbs-up had been passed from Diamond 04, the last F-15E, to Diamond 01, the lead keyed his mike one last time.

"Tower, Diamond 01, ready for take-off."

"Diamond 01, you're cleared for take-off, contact departure control."

"Tower, Diamond 01, cleared and switching."

"Two."

"Three."

"Four."

Diamond 01 selected military power, and accelerated one thousand feet down the runway, where he jammed the throttles forward into full afterburner. At ten second intervals, the rest of the Diamonds did likewise, selecting the necessary thrust to get their lumbering war machines airborne in the available ten thousand feet of runway. The noise was deafening, and the blast even shook Linda's picture on Bama's makeshift table.

The clamor caused Bama to jolt upright, and he promptly smashed his alarm clock in anger. The face of the clock ricocheted off the side of the tent, and the base knocked a tiny newspaper clipping from his improvised nightstand onto the floor. The clipping was yellow, faded, and from *The Tuscaloosa News* dated January sixteenth of 1985. Its entire first line was smudged with a blot of ink or something, but the rest was legible.

> *...who was an all-SEC offensive tackle last season, has decided to forego the 1986 NFL draft, and become an Officer in the U. S. Marine Corps upon graduation. "I want to be a fighter pilot, and serve my country," he stated. "America doesn't have real heroes any more, and that's what I want to be – an American hero." Bear Bryant was unavailable for comment, however the University of Alabama has released a statement wishing this former gridiron great a successful military career.*

Meanwhile, in Buick's tent, he was sleeping off another bender. He snored over the engine noise and drooled a wet spot on his pillow. The roar of the four F-15E afterburners actually rattled his primitive nightstand, knocking an empty beer can onto the floor, next to an open scrapbook. The front page contained a single, yellow letter from a Probation Officer in some rinky-dink, rural American town.

> *In light of your third arrest for underage drinking, I sincerely cannot express my disappointment in you. Today, when Judge Ammer asked me to approach the bench and then talked to me, his Honor sincerely desired to send you to the Boy's School in Steinville. However, I talked him out of it, and promised that he would never see you in his courtroom again. I feel as if I am more than just your Probation Officer. I want to be your mentor and your teacher, and the father that you never had. You're a good kid, but your life needs restructuring and discipline, young man. I feel as if your only*

salvation is to do the same thing that a certain Probation Officer did in his misguided youth. Enlist in the United States Marine Corps.

* * *

The morning sidestep

Remember the Tin Man in the *Wizard of Oz*? Remember the herky-jerky manner in which he maneuvered his tin frame down the yellow brick road? Well, then imagine two hundred tired Tin Men squished shoulder-to-shoulder while holding a cardboard tray and maneuvering through a food service line. That was breakfast in Tent City, affectionately known as the morning sidestep. It was deemed as such for the robotic, mechanical way that the squadron's Marines filed through the line.

0627 Tuesday
The Dining Tent
"Look at that disgusting shit."

Ghost and Pope tried to sleep, but were still too wound up to achieve good REM. Needless to say, the 0600 take-off of four Diamonds didn't help. Thus, they decided to roll out of their racks and partake of breakfast in the dining tent, hoping that a full stomach would dull their brains and aid their efforts to sleep. Ghost led the way into the dining tent, which was divided into two compartments - a service section, and a dining section. Ghost grabbed his cardboard tray and packet of plastic silverware. At least today his packet had a fork. Yesterday, he had to eat his pancakes like a taco, dipping them into the syrup. Ghost then began to dance the morning sidestep, assuming his position in front of the first server. He held his tray out at arm's length.

"Eggs, please," stated Ghost.

"Plain or mixed?" asked the server in a dirty white t-shirt and a hair net. What a waste of material - a Marine wearing a hair net.

"Plain, please," replied Ghost.

The plain scrambled eggs are hard enough to stomach, thought Ghost. *How in the world could anybody eat their scrambled eggs with jalapeno peppers mixed in?*

The server placed a dollop of yellow scrambled eggs onto Ghost's tray, and he quickly sidestepped to the left.

No sooner had the jalapeno thought exited Ghost's brain, then Pope sidestepped to the left in front of the same server, and held out his tray. Pope didn't even give the server time to ask the question, stating, "mixed eggs, please."

Ghost just stared at his squadron mate, who gleefully accepted a dollop of yellow scrambled eggs with green specks throughout.

"Bacon, ham, or sausage," asked the next server, also wearing a dirty white t-shirt and a hair net. His face was bland and expressionless like the first.

"No, thank you," said Ghost, as he sidestepped to the left once more. Ghost was the most serious gym rat of *all* the squadron's Officers; consequently, he carefully monitored everything that he put into his Adonis-like body. The only reason that he tolerated the scrambled eggs was as a source of protein. The key verb was tolerated.

Pope quickly sidestepped in front of the same server, and held out his tray.

"Bacon, ham, or sausage," asked the server.

"Yes, please," replied Pope. "All of the above."

Again, Ghost just stared at his WSO, while the server piled three slices of yesterday's stiff bacon, a pink piece of Spam, and two gray sausages on Pope's tray.

"Man," said Ghost. "You are just a heart attack waiting to happen."

Pope couldn't counter-attack because he had already stuffed one of the bacon strips into his mouth. A drop of grease ran down his chin, which Pope promptly wiped on the sleeve of his flight suit.

Ghost sidestepped to the left again, and held out his tray.

"Pancakes or French toast," asked a server whose hair net was down in his eyes.

"French toast, please," answered Ghost, figuring that at least the bread would provide the day's carbohydrates.

The server placed two yellow slices of yesterday's French toast on Ghost's tray, and then added a plastic packet of syrup that had been floating in a metal container of tepid water. Ghost never ceased to be amazed at how French toast could be yellow instead of orange. Why was *everything* yellow? Even the orange juice was yellow. He sidestepped to the left once again, and then turned to go to the self-service line.

Pope sidestepped to the left, and promptly accepted three pancakes on his tray, before joining Ghost at self-service. He noticed that Ghost had frozen in his tracks.

"Hey, Ghost," he asked. "What's the matter?"

"Look at that disgusting shit," said Ghost.

The self-service portion of the line had a clear, plastic sneeze guard in front of the food selections, and it was a good thing. Someone had actually sneezed on the guard, and no one had bothered to clean it yet. The dried spots and speckles of moisture and mucus partially blocked the view of the food beneath the plastic.

Ghost filled his tray with a bagel, yogurt, and some fruit, while Pope grabbed two doughnuts and three pats of butter. Both tired aviators sidestepped to the left, and then walked into the dining portion of the tent. They walked by Ping, eating his standard breakfast staple of chocolate milk on corn flakes, and Hick Boy, the only aviator who loved grits more than Bama. Ghost and Pope ate silently, before returning to their tents, and crawling into the rack.

* * *

Urinal etiquette, or Joisey's pissing rules

No males in the world are funnier at urinals than Marine F-18 aircrew. Nowhere in the world was this more evident than in the Tent City bathroom building. Some aviators called it "urinal etiquette", for there was an unwritten code of conduct that existed amongst pilots and WSOs using the urinals.

The male bathroom building in Tent City had three urinals, which had both advantages and disadvantages. It all depended on timing. If you walked into the bathroom, and all three urinals were empty, then that was a good thing. You used one of the two urinals on either end - never the one in the middle. This allowed any follow-on users to go to the free urinal on the other end, thus placing a one-urinal buffer zone between the two male bodies.

The code went on to further state that you never talked to another male while using a urinal. You maintained complete silence, and stared straight ahead at the wall. Urinal-to-urinal conversation was strictly forbidden.

If you walked into the bathroom and just happened to be one of those follow-on users, meaning that one urinal was already occupied, then the code further guided your actions. As stated, if one end urinal was in use, you simply went to the other end. However, if a user was unaware of the code, and currently occupied the *center* urinal, then it got tricky. The only ignorant boneheads who always seemed to be unaware of this "center urinal rule" were FNGs and visiting Generals. In any case, you never went straight to one of the urinals on either side of the bonehead and used it, because then no buffer zone would exist. Instead, you killed the precious minute or two that the bonehead had left at the center urinal. You faked blowing your nose with some toilet paper. You faked washing your hands at the sink. You faked combing your hair in the mirror. You did anything, until he was zipped up and gone. Then and only then, could you safely go to one of the end urinals.

Despite the ban on urinal-to-urinal conversation, there *were* times in the bathroom when Marines could talk. However, these conditions only existed in situations where the Marines couldn't see each other's faces, or witness the vulnerability of their position. In accordance with the code, it was authorized to talk from urinal-to-toilet or toilet-to-urinal. Furthermore, it was fine to talk from urinal-to-sink, and from sink-to-urinal.

0632 Tuesday
The Bathroom Building
"I promise that I will never drink again.
Really. I mean it this time."

With only his bathrobe wrapped around him, and wearing flip-flops, Buick staggered his way to the bathroom for his morning piss. Last night consisted of too much beer for him to remain in his horizontal time accelerator a minute longer. He opened the door to the bathroom, and leapt over the two stairs, fighting back a bulging bladder. Damn the luck. Buick couldn't believe his eyes. The far urinal had masking tape across the opening, and a cardboard sign taped above it, stating, "Out of order - do not use." Furthermore, as luck would have it, there was Spine Ripper currently occupying the center urinal. Thinking quickly on his feet, Buick veered right and ducked into a toilet stall. He would fake having to use the toilet until he heard Spine Ripper exit the bathroom. Buick certainly couldn't piss while sitting down - how unmanly. Plus, Spine Ripper would hear it and know. Buick *knew* Spine Ripper. He would tear the door off the stall just to identify the wuss who sat to piss.

"G'd morning, Spine Ripper."

"Hey there, Buick."

Then there was silence for an eternity - only the sound of Spine Ripper's piss bubbling into the urinal could be heard. Suddenly, the bathroom door creaked open. Behind the shelter of his stall door, Buick recognized Butt Munches' heavy feet tramping across the floor. He then heard Butt Munch momentarily halt as he noticed Spine Ripper at the center urinal, and then Butt Munch continued to the far sink. Unbeknownst to Buick, Butt Munch was now staring into a mirror, faking like he was checking his teeth.

"What's up, Spine Ripper."

"How ya doin', Butt Munch?"

Buick's worst nightmare was coming true - he was trapped like a rat, and had a bladder that was about to explode. Buick heard Spine Ripper flush the urinal. Immediately, Butt Munch finished checking his teeth - imagine that - and wheeled about to go to the vacant urinal next to the center one that Spine Ripper just vacated. The code *also* contained a clause about not using the same urinal immediately after another aviator. Without washing his hands, Spine Ripper headed out of the bathroom. As he passed by Buick's stall, he rapped on the wooden, splintered door.

"See ya, Buick," said Spine Ripper.

Then he was gone.

Shit, thought Buick. Now Butt Munch knew that he was sitting in a stall, so he had to continue to fight back his bladder. It would almost be as heinous a crime for Butt Munch to hear him piss while sitting in a stall, as it would've been for Spine Ripper.

"Hi, Buick."

"Hello, Butt Munch."

Buick sat there on the toilet, now crossing his legs. He watched a fly orbit overhead. He counted cracks in the stall door. He read graffiti. He unrolled some toilet paper extra loudly so that Butt Munch would think Buick was otherwise employed.

C'mon, Butt Munch, c'mon, thought Buick. *Hurry up.*

There was only the sound of constant bubbling and gurgling in the urinal.

"Please, God," prayed Buick. "Make Butt Munch finish, and I promise that I will never drink again. Really. I mean it this time."

Eventually, Buick heard the bubbling stop and Butt Munch flush. Then Buick counted Butt Munches tramping steps until he was out the door.

Finally. Buick jumped off the toilet and flung open the stall door. He covered the distance to the center urinal in three steps and flung open his robe. Ahhhhh, it was ecstasy. No sooner had Buick stepped in front of the center urinal, then the bathroom door opened, and in walked Brooklyn's diminutive Italian, Dago. Without any hesitation or thought,

Dago walked straight to the vacant urinal next to Buick, unzipped his flight suit, and began to urinate. It was a clear violation of the code.

An awkward silence fell over the porcelain. Here was two hundred pounds of an angry, hung over WSO pissing next to one hundred and twenty pounds of a half-awake Italian - with no buffer zone between them. God forbid, there was even almost skin-to-skin contact, as Buick's right elbow came within a hair of Dago's left shoulder.

Finally, Buick just couldn't take it any longer. He violated the code by speaking. With eyes affixed straight ahead, and still urinating, he stated a simple question through clenched teeth, asking, "Dago, what the hell are you doing?"

Dago, likewise staring straight ahead, sarcastically answered, "I'm taking a piss. What does it look like I'm doing?"

With eyes still fixed on the wall, Buick continued. "I can *see* that you are taking a piss. I just want to know why you couldn't wait until I was done."

"I had to go," stated Dago. "What kind of an idiot holds his piss?"

0730 Tuesday
On the newsstand at the Commissary
"...speaking on conditions of anonymity..."

The European Stars and Stripes

Printing all the news that *is* news for our men and women in uniform

Volume XIV	Issue 24

Friendly Fire Incident kills U. S. Marine

The Headquarters of the Allied Tactical Air Force is commencing an investigation into a friendly fire incident that resulted in the death of a Marine Lance Corporal and wounded several other U. S. Marines. The incident occurred yesterday in the late afternoon at an undisclosed location in Bosnia-Herzegovinia. Sources at the ATAF Headquarters, speaking on conditions of anonymity, were quoted as saying the death was a result of a breach in security. The release of the Lance Corporal's name is pending notification of the next of kin.

* * *

FOD

The term FOD was an interesting little acronym. FOD was originally coined for "foreign object damage", to denote the havoc that was wreaked upon a jet engine when it accidentally ingested a bolt or a screw or a bird or anything *else* that didn't belong down the intake of a jet engine. Thus, FOD was a simple noun describing the damage caused by a foreign object. It made sense. For example - "The FOD resulting from the right engine sucking down a bolt was the near destruction of the first two rows of blades".

However, over the years, the acronym FOD evolved into several other permutations that would've had English teachers wincing across the country. At some point in Marine aviation history, FOD became a noun describing, not the damage to the engine itself, but the tiny foreign object that actually *caused* the damage. As an illustration, if a pilot was to say, "This morning I found a tiny bolt on the flight line. What a classic piece of FOD," then it was completely understood in aviation circles.

That permutation gradually changed into a noun describing a tiny object that could possibly damage *any* part of the aircraft - not just the engine. The object didn't even have to be found anywhere *near* an engine. In this case, say that a pilot walked into Maintenance Control after a flight and stated, "Staff Sergeant, the rotary knob came off the radar control and went under the front seat. There's FOD in the cockpit."

Later, the acronym FOD became a transitive verb. Maintenance personnel would use the acronym to describe the action of something causing foreign object damage. A prime example would be, "That bird FOD'ed the left engine of aircraft 04."

Lastly, FOD became a derogatory term amongst the aircrew to describe a worthless, piece of shit, pilot or WSO. For instance, "Do you know Bob Jones? What a piece of FOD that guy is."

With so many colorful and varying uses for the acronym FOD, Marine F-18 aviation forged onward with its daily routine. Every single morning in every single fighter squadron started the exact same way. At 0730, every swinging dick in the maintenance department, and all available Officers, lined up on the flight line at arm's length intervals, and conducted what was called a FOD walk. From one end of the flight line to the other, the FOD walk proceeded, scouring the deck for tiny pieces of *anything* that could possibly get sucked into an intake and damage an engine. The man-hours spent searching for such tiny debris was a small price to pay versus the time and effort in having to change an engine damaged by FOD.

0736 Tuesday
On the Flight Line for Morning FOD Walk
"Are you up for doing another skit?"

"DAMN IT. SLOW DOWN ON THE LEFT," bellowed Gunnery Sergeant Morris. "THIS AIN'T A DAMN RACE."

Gunny Morris was in charge of this morning's FOD walk, and he ran a tight ship. He had been fixing jets since Christ was a Corporal, so he knew his shit.

The Officer representation at this morning's FOD walk was weak, but that was not unusual considering the ten pounds of shit in the five pound bag. Standing at arm's interval, walking in slow motion, and staring down at the tarmac, Jock, Frap, Hollywood, and Shitscreen carried on a conversation to pass the time while searching for FOD. Jock was barely awake, and it was all he could do to put one foot in front of the other. Shitscreen was in the same, zombie-like trance.

"Hey Shitscreen," asked Frap, "What in the world are you and Jock doing here if you had the all night alert with Bama?"

The sixty-minute alert was the dreaded bane of every aviator. Starting one day and lasting for twelve hours until the next morning, the aircrew were forced to brief their potential mission, and then hang around in the Ready Room, and just wait. And wait. And wait. And wait. If shit hit the fan, and the call came from the CAOC to launch the alert, then they had to have their jets airborne in sixty minutes.

"Anytime I have the alert sixty, I do the same routine," answered Jock. "After the alert ends, I gut it out until breakfast, cram my stomach full of food, do the FOD walk, and then crash in my tent. It makes for some excellent REM."

"Yeah, me too," added Frap. "I do the same thing."

"You obviously didn't get the call last night to launch, huh?" asked Hollywood.

"Nope," replied Jock. "The CAOC didn't cry wolf."

"Marine deployments in a nutshell," stated Jock, shaking his head. "An exercise in sleep depravation."

"Whoa. Look at that," said Hollywood.

He stopped and bent over to pick up a tiny screw lodged in the crack between two adjacent slabs of concrete.

"Oooo, what a great piece of FOD," stated Shitscreen.

"Yeah, can you imagine taxiing out of the line," said Jock, "and sucking *that* thing down an intake? You'd FOD your engine big time."

"Nice job, Hollywood," added Frap. "That's the way to put that pilot 20/20 vision to good use."

When Hollywood had caught back up with his fellow FOD walkers and resumed the slow motion trek, he changed the topic of the conversation.

"Did you guys hear that the General is coming down?"

"Oh shit."

"Damn it."

"Well, fuck me naked."

"Yep," continued Hollywood. "It's supposed to be one of those 'unannounced inspections', but you know how *that* goes."

"Yeah, for sure," said Shitscreen, "Generals always announce when they're going to do an 'unannounced inspection', because they're afraid of what they might see."

The foursome laughed while continuing to walk in slow motion and scour the tarmac. With their gaze fixed down upon the concrete, the four aviators failed to notice a clear sky and a glorious Italian sunrise. It was starting out to be a perfect day for flying.

"Well, well, well," said Frap. "What do we have here?"

He momentarily halted, bent over, and picked up a small spring.

"Another classic piece of FOD," stated Frap, triumphantly holding up his trophy.

"Nice eyes," said Jock. "Not bad for a WSO."

"If I wasn't so tired right now," returned Frap, "I'd kick your ass."

Frap caught back up with his squadron mates and continued the walk.

"So what do you guys think of NATO and this no-fly zone?" asked Shitscreen.

"NATO?" laughed Hollywood. "You mean 'No Action, Talk Only'?"

"No, it stands for 'Needs America To Operate'," said Frap with a smile.

The foursome laughed, though their daily life was an acronym hell.

"Man, listening to you guys bitch," continued Shitscreen, "you'd think that you didn't like it here."

"Aw, we're just typical aviators," replied Hollywood. "We're not happy unless we're bitching."

The foursome continued to plod along the flight line, staring down at the concrete with approximately fifty other Marines. Silently, Hollywood gave a signal to Shitscreen that went unnoticed by Frap and Jock. Hollywood stopped and bent over, faking as if he had found a piece of FOD. Seconds later, Shitscreen did the same. Once the two were safely behind the long procession and out of earshot from Frap and Jock, Hollywood approached Shitscreen in a low voice.

"Shitscreen, I saw the rough flight schedule for Wednesday. You and I are paired up for the 0030 brief."

"Good," whispered Shitscreen. "Who else is in the flight?"

"Joisey and Pope are in the other jet."

"That's cool."

"So what do you say?" inquired Hollywood. "Are you up for doing another skit?"

"Shit yeah. Let's go for it."

"Roger that."

The two scheming aviators returned to their original positions in the FOD walk, and no one was any the wiser.

0801 Tuesday
In the Ready Room
"That doesn't make a lick of sense to me."

Just then, Hick Boy walked up and joined the gaggle of Easy aviators arguing underneath SPEED IS LIFE, MORE IS BETTER.

Screech, Buick, and Ping were huddled over the Intelligence clipboard that was required reading for every aviator, every day. After Hick Boy poked his nose into the circle, the Officer representation from the FOD walk entered the Ready Room. Jock and Frap came in first, with Hollywood and Shitscreen whispering behind them.

"What are you guys reading?" asked Jock.

"It's today's Intell board," said Buick, tactical and serious when he was sober.

"Intell Board?" replied Jock.

"Yeah, that's right, the Intell board," said Screech, dripping with sarcasm. "You're only supposed to read it every day."

"Oh," mumbled Jock, rather sheepishly.

He quickly turned away to get a cup of coffee at the Ready Room mess.

"Damn it," Jock whispered under his breath while clutching his fist. "It's always *something*."

With his back to the other aviators in the Ready Room, he violently stabbed a spoon into the sugar, muttering, "Damn it. It's just too much shit, that's all."

Jock briefly massaged his temples while all of the Ready Room's attention was devoted to the clipboard that ruled their lives.

"Man, I've *got* to do something about this depression. I've been on a downward spiral since the beginning of the deployment."

Then he quietly inhaled, and turned around from the coffee mess. Jock returned to the crowd around the clipboard with his morning cup of Joe.

"Today's Intell board has an update to our Rules of Engagement," said Buick.

"Let me see," stated Hollywood.

Buick handed the clipboard to Hollywood, who perused it with Jock looking over one shoulder, and Hick Boy the other. Their six eyes resembled typewriters, scanning from left to right, left to right, left to right. Only the typewriter's "dings" were missing.

FROM: COMMANDING GENERAL, ALLIED TACTICAL AIR FORCE

TO: DISTRIBUTION LIST

SUBJ: ROE UPDATE

REMARKS: THIS MESSAGE OVERRIDES ALL PREVIOUS INSTRUCTIONS.

1. RECENT INTELLIGENCE INDICATES THAT ROGUE SERBIAN FACTIONS HAVE DECLARED A HOLY WAR UPON WHAT THEY DEEM TO BE NATO AGGRESSORS. INTERCEPTED TRANSMISSIONS HAVE DIRECTED SERBIAN SURFACE TO AIR MISSILES (SAMS) AND ANTI-AIRCRAFT ARTILERY (AAA) TO ENGAGE ANY AND ALL NATO AIRCRAFT THAT ARE AIRBORNE OVER YUGOSLAVIA. HOWEVER, THE PRESIDENT OF THE UNITED STATES REMINDS ALL AMERICAN FORCES THAT THE UNITED STATES IS NOT - REPEAT NOT - PRESENTLY AT WAR. THUS, THE SECRETARY OF DEFENSE DESIRES THAT ALL COMMANDERS ENSURE THAT THE FOLLOWING UPDATE TO THE RULES OF ENGAGEMENT (ROE) IS STRICTLY ADHERED TO UNDER ALL CIRCUMSTANCES.

2. AIRCRAFT THAT ARE HERETOFOR ENGAGED BY A SAM AND/OR AAA RADAR(S) ARE NOT TO FIRE ANTI-RADIATION MISSILES AGAINST SAID RADAR(S) UNTIL OBTAINING AT LEAST THREE POSITIVE CONFIRMATIONS FROM EXTERNAL SOURCES THAT INDICATE SAID RADAR(S) IS/ARE ACTUALLY A SAM OR AAA FIRE CONTROL RADAR UNDER SERBIAN

CONTROL WHICH HAS ACKNOWLEDGED SAID INTERCEPTED TRANSMISSIONS WITH A STATED HOSTILE INTENT TO DOWN NATO AIRCRAFT.

Hollywood momentarily looked up from the board and scratched his head. The rest of the Ready Room cowboys only looked at each other.

A. THE PREVIOUS SECTION 2. DOES NOT APPLY ON SATURDAYS BETWEEN THE HOURS OF 1000 AND 1200 AND TUESDAYS BETWEEN THE HOURS OF 1800 AND 2000, WHEN THE SERBIAN POPULATION OBSERVES TWO HOURS OF WORSHIP. RADARS OPERATING AT SAID TIMES WILL BE BOSNIAN, UNLESS PREVIOUSLY DESIGNATED AS CROATIAN IN SECRET MESSAGE TRAFFIC RELEASED NO LATER THAN THE THURSDAY PRIOR.

B. THE PREVIOUS SECTION 2. DOES NOT APPLY IF WEATHER CONDITIONS ARE WORSE THAN A SIMULTANEOUS CEILING OF TEN THOUSAND FEET AND A VISIBILITY OF SEVEN MILES.

(1). SECTION 1.A MAY NOT APPLY TO SOME SERBIAN FACTIONS WHO ARE ROGUE TO THE ORIGINAL ROGUE SERBIAN FACTIONS, FOR THEY MAY OR MAY NOT PARTICIPATE IN RELIGIOUS OBSERVANCES. AIRCREW ARE ADVISED TO BE EXTRA CAUTIOUS DURING SAID DAYS AND TIMES, AND IF IT IS RAINING.

"That doesn't make a lick of sense to me," said Hollywood, looking up from the clipboard with a dazed expression.

"What are they trying to say?" queried Hick Boy.

Jock simply shook his head. *Typical*, he thought.

Screech, who happened to be the Duty Officer at the time the message came in, merely sat at the desk at the front of the Ready Room and observed the confusion. He didn't really care about their confusion because he was about to fly a SEAD mission.

"Hey, Screech, what the fuck?" said Buick. "This is *insane*."

"Hey, man, don't shoot the messenger," returned Screech. "I just posted that shit. I didn't write it."

Hollywood continued to scan down the Intell board, flipping the pages, and moving his fingers across the printing as the typewriter eyes continued to ding back and forth, back and forth, back and forth.

32. SECTION 8.A.(24).p. ANY AIRCREW THAT OBSERVES A SAM FIRED INTO THE AIR MUST VISUALLY CONFIRM THAT SAID SAM IS ACTUALLY PROSECUTING AN ATTACK AGAINST HIS OWN AIRCRAFT BEFORE DELIVERING ANY TYPE OF AIR-TO-GROUND ORDNANCE UPON SAID SAM SITE. AIRCREW MUST VISUALLY OBSERVE SAID SAM SITE, AND MAY ONLY DELIVER SMART ORDNANCE UNDER THE POSITIVE CONTROL OF A FORWARD AIR CONTROLLER (FAC) IN A TIMELY AND EFFICIENT MANNER.

33. SECTION 8.A.(24).q. OBSERVING A SAM ATTACK UPON A DIFFERENT AIRCRAFT OTHER THAN YOUR OWN DOES NOT CONSTITUTE A CLEARANCE TO ATTACK SAID SAM SITE.

Buick realized that such restrictive measures handcuffed the squadron, but vowed to remain positive in front of his squadron mates. He dared mention the fact that, for all he knew, the old, Italian geezer who cleaned the Ready Room every night probably knew the combination to the safe, and was funneling these ridiculous rules in-country.

That elderly, Italian janitor didn't speak a word of English, and he looked like a poster boy for Osteoporosis. The boys from Easy had cruelly tagged his as "N.D." - for "Notre Dame" - and the way that the poor soul hunched his back over his cart of cleaning supplies. All N.D. ever did was harmlessly go about his business cleaning.

"Hey, Buick, I quit," fumed Hollywood, tossing the clipboard back into Buick's ample gut. "Just tell me whether we have the same mission or not."

"Well," said Buick to a confused but attentive audience as he scratched his head, "as near as I can tell, we still have the same mission."

"Whew," sighed Hick Boy, wiping a fake bead of sweat from his brow. "Man, they've got to put that shit into language that a Tennessee boy can understand."

"Oh, yeah, I can see it now," said Ping. "See Dick drop bombs on the SAM."

"Shut up, Ping."

"Drop, Dick, drop. See Dick drop."

"Eat me, Ping."

"See Tennessee Jane back home boinking the mail man."

"Knock it off, you two," said Buick, who then returned his attention to Hollywood, stating, "We still have the same mission as before."

"Good," sighed Hollywood.

"In layman's terms," explained Buick, "we are to not allow any aircraft to fly in our designated zone in order to maintain peace between the Serbs and the Bosnians."

"The Serbs and the Bosnians?" interrupted Screech from the Duty Desk. "I thought that we were separating the Serbs and the Croats."

"No, no, no," said Shitscreen. "We're keeping peace between the Bosnians and the Croats."

"You idiots," said Hollywood. "There's more to it than that. We're separating the Serbs and the Croats from the Muslims."

Then the Ready Room interrupted into a true food fight.

"I thought that we were on the side of the Bosnian, Serb-hating Muslims."

"No, I thought that we were supporting the Bosnian-hating Croats and Serbs."

"Shit, all along we've been backing the Serb-hating Croats and Muslims."

"Well, then who's supporting the Muslim, Croat-hating Bosnians?"

Buick simply dropped the clipboard on the floor, shaking his head as he departed the Ready Room. If only Easy Eddie could talk.

* * *

Dick the Dog

F-18 aviators had a favorite expression for whenever one of their brethren committed a royal faux pas. This colossal error could occur anywhere, at any time, under any possible number of conditions. For example, it could occur flying, like if a pilot failed to put a switch in the proper position, resulting in some type of minor damage to the jet. Or this massive mistake could transpire on the ground, like if a WSO got arrested for driving under the influence, thus ending his Marine Corps career. Or it could happen in a social situation, as when an aviator blew it with a gorgeous blonde at the bar. In all of these scenarios, by committing such a foul-up, the aviator was said to "dick the dog" or "screw the pooch".

0830 Tuesday
In the Center of Tent City
"This is Dick."

Booger, piece of rope in hand, was enjoying the quiet of an Italian summer morning while sitting on a makeshift wooden bench located at the very center of Tent City. Behind him, the dining tent was closing down the morning sidestep. Booger could hear the sound of spatulas scraping this morning's leftovers into huge containers to be reheated and served again tomorrow. To his right were the Marine Corps bathroom building and adjacent shower tent. Cursing Leathernecks departed that area, bemoaning the showers having just been shut off and the lack of toilet paper in the bathroom. To his left was the sidewalk that ran into the Air Force portion of Tent City. Down that sidewalk streamed a gaggle of Marines with shower kits and towels, opting instead for the hot water of the Air Force showers. The Air Force hated the invasion. In front of him, stood a flagpole with Old Glory proudly waving in the breeze, and behind that was the laundry tent. Frustrated jarheads smoked cigarettes outside, waiting for an empty dryer. It was just another morning in Tent City.

Booger relaxed before going to his annual flight physical with his best friends on earth - two dogs. At the beginning of the deployment, two stray canines had wondered into Tent City, and Booger immediately adopted them. A dog lover from his boyhood days on an Iowa farm, Booger fed them with food smuggled from the dining tent. The larger of the two was a male mutt, your classic "Heinz 57" variety that would get laughed out of Westminster in a New York minute. The second was a pure black Cocker Spaniel with floppy ears and big, brown eyes that melted your heart.

Booger sat there, petting both of them. The mutt was sitting at his feet with his head on Booger's knee, and the Cocker Spaniel was lying on the bench with her head in Booger's lap.

This is nice, thought Booger, as he tied and untied a clove hitch knot with his piece of rope.

As the trio was enjoying the morning sun, an Air Force Lieutenant Colonel came scurrying down the sidewalk with a briefcase in one hand

and a walkie-talkie, or "talking brick", in the other. He was obviously in a hurry.

"Good morning, Sir," stated Booger, rising from the bench and sharply saluting.

"Good morning, Marine," returned the Lieutenant Colonel. "Lovely pet dogs."

Booger patted the mutt on the head, stating, "This is Dick."

"Dick?"

You could just see the question marks above the Lieutenant Colonel's head. He even cocked his head to the right like a dog does when puzzled.

"Dick, the dog," said Booger.

"Then what is the Cocker Spaniel's name?"

"Screw."

"Screw?"

"Yes, Sir. Screw, the pooch."

The Air Force Lieutenant Colonel stared at Booger, then Dick, then Screw, then back at Booger.

"Have a good day, Marine," he stated, and resumed his harried trek

Booger stood and saluted once more, with Dick the dog and Screw the pooch faithfully at his feet. Yep, it was just another morning in Tent City.

* * *

Downtown, in-country, whatever

All of the old farts used to talk about "going downtown", meaning Hanoi. Those flights were during a definite war, so the adrenaline must've really been pumping when their F-4s went screaming downtown with all the Mig-17s and Mig-21s and SAMs and shit. However, just because the boys from Easy were only covering a no-fly zone, it was certainly no less exhilarating to fly over bad guy country. The only difference was that it was called it going "in-country".

Going in-country to enforce the NATO no-fly zone actually meant that you could be assigned one of three possible missions. A daily order came down from the CAOC, and specifically tasked Marine Corps F-18s with those missions. The missions assigned governed the squadron's daily flight schedule, the ordnance loaded, aircrew hours, and the maintenance agenda - indeed every facet of the squadron's life

The first of these three missions was SEAD, employing the HARM. Because of the large amount of "heads down" time involved in working the HARM display, this mission was ideally suited for a two-seat aircraft like the F-18D. The F-18D aircrew worked feverishly to meet the criteria required by the ROE to unleash a HARM down range upon an unsuspecting SAM site. However, it was not that easy. The SEAD mission was a game of cat-and-mouse, catch-me-fuck-me, played between the WSO working the HARM display, and the operator of the SAM site's radar.

0852 Tuesday
Easy 01 and 02, SEAD mission,
proceeding to the Tanker Track
"I love it when a plan comes together."

Spine Ripper had a personal vendetta against the SA-2 SAM site in their zone's northwest corner. It was an SA-2 that had bagged his Dad's F-4J over Hanoi, causing him to endure six years of hell as a POW. Thus, Spine Ripper was on a mission from God to launch a HARM against that SA-2, and he was going to do it if it was the last thing he did on earth.

"Sky Eye, Easy 01," stated Spine Ripper with an air of confidence from the back seat of his F-18D.

"Easy 01, this is Sky Eye, go ahead."

Spine Ripper absolutely loved Sky Eye, the American AWACS. Having a good AWACS controller was better than sex, and Spine Ripper recognized the voice as one of their best and brightest.

"Sky Eye, Easy 01 is a flight of two Hornets, checking in."

"Roger, Easy 01, Sky Eye has you radar contact. Proceed to Texaco. He is presently on station, bearing one five six, for five one miles."

Texaco today was supposed to be Bastion 41, an Air Force KC-10. Getting gas from the KC-10 would be a piece of cake. Then after aerial refueling with Bastion, the two F-18Ds would go in-country for their SEAD mission.

Spine Ripper's pilot, Butt Munch, steadied Easy 01 on a heading of one five five as Spine Ripper readied the HARM in the back seat. He ran through the numerous built-in-tests that the missile required, and was ecstatic when the left screen showed the HARM was a 'go'. Maybe today would finally be his lucky day against Mr. SA-2. In a perfect combat spread position, Screech, the pilot of Easy 02, maintained formation on Easy 01, while in the back seat, Fig commenced the same preparations for their HARM.

Masterfully working the radar from the front seat, Butt Munch mimicked Sky Eye's call, stating, "Sky Eye, Easy 01, radar contact Texaco, one six zero, four eight miles, request switch."

Sky Eye knew F-18Ds as if he was right there in the cockpit, and he quickly responded to Butt Munch, saying, "Easy 01, Sky Eye, you're cleared to switch frequencies. Report back when done with Texaco."

Damn, he was good.

"Sky Eye, Easy 01, switching. Flight go."

"Easy 02, switching."

Butt Munch switched the number one radio to the tanker primary frequency, while Spine Ripper continued to program the HARM.

"Bastion 41, Easy 01," said Butt Munch.

"Easy 01, Bastion 41, go ahead."

"Flight of two Hornets, four five miles out, we're radar contact."

"Easy 01, Bastion copies. Report the starboard observation position with switches safe and nose cold," instructed the Air Force KC-10, demanding that all of the F-18's switches be placed to the 'safe' position and the radar turned to 'standby' for safety purposes. "Be advised, we've got two chicks presently in tow. Black 21 is waiting to get their gas after you."

"Bastion 41, Easy 01, roger, copy Black 21. I'd like to call your turn at twelve miles if that's ok with you."

"Easy 01, Bastion 41, no problem, call our turn."

To rendezvous with an aerial refueling aircraft was a tricky business, and Butt Munch knew it. Thus, instead of maneuvering his F-18Ds to roll out behind the KC-10, Butt Munch always preferred to do the *opposite* – have the KC-10 turn in front of them. To complete such a ballet, he intended to make a radio transmission at twelve miles telling the KC-10 to turn in front of the F-18Ds, thus expediting the whole rendezvous.

Now down to thirty-five miles and armed with the new information about Black 21, Butt Munch broke the radar lock on the KC-10 and put the radar into a different search mode. In the back seat, Spine Ripper checked his copy of the CAOC's mission assignment order.

Hmmmm, thought Spine Ripper. *Black 21 flight is early.*

Black 21 was a flight of two French Mirage 2000s tasked to share the morning air-to-air mission with some Dutch F-16s. Black 21 couldn't go in-country until the Marine F-18D HARM shooters were on station, and Easy 01 showed themselves to be right on time.

Just then, Butt Munch broke out two smaller blips on the radar in trail of Bastion. A quick call to Easy 02 on the number two radio confirmed the radar picture that Butt Munch was painting - two Mirage 2000s trailing Bastion 41. Things were going so well that nobody talked on the radios for the next minute, until the next Easy flight of Hornets checked in with the KC-10.

"Bastion 41, Easy 03."

"Easy 03, Bastion 41, go ahead."

"Flight of two F-18s, fifty miles out, radar contact."

"Easy 03, Bastion 41, roger. Report starboard observation with switches safe and nose cold," commanded the KC-10. "Be advised, two chicks in tow, Black 21, waiting to get gas after your playmates, Easy 01 and 02, who are presently about twenty miles out."

"Bastion 41, Easy 03, copy all."

Easy 03 and 04, like Black 21, were not allowed in-country until Easy 01 was established on station with his HARM.

"Spine Ripper, it looks like all the players are here," declared Butt Munch on the ICS. "I love it when a plan comes together."

"Roger that," replied Spine Ripper. "It would be even better to go back home with one less HARM."

Butt Munch only shook his head in the front cockpit, imagining Spine Ripper in the back seat, with that vein popping out of his forehead like it always did.

"Today's the day," said Spine Ripper. "We're going to nail that bastard SA-2."

Now down to fifteen miles separation and with seven hundred knots of closure towards each other, the aerial ballet was about to begin.

"Bastion 41, Easy 01, fourteen miles, standby."

Easy 01, Bastion 41, standing by."

That transmission was followed by an anxious moment of silence for Butt Munch. Tuna always preached turning the tanker at fifteen miles, and Screech swore by ten. Butt Munch would split the difference and see what happened. He certainly didn't want to dick the dog on this rendezvous with the tanker.

"Bastion 41, Easy 01, twelve miles, start your turn."

At Butt Munches command, the KC-10 began a standard rate left turn. If Butt Munch had timed it correctly with the twelve mile call, the KC-10 would roll out directly in front of Easy 01, on the same heading and airspeed. Butt Munch slowed his Hornet down to three hundred knots, and ensured compliance with the KC-10's two requests - switches safe and nose cold. Lastly, Butt Munch flipped the refuel probe switch, and the F-18D's refueling probe emerged out of the right side of the fuselage just below the canopy and a little forward. Easy 02 remained silently perched on the right side of Easy 01, and the two Mirage 2000s climbed one thousand feet higher and lagged the KC-10's turn to stay safely out of the way.

Butt Munch, now looking at the KC-10's belly from seven miles, jockeyed his throttles to control the separation and closure that he would have when the KC-10 rolled wings level. He keyed the ICS once more, noting, "God, Spine Ripper, look at the length of the hose on that baby. Isn't that a thing of beauty? It beats the shit out of a KC-135."

Spine Ripper could only laugh before adding, "Yeah, Butt Munch, I *hate* getting gas from the 135."

Pilots simply loved the Air Force KC-10. This refueling would be duck soup. And it was all because of two simple things – the longer length of the KC-10's refueling hose, and the forgiving flexibility of the KC-10's larger refueling basket. The KC-10 made aerial refueling damn near effortless.

Butt Munch didn't even have to key the ICS in the front seat, for Spine Ripper could already hear the jubilant yelling in the back seat anyway.

"Whoo, hoo," yelled Butt Munch. "Just look at this shit. Am I good or what?"

As the Air Force KC-10 rolled wings level, Easy 01 came out in the perfect starboard observation position. At one thousand feet above and one thousand feet behind the KC-10, Butt Munch had completed a textbook rendezvous. He would definitely let Tuna and Screech hear about this one.

"Bastion 41, Easy 01, starboard observation, switches safe, nose cold."

"Easy 01, Bastion 41, you're cleared to the pre-contact position."

Butt Munch slowly maneuvered his F-18D down and to the left, to arrive at a stabilized position behind the hose's refueling basket.

"Bastion 41, Easy 01, pre-contact position."

"Easy 01, Bastion 41, cleared to plug."

Butt Munch goosed the throttles forward ever so slightly, and his Hornet inched its way toward the basket with the required three to four knots of closure. The refueling probe nicked the inside of the circular basket at the two o'clock position, and Butt Munch immediately tapped left rudder to drive the probe into the center. The refueling probe made the familiar clunk, indicating that it was locked into the basket, and the

KC-10's take-up reel sucked in a tiny amount of the hose to maintain constant tension.

"Bastion 41, Easy 01, contact."

"Easy 01, Bastion 41, good fuel flow."

On the underside of the KC-10's fuselage, a tiny green light illuminated to confirm the radio call just made by Bastion 41. The two aircraft were now connected at the basket with good fuel flow from the KC-10. Spine Ripper checked the fuel gauges down by his left knee, and confirmed the same. The digital numbers showing total fuel were slowly clicking upward.

"Concur with Bastion," said Spine Ripper. "I show good fuel flow back here."

"Roger that," replied Butt Munch. "Thanks."

"Nice job – in on the first try," added his WSO.

"Thanks, Spine Ripper."

It would take a good five minutes to top off the F-18D with gas, so Spine Ripper liked to talk to both his pilot and the KC-10 crew to pass the time.

"Hey Butt Munch," queried Spine Ripper on the ICS. "Did you happen to notice the markings on Bastion's tail?"

That Spine Ripper is just a packet of wound up energy, thought Butt Munch.

Since he was concentrating so intently on maintaining position on the KC-10, and simultaneously staying plugged into the basket, there was no way that Butt Munch could see the markings on the KC-10's tail. He simply replied, "No. What were they?"

"Wisconsin Air National Guard," stated Spine Ripper. "They're *cheese-heads*."

That was all the more reason for Butt Munch and Spine Ripper to bullshit with the KC-10 aircrew. Air Force Reservists and members of the Air National Guard frequently filled the refueling track with KC-10s and KC-135s for their annual two-week stint of active duty. Thus, they were always abreast of the latest news from back in the real world, and they were actually quite eager to spread the word to inquisitive ears.

Butt Munch, the son of a Polish butcher from the south side of Chicago, absolutely loved his beer, his brats, and his Bears. Thus, he just *had* to ask, "Hey Bastion, any Packer fans on board?"

That opened the floodgates. For the next few minutes, as the conversation ranged from Brett Favre and the frozen tundra of Lambeau Field to Mike Singletary and his psychotic eyes, Screech and Fig could only wonder what the Mirage 2000 pilots were thinking. Most of the

French pilots spoke a bastardized English at best, so Spine Ripper's imitation of Chris Berman on "ESPN" probably went right over their heads.

"He could - go - all - the - way."

* * *

The Finger Wave

There was a bitter irony that existed in the relationship between Marine F-18 aviators and their Navy Doctor. In the *real* world, whenever a person got sick, the first person that he saw was his doctor. Not so in Marine Aviation. Whenever an aviator got sick, the doctor was the LAST person on earth that he wanted to see, for fear of getting grounded. Was that crazy or what?

For Booger, it was that time of the year again for the most dreaded requirement in Marine Corps aviation - the annual flight physical. Every year within a sixty-day window around an aviator's birthday, he was required to get a complete flight physical from head to toe. Administered by the squadron's Navy doctor, called a flight surgeon, this annual hurdle was more like an aviator throwing his body to the mercy of Navy Medicine, so that they could find something - indeed *anything* - that would ground him.

Affectionately known as "Doc", each squadron had one flight surgeon. These doctors were Navy Lieutenants who had graduated from the Armed Forces Medical College. However, instead of being massively in debt like their civilian counterparts graduating from civilian Med School, these Navy doctors merely owed time back to Uncle Sam as a payback for his medical degree.

Whatever possessed a young man to become a doctor in the Navy was beyond most aviators. He could be making a gazillion dollars in the real world, and have a normal life to boot, but instead he chose to endure the rigors and hardships of life with the Marine Corps. God bless all of the Navy's flight surgeons, for they all had hearts of gold, and really *did* have the aviator's best interests in mind - despite having to administer these annual physicals.

Hopefully, the end result of this annual abuse and mental anguish was the ever elusive "up chit" - a simple, five inch by nine inch, standard Navy form in triplicate. Once the squadron's flight surgeon had applied his signature at the bottom, it guaranteed the aviator of at least one more year of flying. Waivers for various physical conditions were difficult to obtain, but not impossible. Once an F-18 aviator had gotten a waiver and squeaked by for another year of flying, the waiver became his own personal scarlet letter. But that didn't matter. He still had the Doc's signature on an up chit.

Standing between most aviators and the flight surgeon's signature was a two-hour hell of having their bodies poked and prodded, felt and fondled, in ways that only Satan could devise. The absolute worst violation of an aviator's body was "the finger wave". Intended as a check for prostate cancer, this humiliating act was always preceded by Doc snapping on a latex glove, while making chatty small talk. Mere words cannot describe the pain that followed. Sometimes, with a little luck, the Doc was a female flight surgeon, whose fingers were no bigger around than a pencil. At least that pain was bearable. But no, usually you got a male flight surgeon with fingers like a cucumber and a sadistic desire to completely check the prostate gland.

Other obstacles between the aviator and Doc's signature were the tests for testicular cancer and a hernia. The classic line "Turn your head and cough" is probably etched in granite on a monument at the Armed Forces Medical College. The earlier good fortune of having a female flight surgeon for the finger wave was always counter-balanced by the bad luck of having to "cough" for her later. After having seen the penis of every other pilot and WSO in the squadron, she knew who was hung like a horse and who was hung like a tuna can.

Every flight physical started the same. The aviator reported to the Hospital at 0730, checked out his medical records, and proceeded to a room called Physical Exams. No flight physical would be complete without reams of paperwork, and the Navy took that to extremes.

First, the hapless aviator was given a standard Navy form called the NAVMED 6120/2 Rev. (11-79) S/N 0105-LF-206-3071, or the Officer Physical Examination Questionnaire. This form contained a laundry list of bodily malfunctions on both the front and back. To the immediate right of each malfunction, he had to check "yes" or "no" as to whether he had experienced any of those symptoms, problems, or difficulties since the last physical. One couldn't help but think that if he *had* experienced any of those difficulties, then this exam was the *least* of his worries, because he was probably near death. Dizziness? Fainting spells? Bloody stool? Loss of appetite? Painful erections? Frequent or painful urination? Jaundice? Hepatitis? Rupture? Hernia? Rectal disease? VD? Lameness? Loss of a finger or toe? Paralysis? Depression? Loss of memory? Periods of unconsciousness? It was all there - even persistent bed wetting since age twelve. Yeah…right. Like an F-18 jet jock was going to admit having *any* of those problems to a Navy doctor, and get himself grounded.

Lastly, after getting blood samples drawn, a stool sample taken, urine samples given, an EKG, and a hearing test, the aviator went into the flight surgeon's office with Standard form 88 (Rev 3-89) NSN 7540-00-634-4038-88-124, or the Report of Medical Examination. The flight surgeon shut the door to his office, and the aviator stripped to his underwear and socks. The chamber of horrors had officially been entered.

0912 Tuesday
U. S. Air Force Hospital,
In The Cramped Office given to the U. S. Navy Flight Surgeons of Deployed Marine F-18 Squadrons
"That's a one way tunnel back there."

As Doc knelt on the floor, frantically searching under the sink, Booger humbly stood in a green t-shirt, underwear, and black socks. He scanned about Doc's office as various objects were tossed out from beneath the sink.

"Now where did I put those damn things?" mumbled Doc from amongst the pipes, as a roll of medical tape flew out from beneath.

The office of a Navy flight surgeon was absolutely *nothing* like that of a doctor back in the real world. In place of the classic Norman Rockwell paintings on the wall, there was only a classic, tattered "Go Navy" poster above the chair containing Booger's flight suit. There were no nicely framed pictures, or volumes of medical text stored neatly in a cabinet. Instead, the walls were covered with a half-finished paint job that matched flimsy, metal cabinets containing old textbooks from the Armed Forces Medical College.

"I *know* that I put them down here somewhere," assured Doc as some sponges and cough syrup were set on the floor next to the scissors and tweezers.

Booger's eyes continued to scan. There was no fancy, framed diploma from an Ivy League medical school, but instead another yellowed poster, this one depicting the hazards of sexually transmitted diseases.

"Remember to wear your rain coat," read Booger, on a poster endorsing condoms.

"Hang with me, Booger," instructed Doc from beneath the sink, tossing out a roll of toilet paper and a box of gauze. "They're down here somewhere."

Booger noted the clutter on Doc's desk, and the running shoes and stinky jock left out on his chair.

"AHA. Here they are."

Booger squirmed, feeling his sphincter muscles tighten just a little.

Doc backed out from under the sink, with a tiny cardboard box in his left hand.

"I knew they were under there somewhere."

The young Navy Lieutenant opened the box and pulled out a latex glove. He wrestled it onto his left hand, tugging and pulling and yanking until it covered down to his wrist and looked like a sickly pale layer of white skin. SNAP. The glove was secure.

God, he's got an enormous middle finger, thought Booger.

"Booger, you have nothing to worry about it. This is a routine medical procedure, and one that should be completed annually by every male over forty."

"Doc, I'm nowhere near forty," sighed Booger. "Besides, I don't care about *any* of that medical shit. As far as I'm concerned, that's a one-way tunnel back there."

"Booger, relax."

"What exactly are you checking for, anyway, when you do the finger wave?"

"It's an examination of your prostate gland."

"And what does my prostrate gland do?"

"No, that's *prostate*, with only one 'r'," corrected Doc. "It's your prostate gland."

"Ok, ok. So what does it do?"

"Your prostate gland manufactures the semen that contains your sperm," lectured Doc, still tugging and pulling and yanking on the white latex glove. "Booger, are you single or married?"

"Single," said Booger, realizing the importance of his prostate gland and the inevitability of the finger wave.

"A male your age should ejaculate at least twice a week to ensure a healthy prostate gland."

"Doc?"

"Yeah, Booger."

"When you ejaculate, your prostate gland doesn't know how many people are in the room, right?"

Doc just looked at Booger in silence.

"Well, Booger, do you want an 'up chit' or not?" sighed Doc.

Damn, thought Booger. *He's got me over a barrel.*

Faced with the possibility of not flying, Booger dropped his underwear to his ankles and turned around. He simply accepted the fact that he was about to be violated. Booger bent over slightly and grabbed the medical table with both hands.

"I said relax," Doc calmly stated. "Relax."

Staring straight ahead at the wall and grimacing, Booger closed his eyes. He felt Doc's left hand on his left shoulder. Booger tensed up, actually crumpling the white sanitary paper that stretched the table's entire length. Then Doc commenced to violate Booger, whose sphincter muscles immediately clamped down around Doc's finger.

"Aaaauuuugggggghhhhh," screamed Booger, diving across the table.

Doc had forgotten to remove a ring.

"What the hell was *that*?" screamed Booger.

Doc, sheepishly embarrassed about his mental lapse, mumbled a weak apology as he noted the ring having ripped through the old latex.

"I'm sorry. Did that hurt?"

"Did that *hurt*? Does King Kong like big bananas? Of *course* that hurt."

"Booger, I'm sorry."

"That's it, Doc," declared Booger. "This flight physical is over."

Booger quickly pulled up his underwear, and stepped from behind the table. He bounded towards the chair that contained his flight suit, but was intercepted by the Doc.

"Booger, listen," implored the Doc, "you're right. Since you're nowhere near forty, I'll dispense with the check of the prostate gland. How does that sound?"

Booger stared away from the Doc, refusing to make eye contact, and tried to slow down his breathing. Doc continued to plead his case, asking, "Is it a deal?"

"Ok, deal," returned Booger.

"I only have one more check to do and this physical will be over."

"Oh, ok. And what is that?"

"It's a hernia check."

* * *

Safety is Paramount – or Safety is Paranoid?

Every now and then, it was a welcome break to *not* be scheduled for a flight in-country, and simply fly a local sortie instead. For one thing, pilots and WSOs didn't have to walk to the jet with all that cumbersome "camping gear" - charts, binoculars, camera, water bottle, food, pistol, ammunition, and so on. It was just the aviator, his normal nav bag, and a blank, five inch by nine inch, card for taking notes.

Secondly, it was a mentally refreshing break from the exhaustive routine of four to six hour flights in-country. A local sortie involved only being airborne for barely an hour, and then returning home. The butt certainly liked that.

Thirdly, fighting in the F-18 was just like an athletic sport, in that pilots and WSOs had to be "in shape" for its grueling demands. The human body required frequent applications of g forces to be able to overcome their effects on a regular basis.

Lastly, and most importantly, air-to-air skills were the aircrew's most *perishable*. It only took a weekend off from fighting, and on the following Monday, a pilot would be just a hair slower in making the requisite split-second decisions. He would be a bit rustier in manipulating the numerous controls on the stick and throttle. A WSO would be just a tad behind in recommendations to his pilot, and in tolerating g's.

Everybody loved to fight. Any idiot could go out in an F-18D and drop a bomb, but it took exceptional skill to excel in the air-to-air arena. Any bozo could turn dead dinosaurs into jet noise on a low level route, but it required a special expertise to triumph over an aerial adversary.

For obvious reasons, pilots loved the one-versus-one. That was their hop. To fighter pilots, the definitive assessment of one's manhood started with two F-18s and a "fight's on" call. With forty-two thousand pounds of jet strapped to his back, it was the ultimate ego trip to execute a max performance turn, feel six times the force of gravity, and then gun the brains out of a fellow squadron mate.

The bragging rights were ratcheted one notch tighter if the one-versus-one was against a dissimilar adversary. Marine pilots absolutely *loved* to fight the Air Force. Whether F-15 or F-16, it didn't matter. As long as the pilot was wearing bus driver blue, the orgasm was heightened even more.

The ultimate orgasm would've been to fight an enemy adversary. With very little intelligence about the innovative Mig-29, but abundant rumors, the aircrew itched for a fight with the mysterious new fighter.

Therein lied the rub. Fighter pilots knew a secret that very few men will ever realize - fighting a good one-versus-one was better than sex. It was the most fun that you could have with your clothes on.

To control this madness, there was a principle in the Marine Corps that stated "safety is paramount". Over the years, this paradigm evolved to be "safety is paranoid". In any case, numerous training rules were written in blood over time to govern the safe conduct of two aircraft fighting each other. It was mandatory that these training rules be read aloud by one member of the brief prior to the flight, and reviewed by all members present. Examples included:

1. For all passes, there was a minimum of five hundred feet of lateral separation allowed between aircraft. This was increased to one thousand feet if an offensive aircraft was tracking a defender with his gun.

2. No head-on gun shots were allowed within forty-five degrees of the target's nose. No head-on missile shots were authorized within twenty degrees of the target's nose, inside one and one half miles. Anytime two jets were inside of one and one half miles, you were to devote your full attention to not hitting the other aircraft.

3. You cleared to the right for a left-to-left pass unless the situation dictated otherwise. Over the radio, always transmit your *own* intentions.

4. The aircraft that is nose high goes high in a dispute for the same airspace, unless unable to do so due to a low energy state.

5. The aircraft up in the sun is responsible for the separation between the two aircraft. If you lost sight of an aircraft in the sun, you were to call "blind" over the radio, break off the attack, and lag his last known position.

6. An offensive aircraft always monitored the defensive aircraft's altitude, and broke off the attack prior to the defender passing through the altitude of the simulated ground.

Anytime an aircraft violated any one of these training rules, the fight was immediately halted for safety purposes with a "knock it off" call over the radio.

0937 Tuesday
Easy 61 and 62 in the Training Area south of the airfield
This is like a knife fight in a phone booth.

"Easy 61 is heading one four zero," stated Tuna, the flight lead.

"Easy 62, heading one four zero," echoed Ham Fist.

For poor Ham Fist, the saga continued. Today, he had been scheduled for another one-versus-one, this time against Tuna, who was the only other pilot in the squadron on the same skill level as Bama. The problem was, Tuna knew it. Aggressive, daring, bold, and smart, Tuna had also come from a background of flying the single-seat F-18C. Like Bama, he didn't like flying with WSOs; however, unlike Bama, Tuna's ego was *totally* out of control. Whereas Bama's ego just involved typical fighter pilot shit, Tuna's ego extended to the clothes he wore, the car he drove, and his sexual prowess. Tuna's ego overflowed into his ability to ski, golf, run, drink, sing, fuck, and fart.

Now Tuna was in the process of humiliating Ham Fist, having shot Easy 62 on the previous two engagements. In Ham Fist's back seat was another experienced WSO, Pope, who was always the cool, calm voice of reason, and a great tactician. However, Pope was running on an hour of sleep, so time would tell. In Easy 61, Tuna was with One Nut, who was rapidly gaining the reputation of being baggage in the rear cockpit.

The third set-up would be a "perch" start with Ham Fist in an offensive position. At an altitude of twenty-one thousand feet, Ham Fist was three thousand feet higher than Tuna. Furthermore, he was positioned on a bearing line at Tuna's left, eight o'clock, at a distance of one and one half miles. Such an offensive start was designed to teach a new pilot the concept of airspeed control, and the important role that a fighter aircraft's turn radius plays in an engagement.

How can I lose? Ham Fist thought. *I'm starting out above him and behind him.*

At eighteen thousand feet, Tuna coolly initiated the start.

"Easy 61, speed and angels on the right," he stated. "Tape's on."

"Easy 62, speed and angels on the left," returned Ham Fist. "Tape's on."

At that moment, Tuna began a left turn to position his jet in front of Easy 62. It was the most unnatural thing for Tuna to do in his life, other than failing to check his hair when passing a mirror.

"You're cleared in," instructed Tuna.

Ham Fist quickly pointed Easy 62's nose at Easy 61, and likewise reversed his speeding F-18D into a left turn. The fight would begin when

Ham Fist reached a position one mile behind Tuna, with both jets being in a left turn. The mileage countdown began as Ham Fist bore down on Tuna.

"One point four," pronounced Ham Fist.

"Roger."

"One point two."

"Roger."

"One mile."

"Fight's on," declared Tuna.

"Fight's on," returned Ham Fist.

In Easy 61, Tuna snapped on the g's and caused his F-18D to execute a hard defensive turn to the left. Simultaneously, he simulated ejecting the decoy expendables that would save his life in a real engagement, stating, "Chaff, flares. Chaff, flares."

"Ugh...ugh...ugh," grunted One Nut under the g's.

In Easy 62, Ham Fist promptly ignored both of the concepts that the fight was designed to enforce. He kept his left elbow locked, jamming the throttles into full afterburner, and pointed his aircraft's nose directly at Easy 61. Pope could see the outcome already.

"Throttle back. Nose off," Pope instructed.

It was too late. Easy 62's F-18D was screaming at Easy 61 like a raped ape, and Tuna knew it. So Tuna reefed on a little more g to ensure that Ham Fist's jet would overshoot Easy 61's flight path.

"Ugh...ugh...ugh."

Easy 62's jet was just a blur as he passed down 61's left side. As soon as the in-close overshoot occurred, Tuna jammed his stick to the right and back into his lap, reversing to a nose-high, right turn. Tuna was the master. Easy 61 had now successfully driven the fight into a slow speed engagement, where the control of one's airspeed and angle of attack would determine the winner.

From the rear cockpit of Easy 62, Pope tried to get Ham Fist back into the fight.

"Ham Fist, reverse left, nose high," he said. "He's nose high at eight o'clock."

Ham Fist wedged his stick to the left and back into his lap, maintaining sight of Tuna's aircraft, as Easy 62 incorrectly zoomed to the moon.

Damn, thought Ham Fist. *This is like a knife fight in a phone booth.*

Like a good WSO, Pope immediately chimed in with an airspeed and angle of attack call over the ICS, so that Ham Fist would not have to bring his head back into the cockpit. His intent was to immediately halt Easy 62's downrange travel and prevent 61 from rolling in behind them.

Shit, thought Ham Fist. *I've gone from an offensive position at Tuna's eight o'clock and above him, to defensive with Tuna now at my eight o'clock and below me. How did that happen?*

In a slow speed, nose-high, right turn, Tuna selected the gun with his weapons select switch. The end was near, and it was every fighter pilot's dream. Easy 61 had a helpless, slow, Easy 62 treed in front of him and above him, passing from right to left.

"Trigger's down," Tuna declared arrogantly.

"Roger."

"Gun's kill, F-18, nose high, heading three one zero."

"Roger. Copy kill."

"Easy 62, Easy 61, knock it off."

0939 Tuesday
U. S. Air Force Hospital,
In The Cramped Office given to the U. S. Navy Flight Surgeons of Deployed Marine F-18 Squadrons
"You may be an azospermic male."

Booger again stared straight ahead at the wall, this time with the Doc bent over in front of him. The flight surgeon dug his pinky up under Booger's right testicle, and uttered the famous one-word command, "Cough."

Booger complied, still staring ahead, with an exhalation of disgust, "Harugh."

Doc maneuvered his pinky to the underside of Booger's left testicle.

"Again, please."

"Harugh."

Next, Doc stood up straight in front of Booger, but stared down to the left at the floor while fondling Booger's testicles. Booger continued to stare straight ahead. Doc then began a memorized recitation on how important it was for a male to check himself for testicular cancer at least once a month, yadda, yadda, yadda. Booger just rolled his eyes and bobbed his head at Doc's ramblings. The flight surgeon completed the fondling and rolling and pinching and tugging, and then stood up before Booger. He momentarily scratched his chin in thought, mumbling, "Hmmmmm."

Doc's thinking went unnoticed, as Booger bent over and attempted to pull his underwear up from his ankles.

"Wait a minute," instructed Doc. "Not yet."

Doc was serious. He was serious as a heart attack.

"Why Doc?" halted Booger. What's the matter?"

"Just a minute, Booger. I need to check you again."

Doc bent over once more and resumed fondling Booger's testicles. In light of Doc having bungled the finger wave just minutes before, Booger silently questioned the Doc's intent for the second fondling. However, Booger sensed a degree of urgency in Doc's tone of voice.

"Booger, as your flight surgeon, can I ask you some personal questions?"

Booger, nervously fidgeting, sighed and then relented, "Sure, Doc, go ahead."

Next, Doc calmly carried on a conversation with Booger as if they were sharing coffee across a table in Starbuck's. The whole time, he was bent over in front of Booger, all the while rolling Booger's testicles in his hand like two dice. Booger continued to stare straight ahead at the wall, unconsciously rocking back and forth on his heels.

"Booger, did you ever have mumps as a child?"

"Um, no, I don't think so."

"As a young boy, did you ever wreck your bike in a manner where your crotch was thrown forward onto the bar?"

"Doc, I had plenty of bike wrecks as a kid, but nothing like that."

"Do you feel that you had a normal puberty?"

"Yep."

"Normal voice change?"

"Yep."

"When did you start shaving?"

"Thirteen or Fourteen. I don't know."

"Now that you're older, have you ever taken steroids?"

"No, Doc, never."

"Do you have a normal sex drive?"

"Doc, I'm an F-18 guy - I'm fuckin' horny all the time."

Again Doc stopped the fondling and stood up, stepping back to scratch his chin. This time, he was deeper in thought, once more muttering, "Hmmmm."

"Doc, what 'Hmmmm'? What's with the 'Hmmmm'?"

Doc began to explain his findings, but he was interrupted by a Booger who was growing increasingly more alarmed, panicking, "Is it serious? Is it anything life threatening? Is it testicular cancer?"

"Well, Booger, if I was you, I wouldn't buy any green bananas," stated Doc with a straight face.

"What?" questioned Booger, with the tone of his voice an octave higher.

"Booger, I'm kidding," assured Doc. "That was just some flight surgeon humor."

Booger stared at Doc and exhaled.

"Booger, sit down. We're done."

Booger pulled his underwear up from his ankles, and sat on the end of the examination table. He was all ears.

"Booger," commenced Doc, "in all seriousness, your testicles don't have the consistency of a normal male."

Doc's words were like a hot razor to Booger's heart.

"They're just a little too soft and squishy," continued Doc. "Plus, they're not exactly big."

Doc reached into a drawer behind him and retrieved something that Booger had never seen before in his life. It was a rosary of wooden testicles. Booger wasn't Catholic, but he had seen Pope's rosary enough to know a rosary when he saw one. Furthermore, since all of the wooden balls were of different sizes, he assumed that they were testicles since that was the topic du jour. The rosary's small end of wooden balls included what Booger felt had to typify a young boy or a poet, for they were no bigger than a grape. God help the poor grown man who had balls *that* size. On the rosary's large end were golf ball sized testicles that Booger figured belonged to NFL linebackers and F-18 pilots.

"I suspect that we may have a problem with your body's hormones," stated Doc, handing the testicle rosary to Booger.

Booger simply stared at Doc, his very manhood having been challenged.

"Doc," pleaded Booger, "what do you think is wrong?"

"Well, Booger, it could be any number of possible signals that the male body employs in its maturation process."

"Go on."

"To start with, the hypothalamus in your brain sends a gonadotrophin releasing hormone from the brain to the pituitary gland."

"Doc," said Booger, "you're going to have to dumb this down - *way* down. Remember, I'm a Marine."

"Roger that," chuckled Doc.

Doc's snicker helped to put Booger at ease, as if maybe things weren't really that bad after all.

"So Booger," continued Doc, "this gonadotrophin releasing hormone, called GnRH, arrives at the pituitary gland."

"Keep going. I'm with you."

"The pituitary gland receives the GnRH, which causes the production of two more hormones, the luteinizing hormone, LH, and the follicle stimulating hormone, FSH."

"I'm still hanging in, Doc."

"Then the pituitary gland sends those two hormones to the same location. The LH goes to the testes, and tells them to make testosterone. The FSH also goes to the testes, telling them to make sperm."

"Doc," said Booger, "don't tell me that this problem might affect my 'boys'."

"Booger, judging from the results of your blood test, your body's level of testosterone is fine."

"Whew," slumped Booger, obviously relieved.

"However, Booger," began Doc, before being interrupted by an anxious Booger.

"However? What 'however', Doc?"

"That only accounts for half of the equation."

"So what are you trying to tell me, Doc?"

"Booger, I'd like you to come back tomorrow morning and masturbate into a cup so that we can get a sperm count."

Booger was stunned.

"Why?"

"You may be an azospermic male."

"What does *that* mean?"

Doc hesitated before stating the most devastating phrase a man can hear.

"Your body may not be producing sperm."

0941 Tuesday
Easy 01 and 02, SEAD Mission,
Complete on the Tanker Track
"I *dare* you to light me up."

"Sky Eye, Easy 01," stated Spine Ripper on the number one radio.

"Easy 01, Sky Eye, go ahead."

"Easy 01 is a flight of two Hornets, mission complete with Texaco, checking in."

"Roger, Easy 01, Sky Eye has you radar contact, two zero miles south of the entry point. Proceed inbound at angels base plus ten."

With a full bag of gas and two programmed HARMs, Butt Munch and Spine Ripper confidently led Easy 02, Screech and Fig, in-country.

Upon going over land, Easy 01 turned left thirty degrees and pointed towards the known location of the SA-2 in the northwest corner. At a pre-briefed point, 01 continued inbound, and 02 executed a one hundred and eighty degree left turn. The Easy flight was now actually flying away from each other as single aircraft. When there was adequate separation between 01 and 02, they both executed a one hundred and eighty degree left turn. That maneuver placed the two F-18Ds on station, yet safely out of the SA-2's range. They would fly this oval racetrack, counter-rotating with each other, so that one aircraft always had his HARM pointed at the SA-2. It was a non-standard, in-your-face maneuver, denying the SA-2 radar any chance to emit.

"Sky Eye, Easy 01, on station," stated Spine Ripper almost as a matter of fact.

"Easy 01, Sky Eye copies."

"C'mon Mr. SA-2, you bastard. "I *dare* you to light me up," said Spine Ripper, challenging the SA-2 radar to lock up their aircraft.

Butt Munch looked in his mirror, and chuckled at Spine Ripper. His WSO's head was buried in the HARM display, as his left hand was fiendishly working the hand-controller. Butt Munch imagined Spine Ripper's vendetta to be like Ahab's quest for the great white whale. Meanwhile, Spine Ripper was praying that they would meet launch criteria.

It wasn't but ten minutes later that Black 21 checked in with Sky Eye on another frequency and began their air-to-air combat air patrol with radars pointed downrange to detect the potential launch of any Migs.

Fifteen minutes after the Mirage 2000s, Easy 03 checked in with Sky Eye to commence their close air support work under the protective umbrella of Easy 01's HARMs and Black 21's air-to-air missiles.

"God, I love it when a plan comes together," said Butt Munch.

He had spoken too soon.

"Easy 01, this is Sky Eye."

"Sky Eye, Easy 01, go," returned Butt Munch.

"Easy 01, Sky Eye regrets to inform you that Red Dog 41 will *not* be on station this morning due to mechanical problems. How copy?"

"Sky Eye, Easy 01, solid copy."

"Damn." yelled Spine Ripper, with his vein enlarging. "Damn. Damn. Damn."

Red Dog 41 was the U. S. Navy EA-6B electronic warfare aircraft that was to share the SEAD mission with Easy 01, 02, 05, and 06.

Without his electronic capabilities on station, Butt Munch and Spine Ripper realized that their workload just increased.

"Easy 01, turning frigid," radioed Butt Munch, meaning that he was turning away from the SA-2 site.

"Easy 02, turning to burn," returned Screech, meaning that that he was turning towards it.

It was this kind of mundane, drilling of holes in the sky that drove Butt Munch crazy. However, to Spine Ripper, the game had just begun. His eyes were riveted upon the HARM display, and he was making smoke come out of the knobs on the left hand controller. As soon as Easy 01 rolled wings level with its tailpipes pointed back at the radar site, Mr. SA-2 came out of the locker room to play.

"Boop."

The tone in their helmets alerted Butt Munch and Spine Ripper to visually check the appropriate displays. Sure as shit, the displays indicated that an SA-2 radar had locked their aircraft.

"Easy 01, is barbed at six o'clock," stated Butt Munch, informing his wingman of their new status.

"Easy 02, we have nothing," returned Screech, meaning that his systems showed no indications of his F-18D being locked.

Easy 01 was helpless. However, they were safely out of the SA-2's range, so Butt Munch and Spine Ripper weren't worried.

"Where's the EA-6B when you need him?" lamented Spine Ripper.

Easy 01 continued frigid away from the SA-2 site, while on the opposite side of their oval racetrack, Easy 02 continued downrange toward it. After the appropriate distance, Butt Munch began a standard rate turn to the left, still locked by the SA-2's radar.

"Easy 01, turning to burn."

"Easy 02, coming frigid," returned Screech.

"C'mon, baby, come to papa," stated Spine Ripper over the ICS. "We're going to introduce Mr. HARM to Mr. SA-2."

"Boop" suddenly rippled through the helmets of Butt Munch and Spine Ripper. No sooner had Easy 01rolled wings level with its HARM pointed *towards* the SA-2, and then their lock indications disappeared. However, "Boop" immediately resounded in the helmets of Easy 02.

"Easy 02, now barbed, six o'clock," radioed Screech.

"Easy 01, now nothing," stated Butt Munch.

Damn, thought Spine Ripper. *That SA-2 is an asshole.*

Mr. SA-2 was adeptly playing the game. The radar operator was only locking up the frigid F-18D that had its HARM pointed safely away. Spine Ripper's mind raced for a solution. He pounced on the left hand-controller again, frantically working the HARM. But it was as if Mr. SA-2 was reading his mind.

"Easy 02, now nothing," stated Screech.

"Easy 01, nothing."

Now, Mr. SA-2 had neither aircraft locked up.

"Aaauuggghhhh," screamed Spine Ripper aloud, pounding his fists on the canopy.

"Easy back there, big fellow," laughingly returned Butt Munch on the ICS. "Everything is cool."

Both aircraft continued on their present headings to their respective turn points with no further changes in status.

"Easy 01, turning frigid," said Butt Munch.

"Easy 02, turning to burn."

"Boop."

"Easy 01, now barbed, six o'clock," said Butt Munch, as once again, Mr. SA-2 locked their F-18D from behind.

"Shit. Shit. Shit," screamed Spine Ripper, raising a blood pressure that was already out of control, and aggravating the vein on his forehead.

"This guy's fuckin' with me, Butt Munch," Spine Ripper proclaimed.

"Easy 02, nothing."

Then the next pair of scheduled dancers interrupted Spine Ripper's ballet.

"Sky Eye, Easy 05."

"Easy 05, Sky Eye, go ahead."

"Sky Eye, Easy 05 is a flight of two F-18s, checking in to relieve Easy 01."

From the rear cockpit of Easy 01, Spine Ripper looked over his left shoulder and flipped the bird in the general direction of Mr. SA-2. The SAM site had successfully evaded Spine Ripper's personal vendetta for another day. Easy 01 and 02 proceeded to the tanker track for more gas.

"Hey, Butt Munch," Spine Ripper said over the ICS, while reaching by his right hip for a bottle of water and a Ho-Ho.

"Yeah?"

"Have you ever noticed anything unusual about these daily bouts with the SA-2?"

"Like what?"

"Well, it's almost like those radar operators know our tactics and our turn points."

* * *

Dodging bullets worse than the real ones

One thing was for sure. If you were a Captain aviator in the U. S. Marine Corps, then you were constantly dodging a bullet. You never knew when the next dick job was coming, or where it was coming from - but some type of a bad deal was always lurking on the horizon. The latest bullet came down late last year, causing the Captains to all hunker down in their imaginary foxholes. The Wing Commander was looking for a new General's Aide. God, what could be worse? Out of the cockpit for a year, and forced to wear the gold epaulet that identified you as a brown-nosed loser, the General's Aide job was nothing more than being the General's twenty-eight year old butt-boy.

"More coffee, Sir? Would you like cream and sugar with that, Sir?

"Sir, General Brass-Ass is holding on line two, and your 0915 is here, Sir."

"Sir, I dropped your uniform off at the cleaners, and I'll pick them up Tuesday."

Aaaaauuuugghhh.

0952 Tuesday
Marine Aircraft Wing Headquarters,
Aide-de-Camp's Office,
On the computer
"Who keeps getting nail polish on my keyboard?"

Dear Protocol Office,

This e-mail is intended as the final reminder of our General's visit to your Air Force base this week. As I've stated before, he intends to conduct an unannounced inspection of the Marine F-18D squadron presently living in tents aboard your base; consequently, no Marines are aware of his coming. The General, our driver, and I should arrive at approximately 2100 tonight.

No special accommodations will be required, as the General desires to stay in the tents with his Marines. However, please be advised that his driver is a female Lance Corporal, and she will have to be billeted as such.

Thank you very much for all of the cooperation and hard work that your office has extended to me over the last eight weeks to ensure that the General's surprise inspection goes off without a hitch. We are looking forward to the visit.

Respectfully,
General's Aide-de-Camp

"Damn it," said the General's Aide, leaning back in his chair. "Who keeps getting nail polish on my keyboard?"

* * *

Type appropriate heading

(fill in the date)

Mr. and Mrs. (fill in the blank),

It is with the deepest and most sincere sympathy that the United States Marine Corps regrets to inform you that...

How do people in the real world deal with a friend or coworker dying a sudden, accidental death? It just *has* to be different at IBM or AT&T. Marines always imagined two guys talking at the water cooler, and one says to the other "Did you hear that Bob died in a car wreck?" And that was it.

However, in the Marine Corps, deployed aviators were more than just friends at a water cooler. They were together more than just nine to five. They were brothers. They ate together, flew together, worked together, showered together, ran together - it was different.

Accidental deaths just came with the turf of flying fighters. Everyone accepted it, but nobody talked about it. By the time that most aviators finally hung up their flight suits after twenty years, they had friends fly into the water, fly into a mountain, fly into the ground, and fly into each other. Most aviators actually quit counting the number of aviator brethren who had died.

There was once this back-seater who rode an F-4S into the ocean with his pilot. There was no radio call, no ejection, no nothin'. The sad part is, he was an FNG, having just joined the squadron. They were out one night doing intercepts with another F-4S, and his more experienced pilot must've gotten disoriented, for they simply flew into the water.

How does that happen - "fly into the water"? Most Marines have seen cloudless, starry nights, where the light's reflections off of a smooth ocean made it impossible to discern a horizon. Maybe it was one of those nights. In any case, his F-4S playmate radioed that he was ready for the next run, and got no answer. Imagine how eerie that must've felt. Two young lives, snuffed out before they even got a chance.

The same thing happened about ten or twelve years later in an F-18D - two friends flew into the water. Again, there was no radio call, no ejection, no nothin'. That accident was a little more understandable, because they were flying low and fast, wearing the night vision goggles, in a circular bombing pattern. It may have been more understandable, but that didn't make in any more acceptable. It was probably the same thing - pilot disorientation. Who knows? In any case, it's still ironic. All that whiz-bang technology in the F-18D, and they *still* flew into the water. Wearing night vision goggles, no less.

Before that accident, Marine WSOs used to pride themselves on the fact that no aircrew had ever died in a two-seat F-18D. They liked to think that the second aviator in the jet exponentially increased the odds of preventing an accident. However, that theory went to shit when F-18Ds flew into the ocean off the coast of Korea, ejected over the Atlantic, and had a mid-air collision over the Arizona desert.

The most mysterious deaths occurred on a night that was just the opposite of the F-4S accident - it was cloudy and rainy with thunderstorms. They were in a lone F-18D about twenty miles off the coast, coming home, when they just disappeared. That's right, they just disappeared. It was pure "X-Files" stuff. It was the same thing as before - no radio call, no ejection, no nothin'. Some theorized that they were dumping fuel to get down to landing weight, and maybe got hit by lightning. Picture *that*.

Of the four services, the Marine Corps always had the highest accident rate. However, the bean counters *had* to expect accidents when you consider that Marine Corps pilots were flying cutting-edge technology like the AV-8B Harrier, and at the same time flying Vietnam era helicopters that were older than the pilots themselves. But still, that didn't explain the accidents in the F-18. Regardless of their aircraft, maybe Marine Corps pilots simply flew them more aggressively to the edge of the envelope.

Yep, accidental deaths just came with the turf of flying fighters.

1053 Tuesday
The Squadron Safety Department
"No, it's a testament to touching banners and stroking fish."

Chunks knocked on the door of the Safety Department, and poked in his head, asking, "Hey Pope?"

"He isn't here right now," returned the Doc, sitting at the computer.

"Do you know where he is?" asked Chunks, stepping inside.

"No, but he had the early launch this morning," explained the Doc, continuing to type. "He's probably still sleeping in his tent."

"Ok, thanks, Doc."

Chunks was about to depart, when he couldn't help looking over Doc's shoulder. He was typing some type of fancy-schmancy letter with the squadron logo.

"What are you working on, Doc?"

"Well, Chunks," Doc explained, "at this pace, the squadron should go over twenty thousand accident-free hours this Thursday."

"Wow. Twenty thousand hours?"

"Yes, Sirree, Chunks, twenty thousand hours without an accident or a death. It's pretty incredible, and a real testament to the aviation skills of the boys from Easy."

"No, it's a testament to touching banners and stroking fish," joked Chunks.

"Anyway, as the squadron flight surgeon, I'm typing an addendum to the award."

"Award? What award?"

"If everything goes without a hitch, we're going to have the General present an award to the squadron Friday morning."

"You mean the same General that we're not supposed to know is coming?"

"Yeah, that's the one."

Doc chuckled, and quit typing long enough to sip his coffee and take a drag on his filter-less Camel.

"Ok, Doc, thanks," said Chunks. "I'll catch Pope later."

"Roger that," replied Doc, as he returned to plinking on the keyboard.

* * *

Piddle Packs

With in-country missions lasting anywhere from four to six hours, aircrew took care of their most basic human needs - hunger and thirst - by walking to the jet with various food items and bottles of water. However, the follow-on problem was the bodily function of waste removal that resulted from satisfying those original human needs. One solution to this dilemma was the "piddle pack", which can best be described as a zip-lock baggie. Made of a stronger, more durable, clear plastic than a baggie, it was intended to hold a man's urine, and then be sealed at the top. However, rather than use the patented zip-lock top, the piddle pack came with a twist-tie, much like the ones commonly used back in the real world to tie garbage bags.

Aircrew kept piddle packs somewhere in the cockpit within easy arm's reach, yet avoided using them until the pain in their bladder became too great to bear. The manufacturer billed the piddle packs as "user friendly", and they were - if you had three hands. For WSOs, who had both of their hands free, employing the piddle pack was less of a chore. It even helped for the WSO to undo his lap restraints and thrust his pelvis up from the seat in order to successfully urinate into the piddle pack. However, for pilots, who had the stick and throttles in their hands, the task was much more difficult. Let it suffice to say, thank God for the F-18's auto pilot system.

For both pilot and WSO, the piddle pack workload greatly increased if you weren't particularly well hung. When you consider that aircrew wore underwear under a flight suit, and then a g-suit, torso harness, and survival vest, it became a major struggle to expose their manhood. First, you had to unzip your flight suit from the bottom up - whoever thought of that second zipper down there deserves a medal - and then fiddle with the entrance to your boxers or briefs. Once you were holding yourself in one hand, you had to ensure the careful placement of the piddle pack with the other. Since the bulkiness of the survival vest prevented actually looking down and seeing the job at hand, this task had to be done entirely by a sense of feel. More than one aircrew thought he was in the piddle pack, only to piss all over the seat and his flight gear.

Once complete with the piddle pack, then it became a question of where to place it. A bulging, plastic bag of yellow urine that is only closed by a red twist-tie is not something that you want lying around the cockpit. Most aircrew placed them on the consoles by their right or left hips, and prayed to God that they didn't break.

1113 Tuesday
The Crew of Easy 42 Walking to Their Jet
"It's a ham sandwich."

Joisey and Shitscreen ensured that they touched SPEED IS LIFE, MORE IS BETTER. before departing the Ready Room. They also stroked Easy Eddie's stringer of fish. After a brief stop in Maintenance Control, they commenced the long trek to their assigned Hornet. Today's in-country flight was going to be a long one, so each had packed extra trinkets in his "camping gear". Shitscreen appeared to be even more laden down with his camera, binoculars, and charts than the normal WSO. Maybe that was because of the extra water bottle and granola bars that he carried in a canvas lunch tote. As Joisey preceded Shitscreen through the door at the end of the hangar, Shitscreen noted that his pilot was carrying next to nothing. Joisey only had his normal nav bag, a water bottle, and some type of a bag in his left hand. Upon a closer inspection of the bag, Shitscreen did a double take, asking, "Joisey, what *is* that in your left hand?"

Unfazed, Joisey simply kept walking and held the bag up so that Shitscreen could get a better view, stating, "It's a ham sandwich."

Shitscreen jogged a few steps to catch up with Joisey.

"I can *see* that it's a ham sandwich," returned Shitscreen, raising his voice. "But what is that bag that it's in?"

"It's a piddle pack," Joisey stated matter-of-factly.

"You gross bastard," said Shitscreen. "I thought so. You packed a ham sandwich in an empty piddle pack?"

"What's gross about it? The piddle pack hasn't been used yet."

"I don't care," continued Shitscreen. "It's the principle behind the thing. You put a ham sandwich in an unused piddle pack. Have you ever heard of a zip lock baggie?"

"Hey, Shitscreen," said Joisey. "I'm a master of efficiency. I'll eat the ham sandwich, drink my water, and voila'. I've got an empty piddle pack at my disposal."

Shitscreen wasn't buying it. He clenched his teeth and stared up into the sky, declaring, "God, what am I? Fly paper for dorks?"

"Hey, Shitscreen, face it. You can't change me."

"True, but I've got to *fly* with you."

"How else can I say it?" continued Joisey. "You're wasting your time. You're farting into the wind. You're trying to push a piece of shit uphill with a sharp stick."

"Ok, ok, you turd merchant, I get the idea," said a frustrated Shitscreen. "I'll just accept the fact that you're a gross bastard and I can't change you. Joisey, you'll never soar with the eagles."

"Shitscreen," Joisey calmly stated, "Eagles may soar, but weasels don't get sucked into jet engines."

The two arrived at aircraft ten, and began their preflight inspection. In accordance with the unwritten code, Joisey the pilot went clockwise, and Shitscreen the WSO went counter-clockwise.

* * *

The weight-on-seat switch

Internal to the F-18, several systems functioned according to whether the Hornet was on the ground or airborne. Some of these more important systems included the master arm switch, the external stores jettison button, the automatic throttle control, the auto pilot, and fuel tank pressurization. To determine when the F-18 was on the ground, a tiny proximity switch - called the "weight-on-wheels" switch - was located on each of the landing gear. Consequently, when this switch sensed that the Hornet's weight was on the wheels, the system disabled some of the aforementioned systems, because they had no business being operational on the ground. When the proximity switches sensed that weight was no longer on the wheels, meaning that the jet was airborne, these systems were automatically enabled. Neither pilot nor WSO could override those switches.

Well, there must've also been a "weight-on-*seat*" switch in the F-18. This tiny switch sensed whenever the aircrew's weight was upon the seat, and disconnected the clutch that existed between his brain and his mouth. This disconnect would cause even the most capable of aviators to suddenly become tongue-tied, and then sound stupid on the radio. No matter what helmet fires were currently occurring in the cockpit, sounding cool over the radios was still paramount in the fighter community. The weight-on-seat switch sometimes prevented that.

An instructor way back in flight school once preached that there were three, key, sequential steps to sounding cool on the radio:
1. Stop and think what you were going to say.
2. Say it once to yourself in your head.
3. Then don't say anything at all.

1201 Tuesday
On the Path from the Ready Room to Tent City
"You're sounding like a real dork on the radios, youngster."

Buick and Dago were walking back to Tent City, with the young One Nut sandwiched in between. The two masters of the F-18D back seat were mentoring the newest grasshopper to the community. Buick walked on the left, as the cool, calm, and collected lug who had seen it all. Without even raising his voice, he could make you feel like shit when you screwed up, yet instruct you in such a way that it never happened again. Dago walked on the right, and was just the opposite. Whenever you screwed up, the feisty little Italian from Brooklyn would just as soon rip off your head and shit down the hole. Stuck in between the two was a tired and defeated One Nut. His neck hurt from this morning's one-versus-one in Tuna's back seat, and he had blacked out under the g's on two separate occasions. However, Buick and Dago didn't care about *those* errors, for they would be corrected with time and experience. Instead, the instruction du jour was on radio communications.

"One Nut," began Buick, "I've got to tell you that you pulled some real boneheads over the radio today."

"I know, Buick, I'm sorry," said One Nut, rubbing his neck.

"Shit, your jet wasn't even out of the line yet," injected Dago, "and you had already messed up big time."

Dago was relating to one of the most embarrassing errors that an aviator can commit - talk on the wrong radio. This morning when Tuna's flight was ready to taxi, One Nut called Ground Control on the number *two* radio, instead of the number one. Thus, when his call to taxi came over the duty radio in the Ready Room, the circling sharks jumped on the radio like a hobo on a hot dog. Dago was the ringleader, assuming the voice of Ground Control, and telling Easy 51 to hold their position, run their seats down, and cycle the canopy up and down. In the front seat, Tuna recognized Dago's voice and just shook his head, but the virgin One Nut was clueless. Tuna just knew that every Officer in the Ready Room was rolling on the floor in laughter.

"Get your foot pedal switches straight, One Nut," continued Dago. "The left is the number one radio, and the right is the number two. Left, number one. Right, number two. Got it?"

"Roger that, Dago."

"So far, you're sounding like a real dork on the radios, youngster," said Dago.

"Listen to the Strike Eagles take-off sometime," instructed Buick. "They are really good. They use very disciplined and professional comm."

The threesome got to perimeter road, and halted, looking both ways. This time of day, traffic was nuts, so they were careful to cross on their trek back to Tent City. Once safely to other side, the mentoring continued.

"One Nut, as a WSO," continued Buick, "You own those radios. You've got to sound like the epitome of cool every time you talk."

"Well, what about the other day?" inquired One Nut.

"What happened the other day?" asked Buick.

"I was in Easy 46, and Pope was the lead WSO in Easy 45. We were on our way back, and Approach Control warned us of heavy bird activity at the west end of the airfield. Pope replied 'Roger, we're radar contact'."

Buick and Dago both bit their lip, trying not to laugh in front of One Nut.

Damn. What a hilarious reply, thought Buick. *I've got to remember that one.*

Shit. I wish I had thought of that, thought Dago. *That is hilarious.*

"Well, youngster," continued Buick, "there's a double standard in fighter radio
communications. Salty aviators like Pope can joke around on the radios like that, but FNGs like you have to talk like you're still in flight school."

In the middle of the corn flakes rocks – named because walking on them sounded like walking on corn flakes - the trio of WSOs ran into Bama going in the opposite direction. He had just rolled out of his green slug after the all night alert and five hours of sleep.

"I see the WSO Protection Union is alive and well," said Bama.

Dago didn't miss a beat, and Buick was ready to accept the challenge. One Nut was clueless to the squadron politics that surrounded him.

"Buick, take care of my light work for me, will you?" said Dago, alluding to Bama and his comment.

"Roger that," winked Buick.

"I've got some more one-on-one counseling to do with our FNG here," said Dago, grabbing One Nut by the sleeve and jerking him towards Tent City.

After Dago and One Nut's departure, the squadron's two icons made small talk in the middle of the corn flakes rocks.

"Hey, Bama. Where ya headin'?"

"I'm on my way down to the Ready Room," he stated. "I'm going to talk with Ham Fist when Tuna gets done debriefing him."

"Then I guess that I could say the *pilot's* Protection Union is alive and well, too, huh?" returned Buick.

"Listen asshole," said Bama, immediately escalating the tension, "you're damn right there's a pilots Protection Union, and it's thriving, thank you."

"You don't have to tell *me*."

"As the informal president of that union," continued Bama, "I am going to do everything in my power to strengthen the pilots in this squadron."

"And what about the WSOs?"

"Fuck the WSOs," said Bama. "WSOs are a crutch for a poor pilot."

"You're in a two-seat 'D' squadron now, Bama. WSOs are a fact of life."

"Yeah, that's right. A fact of life that I don't need."

"Did you even say a word to One Nut during yesterday's fight?" queried Buick.

"No," returned Bama, inflating his chest, "because a one-versus-one is a pilot's hop. The WSO is just a piece of American Tourister that's along for the ride."

"What about after the hop?"

"No."

"During the debrief?"

"No."

"After the debrief?"

"No. What's your point, Buick?"

"Then how is a young WSO supposed to learn?" asked Buick. "*That's* my point."

"I don't give a rat's ass."

"Bama, someday, a good call from the back seat is going to save your ass, and I hope that I'm there to see it. Good day."

Buick stepped aside, and continued his trek across the corn flakes rocks.

"You fat piece of FOD," muttered Bama, before continuing to the Ready Room.

* * *

Bitchin' Betty

The F-18D was actually smarter than *any* pilot or WSO who ever crawled into its cockpits. One of the Hornet's systems that continuously proved this fact was the voice alert system. When certain critical warnings or cautions occurred, a female voice was heard in the aircrew's helmets, advising them of the problem. Affectionately known as "Bitchin' Betty", she promptly repeated the message twice to the aircrew. The tone of her voice didn't scream, didn't shriek, and didn't yell. She just calmly - well, bitched. It had to be like flying with your wife. For example, if the F-18 experienced a left engine fire warning, Bitchin' Betty coolly stated, "Engine fire left, engine fire left". If the F-18 dipped below a preset altitude and triggered a low altitude warning, Bitchin' Betty let the aircrew know with a casual, "Altitude, altitude". You get the idea.

When less serious cautions occurred, Bitchin' Betty was there too. She constantly monitored the flight control system, and if any flight control surface suddenly became inoperative, like the flaps or the ailerons or the rudders, then Betty bitched, "Flight controls, flight controls." Bitchin' Betty also kept an eye on the cautions for various engine systems. For example, if the right engine's oil pressure suddenly shot out of limits, or the right engine's exhaust gas temperature became too high, she promptly bitched, "Engine right, engine right".

The F-18's big blue bible had an entire chapter dedicated to emergencies, including the required curative procedures. Those corrective actions contained several steps, the first of which were called "immediate action" items. The aircrew memorized these items, so that they could be performed immediately upon Betty's bitching; thus halting the emergency and possibly saving the aircraft - if not their lives. Then more steps followed the immediate action items, and those steps required completion to resolve the problem. These secondary steps just weren't as urgent as the immediate action procedures, but they were still important.

All of the emergency procedures contained in the big blue bible were condensed into a smaller, blue, pocket checklist - or PCL, for short. All aircrew flew with this five inch by nine inch life saver, and they kept it at their ready disposal in case of emergency.

Once Betty bitched, it became an exercise in crew coordination to quickly handle whatever emergency it was that Betty had detected. Since most emergencies required an action upon some type of a knob or switch or button in the front cockpit, pilots were responsible for the immediate action procedures. Meanwhile, the WSO broke out the PCL in the back seat. He first verified that the pilot had completed the correct immediate action procedures, and then read the secondary steps to the pilot.

1250 Tuesday
Easy 99, in the Training Area South of the Airfield
"I'm breaking out the book."

Screech and Dago were airborne in aircraft 02 on a post maintenance check flight. These flights were designated by the acronym PMCF, and were called "test hops" for short. A running gripe had been in the books about 02's engine bleed air system, and the Maintenance Department swore that they had finally located the problem and fixed it. Thus, before the aircraft could be placed back on the flight schedule, it had to be flown on a test hop by experienced aircrew. This pilot and WSO followed very specific procedures in a tiny PMCF booklet from start to finish to ensure that the problem had actually been corrected. Thus, Screech and Dago were airborne to verify that the problem with 02's engine bleed air system had been fixed. However, they had no sooner entered the warning area when Bitchin' Betty made her presence known.

"Bleed air left, bleed air left," she bitched, detecting a bleed air leak on the left side of the F-18D.

"Shit," said Screech, promptly beginning the memorized, immediate action procedures. *"Throttle affected engine - IDLE."*

Screech retarded the left throttle to the idle position.

"Bleed air knob - OFF affected engine. (DO NOT CYCLE)"

In the same motion, Screech reached down by his left hip and rotated the bleed air knob to the 'off' position. Almost simultaneously, Dago's voice entered Screeches helmet from the back seat, stating, "I'm breaking out the book."

"Roger that," returned Screech, already turning the jet around for the trip home.

"I'm on page three, looking at left bleed warning," said Dago.

"Concur, Dago. What does it say?"

"Step one. Throttle affected engine- Idle."

"Got it."

"Step two. Bleed air knob – Off affected engine. (Do not cycle)."

"Got it."

"That's it for the immediate action procedures, Screech."

"Roger that. What's next?"

"Step three. If the light goes out, land as soon as practical."

"I show the light out in the front seat. Do you concur?"

"Concur. The 'L bleed' warning light is out in the rear seat."

"Roger, that," returned Screech. "Looks like we're heading home with a jet that's still broken. Shit."

* * *

Fuck dropping bombs – *this* is why Bama flew

The second possible in-country mission that the F-18D could be assigned involved actually enforcing the no-fly zone. These hops meant endless hours of drilling holes in the sky, listening to AWACS, working the radar, and praying to God for that one-in-a-million chance to shoot down a Mig. Actually, *any* aircraft would do. Jet, prop, helo - it didn't matter. Even a tiny Cessna bug smasher would've been toast if the CAOC cleared Marine F-18s to kill it.

F-18Ds flying this particular mission were loaded wall-to-wall with air-to-air missiles, and all they wanted to do was return home with one less missile and one more story. Bama came up with an excellent idea that would've achieved just such an objective. He vowed to shoot down the very first Mig he saw without waiting for a clearance to fire, and then report to the AWACS, "I just witnessed a Mig crash. I'll mark the spot where it went down with a missile."

1302 Tuesday
Easy 42 and 43 on an in-country, air-to-air mission
"Man, wouldn't that be the cat's ass?"

Easy 42, Joisey and Shitscreen, with piddle packs properly stowed, and Easy 43, Jock and Pope, proceeded towards Point Charlie on a beautifully glorious day. In fact, sunlight actually glistened off of the heat-seeking Sidewinder missiles affixed to their wingtips. With any luck, maybe today would be the day when they would return home without them.

"Pierre, Easy 42," said Joisey.

"Easy 42, Pierre, go ahead," returned the French AWACS currently on station.

"Pierre, Easy 42 is a flight of two Hornets," continued Joisey, "mission complete with Texaco, and ready for your control."

"Easy 42, Pierre copies. Picture is clean."

"Pierre, Easy 42. Picture clean."

"Picture clean," sighed Shitscreen on the ICS as he manipulated the radar, "there's a shocker. Alert the media."

"Yep," laughed Joisey, "another day of drilling holes in the sky."

Positioned on their right, Easy 43 was also attempting to combat the boredom.

"Hey, Jock," stated Pope over the ICS.

"Yeah, man?"

"Take the radar for a minute," instructed Pope, "while I eat a Ho-Ho."

"Roger, my radar."

Pope retrieved a packet of Ho-Hos from the map case at his right hip, and scooted his butt forward on the seat. The change in body position allowed blood to better circulate through his tired butt muscles while he removed the oxygen mask from his face.

"Hey Pope," said Jock, as he adjusted the radar's search parameters.

"Yeah?" returned Pope, as he ripped the plastic Ho-Ho package with his teeth.

"You never know," continued Jock, "today could be the day."

"The day for what?"

"The day that a Mig finally gets airborne, and I blow him out of the sky."

"Don't hold your breath," returned Pope, who then made the sign of the cross and barely whispered the mandatory pre-meal Catholic prayer.

"Bless us oh, Lord, and these thy gifts, which we are about to receive, from thy bounty, through Christ our Lord, amen."

Pope wasn't sure if the Catholic Church considered a Ho-Ho to be a meal, but he figured that he would be safe anyway. He just couldn't escape that classic Catholic guilt.

"Easy 42, Pierre, picture clean."

"Pierre, Easy 42, picture clean," returned Joisey in the other F-18D.

"Man, wouldn't that be the cat's ass?" cooed Jock in the front seat of Easy 43.

"Yep," yawned Pope, wiping whipped cream from the corner of his mouth.

"Shooting down a Mig - the perfect thing to shove up Bama's and Tuna's asses."

Damn it, thought Pope, as he attempted to pick a tiny chunk of chocolate icing from between his two front teeth. He was barely paying attention to Jock's dreaming.

"Plus," continued Jock, "I'd be a hero. That would certainly pull me up."

The last statement caught Pope's attention.

Pull me up? Pope thought.

"Easy 42, Pierre, picture clean."

"Pierre, Easy 42, picture clean," said Joisey.

"Hey, Jock," said Pope, "are you *still* feeling bummed like you were when we talked last week?"

There was no immediate answer on the ICS.

"Hey, Jock."

There was still no answer.

"Yo, Jock?"

"I heard you the first time, Pope," injected Jock, rather irritated at himself that he had dreamed aloud over the ICS.

"Well?"

"Oh, I don't know," confided Jock, "my depression comes and goes."

"We can't talk right now," said Pope, "so how about if we talk after the debrief?"

"Roger that," agreed Jock, still fingering the radar's controls.

"Easy 42, Pierre, picture clean."

"Pierre, Easy 42, picture clean," droned Joisey.

"Yep, today could be the day," mumbled Jock. "Something big is going to happen. I can feel it."

* * *

What you see depends on where you sit

The Pentagon's fancy-schmancy term for it was anti aircraft artillery, or AAA. However, for those who lived on the tip of the spear, they were bullets, and it was bullets that really scared F-18 aviators.

It's been that way long before Jesus was a General. Back in World War Two, the bombers over Germany called it "ack-ack", and they feared nothing more. In the first Gulf War, "CNN" brought the lethality of AAA into America's living room with grainy, green footage of bullets streaming into the night sky over Baghdad like a seething Cobra.

Yep. F-18 aviators trusted that chaff would deceive an enemy radar, and the missile that it was guiding; likewise, that flares would decoy a heat-seeking missile. But nothing would stop a well-aimed bullet.

1357 Tuesday
Easy 42 and 43 on an in-country, air-to-air mission
"What could possibly happen?"

"Easy 42, Pierre, picture clean," droned the French AWACS for the millionth time this afternoon.

"Pierre, Easy 42, same," yawned Joisey.

"Hey Joisey," said Shitscreen on the ICS.

"Yeah?"

"I'm about to cry 'uncle', man."

"Yep, me too," returned Easy 42's pilot, "but that's ok. Our time on station is almost over."

In Easy 43, their fun meters were completely pegged too.

"Yo, Pope."

"Speak to me, Jock."

"Looks like another day of no Migs getting airborne, huh?"

"Yeah, that's flying," stated Pope, "hours of maddening boredom punctuated by seconds of sheer terror."

"Easy 42, Pierre."

"Pierre, Easy 42, go ahead," returned Joisey.

"Easy 42, Pierre has a request. Are you ready to copy?"

"Pierre, Easy 42, send it."

"The CAOC reports possible convoy activity twenty miles south of present position. Can you investigate?"

"Pierre, do you have a grid or a latitude and longitude?"

"Easy 42, Pierre, negative."

Well, that's just peachy, thought Joisey.

"Easy 42, Pierre. The CAOC only reports the possible convoy activity to be in the vicinity of the town of Grobnev."

"Where the fuck is THAT?" asked Shitscreen, unfolding map after map after map in the rear cockpit.

"Pierre, Easy 42," returned Joisey, "stand by one."

Suddenly, Pope saved the day on the number two radio, calling, "Joisey, Pope."

Joisey immediately thumbed the transmission rocker on the throttle to the down position, keying the number two radio.

"Pope, Joisey, go ahead."

"I know where Grobnev is," Pope stated. "I had to do the same thing one day last week as Easy 73. Do you want us to take it?"

"Pope, Joisey, stand by."

While the gears in Joisey's head ground away in trying to weigh the pros and cons of such an impromptu, unbreifed mission, Pope grilled Jock in Easy 43.

"Jock, what do you say? Are you up for it?"

"Sure, Pope. I'm bored out of my gourd anyway."

"Roger that," returned his WSO. "What could possibly happen?"

There was an eternity of silence before Easy 43 finally heard, "Jock, Joisey, on the number two."

"Joisey, Jock, go ahead."

"State your gas."

"Easy 43 is nine point five," stated Jock, meaning ninety-five hundred pounds of fuel remained.

"Roger that," returned Joisey, "Easy 42 is eight point eight. Stand by."

Again, Joisey attempted to put out a helmet fire in his cockpit while the pilot and WSO in Easy 43 relished at the possibilities.

"We just may salvage some fun out of this day yet," said Pope.

"I'd rather salvage a Mig," laughed Jock.

Again, there was an eternity of silence.

C'mon, Joisey, thought Jock. *What's the hold up?*

"Jock, Joisey, on the number two."

"Joisey, Jock, go ahead."

"You've got it," replied the flight lead. "You know where Grobnev is, and you've got seven hundred more pounds of gas. Take us there."

"Roger that."

"Pierre, Easy 43," stated Jock confidently, already turning his aircraft to the left and beginning a slow descent.

"Easy 43, Pierre has you loud and clear."

"Pierre, Easy 43 now has the lead and is proceeding to Grobnev as requested."

"Easy 43, Pierre copies. Picture is clean."

Jock steadied Easy 43 on a heading that Pope directed.

"Jock, Joisey on the number two. We'll stay in the high cover position to check your six as you go down to look for the convoy."

"Jock copies."

Passing twenty thousand feet, Pope retrieved the binoculars from their resting place by his left hip, in anticipation of looking for the convoy. In the front seat, Jock turned down the brightness and the gain in his HUD.

"Easy 43, Pierre, picture clean."

"Jock, Joisey, six is clear."

"Easy 43 copies," returned Jock.

Descending through fifteen thousand feet, Pope split his time between the binoculars and the infrared display, with his head going back and forth, back and forth, and back and forth like he was at a tennis match. Meanwhile, Jock's head was doing the same thing in the front, trying to look in vain around the left and right sides of the HUD.

"Easy 43, Pierre, picture clean."

"Jock, Joisey, six is clear."

"Easy 43, copies."

Then an unwanted female voice tip-toed into Easy 43's helmets.

"Flight controls. Flight controls," bitched Betty.

Shit, thought Jock.

"Damn," said Pope.

Both aviators instinctively glanced at the left display as their F-18D continued to descend. Sure as shit, there it was, an FCS caution. Bitchin' Betty had detected something amiss with the flight control system, and alerted the crew. That particular caution had no immediate action procedures to perform, thus there were no memorized steps to be instantly completed to save the jet. An FCS caution was just that - a routine flight control caution.

"I'm breaking out the book," Pope calmly stated from the rear, as he retrieved the F-18D pocket checklist from his nav bag.

"Roger that," replied Jock, bringing his head into the cockpit, and temporarily removing altitude and airspeed from his visual scan.

"You ready?" inquired Pope.

"Ready."

Pope read the procedures word for word, straight from the pocket checklist.

"Step one. Menu FCS – Identify Failure."

"Roger that," returned Jock as he punched up the FCS display on the right screen. "I'm showing a pitch rate gyro, four channel failure. Do you concur?"

"Yep, I concur, man," returned Pope. "I've got x's in all four channels next to the letter 'P'."

"No sweat," returned Jock, already reaching for the FCS reset button, which was used to reset the flight control computers after a transient malfunction.

"Step two. FCS Reset," recited Pope.

"I'm resetting," coolly stated Jock, pressing the FCS reset button as their F-18D descended through twelve thousand feet.

"Easy 43, Pierre, picture clean."

"Jock, Joisey, six is clear."

There was no reply from Easy 43, which piqued the interest of Joisey and Shitscreen in the other jet. Obviously, Jock and Pope were busy.

Why didn't they answer? Joisey thought.

Meanwhile, Jock's eyes were glued to the right display, waiting for the four x's to go away, while Pope continued to read from the back seat.

"Jock, with a pitch rate gyro, four channel failure, we now have no pitch augmentation. Our autopilot and automatic throttle control are both inoperative, and with the flap switch in the auto position, we will have poor pitch stability."

Pope's advisory information went into Jock's one ear and right out the other. Jock was glued to the right display.

"Hey, Pope. Do you see what I see?"

"What's that?"

"The FCS button didn't reset the flight control computers," stated Jock, his voice slightly higher. "Shit. We still have all four x's."

"You're right," added Pope.

"What does the book say to do now?"

"*Step three. With no reset, maintain 200 to 300 knots, minimum sideslip, an angle of attack less than ten degrees, and a maximum of two g's.*"

"Man, we can't do that in-country," said Jock as they passed ten thousand feet.

"Good call," agreed Pope. "That's too slow."

SPEED IS LIFE, MORE IS BETTER.

"Easy 43, Pierre, picture clean."

"Jock, Joisey, six is clear."

Again, there was no answer from Easy 43.

"Hey, Jock. This is Joisey on the number two. Is everything ok?"

Then all hell broke loose. A Cobra of red, twenty-three millimeter tracers suddenly ripped the sky next to Easy 43's right wingtip. Jock instinctively jammed the stick into his left thigh and back into his lap. Easy 43's F-18D had no problem with its roll authority, but the lack of a good pitch capability failed to maneuver their nose adequately across the horizon.

"FUCK."

"Holy shit," said a stunned Joisey from above, "they're shooting at 'em."

"Easy 43, Pierre. Do you have a problem?"

"Damn it."

A second Cobra of tracers pierced the sky on the other side of Easy 43.

"FUCK."

Jock jammed the stick into his right thigh and back into his lap.

"Jock, Joisey, on the number two radio."

Pope's helmet was slammed into the canopy.

SPEED IS LIFE, MORE IS BETTER.

Such a tiny diameter of twenty-three millimeters never looked so big.

"Flight controls. Flight controls," bitched Betty.

"Shitscreen, did you see where the bullets came from?"

"Damn."

"Easy 43, Pierre, how do you hear?"

Another Cobra zinged by the canopy.

"FUCK."

"They're coming from the hill by the red barn."

"Jock, have you got it?" asked Pope.

"Damn."

SPEED IS LIFE, MORE IS BETTER.

"Easy 43, Pierre, radio check."

"Jock, get some knots," instructed Pope.

"Pierre, shut up," commanded Joisey.

"Oh, God."

"WHAT red barn?"

Jock jammed the stick full forward and slammed the throttles into full afterburner. The negative g's caused the contents of their nav bag's to explode into the cockpit.

"Flight controls. Flight controls."

A fourth Cobra of red tracers barely missed the rear horizontal stabilators.

"FUCK."

Maps and charts and checklists and Ho-Hos scattered throughout both cockpits.

"THAT red barn."

"Aircraft calling Pierre, say again, your transmission was broken."

"Shit."

SPEED IS LIFE, MORE IS BETTER.

"Flight controls. Flight controls."

"I don't think we're cleared to drop because it's Tuesday," stated Shitscreen.

Easy 43 rapidly accelerated through five hundred knots as an old fighter axiom suddenly came true - I'd rather be lucky than good. The crew of the twenty-three millimeter AAA gun had to reload.

Jock rapidly whipped the ponies through six hundred knots and then gradually pulled the stick back into his lap to commence a climb. Pope's head was on a swivel in the rear seat, checking for additional threats. Overhead, Joisey and Shitscreen maintained the altitude sanctuary afforded by their high cover position.

"Jock, Joisey, six is clear. Continue your climb."

There was no answer.

"Jock, Joisey."

There was still no answer.

Without bringing his head into the cockpit, Pope quickly advised his pilot of Joisey's transmission, in case something was wrong with Jock's oxygen mask or microphone or helmet or whatever, causing him to miss the call.

"Hey Jock," stated Pope on the ICS, "Joisey is calling you on the number two."

"Pant. Pant. Pant."

The only thing that Pope could hear was Jock's heavy breathing, as their F-18D climbed through eleven thousand feet.

"Yo, Jock."

"Pant. Pant. Pant."

"Jock?"

"Pant. Pant. Pant."

"Jock, this is Joisey, on the number two. Your six is clear. Continue your climb."

"Wilco," replied Pope, answering for his pilot.

"Hey, Jock," queried Pope on the ICS, "are you alright?"

"Pant. Pant. Pant."

"Easy 43, Pierre."

Pope hesitated momentarily to see if Jock would reply to the AWACS from the front seat. There was nothing, but their F-18D continued to climb, passing sixteen thousand feet.

"Pierre, Easy 43, go ahead," replied Pope for Jock.

"Easy 43, state your intentions."

Pope had to stop and think for a moment. He didn't want to go external to his jet with a radio communication that his pilot might have freaked out. He didn't know how Jock felt in the front seat or what he was doing, yet the aircraft was continuing to climb and the nozzle position indicators showed that he was still in full afterburner. Pope had no stick or throttle in the back seat, and wasn't sure what he would do if he actually *did*. Pope was pondering his dilemma, when Joisey broke radio silence.

"Jock, this is Joisey on the number two."

"Joisey, Jock, go ahead."

Pope was stunned. Jock had answered.

"Is everything ok?"

"You've got the lead," coldly stated Jock. "Take me home."

"Roger that," replied Joisey. "I've got the lead."

A final Cobra of red tracers fell harmlessly to the earth behind Easy 43.

* * *

Bada-boom-bada-bing

Remember the explanation of the three possible missions that F-18Ds could be assigned? Well, in addition to the SEAD mission, and the air-to-air mission, the third possibility was a simulated close air support, or CAS, mission. With the southern half of Easy's zone divided into smaller operating areas amongst all of the participating NATO nations, it meant that there were infantry troops on the ground. These peace-keeping forces had FACs, and Marine F-18Ds practiced CAS under FAC control.

These Hornets carried an air-to-ground ordnance mix ranging from dumb, gravity bombs to smart, laser-guided bombs. Furthermore, these Marines were the best in the world at CAS, with the capability to deliver ordnance within meters of friendly troops. But who was really smarter - the pilot or the bomb? Bada-boom-bada-bing.

A Marine Corps FAC was a Captain aviator who was removed from a flying squadron, and assigned to an infantry battalion for one year. A FAC tour was hard, demanding, sweaty, dirty, work. He was bounced around the various companies in the battalion with one mission in life - to control close air support. Thus, a FAC was constantly in the hip pocket of the Company Commander, with the heavy tools of his trade slung over his back. These included three radios - the antiquated PRC-77 for lower frequencies, the unreliable PRC-104 for high frequencies, and the trusty PRC-113 for ultra-high frequencies.

Thus, when it came down to accepting a FAC tour, it was advantageous for the aviator to "pick his poison". That is, volunteer for the one-year-out-of-the-cockpit that would be the least painful. If an aviator knew a FAC tour bullet had his name on it, then it was best to volunteer for one that was non-deploying. That way, he still spent a year with the infantry, but he did it in the good ol' U. S. of A. Whereas, a deploying FAC tour guaranteed him six months on Okinawa, or floating on some type of a Naval amphibious ship. Regardless of whether it was non-deploying or deploying, a FAC tour was a far cry from setting his hair on fire in the F-18D.

Secondly, it was wise to volunteer for a FAC tour based on the type of battalion that he would be supporting. FACs assigned to a Tank battalion or a Light Armored Reconnaissance battalion had one distinct advantage over those assigned to a "straight-legged" infantry battalion - they *rode* wherever they went. Infantry FACs humped their radios, in addition to their pack and other gear.

All of the squadron's Majors and Lieutenant Colonels insisted that a FAC tour was absolutely necessary for promotion. It demonstrated to the grunts that an aviator was a "team player". They insisted that a good fitness report from the grunts was a necessary ticket to be punched. However, that fact still made a FAC tour a tough sell to the strapping, twenty-eight year old bucks flying the F-18D. Their forward vision only went as far as tomorrow's flight schedule.

1427 Tuesday
Easy 23 and 24 in-country on a simulated CAS mission
"This is a mission abort. We're turning around and goin' home."

"Pierre, Easy 23," said Ninja.

"Easy 23, Pierre, I have you radar contact," replied the French AWACS. "Go."

"Pierre," began Ninja, "Easy 23 is a flight of two Hornets, mission complete with Texaco, assigned to work with Gunner 14."

"Easy 23, Pierre copies all. Proceed to Point Echo."

"Pierre, Easy 23, Echo, wilco."

Easy 23, Hollywood and Ninja, instantly commenced an energy-sustaining left turn to the west at twenty three thousand feet. As Hollywood rolled wings level, Ninja selected the steering to Point Echo. Then Ninja ran Hollywood through his combat checklist via challenge and reply.

Easy 24, Hick Boy and Frap, floated their left turn and climbed slightly, assuming a perfect wingman's position   Hick Boy maintained sight of his lead throughout the turn, while Frap manipulated the radar controls to ensure clear airspace downrange.

It looked like just another day of simulated CAS as two Marine F-18Ds droned towards Point Echo. In fact, nothing was said for a minute or two.

"Easy 23, Pierre."

"Pierre, Easy 23, go ahead."

"Easy 23, Pierre shows you at Point Echo. You're cleared to switch Gunner 14 on Magenta."

"Pierre, Easy 23, switching Gunner 14 on Magenta."

In reality, Gunner 14 was Yeti. He was a pilot in the squadron a short year ago, and was now a FAC with the First Battalion, Third Marine Regiment. An aggressive, rising star, Yeti was one of the squadron's front-runners, and he was sure to pick up a Top Gun quota. Then he sucked up a FAC tour with the grunts. Ouch. It would be good to talk to an old friend again.

As soon as the two Hornets switched to Magenta, an aggressive Gunner 14 was already on the net.

"Easy 23, Gunner 14."

Ninja didn't reply right away, for he wanted to listen again. Something was afoul.

"Easy 23, this is Gunner 14."

"Hey Hollywood," Ninja stated on the ICS.

"Yeah?"

"Does that sound like Yeti to you?"

"No," returned Easy 23's pilot, "but he's probably got a cold or something. You know, from sleeping in the mud and rain."

"Yeah, I guess you're right."

Easy 23's WSO resumed his duties.

"Gunner 14, Easy 23 has you loud and clear," said Ninja.

Then Ninja dropped all semblance of radio discipline in an effort to talk to his former squadron mate, asking "Hey Yeti, how are ya doin'?"

Ninja was greeted with only silence, but he still continued his attempt.

"Yeti, Easy 23 is Hollywood and Ninja. Easy 24 is Hick Boy and Frap. Remember us?"

Again, there was silence.

"Hollywood, what's Yeti's bag?" asked Ninja on the ICS. "He acts like he doesn't even know us."

"Man, I don't know."

Then Gunner 14 finally spoke in a serious monotone, stating, "Easy 23, Gunner 14, I have an immediate mission for you. Ready to copy?"

Behind the power curve but sensing the urgency, Ninja resumed radio discipline.

"Gunner 14, Easy 23, go ahead."

"Easy 23, Gunner 14, you are cleared for an immediate attack upon the following grid coordinates."

As Gunner 14 read the coordinates, the hair stood up on the back of Frap's neck in Easy 24. He recognized those coordinates from *somewhere*, but didn't know where. He grabbed his nav bag from the left console and instantly began digging.

"Gunner 14, Easy 23 copies all, proceeding inbound," stated Ninja.

"Easy 23, Gunner 14, I'm standing by."

"Hey Hollywood," Ninja said over the ICS. "Something's not right. Those coordinates don't make sense."

Then Frap keyed the number two radio, knowing that Gunner 14 could not hear on that frequency, and said, "Easy 23, this is Easy 24 on the number two."

"Go ahead, Frap," said Hollywood.

"Those coordinates belong to the Marines' Third Regimental Command Post."

What a *great* call from a young WSO.

"Are you *sure*?" asked Hollywood.

"I'm lookin' right at it, Hollywood," asserted Frap. "Let's validate that Yeti."

Frap was definitely on his game, for that was *another* great call.

Ninja immediately jumped back onto the frequency, saying, "Easy 24, 23, got it."

As the lead WSO and having both hands free, Ninja rifled through his own nav bag, and broke out the classified validation card for the day. An appropriate response from the mysterious Gunner 14 would clear up any doubts as to his true identity.

"Gunner 14, Easy 23," said Ninja.

"Easy 23, Gunner 14, go ahead," returned the voice that wasn't quite Yeti's.

"Gunner 14, Easy 23 requests that you validate Chicago Tampa."

An eternity of silence followed on the number one radio. The correct response was Denver.

"Gunner 14, Easy 23, I say again, validate Chicago Tampa."

Again, there was only silence.

Then Hollywood jumped onto the number one radio with the failsafe question that every Marine aviator would know.

"Yeti, this is Hollywood. What's the shittiest part about deployments to 29 Palms, California?"

Again, there was no reply.

Hollywood, the flight lead, instantly took charge, calling, "Easy 24, Easy 23."

"Easy 23, Easy 24, go ahead," replied Hick Boy.

"Easy 24, this is a *mission abort*. We're turning around and goin' home. Flight switch to Pierre, go."

"Easy 23, Easy 24 copies, switching Pierre."

"Hick Boy, Hollywood on the number two radio," said Easy 23's pilot, knowing that the alleged Yeti could not hear that frequency.

"Hollywood, this is Hick Boy, go ahead."

"That wasn't Yeti," declared Hollywood.

"Hollywood," said Ninja on the ICS. "Who *was* that?"

"I don't know. And how did he get our frequency and those coordinates?"

1538 Tuesday
Easy 42 Returning Home
"You just do your WSO shit,
and leave the pilot shit to me."

Their mission was over, and Shitscreen was in that mindless state that aircrew entered as they flew the profile back home. Once again, an Easy flight was returning to base with no ordnance expended, but after having been fired upon. However, other than Jock's fiasco, it had been a great flight. Joisey and Shitscreen were both very experienced in the F-18D; consequently, the mission progressed smoothly, and the aircrew coordination was flawless.

Shitscreen's butt hurt from the four hours of drilling through the sky, thus, he pounded his left thumb up and down on the g-suit test button by his left hip. The alternating inflation and deflation of his g-suit forced the blood to circulate a little more in his legs and lower abdomen, which felt good. He pressed his toes hard against the foot pedals to tense his leg muscles, and twisted his torso to relieve the stiffness. In the front cockpit, Joisey performed the same gymnastics to increase the blood flow to tired muscles. Eventually, Joisey interrupted his exercise session with a humble call on the ICS, saying, "Hey, Shitscreen."

"Yeah, Joisey, what do you want?"

"Do you. . . um. . . have an extra piddle pack?"

Shitscreen furrowed his brow in thought for a moment, then asked, "Why? What happened, 'Mr. Efficiency'? Did you fill the one you brought with you after eating your ham sandwich?"

There was silence from the front cockpit. Then came the embarrassed reply, "No. After taking a bite out of my ham sandwich, I accidentally dropped both it and the piddle pack on the floor, and now I can't reach either one."

"Ohhhhhhhhh," returned a smug WSO. "So are you telling me there's FOD now in the front cockpit?"

"Oh, cut the shit, man," said Joisey. "Do you have an extra piddle pack or not? My bladder is killing me."

Shitscreen reached by his right hip, and grabbed the piddle pack that he had filled thirty minutes ago. Knowing that the plastic was very sturdy and that he had securely tied the twist-tie, he tossed the bulging piddle pack to the front cockpit and hit Joisey on the back of the helmet.

"You want a piddle pack?" asked Shitscreen. "Well, here's a piddle pack."

Joisey violently jerked in the front seat, accidentally hitting the stick, and knocking the jet out of autopilot.

"Auuuggghhhh," Joisey yelled. "Who's the gross bastard *now*?"

Meanwhile, Shitscreen was laughing so hard in the rear cockpit that he got a side stitch. Joisey tossed the used piddle pack over his left shoulder into the back seat, and Shitscreen caught it like he was at an egg toss, cradling it to a soft landing on his lap. Then, he carefully returned it to its original resting place on the right console. In between chortles, Shitscreen reached into his left bicep pocket, and pulled out a new piddle pack.

"Hey, Joisey," stated Shitscreen. "I've got an extra piddle pack. Reach back over your right shoulder."

Joisey followed his WSO's instructions, stretching to the extreme physical limits of his body. In the back seat, Shitscreen undid his right shoulder harness to allow a few precious extra inches of reach, and slipped the piddle pack into Joisey's waiting grasp. That's how everything was passed between cockpits. Maps, charts, approach plates, airfield diagrams, Twinkies - it didn't matter.

"Thanks, Shitscreen. Remember to redo your shoulder harness."

"Got it. Thanks Joisey. Good call."

Shitscreen reconnected his right shoulder harness, and then he went back to that mindless, returning home state of mind, playing with the infrared display by trying to lock up fishing boats. At one time or another, the entire Italian fleet of fishing vessels had probably been under the tracking symbology of an F-18's infrared system. In between acquisitions, he cocked his head to the right so that he could somewhat see around Joisey's head box. Shitscreen could see that Joisey had his head buried in this chest, so he knew that his pilot was busy with the task at hand of trying to use the piddle pack. Suddenly, their Hornet jerked violently with a roll to the right.

"Sorry, man," Joisey said on the ICS. "My knee accidentally hit the stick."

"Hey, bonehead," returned Shitscreen. "Have you ever heard of autopilot?"

"Shitscreen, you just do your WSO shit, and leave the pilot shit to me."

Then Shitscreen noticed the text illuminating on the key pad, indicating that Joisey had selected autopilot, on the advice of his WSO. Shitscreen continued his search for fishing boats, content with the realization that it would only be a matter of time before Joisey was done filling his piddle pack. After a few moments, Joisey keyed the ICS, stating, "Hey, Shitscreen, look up front on the right side."

Shitscreen diverted his attention from the infrared display, and glanced into the front cockpit over Joisey's right shoulder. Joisey was holding up a bloated piddle pack full of yellow urine as if it was some kind of a trophy. Shitscreen laughed, because Joisey was exhibiting the same pride demonstrated by a two year old being potty-trained. Rightly so, for a pilot to use a piddle pack was a monumental undertaking.

"Not a drop on me," Joisey proudly boasted from the front seat.

"All this talk about piss has made me have to go," returned Shitscreen.

"Oh, oh. Was that your last piddle pack that you gave me?"

"No," answered Shitscreen. "I've got one more."

"Damn, Shitscreen," said Joisey, "think of how many ham sandwiches you could've brought with you."

Shitscreen reached into his left bicep pocket one final time, and retrieved his last piddle pack. This was going to be duck soup, for although still a challenge, it was much easier for a WSO to use a piddle pack. Shitscreen undid both of his lap restraints, and thrust his pelvis up and forward, lifting his butt off of the seat. Then he wrestled open his flight suit zipper, and struggled to remove his manhood out past the straps of his torso harness. Once satisfied that he was in the piddle pack, Shitscreen settled his butt back onto the seat cushion, and opened his body's internal piss valves. It actually felt good, until he suddenly felt a warm wetness on the seat cushion.

"Damn it," said Shitscreen.

He had obviously miscalculated on the angle to hold the piddle pack, and spilled urine onto the seat. He immediately closed his internal piss valves, but it was too late. His seat cushion was soaked, and Shitscreen was forced to sit in his own urine for the duration of the flight home.

Joisey was just like most pilots, and flew with his mask off on the way home for comfort. After a few moments, he keyed the ICS, asking, "Do I smell piss?"

"Oh, eat me, Joisey."

"No, thank you," returned Joisey. "I've got a ham sandwich to eat up here that I was able to retrieve from the floor."

Joisey cranked up the cockpit airflow, which blew from front to rear, and kept the smell of urine in the rear seat. He smugly took a big bite of his ham sandwich.

* * *

The Jesus Chain

Someone once said that there are no atheists in foxholes. That's probably true. However, that same statement probably didn't apply to F-18D cockpits. In an environment where you could be fat, dumb, and happy one minute, and then in a smoking hole the next, there were surprisingly quite a few aviators who never acknowledged a belief in God. In the military, and especially in the egotistical kingdom of Marine fighter aviation, a belief in God was perceived to be a weakness. Religion was thought of as a crutch. In the world of Marine Corps fighter pilots, where the slightest chink in your armor caused a feeding frenzy, a crutch was the *last* thing anybody needed. Fighter pilots felt that they could do it all themselves. Thus, they had precious little need for silly religious trinkets like a Catholic rosary, dubbed "the Jesus chain."

1702 Tuesday
The Chapel Tent
"Fellows, never lose the faith, and pray the rosary daily."

Pope slumped down in his chair, a frustrated man, sighing, "Not again."

For the entire length of the deployment, he had tried to organize a group of Catholics to pray the rosary every Tuesday night at 1700. For the entire length of the deployment, he had suffered through a disappointing turnout. Was that so much to ask? Twenty minutes on a Tuesday evening?

Tonight's only attendee was Jock. Of course, that was no surprise. Jock was still shaking from this afternoon's incident with the flight control caution and the AAA. It was yet another straw laden upon his weakening back, thus, he sought strength in his fellow Catholics. Jock confided only in Pope about his depression, and Pope kept the pilot's problem strictly in confidence. However, Pope also secretly worried about Jock, not only for his safety, but also for the safety of those who flew with him.

Every month, the squadron's Director of Safety and Standardization, the DOSS, chaired a "Human Frailties Board" amongst all of the squadron's bigwigs, except for the Commanding Officer. At this super-secret, closed door meeting, the DOSS methodically covered a list containing the name of *every* aviator, and asked if the board members knew of any personal problems that the aviator might be having. It didn't matter what the problem was. A divorce, adultery, a separation, financial difficulties, the pursuit of a masters degree, an upcoming move, Johnny's performance in school, Suzy's need for braces - anything - weighing on the mind of an aviator could cause him to lose his mental edge, and subsequently crash his F-18. If the Human Frailties Board deemed it necessary, an aircrew was grounded - for his own good - until he resolved the problem.

Pope was torn apart inside. On one hand, he didn't want to expose the chink in Jock's armor, and leave him to the mercy of the sharks. After all, it was only depression and loneliness. Shit, everybody in the squadron felt those emotions at one time or another on deployment. If the Marine Corps grounded every aviator who was combating depression and loneliness, not a single jet would ever get airborne. Then on the other hand, Pope feared for the lives of those who flew with Jock, not to mention Jock's *own* life. Was Jock an accident in the jet just waiting to happen? Was Jock a suicide risk?

"Aw, don't worry about the turn out, Pope," stated Jock. "We'll eventually get more Marines coming once the word gets out."

To Jock, it felt good for the helping hand to be reversed, extending from himself to Pope for once. It had been the other way around since the beginning of the deployment. Today's flight over Grobnev certainly didn't help matters.

"Once the word gets out?" asked Pope. "I've put it in the daily plan, I've put it on the training plan, I've announced it at formations - I don't know what else to do."

Just then, the entrance flap to the Chapel tent flipped up, and Ghost ducked in, rosary in hand. Pope smiled. Ghost was rock solid in his Catholic faith. He was the epitome of all those characteristics that the Marine Corps espoused - honesty, integrity, and faithfulness. Back in the real world, Ghost attended mass on a daily basis; furthermore, he went to confession twice a month. Lastly, Ghost was the only Officer in the squadron who humbled himself every night by kneeling down beside his bed and saying prayers to the Lord. Of course, he didn't make that common knowledge amongst his squadron mates. In any case, nothing ever rattled Ghost's faith, and Jock secretly tried to emulate him in every facet of his life. Pope, on the other hand, was just a good Catholic, if not a well-practiced one. He couldn't remember who was President the last time that he went to confession.

"Hey, guys. Sorry I'm late," said Ghost. He looked around at the sparse attendance. "Is this it again?"

"Yep, this is it," replied Pope, the frustration showing in his voice.

"Well, that's the problem with a lot of Catholics," smiled Ghost. "They only go to church three times in their life - when they're hatched, matched, and dispatched."

Pope laughed and nodded his head.

God, how can Ghost always be so positive? Jock thought in admiration.

"Yeah, I once knew a Catholic priest who wanted to get rid of the bats in the churches belfry," added Pope, "so he baptized them, and he hasn't seen them since."

It was Ghost's turn to laugh in agreement.

Inside, Jock felt as if he was struggling to be as cool as Ghost and Pope. Wanting to be one of the boys, Jock added one last playful jab at the world's Catholics, saying, "That's nothin'. My parish church back home had a big sign above the door on the inside that said 'Go ahead. Judas left early too'."

Pope chuckled, but Ghost actually laughed out loud, which pleased Jock.

"Well, we might as well get started," continued Ghost. "We want to make it to the evening sidestep in time to get the good ranch dressing."

"And the first batch of chicken," added Pope.

Jock wanted to be part of the conversation so badly. He was tired of the depression and loneliness. He was searching for something - indeed anything - to make him feel like he belonged to the fighter community.

"You don't have to do the evening sidestep tonight if you don't want to," stated Jock. "I thought I heard Butt Munch and Ping say that they were taking the van out into town to eat tonight."

"Nah, I'll pass," declined Ghost. "I have to work-out yet tonight after I eat."

"I'll skip it, too," said Pope. "The last time I did that, we went to a Chinese restaurant, and it was like watching a bad movie. Every time the Chinese waitress moved her lips, Italian words came out."

"Yeah, let's get started," stated Ghost.

"Ok, what Mysteries do we want to say tonight - the Glorious, Joyful, or Sorrowful?" asked Pope. "Catholic doctrine says you say the Sorrowful on Tuesday."

"You know my view on that, Pope daddy," said Ghost. "The Sorrowful Mysteries are too damn depressing. I always vote for one of the other two."

"Jock, do you give a rat's ass?"

"Let's do the Joyful Mysteries," he answered. "They're very uplifting."

"Then the Joyful Mysteries it is."

Pope reached down into the flight suit pocket on the outside of his left shin, and pulled out an antique, black rosary. He constantly kept his rosary there, and always reached down to touch it when his F-18D was cleared for take-off. His old, black rosary with the huge wooden beads was originally his Grandpa's, and Pope's mom had given it to him on the day that Pope graduated from flight school. She told Pope the story of how his Grandpa would come in from the fields every night, tired and dirty. He would drink a long neck Blatz with his supper, and then sit in the dark at the kitchen table, all by himself, and pray the rosary before going to bed. Pope never forgot what his mother told him on that day, and he always started the Tuesday night rosary sessions with the same statement, "Fellows, never lose the faith, and pray the rosary daily."

"Roger that."

"Will do."

"Everybody ready?" asked Pope.

"I'm ready," stated Ghost, clutching his white ivory rosary from the first grade.

"Go for it," returned Jock, holding a tiny rosary with brown wooden beads.

"In the name of the Father, and the Son, and the Holy Spirit," began Pope, blessing himself.

1711 Tuesday
In the Dining Tent
"I'm a normal, healthy male."

"You mind if I join you?" asked Frap, holding his cardboard tray.

"No, pull up a chair, my man," answered Booger with a cynical grin, for the dining tent contained only booths. "Sometimes a chair can come in very handy."

Booger cleared two empty milk cartons from Frap's side of the booth, and returned the piece of rope to his lap.

"Thanks," said Frap, sliding into the booth, and ignoring Booger's weird chair comment. "Where's Dick and Screw?"

"They're waiting outside," returned Booger. "I've got their supper hidden in my lower flight suit pocket."

"That's cool," smiled Frap. "Why are you sitting over here all by yourself?"

"Oh, I don't know," said Booger, stirring his peas with a plastic fork.

"Well, you ought to be happy, with the chow hall serving the 'halfway-to-home' meal tonight. Didn't you get your crab leg?"

"Yep, I got my crab leg - singular," answered Booger, "while people back in the real world get to enjoy crab legsssss - plural." Booger phonetically emphasized the 's' with a sarcastic tone of voice.

"That's the breaks of Naval Air," returned Frap.

"Yeah, I guess so," sighed Booger, unable to make eye contact.

"Can you believe it?" asked Frap. "Only three months to go. Man, you'll be back in the real world before you know it, and have crab legsssss out the ass."

Frap's mocking emphasis of the 's' made Booger realize how immature he had sounded in bitching. Maybe he shouldn't be so worried about his physical. After all, he only had to do a routine follow-up tomorrow morning at the hospital, and then everything would be fine.

"I know," continued Booger, "where has the time gone? I wanted to take some leave while I was over here, but I haven't done so yet."

"Really? Where do you want to go?"

"I hear Austria and Switzerland are nice," answered Booger. "I don't know, maybe go hiking in the Alps."

"Have you ever been to Paris?" asked Frap, cracking his crab leg.

"No, I never have."

"Do you know why all the boulevards in Paris are lined with trees?"

"No, but I'll bite. Go ahead," said Booger.

"Because the Germans like to march in the shade."

Booger chortled and shook his head. Talking to Frap was good. He was definitely a 'glass is half full' kind of a guy. Furthermore, Frap was good at keeping secrets. Booger momentarily pondered confiding in Frap.

"Didn't you have your flight physical today?" asked Frap.

Oh no, thought Booger. *Frap already knows.*

"Yep. Why do you ask?" he inquired, fearful that Frap had heard something.

"I ask because, while you were at Dental, did you see the cute hygienist in the last room on the right?"

Whew, thought Booger. *Frap doesn't know anything.*

"Nope. What about her?" he asked, hoping to steer the subject away from his flight physical.

"Man, you talk about *hot.* For my flight physical last month, I had to go back to her the following week for a cleaning. Well, before going, I intentionally ate a whole damn box of Oreos."

Booger chuckled as he formed a mental picture of Frap's teeth.

"So how did the physical go?" inquired Frap.

Shit, thought a paranoid Booger. *Why is he digging?*

"Oh, you know," he explained. "It was your typical flight physical. The Doc has one hand down your throat, the other hand up your ass, and it feels like he's trying to shake hands."

Frap laughed, asking, "Did he find anything?"

God, thought Booger, *he must know something.*

"Oh no, he found nothin'," lied Booger. "I'm a normal, healthy male."

"Good," returned Frap, "because personally, if they found something wrong with me, and declared that I couldn't fly, I'd kill myself."

"I would too," admitted Booger. "I would too."

1722 Tuesday
The Chapel Tent
"…you've got to be like Teflon, man.
Shit just doesn't stick."

"In the name of the Father, and the Son, and the Holy Spirit," concluded Pope, blessing himself, and then kissing the cross on his rosary. "That's it for another rosary."

"Let's eat," said Ghost.

Pope and Ghost arose from their chairs, but Jock interrupted their escape, asking, "Um…Ghost, can I ask you a question?"

"Sure, Jock. What's on your mind?"

Jock dropped a bombshell.

"How do you combat depression while on deployments?"

Ghost just stared at him in bewilderment, unaware of Jock's depression. Furthermore, he hadn't heard about Jock's AAA incident just hours earlier.

Oh shit, thought Pope. *Is Jock going to spill his guts?*

"What do you mean?" asked Ghost.

Oh shit, thought Pope. *Here it comes.*

"Well, deployments are hard," continued Jock. "I certainly don't have to tell you *that*. Yet you're always so upbeat and positive. How do you do it?"

Whew, thought Pope, wiping his brow. *That was nothing.*

"You're serious, aren't you?" asked Ghost.

"I'm serious as a heart attack. I miss my wife. I can't take the bullshit. All I want to do is get out of the Marine Corps and fly for TWA."

Oh shit, thought Pope. *He opened the floodgates now.*

Ghost glanced over at Pope, and then looked back at Jock. There was a moment of silence. Jock sounded pathetic and weak.

"Jock, my man," began Ghost, "first of all, you have to enter what I call a 'deployment mindset'. You have to mentally numb yourself to holidays and birthdays and anniversaries and fun. They simply don't exist. Each one is just another day."

"I understand."

"Also, you have to mentally numb yourself to the bullshit."

"Numb myself to the bullshit?" asked Jock, his voice cracking. "How?"

Oh God, thought Pope. *He's going to lose it right here and now.*

"How do I numb myself to sleeping in a tent that's three hundred yards from a runway? How do I numb myself to cold showers, Strike Eagle take-offs, oh-dark-thirty briefs, and washers that don't work?" sniffled Jock, as a tear rolled down his cheek.

This was interesting. Pope had never witnessed a nervous breakdown before.

Ghost held his ground, refusing to put his arm around Jock or comfort him. He kept the same steady tone of voice and continued to lecture, saying, "Jock, you've got to be like Teflon, man. Shit just doesn't stick."

Pope was embarrassed by Jock's dismal display of helplessness. Maybe he shouldn't have held Jock's depression in confidence over the past few months. Maybe now it was time for Jock to see a doctor. Maybe Pope should expose him to the sharks.

"Secondly, you have to have a sense of humor," instructed Ghost. "Laugh at everything. I say again, laugh at everything."

Jock was beginning to listen, and not question Ghost's fatherly advice.

"Thirdly, Jock, find yourself something to do besides flying. Make it something that will totally take your mind off of the deployment. Exercise, read, paint, write, for Christ's sake, collect stamps, I don't care - but do *something.*

"Yeah," added Pope. "Most guys go overseas on deployment, and they become one of two things - either a work-out animal or an alcoholic. Ghost and Buick are perfect examples."

Ghost cast a glance as if to say, "You're not helping," then returned to Jock.

"Jock, I lift weights every single day. That's *my* time. That's *my* thing. The Marine Corps can't take it away from me. In fact, it's an escape from the Marine Corps."

"Really?" sniffed Jock, "Do you think that maybe I could give it a try?"

"Sure, join me in the gym tent anytime," said Ghost.

Jock wiped the tears from his face, mumbling, "Thanks, Ghost."

"Now, what do you say we go eat?" asked Ghost.

"Ghost, I think I'm going to run and see if I can catch Butt Munch and Ping in the van," said Jock. "It's time that I start living. Thanks again."

Jock whirled about, lifted the flap, and exited the Chapel Tent. Pope and Ghost heard the clopping of his flight boots as he ran down the sidewalk towards the parking lot. Ghost reached for the flap to do the evening sidestep, but Pope grabbed his sleeve and tugged Ghost's arm back slightly. Pope stared into Ghost's eyes.

"Are you going to tell the Human Frailties Board?"

"Nope."

"Why not?" Pope asked.

"Let's just wait and see how his foray into a new lifestyle works out."

"Of course, you realize, that may take too long. He could kill himself and a WSO before then."

"I'll take him under my wing. I won't let that happen."

1731 Tuesday
Tent City, Tent 11
"It's always *something*."

Jock raced from the Chapel Tent through downtown Tent City. He adeptly avoided N.D., who was struggling to push his cleaning cart on the bumpy sidewalk as he slowly made his evening rounds through the shower and bathroom buildings.

Jock checked his Rolex as he lifted his tent's flap. Nobody was in tent eleven, so his tent mates must've been doing the evening sidestep. At this hour, they would be early enough to get the good ranch dressing.

I can still catch Butt Munch and Ping in the van, he thought.

He quickly bounded to his masterbatorium, and entered it. Jock raced to change from his flight suit into civilian clothes. He combed his hair to get rid of the "helmet head", and dabbed some cologne to hide the stink.

"Yeah . . . mentally numb myself," mumbled Jock. "Teflon . . . be like Teflon."

Jock sat on his rack to tie his shoes, when he noticed a letter on his pillow.

"Hmmmm. What's this?"

One of Jock's tent mates must've gotten his mail from the Ready Room and dropped it off for him. Jock noted that the return address was the Department of the Treasury's Internal Revenue Service Office, in Atlanta.

"What the hell?"

Jock grabbed the letter, and ripped it open.

Request for Tax Payment

According to our records, you still owe $6,505.07 on last year's income tax. Please pay the full amount by August 22. Mail your check or money order, with the tear-off stub from the last page of this letter, to the address below. Make your check payable to the United States Treasury and include your social security number. If you can't pay in full, please call us to discuss payment.

Jock couldn't believe his eyes.

"Damn it," stated Jock. "It's always *something*."

Jock placed his head in his hands, as the letter fell to the floor.

"It's always *something*."

Jock began forcibly inhaling and exhaling in an attempt to regain his composure.

"Pant....pant....pant."

"Teflon."

"Pant....pant....pant."

* * *

You just wanna go somewhere where everybody knows your name.

The Officers' Club tent was an island of sanity in a sea of bullshit. Open 24/7 and run totally on the honor system, it was a Marine Corps version of the sitcom "Cheers" - you only wanted to go somewhere where every body knew your name. To do so, you lifted the flap and ducked through the canvas entrance into the very center of what little social life an Officer had.

After entering, immediately on the left, was a makeshift wooden bar with six rickety stools, none of which matched. One had been built by Buick's handy work, and two of them had been stolen out of a dumpster behind the Air Force Officers' Club. At the corner stool down by the CD player, you could always find Buick. He was Norm from "Cheers". When he wasn't flying, his fat butt was permanently glued to that corner stool. His partner in crime was Screech, the Citadel graduate. Screech was Cliffee the mailman, hands down. That guy could spout more useless trivia than *any* man.

Behind the bar was a refrigerator, which was always stocked. It contained the standard brands of beer, with the occasional German lager. Sodas were placed on the bottom shelf, back in the rear, mixers were placed in the door's shelves, and milk was not allowed. At one time or another, there was usually a jar of olives, a baggie of limes and lemons, and the occasional leftover submarine sandwich that someone hoped to save. In the freezer above, there were always empty ice trays, because aviators were notoriously wicked at not re-filling them. There was also a tupperware container with a frozen daiquiri mix that had been there since the *last* deployment.

On top of the refrigerator was an empty coffee can, which was the receptacle for whatever cash donations were deemed appropriate when you grabbed a beverage. Next to the coffee can sat the obligatory brown dice cup, which only contained four of the five required dice. Everybody blamed Joisey for losing the one.

Both the bar and the refrigerator were covered with a multitude of stickers from the various squadrons in this crazy business. Any visitors to the club were required to place one of their squadron's stickers somewhere in the bar.

Planted behind the bar were Hick Boy and Dago. They were as close a match to Woody and Carla as you will ever find. Hick Boy wasn't from Indiana, like Woody on "Cheers", but was instead from the backwoods of eastern Tennessee. Dumber than a box of hammers, but with a heart of pure gold, he put Jack Daniels in everything. Hick Boy, with his trademark towel draped over his shoulder, assumed the monumental task of keeping the refrigerator stocked, and never let the squadron down. Dago, a spunky Italian from Brooklyn who barely stood five feet tall, possessed a rapier wit and a sarcastic tongue that would cut you at every opportunity. He even had curly brown hair like Carla, and the same fiery temper.

Pope rounded out the "Cheers" crowd. Philosophical and deeply religious, he was as close to Doctor Frazier Crane as anyone. Even though Pope was single, the scary part was that his girlfriend back in the real world was also the spitting image of Lilith. She was cold and calculating, and Shitscreen used to joke that she was so uptight, you couldn't drive a needle up her ass with a sledgehammer.

Immediately to the right as you entered the Officers' Club was a card table and four lawn chairs. It was here that wicked games of Dominoes, Risk, Clue, and Monopoly were waged on lonely Friday and Saturday nights, or on rainy afternoons when the flight schedule was cancelled. However, the real game of choice was Hearts. Everyone loved that game - especially Ping - and it was a pure joy to stick Joisey or Dago with the Queen of Spades. Affectionately known as "the bitch", the Queen of Spades caused more contention at that table than *any* houses on Boardwalk Avenue.

The far end of the tent contained an eclectic mixture of scavenged chairs and sofas arranged theater-style in front of a big-screen TV and VCR. Every Thursday night back in the real world, One Nut's wife would tape "Seinfeld", "Friends", and "ER", and then mail it to him. The tape always seemed to arrive on the following Wednesday, and everyone would huddle in front of the TV on Wednesday nights for a little taste of the real world. Wednesday nights were always a big production in the Officers' Club.

Finally, you might wonder, who was Sam Malone? Most all of the Officers were former athletes like Sam, some had drinking problems like him, and *all* of their egos thought that they were lady-killers. They *all* thought that they were Sams.

It was too bad that there was no Diane or Rebecca around.

1816 Tuesday
In the Officers' Club Tent
"Football is a metaphor for life."

It was just a typical night in the Officers' Club tent. With supper in their stomachs and nothing else to do, several aviators had migrated down to their canvas escape. Behind the bar, Hick Boy was serving up cold Jack Daniels, and Dago was serving up caustic insults. In his seat at the right end of the bar, Buick preferred beer instead of liquor, as he controlled the CD player. Buick actually surprised the younger crowd, by not playing a lot of classic geezer rock, but instead, the latest, cutting edge stuff from the nineties - the Red Hot Chili Peppers, Jane's Addiction, Jesus Jones, and so on. At the bar sat Bama and Screech, debating some topic that couldn't be heard over the music. Maybe it was football. Bama was already on a roll, pounding down Hick Boy's offerings one right after another, while Screech remained more discreet and under control. At the card table, Pope, Frap, Doc and Butt Munch were into a wicked game of Hearts. Between deals, Butt Munch and Frap laughed about Spine Ripper's mission in life to shut down the SA-2, and Doc just listened. He had no choice. Pope was hanging pretty well for someone who had been up since midnight. Meanwhile, Ninja and One Nut were watching "CNN" on the Armed Forces Network. AFN carried the same shows that were popular back in the real world, but sandwiched them in between poorly made commercials about America that were designed to motivate service men. The cacophony of sounds could not be described.

"How about another Jack-n-Coke?" asked Hick Boy.

"Shit yeah," demanded Bama, pounding his fist on the bar.

"No, thanks," returned Screech. "I've had enough."

"I'm telling you, Screech," said Bama, "football is a metaphor for life."

"Screech, the best part of you is still running down your mom's leg," said Dago.

The Red Chili Peppers sang about never wanting to feel like they did that day.

"Ping, what are you always writing in those little red books?"

"Whose deal is it?" inquired Butt Munch.

"It's Doc's," answered Frap.

"I dealt the last hand. It's Pope's deal."

"What am I?" asked Pope, grabbing the deck, "a pass right, left, or across?"

"Pass across."

"Good evening. Today, American F-15s and F-16s from the U. S. Air Force continued to systematically enforce the NATO no-fly zone over Bosnia with missions 'round-the-clock, aided by F-18s from both the U. S. Navy and the Marine Corps."

"Tell me about it," grumbled Ninja.

"How come the news makes us sound like the second string?" asked One Nut.

"Do you want Joan Osborne or the Dave Matthews Band next?" inquired Buick.

"Whatever," One Nut replied over his shoulder.

"I missed my calling. I should've been a D. J."

"If you can be a winner at football, then you'll be a winner at life."

"Hey asshole," said Butt Munch, "will you quit leading spades?"

"Man, I'm just trying to sniff out 'the bitch'," replied Frap.

"Furthermore," said Bama, "our squadron logo - speed is life, more is better - applies to *real* life."

"Where the hell is the latest CD of the Dave Matthews band?"

"We already know that 'speed is life, more is better' will save your ass in the cockpit. When everything is going to shit all around you - SAMs, Migs, AAA - as long as you are hauling balls, you'll survive."

"Damn! *I hate* that Queen of Spades!"

"But also in *real* life, when everything is going to shit all around you - death, divorce, taxes - just put your head down and keep up your speed. You'll make it."

"Put something on the boob tube besides the news."

"I'm leaving. I've got to go to the bathroom," stated Bama.

"Don't worry,' replied Dago, "we're not going to follow you."

"You don't have to," returned Bama, "I'll be back. Hick Boy, pour me another Jack-n-Coke and have it waiting."

"Roger that."

"Back in a flash, fellas."

"We await your return with baited breath," snickered Dago.

"Think about what I said concerning football," said Bama over his shoulder.

Jesus Jones sang that there was no other place that they wanted to be.

"Man," confided Butt Munch, "you guys should've heard Spine Ripper yelling in the cockpit today at that SA-2."

"Oh, shit, not 'the bitch' again," said Doc.

"That's about the millionth time you've got the Queen of Spades tonight."

"That's it. Game's over," stated Frap.

"It's just as well," returned Pope. "I've got to hit the rack because I've got the early breif tomorrow morning."

Jane's Addiction sang about having been caught stealing.

"Somebody else can take over the music. I'm hitting the rack too."

"Today, the President continued to emphasize the pride he has in those courageous Service members enforcing the NATO no-fly zone."

* * *

They blew it

They blew it. That's all there is to it. They simply blew it. During the height of the Cold War, the Russian Bear and its KGB probably spent a gazillion Rubles on spy satellites and wire taps and covert spying operations and the like. However, if they *really* wanted to know what was going on - both in-country and in Tent City - all they had to do was bug the toilet stalls of a Marine Corps bathroom.

1902 Tuesday
Tent City Bathroom Building
"Can you spare any paper?"

Spine Ripper was enjoying the quiet solitude of sitting on the toilet all by himself. It was actually kind of peaceful. He had a nice, quiet stall, and was all alone - save for N.D.'s cleaning cart out by the sinks. N.D. was nowhere within sight. Spine Ripper actually had a tiny - very tiny - soft spot in his heart for that old, Italian janitor.

"That poor, hunch-backed bastard," said Spine Ripper. "Right now, he's probably scraping soap scum in the shower."

Additionally, Spine Ripper was enjoying the graffiti.

Here I sit, broken hearted, I came to shit, but only farted.
Why are you looking up here? The joke is between your legs.
He who reads these lines of wit, shall eat my little balls of shit.

As Spine Ripper laughed, the noisy door to the bathroom creaked open. The heavy footsteps that walked into the next stall belonged to only one person. Spine Ripper heard a long unzipping, then Bama's flight suit and underwear dropped to the floor. The tiny toilet seemed to groan under his massive weight. It seemed unnatural to Spine Ripper for the almighty Bama to be in the vulnerable position of having his pants down around his ankles.

"Bama? Is that you?"

"Yep. How are you doing Spine Ripper?"

"Fine, my man."

"Did you get Mr. SA-2 today?"

"No, that bastard dodged another bullet."

"Keep at it, Spine Ripper. You'll get 'im."

"Yeah, I know, Bama. But you know what?"

"No, what?"

"I can't explain it, but something goofy is going on in-country."

"What do you mean?"

"Oh, I don't know," said Spine Ripper. "It's like they know our every move."

"Yeah, Spine Ripper, now that you mention it, I know what you mean."

"For example, they know we need three positive confirmations to fire a HARM and they know that Yeti's frequency is always Magenta and they know our ROE is so worried about collateral damage."

"Yep, you might be right."

Bama fidgeted on the seat, and Spine Ripper scratched.

"Oh, Spine Ripper, speaking of Yeti," said Bama, "did you hear about what happened to Hollywood and Hick Boy today?"

"No, Bama. What happened?"

"They think they ran into the same Yeti imposter who cleared Viper 61 to drop on those Marines yesterday."

"No shit?"

"Yeah, no shit, Spine Ripper."

"That fucker."

There was another reflective moment of silence while Spine Ripper scratched again and Bama grunted. Relieved of their burdens, the mood shifted to a lighter tone.

"What are you doing tonight, Bama?"

"Oh, I'm just hanging out at the club. And you?"

"Oh, I'll probably just read *Stars-n-Stripes*, and then hit the rack."

"Spine Ripper, did you happen to see tomorrow's flight schedule yet?"

"No, Bama, not yet. Why?"

"Spine Ripper, the schedule writer put Hollywood and Shitscreen together again in the same jet tomorrow morning. In fact, they're briefing and leading the flight."

"No shit?"

"Yeah, no shit."

"Oh, man, Bama. I caught their act one morning last week. It's awesome."

"Yep, I was in one of their briefs the other day. It was truly unbelievable."

"Who are the lucky bastards in the other jet tomorrow?"

"Joisey and Pope."

"They'll love it, especially Joisey."

"Yep."

"Bama, do the Safety Nazis know that they're doing those skits?"

"Nope."

"What about the Commanding Officer?"

"Nope."

"Man, there really is a God."

"Yep."

There was another moment of silence.

"Hey Spine Ripper."

"Yeah?"

"Can you spare any paper?"

1923 Tuesday
At the pay phone next to the laundry tent
"Well, Babe, I can't be a real Daddy and a deployed Marine Corps Officer at the same time."

Buick was hunched over Tent City's lone pay phone with his flight suit unzipped to the waist. With the phone receiver to one ear and a finger firmly plugged in the other, he was desperately trying to drown the din that was Tent City in the evening. Fat, dumb, and happy from the evening meal, he was absolutely stuffed - but not so full that he didn't have a cold Budweiser sitting on top of the phone.

"Operator, I'd like to place an international credit card call, please."

After a series of boops and beeps, Buick heard the familiar ring of his in-law's telephone back in Virginia. His wife, Jenny, had packed their three kids and returned to her parent's home for the duration of Buick's deployment. Buick had decided to surprise both her parents and Jenny with a call. But more importantly, Buick felt as if he had to smooth over a couple of speed bumps that had arisen in their marriage. After the fourth ring, Buick began to grow worrisome.

"C'mon, Jenny, pick up," he said aloud, after sipping his beer. "Please, please."

Then he heard that sweet, familiar voice, and said, "Hello? Jenny?"

"Honey, what are you doing answering the phone?" asked Buick.

"What? Your Mom and Dad took the kids to a movie?"

"Yeah, I know, Babe. It's been *years* since they even set foot in a theater."

Sip, then, "Damn. I wish I was there - we'd have the whole house to ourselves."

"Pardon?"

"I said, that I wish that I was there. We'd have the whole house to ourselves."

"Of course."

"Jenny, sure, I can talk."

"Seriously, sweetheart. What's on your mind?"

"No, it *shouldn't* wait until I come home."

Sip, then "WHAT? You want a *what*?"

"Honey, are you *sure* that's what you want?"

"Jenny, a divorce would kill me."

"Yes dear. I'll quit drinking. I'll lose weight. I'll fly less. I promise."

"Well, what about the kids?"

"Babe, we can't do that to them."

"Yeah, sweetheart, I know, I know."

"Well, Babe, I can't be a real Daddy and a deployed Marine Corps Officer at the same time."

"No, I did NOT snip at you."

"Soon, honey, soon. Only three months to go."

Sip, then, "Babe, what's the matter?"

"Don't cry. Jenny, why are you crying?"

"Honey, I do *not* put the squadron ahead of you."

"Yes, you and the kids *always* come first."

"Sure, Babe, I remembered Timmy's birthday on Thursday."

"Yes, dear, a card is already in the mail."

"Yeah, I'll call again on Thursday."

Sip, then, "Ok, ok, I understand. You have to go."

"Despite your desires, Jenny, I still love you and miss you, honey."

"Before you go, I'll tell you what. There's a romantic bed and breakfast Inn called Stefano's near our base. Maybe we can work out you taking a little trip over here later in the summer."

"No sweat. My Mom and dad will gladly watch the kids."

"Jenny, don't worry - we can afford it."

"It will be good for us, sweetheart. Maybe we can patch things up."

"Well, honey, think about it, ok?"

"I love you more than life itself, Jenny."

"Remember. Tell your Mom and Dad and Timmy that I'm going to call again Thursday night."

"Ok. Bye, bye. I love you."

Click. Pmmmmmmmm. A dial tone is the loneliest sound in the world.

2109 Tuesday
Out in the Ville
2716 Petrone Avenue, Apartment 5B
"In a weird kind of way, he has my life in *his* hands, too."

Fig skidded the Commanding Officer's car to a screeching halt. What the hell? Why not? The car was a loaner from the Air Force, so who cared about the brakes? Chunks and Fig were just thankful that the Skipper was cool enough to lend them his official car for the evening.

"Here you go," stated Fig.

But Chunks was already out the passenger side door and double-checking his Rolex watch.

"Thanks for the lift, Fig," returned Chunks, running towards the stairs. "Pick me up at 2300."

"Hey," yelled Fig, leaning out the window. "How about a tip for your driver?"

"Ok," Chunks said over his right shoulder. "Don't smoke in bed."

Fig chuckled, and stepped on the gas, burning rubber. Who cared about the tires too?

"It must be love," he said to himself, shaking his head.

As Fig roared away down Petrone Avenue, Chunks stopped at the top of the stairs, and exhaled. He quickly leaned to the right to gauge his appearance in the window's reflection, and checked his Rolex one last time, before ringing the doorbell.

Riiiiiiiiiiing.

Chunks knew exactly how many steps it was from the kitchen to the front door, and he impatiently counted down.

"…five…four…three…two…one."

The door opened to reveal a picture of beauty. Angela Giancarlo's gorgeous brown eyes lit a fire in Chunk's heart. A glistening smile revealed her happiness to see Chunks again, as thick, luscious brunette hair fell down upon the smooth olive skin of her exposed shoulders. Chunks aggressively placed his right hand around her waist and his left hand under her chin, gently guiding her soft lips to his. Angela's kisses were Heaven on earth, and Chunks wished he could freeze this moment in time.

"Mmmmm," cooed Angela, throwing her arms around Chunks' neck.

Their lips parted, and Chunks dropped his left arm down to join the right that already encircled her tiny waist. They stared into each other's eyes.

"Babe, it's great to see you again."

"I was so worried about you, honey," said Angela, in surprisingly good English.

"Yeah, Babe, I'm sorry I'm late."

Angela merely gazed into Chunk's eyes.

"We landed late," explained Chunks.

"Again?"

"Yeah, and then the debrief from hell went way over."

"Oh, that's ok," sighed Angela.

God, she was so patient and understanding and supportive and caring.

"I didn't have time to take a shower, honey," he continued, "because Fig had to drop me off and get right back for a meeting."

Angela had heard it all a million times before. Such was the lifestyle of dating a deployed Marine Officer.

"Fig?" questioned Angela. "Who is Fig?"

"Oh, you know, Captain Tom. He's my WSO. Remember? He was with me on the night that we met."

"Oh, *that* Captain Tom. I like him. He's sweet."

"Yeah, Fig is a great American."

"Oh, Bill," said Angela, relaxing her grip around Chunk's neck, "I don't understand why you Marines call each other by those silly names."

Sensing the formation of ice, Chunks slightly cinched his grip around Angela's waist, and intensified his gaze, saying, "Sweetheart, it's part of flying. That's all."

"Sometimes I don't think I know you, Bill. You talk about touching banners and stroking wooden fish and I just don't understand."

Chunks realized he was fighting a losing battle.

"Plus," continued Angela, "you say 'he's *my* WSO' like you *own* him."

"Honey, I don't think you understand. I have his *life* in my hands."

Angela gazed into Chunks' eyes.

"Plus," continued Chunks, "I could probably say that the reverse is true. In a weird kind of way, he has my life in *his* hands too."

"Bill, you're talking scary again," scolded Angela, trying to push away.

"Babe, in most emergencies, it's the WSO who pulls the ejection handle first, thus saving both aircrew."

"Bill - emergencies, ejections - I don't like to hear you talk about such things."

"Honey, I'm sorry."

"And I don't want to fight with you either."

"I don't want to fight with you, Babe."

Again, the two engaged in a Norman Rockwell kiss under the moths that flittered around the porch light. They remained in a tight embrace for a silent eternity, and then faced each other once more.

"Ok, Babe. What's for supper?"

Bad move on Chunks' part - ruining the moment. Angela dropped her arms and pushed herself away from the insensitive and socially inept pilot.

"Chicken Cacciatore," stated Angela, folding her arms across her chest, "but it's cold now."

With a basic understanding of body language 101, Chunks recognized that the Chicken Cacciatore wasn't the only thing that was getting cold. He reached out to take Angela into his arms once more. She stepped back again.

"Bill, I never get to see you."

"Sweetheart, there are just some things that I can't control."

"Is it going to *always* be like this?" she asked, with tears welling in her eyes.

"Stick with me, Babe," pleaded Chunks, "stick with me. I promise. Life will be better once we get back to the real world and I get out of the Marine Corps. I promise."

2114 Tuesday
In the Aircrew Van
"You'd probably have to pet him first."

Butt Munch, Ping, Ham Fist, and One Nut were piled into the aircrew van, returning back to the base. Jock had failed to catch the van for some reason. That was too bad for Jock, because it was nice to get out into town every now and then for a quiet evening of pasta and wine. No sidestepping robots, no dirty messmen, and no stains on a sneeze guard - just a portly waiter with a moustache like the fat steward who served *Lady and the Tramp*.

Butt Munch was in the driver's seat - speeding by Italian standards - and enjoying how great it felt to drive again. He missed his fighter pilot car, a BMW. Ping was in the passenger's seat with the window down, gazing up at the stars and making his hand into an airfoil in the air stream. Ping was still a kid at heart.

Despite the relaxed atmosphere emanating from the two front seats, the two passengers in the rear were going head to head. Ham Fist, the FNG pilot, and One Nut, the FNG WSO, were jokingly taking pot shots at each other's profession. This was sure to be a credible and fact-filled debate, considering that there was a whopping total of two hundred hours in the F-18D between the two. So Butt Munch and Ping were fat, dumb, and happy to simply listen to the bullshit flowing from the back seat. I guess a stomach full of pasta and wine makes older men pensive, and younger men bellicose.

"How hard can it be to be a pilot?" asked One Nut. "You push forward on the stick, and houses get bigger. You pull back on the stick, and houses get smaller."

"How hard can it be to be a WSO?" countered Ham Fist. "You type in some nav points, and then you're just along for the ride like a piece of luggage."

Butt Munch and Ping looked at each other and laughed, as Ping adjusted the rear view mirror to check their expressions.

"Ping, will you kindly quit moving my mirror?" requested Butt Munch. "I'm trying to drive here."

Butt Munch reached up with his right hand and readjusted the rear view mirror that Ping had skewed, while Ham Fist punched the upper arm of his fellow FNG.

"Have you received last Thursday night's tape from your wife yet?" asked Butt Munch, changing the subject.

"Nope," replied One Nut. "It usually comes in Wednesday's snail mail, so it should be here tomorrow."

"What a cool wife you have, One Nut," said Ping, adjusting the rear view mirror.

"Will you leave my mirror alone?" cried Butt Munch. "Driving in Italy is hard enough without you screwing with my mirror."

Ignoring Butt Munch, Ping jockeyed the mirror again to see One Nut's face.

"If you touch my mirror one more time, I'm going to rip off your left arm and hit you with the wet end."

Suddenly, the extra attention that Butt Munch was devoting to Ping and the rear view mirror caused him to blow through a sign at an intersection. Luckily, there was no traffic coming from the right or left, and the white Air Force van skittered through the intersection unscathed.

"Shit," said One Nut as he grabbed the armrests.

"What was that sign back there?" questioned Ping, contorting his body around in the seat and sticking his head out the window.

"It had red on it," added Ham Fist. "That's all I know."

"Was it a 'stop' or a 'yield'?" asked Butt Munch, speeding away from the scene of the crime.

"I can't tell," replied Ping, with the air stream muffling his words. He returned his head back inside, only to take a verbal face shot from Butt Munch.

"What kind of a WSO are you?" screamed Butt Munch. "Allowing your pilot to run through an intersection like that?"

"I was all disoriented in the front seat," joked Ping. "I'm not used to having all this glass in front of me."

"We were lucky back there," said Ham Fist, wide-eyed and fearful.

"Yeah, we could've broad-sided somebody," said One Nut, master of the obvious.

"Oh man. If we had gotten pulled over, the Italian Carabinieri would've smelled that wine on your breath," sarcastically envisioned Ping, "and you'd have been toast."

"It would've been *your* fault," said Butt Munch. "You were my navigator."

"Oh yeah, blame it on the WSO. Isn't that just like a pilot?"

"Ping, you're a bonehead."

"No, I'm just an average guy with a small penis."

"Ping, are you ever serious?"

"Butt Munch, "CNN" would've had a field day with *that* one - 'Drunken Marine in Air Force van plows into bus from Italian orphanage'."

"Oh, yeah, Ping? Then they would've *also* had a related, follow-on story, with the headlines reading, 'Marine F-18D pilot chokes his bonehead WSO'."

Ham Fist and One Nut sat silently in the back seats, unsure of what to make of the verbal sparring in front. Were they serious? Ham Fist and One Nut's heads bounced back and forth like they were seated on center court at Wimbledon.

Finally, Butt Munch and Ping looked at each other, poo-poo'ed the other's existence, and then returned to their previous activities. Butt Munch steered the van, and Ping made an airfoil in the air stream.

"Ham Fist," said Butt Munch, "how did your one-versus-one go against Tuna?"

"Oh, not so well," replied Ham Fist, looking down at the floor mat in the back seat. "I got shot on *every* engagement."

"Hey, been there, done that, got the t-shirt," confided Butt Munch. "Tuna is probably the best pure fighter pilot in the squadron, after Bama."

"I was in Tuna's backseat today," said One Nut, "and I learned so much. That is, when I wasn't blacked out from the g's."

Butt Munch glanced into the rear view mirror to talk to Ham Fist, while signaling a lane change and down shifting.

"Who was your WSO today, Ham Fist?"

"Buick."

"Shit hot. Buick is a damn good WSO. Listen to what he says."

"Buick is the *best*," concurred Ping, staring out at the moon. "I can only aspire to such greatness."

"Have you seen tomorrow's flight schedule yet?" asked Butt Munch, again looking into the rear view mirror.

"Yep," replied Ham Fist. "You and I are fighting tomorrow afternoon."

"Who's in your back seat, Ham Fist?"

"Dago."

"Another good WSO," confided Butt Munch, nodding his head. "Use him."

"Just don't ask him anything about the state of New Jersey," said Ping, winking at Butt Munch.

Butt Munch stopped the van at the flashing red light, and made an immediate right turn towards the base's front gate. He shut off his lights, and left on his parking lights, concurrently fishing for the green military ID that the Air Force MP would require.

"What's the matter?" whispered Ping. "Can't you find your ID?"

"Standby," returned Butt Munch. "I've got it somewhere."

"You want to use my American Express card?" asked Ham Fist, referring to the stunt pulled one night by a drunken Buick. He was lucky he didn't get caught.

"No, I've got it," answered Butt Munch. "I just can't get it out of my pocket."

He slowly brought the van to a halt, seeming to be extra careful because of the Italian Carabinieri with the sub-machine gun who was sharing gate duty with the Air Force MPs. Butt Munch rolled down his window, and cracked a friendly smile at the Carabinieri. However, a paranoid Butt Munch kept his mouth shut and momentarily held his breath, as if wine molecules could jump off his tongue and leap fifteen feet through the air to the Carabinieri's nostrils. The Air Force MP stepped out of the guard shack and rendered a sloppy salute, even by Air Force standards.

"Good evening, Sir."

"Good evening, Tech Sergeant," returned Butt Munch. It was tough to talk without exhaling.

Butt Munch handed his ID to the MP. While the MP was inspecting the ID, Butt Munch couldn't help but notice the guard's German Shepherd. His canine friend sat in the open entrance to the guard shack, with one of his rear legs hiked up into the air. The guard dog had contorted his body around in such a manner to be licking himself as male dogs are prone to do. Butt Munch chuckled and nudged Ping, pointing at the dog.

"Ping, I wish I could do that."

Without missing a beat, Ping quickly replied, "Well, I'm sure that you could, but you'd probably have to pet him first."

* * *

Alcohol and Testosterone did not mix well

Liquor was an escape. It temporarily numbed the senses and made one forget that he was drinking in a green, canvas tent. However, liquor was also an instigator. A few beers under the belt of even the most docile aviators often led to disagreements, arguments, and even fights. Not to mention liquor's effect on someone who was already big and cocky. Alcohol and Testosterone did not mix well.

2354 Tuesday
Officers' Club Tent
"Boneheads like me are four feet behind you with *one* purpose in life - to keep your ass alive."

The liquor bottle was nothing but trouble to deployed aircrew; however, most still knew when to say when. There were those who pushed the envelope - like Buick - but the squadron's giant teddy bear never bothered anyone after he had imbibed. However, unlike Buick, who was just a loveable lug when he was sober, and even more so when he was drunk, Bama got belligerent. He was quick to point out his past history in the single-seat F-18C, and didn't hesitate to put his finger in the chest of younger pilots and WSOs, challenging their skills, if not their very manhood. The last thing you needed was a former offensive tackle for Bear Bryant to be drunk and in your face.

Most everyone had scattered from the Officers' Club tent. Some hit the rack, for tomorrow was another busy day, and a good session in the horizontal time accelerator would only help. Others went down to the Ready Room to brief a hop that would later launch into the black morning darkness. They were the poor saps that couldn't drink, while the rest of the aircrew set their hair on fire. Left behind in the Officers' Club, Bama, Screech, and Hick Boy were having another late night conversation over too many drinks. Maybe Hick Boy was partly to blame. He was holding down his usual position behind the bar, and allowing the Jack Daniels to flow a little too freely. Screech sat on the only stool with arm rests, flipping through his Citadel alumni magazine. Bama, seated on the stool next to Buick's throne, was already on a roll.

"I'll tell you what, boys," slurred Bama, "So far, this F-18D has been a big disappointment for me. I don't like two seats."

"What are you talking about?" asked Screech. "Good calls from a WSO have saved my ass on more than one occasion."

Bama unzipped his flight suit to the waist and accepted another Jack Daniels.

"Shit," Bama said with the glass to his lips. "I'd rather have the eight hundred pounds of gas."

Ouch. There were no WSOs in the club to defend their fraternity, and it would've taken a very ballsy WSO - not to mention a *big* one - to stand up to a drunken Bama.

Screech, forever the reasonable man, searched for a way to avoid escalation, calmy asking, "Bama, what do you say we call it a night?"

But Bama wasn't about to slow down.

"Shit, Screech," continued Bama. "Everything that I heard about the WSO before coming over from the 'C' ain't true - the second set of eyes in a dog fight, the help at night on the goggles, the Godsend to have in emergencies. None of it is true."

"Bama," said Screech, biting his tongue. "C'mon, it's late."

"I did everything by myself in the F-18C," said Bama, "and by God, I'll continue to do it by myself in the 'D'."

Bama's drunken chest thumping was not about to be stopped by Screeches calm, casual approach.

"You know what else?" ranted Bama. "The Ready Room sucks."

"What are you talking about?" asked Hick Boy. His question didn't help Screeches efforts to settle down Bama.

"I'm talking about the environment in the squadron," rambled Bama. "It just doesn't *feel* like a fighter squadron."

"Oh, I don't know," said Hick Boy. "I like the - "

"Yeah, you're damn right, Hick Boy," interrupted Bama, raising his voice. "You hit the nail on the head - you *don't* know."

Hick Boy was dumbfounded. Being the junior pilot in the crowd, a little voice whispered into his right ear, telling him to simply disregard Bama's attack. However, the fighter pilot in his young Tennessee ass talked louder into his left ear. Hick Boy removed his elbows from the bar and stood up tall, inflating his chest.

"Sir, as a fellow Marine Officer, pilot, and southern gentleman," he stated, "with all due respect, I don't take too highly to your comment."

Bama rose slightly from his stool, and poked Hick Boy in the chest with a crooked right forefinger that had been broken on a 'rip right, thirty-two, counter trap'.

Behind the bar, Hick Boy reeled from the force of the blow, even more surprised.

"Hey, c'mon, Bama," said Screech. "Throttle back, man."

Bama jumped from his stool, and violated the one-stool buffer between himself and Screech. He poked Screech in the chest with the same crooked finger, and a bottle fell to the floor, shattering to pieces.

"No, *you* throttle back, asshole." returned Bama, slobbering on himself.

Suddenly, the flap of the Officers' Club entrance was raised, and a crusty-eyed Buick entered. With a pot-belly hanging over his wrinkled boxers, he was hardly a threatening figure. His hair was a mess, and he wasn't even wearing the same two sandals.

Buick looked at Bama. Bama looked at Buick. Hick Boy alternated gazes between the two, and Screech just sat back down for another sip. He had tried. He knew what was about to take place.

"Fellas," began Buick, "*this* asshole is trying to get some sleep in the tent next door, so your late night conversation is *over*."

Screech was smart enough to take his cue. He chugged the last of his Jack Daniels, and hopped down from the stool. As he exited under the flap, he threw a cursory salutation over his shoulder without looking back, saying, "G'd night."

In reality, Screech just wanted to get out of the frag pattern of the bomb that was about to explode.

"Hick Boy," Buick stated calmly, "you need to hit the rack too."

Hick Boy grabbed the towel that was over his shoulder, and began to wipe down the bar as fast as he could, stating, "Yes, sir, as soon as I'm done with the bar."

"NOW," Buick added, raising his voice.

Hick Boy threw the towel on the refrigerator, scooted out from behind the bar, and quickly ducked under the tent's flap, saying, "Good night, gentlemen."

Buick pointed his right forefinger, broken in a bar fight in the Philippines, within inches of Bama's chest, without making physical contact.

"Bama," he began. "Let me tell you a little story. On the first night of Desert Storm, I was crewed up with a single-seat guy from the Group Headquarters. He basically told me to just get in the back seat and shut up. Well, I won't go into the details of what happened that night. But let it suffice to say, that after we landed, and we were doing our post flight inspection, we met back at the exhausts. He looked into my eyes, and said "Thanks, Buick." That's all he said. But he didn't have to say anything else. He knew. I knew. That's all that mattered."

Buick hesitated to take a slow breath before his summation.

"Bama, I am convinced that the only way to go into combat is with two seats and two engines. You're in a 'D' squadron now. Boneheads like me are four feet behind you with *one* purpose in life - to keep your ass alive. Get used to it."

Buick turned around and left the Officers' Club.

There was a moment of silence, and then Bama inhaled. He crushed the shot glass in his left hand, and blood dripped onto the floor.

"I swear, before this is over, I'm going to deck that drunken, fat ass."

Wednesday

0030
Easy 27 and 28 Brief for in-country Close Air Support
"It beats the shit out of being that desk jockey
back at the Pentagon."

Each of four different aviators tried their own special method of mental preparation before walking down to the Ready Room. Pope read the new issue of *Stars-n-Stripes* by flashlight in his masterbatorium, because the electricity was out in his section of Tent City. Hollywood walked into the Officers' Club to grab a Coke, just as Buick left in a huff and Bama crushed a shot glass. It took an awful lot to piss off Buick, so Hollywood just figured that he would probably hear about it tomorrow. Joisey had tried to take a pre-brief crap, but a full septic tank had caused all of the toilets to back up, so he walked over to the Air Force bathroom. Shitscreen grudgingly draped wet flight suits and t-shirts over a taut rope in his tent, because none of the dryers were working.

At 0030 was the squadron's daily "oh-dark-thirty" brief to go in-country for a close air support mission. The routine of flying these missions on the night vision goggles was unlike anything the aircrew had ever done before in their lives. Unlike the day missions, where aviators got a full night of sleep, didn't miss any meals, and got to take a shower, the night schedule was the dreaded bane of every aviator. The night page involved the evening sidestep, setting an alarm for midnight, and then trying to crash for some sleep. The night missions invariably led to finishing the flight, shoveling down a breakfast, waiting for the F-15Es to take-off, and then trying to sleep until lunch while grenades exploded one hundred yards to the east.

Thus, Hollywood, Shitscreen, Joisey, and Pope were gathered in the Ready Room, with the former two doing last minute preparations prior to giving the brief. Easy 27 consisted of Hollywood and Shitscreen;

consequently, Easy 28 couldn't wait for the secret brief to begin. Easy 28, Joisey and Pope, had only heard the underground stories. Yep, despite the previous hour's adversities back in Tent City, the mood in the Ready Room was very upbeat and positive. Joisey and Pope had fresh cups of coffee, and were nestled down into their front row chairs, ready to be entertained. Meanwhile, N.D. slowly exited the Ready Room, hunched over his cart, having completed another long day of unappreciated cleaning.

Anytime that Hollywood and Shitscreen were paired together in the lead jet, the brief was more of a production than an instruction. Hollywood and Shitscreen played off of each other like Abbot and Costello, and their squadron mates loved it. Even the poor bastards on the sixty-minute alert - Easy 27 and 28 couldn't tell who they were - rolled over in their blankets on the couches at the back of the Ready Room to listen.

Of course, you would expect such a production from a pilot called Hollywood. But Shitscreen was the real Cinderella of their skits. Normally wearing a ruffled flight suit and dirty flight boots, he also kept his hair at the maximum length allowed by Marine Corps regulations. Possessing a callsign like Shitscreen led the other boys in Easy to realize that at some point in his career - the Naval Academy, the Basic School, flight school, *somewhere* - he had bore the brunt of some terrible tormentors. One would expect such a man to be bitter from having lived such a hell, but Shitscreen was just the opposite. He was full of life. He felt that flying should be fun. He felt that life in a fighter squadron should be fun. He *tried* to make the Marine Corps fun. Guys like Shitscreen never became squadron commanding officers, but they were the backbone of a deployed fighter squadron.

Beneath SPEED IS LIFE, MORE IS BETTER., Shitscreen kicked off the brief.

"Hollywood, Joisey, Pope," he began, "stand by for a time hack."

The purpose of this exercise in futility was to synchronize all of their watches with the official "game clock" of the entire no-fly zone operation. Whereas, fighter pilots were notorious for having monstrous Rolex watches, there stood Shitscreen, with his twenty dollar, black Casio that he held together with a bent paper clip.

"Standby. Five . . . four . . . three . . . two . . . one . . . hack. It's Wednesday morning," stated Shitscreen, staring at his Casio.

"Now, without further adieu," he continued, "I introduce your Easy 27 flight lead, and one of the most talented homosexuals that I have ever met."

After the laughter from Joisey and Pope had subsided, Shitscreen apologized.

"No, no, wait a minute. I take that back. That's not true," he stated, setting them up like a bowling pin. "He's really *not* that talented."

Hollywood stood up and accepted the brief's baton from his WSO.

"Thank you, Shitscreen."

He removed a pair of aviator's sunglasses from his face, only to reveal yet another pair underneath.

"Gentlemen, I'd like to read you a little poem, that expresses my feelings on this whole operation."

Hollywood reached into his breast pocket, and pulled out a sheet of yellow legal paper that contained blue ink chicken scratching. He cleared his throat once, and began.

"Gentlemen, I've smoked dope, chewed rope,
dirty danced, and French romanced.
I've farted, fought, and got great fucks,
I've shot the moon, and drove big trucks.
I've been to Maine, Spain, Spokane, and Fort Wayne,
I've seen three world's fairs, and felt love's pain.
I've been around the world twice, and looked death in the face,
I've seen goats fuck in the marketplace,
But I ain't *never* seen no shit like what goes on around this place."

Joisey and Pope hooted and hollered, clapping their hands, causing Pope to accidentally kick over his coffee. Even a muffled voice came from underneath the alert sixty blanket on one of the couches, stating, "Here, here."

"Attention to brief," began Hollywood. "Our callsigns this morning are Easy 27, Hollywood and Shitscreen, and Easy 28, Joisey and Pope. The air-to-air positioning aids, radar channels, and radar looks are listed on the board. We are event one on the flight schedule, and have mission number one four tack zero one. Our friend-or-foe identification codes are also on the board. The assigned aircraft are ten and zero two, with a back-up of lucky seven."

The brief momentarily turned serious as Shitscreen, Joisey, and Pope frantically wrote data on their kneeboard cards.

"Gentlemen," continued Hollywood, "our flight this morning is an in-country close air support mission on the night vision goggles. We have been assigned to support the Marine's First Battalion, Third Marine Regiment, which is in the vicinity of Grobnev. Need I remind you that we are at the sixth and final step of any military program?"

The three aviators quit writing and looked up at Hollywood, for they knew that some more shit was about to flow. One of the blankets even stirred. Without missing a beat, Hollywood continued, stating, "My WSO will explain."

In a perfectly choreographed maneuver, Hollywood sat down and Shitscreen stood up at the front of the Ready Room. Yep, you certainly didn't have to worry about the sun's glint off of Shitscreen's boots hurting your eyes. They were filthy.

"As you all know, the six steps in any military program are: Step one - Wild enthusiasm. Step two - Disenchantment. Step three - Total confusion. Step four - The search for the guilty. Step five - The punishment of the innocent. And lastly, step six - The promotion of non-participants."

Joisey especially liked that list, and he poked Pope in the side.

"Yes, today, in the bowels of the Pentagon, the five-sided-puzzle-palace, the wind tunnel-on-the-Potomac," continued Shitscreen, "Step six will take place. Some desk jockey will receive a Navy Achievement Medal for his non-participation in enforcing this no-fly zone. Let's offer him a round of congratulatory applause."

All four members of Easy 27 flight applauded, and then returned to the matter at hand. Once more, the same tired, muffled voice resounded from beneath the blankets at the back, toasting, "Here, here."

"For the weather and the Notice to Airmen," continued ShitScreen, "both are looking good."

Shitscreen briefed Easy 27 and 28 on the weather both at the airfield and in-country, then also covered all of the moon data required for the night vision goggles. He covered the moon's azimuth and elevation, as well as its size and luminance. The Notice to Airmen included the construction that was currently taking place on taxiway Bravo at the far end of the runway, which was no big deal.

The brief smoothly continued, with Shitscreen at the helm.

"We have a 0230 take-off, so let's walk to the jets at 0140 to make a 0210 start-up and a 0225 taxi. When you walk through Intelligence, remember to check the latest threat board and review the last flight's debrief sheets. WSOs, sign out a camera, and ensure that you have a complete packet of one-to-fifty maps. Pilots, just do what you normally do - stand there and look pretty with sunglasses and a big, fancy watch."

Hollywood bolted up from his seat in a feigned anger, pointing his right index finger at Shitscreen.

"Hey," he said, "I resent that remark."

"No," stated Shitscreen, "you *resemble* that remark."

"By God, I'm a fighter pilot, and I won't stand here and let you disparage my community."

Shitscreen took his cue.

"Hollywood, how do you tell if there's a fighter pilot at your party?"

"I don't know, my friend, how *do* you tell if there's a fighter pilot at your party?"

"Don't worry - he'll tell you. Bada-boom-bada-bing."

"Hollywood, what's the difference between God and a fighter pilot?"

"I don't know, my WSO, what *is* the difference between God and a fighter pilot?"

"God doesn't think that he's a fighter pilot. Bada-boom-bada-bing."

"Hollywood, what does a fighter pilot use for birth control?'

"I don't know, my able aviator, what *does* a fighter pilot use for birth control?'

"His personality. Bada-boom-bada-bing."

"Hollywood, what's the difference between a fighter pilot and a jet engine?"

"I don't know, what *is* the difference between a fighter pilot and a jet engine?"

"A jet engine quits whining when the F-18 finally parks. Bada-boom-bada-bing."

The rapid fire staccato of pilot jokes had Joisey and Pope in stitches. Such a well-choreographed event could never have been pulled off with the egos of Bama or Tuna. But Hollywood, flashy and shallow as he could be, was the ultimate team player – he would play straight man to a WSO.

"For the communications plan," said Hollywood, "we'll start up on ground control in the number one radio and base frequency in the number two. Comm will be standard operating procedures up until we take the runway, when we'll switch to our tactical frequency in the number two. This morning, that will be Tac three."

Again, heads were down and pens were scratching as the brief progressed.

"We'll have Italian air traffic control in the number one radio until we switch to the AWACS, Sky Eye 03, on yellow for vectors to the tanker. We'll remain on yellow until we are tally on the tanker, then we'll switch to tanker primary. The tanker today is a damn KC-135 - shit - with the callsign of Castle 21, and he'll be on blue as primary, with orange as a back-up. Our FAC this morning will be Gunner 14 on Violet. I guess they've had some security problems on Magenta, so we'll see. Any questions?"

Joisey and Pope just shook their heads, not realizing that 'Any questions?' was actually the next cue for Shitscreen.

"Hollywood, why does getting gas from a KC-135 bother you? Have you forgotten number three of Marine aviation's seven rules to live by?"

"Why no," said Hollywood. "Do you mean 'Hindsight is 20/20'?"

"Nope."

"Don't fight with a bear in his own cave?"

"No sir."

"Never argue with an idiot?"

"Not that one."

"When you wrestle with a pig, he likes it and you just get dirty?"

"No. I said number three."

"It's easier to get forgiveness than permission?"

"Nope."

"Never underestimate the power of stupid people in large groups?"

"No sir. Number three."

"Well then, refresh my memory."

"Where you sit determines what you see."

"Ah, yes, now I remember."

How did Hollywood and Shitscreen do it? Joisey thought, as he held his side. Pope accidentally kicked over his coffee again.

"Here, here," came out from under the blanket again.

"Yes. Where you sit determines what you see. This morning, we may be sitting ten feet under a KC-135 getting gas and then be at fifteen thousand feet straining to find a target on the ground. But you know what? It beats the shit out of being that desk jockey back at the Pentagon. We really ain't got it so bad over here."

"Here, here."

The brief continued. Bada-boom-bada-bing.

Was that a smile on Easy Eddie's face?

0553 Wednesday
Tent City, Tent 03
"Saint Jude, the Church invokes you universally as the Patron Saint of hopeless causes and things despaired; pray for me..."

Pope was dead to the world, after flying all night on the night vision goggles. It wasn't so much the usual obstacles encountered on the tanker track and in-country, as it was the crazy, awake-all-night lifestyle that messed with his mind. It was so counter to his circadian rhythm, and it definitely took its toll, both mentally and physically. Looking through night vision goggles gave Pope a tremendous headache, no matter how he adjusted the numerous knobs that controlled variables like interocular distance.

Pope said good night to his pilot, Joisey, who stayed behind in the Ready Room to read a letter from his mom. Hollywood and Shitscreen huddled in the corner by the refrigerator, debriefing this morning's production. Pope departed the Ready Room by himself for the long trek back to his tent.

Pope didn't even remember crossing perimeter road, or cutting across the corn flakes rocks. It wasn't until he turned the sidewalk's corner by the dining tent that he noticed he was shuffling his tired feet, obviously scuffing the bottom of his flight boots. Pope continued down the sidewalk, and met Screech and Hick Boy on their way to the showers. It was like the changing of the guard.

"Hey, Hick Boy. Hey Screech."

"Hi Pope. How was the brief with Hollywood and Shitscreen?"

"Classic," replied Pope, grinning from ear to ear, and shaking his head.

"Yep," added Hick Boy, "if the Commanding Officer ever found out they were giving briefs like that, the shit would hit the fan."

"The C.O.?" said Screech. "What about the Safety Nazis? They'd have a cow."

"And how was the flight?" asked Hick Boy.

"Quiet, as usual. Nothing erupted."

"I know what you mean," said Screech. "I think we need to do a strong reality check on those early morning CAS missions."

"It wouldn't help," returned Pope. "My reality check has bounced."

The threesome laughed, and then said their farewells.

"See ya, Pope," said Hick Boy. "We have to run if we want to get any hot water."

"Yep," added Screech, "the early bird gets the worm."

"Well, remember, the early bird may get the worm," said Pope, "but the second mouse gets the cheese."

"Roger that."

"Ok, I'll see you two guys later."

Pope shuffled his way down the sidewalk to his tent. He quietly lifted the entrance flap, and ducked inside. He counted the eight steps in the dark to his left turn, and then the three steps to his masturbatorium. Pope lifted the white sheet, and sat on the edge of his rack, knocking an issue of *Stars-n-Stripes* to the floor. He reached under his pillow, and found his tiny flashlight. After clicking it on, he placed it on the pillow so that it cast its glow over his rack. Pope didn't untie his boots. Pope didn't unzip his flight suit. Pope didn't remove his glasses. He just sat there, and sighed.

Pope reached toward the rickety bedside table that he had made from scrap lumber, and grabbed a book from the bottom shelf. It was a book on Vince Lombardi. Pope found strength in the former great coach of the Green Bay Packers. Pope was a strong Catholic who believed in a loving God. So was Vince. Pope prayed daily to Saint Jude, the patron saint of lost causes, hopelessness, and despair. So did Vince. Pope believed in the disciplined repetition of fundamentals at practice in order to achieve superiority in the game. So did Vince. Pope didn't believe in the consumption of alcohol and cigarettes, which tore down the Lord's temple here on earth. Oh well, three out of four wasn't bad. Pope sat there in the semi-darkness, holding the book, and staring at a picture of a common man with a gap in his front teeth, wearing birth control glasses, and sporting an old fedora.

Then Pope reached down into the flight suit pocket on his left shin. Like Ghost, he kept a token of strength there too, pulling out a laminated card that contained the Catholic prayer to Saint Jude. Placing the card upon the book, he began to silently mouth the words. Pope whispered aloud the phrase that meant the most - *Saint Jude, the Church invokes you universally as the Patron Saint of hopeless causes and things despaired; pray for me, who is so miserable, pray for me, that finally I may receive the consolations and the succor of Heaven in all my necessities, tribulations, and sufferings.*

Meanwhile, three hundred yards to the west, four Air Force F-15Es taxied into the hold short area.

"Tower, Diamond 01, take-off four Eagles."

"Diamond 01, Tower, taxi into position and hold."

The lead Strike Eagle jockeyed his throttles forward, and led the first three F-15Es onto the runway. They formed a forty-five degree echelon to the left based on the winds, while the fourth F-15E patiently waited in the hold short area.

"Tower, Diamond 01, ready for take-off."

"Diamond 01, Tower, cleared for take-off, contact departure control."

"Tower, Diamond 01, cleared and switching."

"Two."

"Three."

"Four."

In order, Diamond 01, 02, and 03 rolled down the runway, selecting full afterburner at the one thousand foot marker. As soon as Diamond 01 began his take-off roll, Diamond 04 replaced him on the runway from the hold short area and followed suit. The thunderous noise rattled Pope's tent, causing him to clutch his Saint Jude card and Vince Lombardi book.

Meanwhile, in his own tent, Ghost was getting dressed for the morning sidestep. He wearily retrieved yesterday's dirty, stinky, green t-shirt from the nightstand, and turned it inside out for another day's wear. The removal of the t-shirt from the nightstand revealed the latest book that Ghost was reading, entitled *Lee's Lieutenants*. Ghost was attempting to understand what made Generals tick.

* * *

A Navy Shower

Water in Tent City was at a premium – let alone *hot* water. Consequently, the Camp Commandant established three different blocks of shower hours during the course of a twenty-four hour day to conserve water. Furthermore, all the occupants of Tent City were asked to take a Navy shower, named from where it originated – aboard Navy ships. The concept was rather simple - get in, get wet, shut off the water, lather up, rinse off, shut off the water, then get out.

The habits of some men in the shower never ceased to be a constant source of entertainment. Tuna used to brush his teeth - water conservation be damned. By God, he would stand there, buck naked, and brush his teeth with the water blasting on him full bore. Pope used to shave in the shower, another habit that probably kept the Camp Commandant awake at night. He claimed the steam gave him a smoother shave. Screech was a clean freak that showered every day - twice.

Some men were gross in the Shower. Dago was so hairy that it looked like he was wearing a sweater. Rumor had it that Joisey liked to use the shower drain as a urinal. That is, he would on the rare occasion that he ever took a shower. Hick Boy never wore shower shoes, which was a gutsy call considering the rumor about Joisey.

Other shower rumors ran rampant amongst the officers. Supposedly, Spine Ripper was hung like a horse. Conversely, Ping always joked that he was hung like the Milky Way - impossible to see with the naked eye. Nobody was ever able to visually confirm if One Nut really *had* one nut.

As previously stated, Joisey never showered. Well, maybe *never* was a little too strong. He would finally break down and shower each time after Bama and Ghost threatened to throw his ass in and scrub him down with a wire brush. Joisey didn't like to shower because he claimed that his body produced natural pheromones, which attracted the female of the human species. In any case, he didn't like to shower, and thus remove the pheromones from his horny body. With such a view on cleanliness, Joisey *still* couldn't understand why his wife had divorced him. Yes, once upon a time, there actually existed a Mrs. Joisey. Shudder, shudder, shudder.

The same conditions that existed over the urinals were also alive and well in the showers. There were three different heads to choose from - one on the left wall, one on the right wall, and one in the middle. Thus, the same unwritten code existed that called for the establishment of a buffer zone between male bodies. Conversation was forbidden.

If an aviator didn't want to deal with the Tent City shower hours, or his schedule simply forced him to miss taking a shower, he always had the option to sneak over to the Air Force showers. They were open twenty-four hours a day, seven days a week, and always had plenty of hot water. Plus, they possessed nozzles that rivaled the best hotels back in the real world.

0603 Wednesday
In the Shower Tent
"FIRE IN THE HOLE."

It had to be the Camp Commandant's worst nightmare - Dago, Hick Boy, and Screech were all in the showers at the same time. Another fruitless morning of water conservation down the drain - no pun intended.

Dago was in the shower with his sweater, ignoring the ape comments. Hick Boy was washing his hair with some type of lye soap that his Grandmother had made. Screech was actually lathering his body with a bar of Lava soap. Remember Lava? That was the sandpaper soap that your Dad always used after working on the car. It might be more appropriate to say that Screech was removing a layer of skin with a bar of Lava.

Meanwhile, Spine Ripper and Frap patiently waited out in the sink area for the next available shower with towels wrapped around their bodies. Spine Ripper was just finishing a shave, and Frap leaned his toweled butt against a sink. The place was full of steam - as usual - because the first ones into the morning showers got all the hot water.

Suddenly, a courtesy warning sounded from the bathroom building next door.

"FIRE IN THE HOLE."

Dago, Hick Boy, and Screech knew how to play the Tent City shower game. They simultaneously stepped out of the shower's hot stream, as the reason for the warning immediately followed.

"Vwoooooosh."

A toilet flushed, sucking the majority of cold water from the shower flow, and turning the shower's stream into a scalding spray.

Dago, Hick Boy, and Screech waited the obligatory count to "three Mississippi's", and then mechanically stepped back into a water stream that had returned to a normal temperature.

"Thanks." yelled Hick Boy, with suds in his eyes, to the anonymous flusher in the bathroom building.

"Yeah, thanks," echoed Screech.

"No sweat," yelled somebody in return. The voice was unrecognizable due to the noise from the running water.

"What's the matter?" bellowed Dago to the phantom flusher. "You can't wait until we're done in the showers to take a shit?"

Spine Ripper and Frap only looked at each other and chuckled in their steamy holding area.

With the water having returned to a tolerable temperature, Dago continued to scrub his sweater, Hick Boy rinsed the soap from his face, and Screech removed some more skin.

Once again, a courtesy warning resounded from the bathroom building.

"FIRE IN THE HOLE."

Dago, Hick Boy, and Screech, like robots, simultaneously stepped out of the shower stream, continuing to scrub a sweater, rinse a face, and remove some skin.

"Vwoooooosh."

A toilet flushed again, depleting the shower stream of cold water.

"One Mississippi, two Mississippi, three Mississippi."

Dago, Hick Boy, and Screech returned back into a normal water stream, without missing a beat in their scrubbing, rinsing, and skin removal.

"Thanks, man." yelled Screech.

"Ditto," returned Hick Boy.

"No problem," returned another anonymous voice, muffled by the flow of water.

"Damn," roared Dago. "What did they serve last night for dinner? Ex Lax?"

The shower ritual continued without any further interruptions, while Spine Ripper and Frap grew increasingly impatient.

Meanwhile, a tired Butt Munch shuffled his way down the sidewalk to the bathroom building. He opened the creaky door, and walked past the stalls to the three urinals. The far left urinal was still out of order, as evidenced by the conglomeration of masking tape and ordnance tape rigged over the opening. The makeshift sign still hung above the broken urinal, too. Butt Munch stepped to the center urinal, and began to relieve himself, staring straight ahead at the wall. No sooner had he started, the door creaked open again, and Buick stepped into the building with the waist tie of his bathrobe dragging on the floor. He strode past the stalls, and noticed Butt Munch at the center urinal. Buick quickly did a left turn, and bent over at the sink, putting his face within inches of the mirror. He pulled up his right eyelid with his forefinger in a fake check for pink eye. Buick was a master of the rules.

What the hell? Buick thought. He had faked everything else at that same mirror, so why not pink eye?

Still, Butt Munch was not done yet at the center urinal.

"Good morning, Butt Munch."

"How ya doing, Buick?"

Buick checked his left eye in the mirror. No pink eye there either. Imagine that. Still, Butt Munch continued at the center urinal.

Shit, thought Buick. *What am I going to fake doing now?*

Thinking quickly, Buick returned to his faithful, old standby - the stall. He stepped back from the mirror, and walked two steps to the first stall, opening the door. As Buick attempted to enter, his left foot accidentally stepped on the dangling bathrobe tie, causing him to trip. He reached out to catch his falling body, with his right hand landing on the black toilet seat, and the left hand landing on the toilet's handle.

"Vwoooooosh."

Oh shit, thought Buick.

He had accidentally flushed the toilet without a courtesy warning. Buick's fat body rolled off the left side of the toilet, and he hadn't even hit the floor yet before he heard the anguished cries coming from the shower building.

"Aaaauuuuuugggghhhh," screamed a scalded Hick Boy.

"Shiiiiiiiiit," cried a burned Screech.

"Damn it," yelled Dago. "I'm going to kill somebody."

A naked Dago, sweater and all, bolted out of the steamy shower room, and ran past Spine Ripper and Frap towards the door.

As the hairy blur blew by Frap, he calmly turned to Spine Ripper, stating, "A shower's open. After you, my man."

"No, thank you," returned Spine Ripper in a rare display of kindness. "You go."

Dago sprinted out of the shower building, and - WHAM - ran headlong into N.D.'s cleaning cart. His hairy body completely flipped, and the little Brooklynite landed flat on his back.

"Ooooooomph."

Hearing the thud outside, Buick deemed it now safe to exit the stall. He coyly opened the building's creaky door, and stepped out of the bathroom. Buick assumed a triumphant position lording over Dago, who was frozen, spread eagle, on his back.

"It's my spine. I can't move."

"Tsk, tsk, tsk," stated Buick, shaking his head.

"Damn you," cursed Dago through clenched teeth. "Go get the Doc. I'm hurt."

"I can't," explained Buick. "He's catching some extra "z's" for his flight this afternoon with Screech. I'd hate to wake him."

"Damn you," gritted Dago. "I'll get you for this."

Dominating the fallen Italian, Buick continued to gloat over his injured comrade, stating, "There's a lesson here somewhere."

But rather than incur Dago's wrath at a later date, Buick finally broke down and decided to aid his fellow WSO, saying, "Here, let me help you up."

Buick knelt down over Dago, carefully repositioned the Italian's body, and then placed his arms around him in the manner of a fireman's carry.

"Are you ready?" asked Buick. "On three."

Dago just nodded while biting his lip.

"One, two, three . . . uuuuggghhhhh," grunted Buick.

He groaned as he stood up with Dago's limp body draped over his shoulder. Buick then stepped back into the bathroom building, and maneuvered Dago into the same stall that Buick had just vacated. He sat Dago's wet, naked body on the toilet, and then stood erect, wiping his hands.

God, somebody ought to shave his back, thought Buick.

"Are you ok, man?"

"I'll make it," whispered Dago, now with tears in his eyes.

Then Buick reached over Dago with his left hand, grabbed the toilet's handle, and slammed it down – without a courtesy warning.

"Vwoooooooosh."

Buick bolted from the stall and exited the bathroom as fast as his overweight body could run, with the cries of pain emanating from the showers next door.

"Aaaauuuugggghhhhh." screamed a scalded Hick Boy.

"Shiiiiiiiiit," cried a burned Screech.

"Damn it." yelled an irate Frap.

Seconds later, just as a panting Buick was ducking into his tent, a wet and very pissed off Screech, with Hick Boy and Frap in trail, slammed open the door to the bathroom building. They plowed in with a vengeance, looking for the culprit. When they spied a hairy Dago sitting helplessly on the toilet, they mercilessly uncoiled on him.

"You asshole," declared Screech.

The three aviators stripped off their towels and began to snap the powerless Dago.

Snap. Thwack. Snap. Thwack. Thwack.

Buick could be heard laughing all the way from his tent.

Polishing Turds

It was crazy. The man-hours that were spent getting ready for an inspection that Marines weren't even supposed to know about were phenomenal. The resultant buffing, washing, cleaning, polishing, and so on only served to make an entity look like it never really did. The Marines were polishing turds.

0618 Wednesday
The Dining Tent
"Mocha mint? Irish crème? Or Paris Morning?"

It was time to dance the morning sidestep once again. Like a robot, Ghost was proceeding through the breakfast line in the dining tent. Pope had joined him because he couldn't sleep. They both noticed that something, somehow, was just different. Ghost could sense it in his sleepy stupor. It started with plastic trays, instead of the usual cardboard, and real silverware, instead of the normal plastic. He mechanically sidestepped to the left and held out his tray.

"I'll take eggs please," he mumbled, still half-awake.

"No eggs this morning, Sir," returned the messman. "It's made-to-order omelets. What would you like? Cheese? Ham? Mushrooms? A western omelet, perhaps?"

Ghost closed his eyes and shook his head, thinking, *am I dreaming?*

He rubbed his eyes, and then re-opened them, having awakened just a little more. There before him, was a heated griddle with broken eggs in clean bowls along the side, neatly lined up in military fashion, next to bigger, cleaner bowls containing all the fixings necessary for any type of omelet. In his sleepiness, he hadn't even noticed the fancy new array. The messman even had a clean t-shirt and wore a chef's hat instead of a hair net.

"Um, ham and cheese, please," said Ghost, hesitantly.

"Right away, Sir," answered the messman. He was happy - unnaturally happy.

Man, what's up? Ghost thought, sidestepping to the left.

A pleasant 'sssssssss' filled the air as the messman poured a bowl of eggs onto the griddle, and grabbed the two bowls containing ham and cheese. He delicately sprinkled Ghost's wish list on top of the sizzling eggs, and flipped his spatula into the air, catching it after a double spin.

Pope sidestepped to the left, filling the hole left by Ghost.

"Western omelet, please," he asked of the happy-go-lucky messman.

Ghost was still confused. Overnight, how did the dining tent go from Huddle House to IHOP?

The messman heaped a gorgeous ham and cheese omelet onto Ghost's plastic tray, and wished him a pleasant day. Ghost sidestepped to the left to the next station. This time, he didn't even ask. He just stared in disbelief.

"French toast, sir?" asked another jolly messman in a clean t-shirt and chef's hat.

There before Ghost, were the thickest pieces of French toast he had ever seen in his life. They weren't yesterday's leftover bread slices, but real, thick pieces of French bread. They were even colored orange like French toast was supposed to be. To the left of the messman, there wasn't the usual packets of maple syrup floating in tepid water, but a mouth watering spread of possible combinations to put upon your French toast.

"Powdered sugar? Cinnamon? Strawberries? Syrup? What would you like on your French toast, sir?" asked the smiling messman.

"Uh, yes, two slices, with strawberries, please."

This guy was acting overly happy too.

What is going on? Ghost thought.

The messman handed Ghost's tray to him with a heaping pile of French toast and strawberries, then added "Sir, if you like, whipped cream is in the self-service line."

Ghost sidestepped to the left, now in a complete daze. Pope sidestepped to the left, right on his tail, except he wasn't like Ghost, and looking a gift horse in the mouth.

"Powdered sugar, please," said Pope, smiling even more than the messman.

The next station was too much for Ghost to handle.

"Coffee, Sir?" asked another messman with another fake smile, another clean, white t-shirt, and another paper chef's hat.

"Yes, please," replied Ghost.

"Mocha mint? Irish crème? Or Paris Morning?"

Ghost stood there in disbelief.

"Whatever," was the only reply that he could muster.

By the time that Pope linked back up with Ghost in the self-service section, Pope was in a heavenly trance and Ghost was in a stupefied daze. The self-service station had piles of fresh fruit, an assortment of cereals, dozens of bagels, doughnuts, and croissants, and cold, fresh yogurt. Oh yes, it also had whipped cream. Someone had even cleaned the remnants of the sneeze off of the sneeze guard.

Ghost filled his tray with ample portions of everything healthy, and Pope just filled his tray. As soon as they stepped around the corner into the dining portion of the tent, a little light bulb illuminated above Ghost's head. There, eating breakfast with his entourage of lackeys, was the Marine Corps General who commanded their aircraft wing.

The General was - well - a General. He just looked the role. He was obviously in his mid-fifties, with gray hair and a slight paunch. He wore glasses, and had rows of ribbons that stretched from his pocket to his shoulder. He had obviously been to the super secret "General's school", because he was cranky and feisty. Ghost swore that there was just such a school hidden in the bowels of the Pentagon, where they taught all of the new Generals how to scowl and frown and be General-like. It seemed as if Marine Corps Generals and Army Generals were all graduates from the same school, unlike Air Force Generals and Navy Admirals. They were more like your grandpa.

Next to the General was some poor Marine Captain. He had a high-n-tight, buzzed haircut normally associated with an infantry officer, and every detail of his 'Charlies' uniform was perfect. With a creased shirt, ribbons in order, a belt tab of one and three quarter inches in length, and polished bars, he looked the classic, poster Marine. Draped around his shoulder was the gold epaulet that labeled him as a General's Aide.

Ghost even told himself that the Aide was probably one of those guys who wore those black suspenders under his pants to hold up his socks. Ghost *hated* those guys. Lastly, Ghost wondered how the Aide was able to still eat his breakfast when he had his nose so far up the General's ass.

Whoa. Who was that? On the other side of the Aide, sat a female Marine, who was the best looking thing that Ghost had ever seen in a uniform. Had Ghost really been overseas that long? Or was this Marine really that hot? He could only make out the name of Heather on her nametag. The car keys by her tray belied the fact that she must be the General's driver.

In any case, her uniform displayed the chevrons of a Marine Lance Corporal, so she couldn't have been a day over nineteen. Petite and shy, she wore the exact amount of make-up, lipstick, and mascara that was in perfect accordance with regulations. Underneath the table, she crossed her legs, revealing just enough of her silky thighs to cause Ghost to stare. Furthermore, she had long, brunette hair that she wore in a bun. Ghost just imagined her undoing that bun in the shower, shaking her head, and allowing that long hair to fall down her back

Ghost couldn't take it. Against Pope's objections, he carried his tray back to the tent to eat.

0716 Wednesday
In the Center of Tent City
"Nah. Just some routine tests."

Booger sat with Dick and Screw on the makeshift bench again. He had some time to kill before his 0800 follow-up appointment at the Hospital, so Booger decided to relax a bit with *yesterday's* issue of *Stars-n-Stripes*. That was certainly status quo for a deployed Marine Officer - you were always a day late and a dollar short. His piece of rope lay across his left thigh, with a perfect clove hitch knot tied in it.

Booger deduced that it must've been an eventful morning in Tent City, for he had heard nothing but screams coming from the shower tent as he walked by for breakfast. Then while eating, he overheard Joisey raving about some production from Hollywood and Shitscreen. Booger tied and untied a square knot.

Booger was very apprehensive about this morning's tests at the Hospital. F-18 pilots and WSOs dreaded *anything* that could possibly down them. This follow-up test was certainly an added stressor in his life. Furthermore, in the high testosterone world of fighter aviation, the last thing Booger needed was a problem in the genital area. He vowed that no one - absolutely no one - would find out about his potential problem. Integrity be damned, for an F-18 pilot or WSO would lie right through his teeth to conceal a possible chink in his armor.

Dick was in his faithful position at Booger's feet, and Screw dutifully assumed his position on the bench. After scratching both of their heads, Booger looked up from the sports pages to notice Dago walking very gingerly toward him.

"Hey, Dago. Are you ok?"

Dago lightly hobbled up to the bench. Upon his arrival, a very frisky Dick the dog jumped upon him. Dago grimaced in pain and slightly doubled over, yet happily petted Dick on the back and forced him back down to his side. Screw the pooch just watched the playful assault with his head in Booger's lap.

"Yeah, yeah, I'm fine," grinned Dago through clenched teeth.

"What happened?" inquired Booger.

"Oh, nothing," lied Dago. "I tripped over N.D.'s cart, that's all. I'm on my way over to see the Doc."

"Well take care, Dago," said Booger, pulling Dick back over to his original spot.

"What about you?" Dago asked. "What have you got going on today?"

"Nothing really," lied Booger, hiding his anxiety. "I have to go over to the hospital for a follow-up appointment to my flight physical."

"Anything serious?"

"Nah. Just some routine tests."

"Good," returned Dago. "You know the deal. Hide everything possible so that you can continue to fly."

"Roger that, Dago."

"Well, I have to run," said Dago. "I told the Doc I would be there at 0800."

"Yeah, my appointment is at 0800, too," concluded Booger. "Catch you later."

* * *

Bitch, bitch, bitch.

All the older guys in the squadron used to say that you weren't really happy unless you were bitching. If that axiom was true, then the boys from Easy were ecstatic. Any time that the Officers had a chance to talk amongst themselves, they bitched about the Marine Corps and being deployed and the food and the cold showers and the lack of sleep and so on and so on. Some bitched about future orders to another assignment, others bitched about whether to stay in or get out. Some even bitched about bitching.

0731 Wednesday
On the Flight Line
Morning FOD Walk
"Yep, trying to do anything is like herding cats."

"DAMN IT," bellowed Gunny Morris, "QUIT YOUR JAW-JACKING AND KEEP YOUR EYES GLUED TO THE DECK."

Gunny Morris hated it when the Marines carried on a conversation while doing the FOD walk. He was afraid that even the most trivial dialogue between walkers would cause a Marine to miss a piece of FOD. Thus, Screech, Butt Munch, and Spine Ripper intentionally positioned themselves on the far left end of the line, where they could whisper amongst themselves. All three Captains were debating their futures.

"Hey Screech," said Butt Munch, "aren't you up for orders when we get back to the real world?"

"Yep," returned Screech, "and I don't have a clue as to what I'm going to do."

"I'm a mover this December," continued Butt Munch, "and I think I'm going to play my cards to be an instructor at flight school. I need to pad my log book with maximum hours before I make the jump to Delta."

"Funny you mention that," said Screech, "I was thinking about United."

"Whoa. Hold that thought," said Spine Ripper as he stooped to pick up a tiny metal washer. He returned to his position between the two pilots.

"Plus, the airlines are really hiring right now," stated Butt Munch.

"Yeah, at some of these airlines, you can't swing a dead cat without hitting a former military pilot," said Screech.

"Remember Pooper?" asked Butt Munch. "He jumped ship, and got snatched up by Continental in a heartbeat."

"Pooper did? No shit?" returned Screech. "That guy was such a piece of FOD."

"Yeah," concurred Spine Ripper. "I think he got into the gene pool when the lifeguard wasn't watching."

"And then there was Rockets," continued Butt Munch. "He got hired by Federal Express, no sweat."

"God, I remember Rockets," reminisced Screech. "What a great American."

"Concur," added Spine Ripper, "He was the kind of a guy that you could trust with your life, your wife, or your wallet."

"Yeah, the Marine Corps lost a good one there," sighed Screech.

"But still," said Butt Munch, "I love it when good things happen to good people."

"Yep," agreed Screech, nodding his head.

"Well, Spine Ripper," said Butt Munch. "What are you going to do when we get back? Are you going to stay in or get out?"

"I don't know. I'd stay in if it wasn't such a red-ass to do everything."

"Yep, trying to do *anything* is like herding cats," laughed Screech.

"Yeah," added Butt Munch, "and life on deployments is like wiping your ass on the tire of a stationary bicycle."

Screech and Spine Ripper split their sides at the visual image, praying that Gunny Morris didn't hear their laughter

"Stand by one, you guys," said Screech, as he bent over to pick up a small chunk of concrete that had broken loose from the tarmac.

Spine Ripper continued with his saga, stating, "I'm facing the biggest decision of my life. I'd hate to get out at the ten year mark."

"You certainly wouldn't be alone," said Screech. "A lot of guys are getting out at the ten to twelve year mark. It's tragic."

"Plus, my wife is riding me like a rented mule," admitted Spine Ripper. "Susan wants me to get out sooooo badly."

"Well, you know what they say," said Butt Munch, the confirmed bachelor. "If the Marine Corps had wanted you to have a wife, they would've issued you one."

"Don't listen to Butt Munch," stated Screech. "Susan is a great woman, and you did the right thing by getting married. It's a documented fact that married men live *longer* than single men."

"That's not true," returned Spine Ripper. "It just *seems* longer."

"Actually, man is incomplete until he gets married," philosophized Butt Munch. "Then he is finished."

The three aviators laughed at the play on words, as they came to the other side of the flight line and Gunny Morris halted the morning FOD walk.

"FALL OUT," he yelled, dismissing the Marines.

0740 Wednesday
Easy 31 and 32 Enroute to the Tanker Track
Closer, closer, closer – dink.

"Sky Eye, Easy 31, flight of two Hornets, checking in," stated Fig.

"Roger, Easy 31, Sky Eye has you loud and clear, state your position."

"Sky Eye, Easy 31 is one zero miles southwest of Bravo, at angels base plus two."

"Sky Eye copies. Standby, looking."

While the AWACS crewmember temporarily searched his scope for the flight of two F-18Ds, Chunks and Fig were going through their combat checklists. Chunks, a stickler for detail, had Fig methodically read the checklist to him item-by-item from the back seat to ensure that nothing was forgotten.

In the other Hornet, it was quite the opposite. FOD and Ninja were listening to Hootie and the Blowfish on FOD's portable tape player that he had spliced into the ICS. FOD and Ninja were both FNGs, but you would never know it. Somehow, these two alternative rockers and laid-back surfer dudes from California had avoided that whole FNG stigma. Furthermore, they both believed that there was "pilot shit" and "WSO shit" in the F-18D; consequently, when one told the other that a checklist was complete, he took him for his word. Trust in a two-seat fighter was imperative.

"Easy 31, Sky Eye."

"Sky Eye, Easy 31, go."

"Sky Eye is now radar contact. Your instructions are to proceed to Texaco. He is presently on track, bearing one six zero, four five miles, angels base minus two."

Chunks steadied the jet on a heading of one six zero, and FOD mimicked his lead from the combat spread position. The race was on. It was always an unspoken contest to try and be the first jet to find the tanker on radar. In Easy 31, Fig increased the range scale in an attempt to do so. In Easy 32, Ninja slightly turned down the volume of Darius

Rucker's voice, and lowered his elevation caret. Ninja won. But since he was in the wingman aircraft, he did not go external to the flight over the primary radio to Sky Eye with his contact call. It was fighter protocol for his lead to make the call.

Instead, Ninja stated the following on the number two. "Easy 31, 32 is radar contact one five five at four two miles." Thus Sky Eye was none the wiser.

"Easy 32, 31 is looking," returned Fig on the number two. It was only a matter of seconds before Fig found the tanker on their radar and then went public to AWACS on the number one radio. Protocol complete – lead's ego was still intact.

"Sky Eye, Easy 31, radar contact Texaco, one five five, four zero miles, request switch to tanker primary."

"Easy 31, Sky Eye, you're cleared to switch. Report when done with Texaco."

"Easy 31, switching. Flight go tanker primary, number one radio,"

"Two."

Both Fig and Ninja put their radars into a different search mode around the approaching tanker. The two pilots, Chunks and FOD, certainly weren't looking forward to the upcoming evolution. According to the schedule, Rocky 51 was a KC-135. Pilots hated the KC-135. The short length of the refueling hose and the rigid basket at the end meant it was no picnic to plug in, let alone *stay* in. Both pilots started to tense up; thus they wiggled their fingers and toes to get the blood flowing to the extremities. Chunks flew with his left hand on the stick to give the right a rest, while FOD relaxed his grip on the stick.

"Rocky 51, Easy 31."

"Easy 31, Rocky 51, go ahead."

"Flight of two Hornets, three five miles on your nose, radar contact."

"Easy 31, Rocky 51, solid copy. Report the starboard observation position with switches safe and nose cold."

"Rocky 51, Easy 31, wilco."

Chunks turned the flight thirty degrees to the left to a heading of one three zero, and instructed FOD to get on his left side. The intent of the displacement turn was to start building lateral separation between the converging flight paths of the Hornets and the KC-135. This lateral separation would later equate to turning room to the right, allowing Easy 31 to roll in behind the tanker and intercept him. Both Chunks and Fig did the math in their heads, and verified with the radar presentation that one three zero was good. Then Chunks had Fig read him the pre-aerial refueling checklist from the back seat, item-by-item. In Easy 32, FOD and Ninja sang along with Hootie.

"Rocky 51, Easy 31, two zero miles," stated Fig with a purely advisory call to the KC-135. Personally, Ninja didn't believe in such sugar calls. He was a big fan of radio silence. Still, Chunks and Fig were the lead, so protocol deemed that Ninja just keep his mouth shut.

At twenty miles, Chunks turned the flight back right to a heading of one six zero. He had successfully built enough turning room between the Hornets' flight path and that of the KC-135, and was now on a reciprocal heading with the tanker to preserve it. Still with his left hand on the stick, Chunks continued to wiggle his fingers and toes while descending down to an altitude of base minus one.

"Rocky 51, Stein 01," said a radio call with a thick German accent.

"Stein 01, Rocky 51 has you loud and clear, go ahead," returned the KC-135, intentionally talking slower and enunciating more clearly.

"Rocky 51, Stein 01, two Tornadoes, fifty miles out."

"Stein 01, Rocky 51, roger, copy all. Easy 31, two Hornets, is in front of you by about three zero miles. Report the starboard observation position with switches safe and nose cold."

"Rocky 51, Stein 01, copy."

Now down to ten miles, it was time for Chunks to counter-turn. He began a standard rate turn to the right to bring the KC-135 to the nose. FOD remained high and to the left in the same turning profile. Both pilots transitioned from the radar display to a heads-out scan of the horizon. Like the earlier race when the WSOs were working the radar, an unspoken race now commenced to be the first pilot to visually pick-up the KC-135. A pilot's vision was his life.

"Easy 31 is tally, KC-135, forty degrees right, seven miles."

"Easy 32, looking – tally now. Good call."

Chunks slightly altered his angle of bank and jockeyed his throttles forward in order to fine-tune the intercept. Easy 31 arrived perfectly at three miles, nose-on the KC-135, with ninety degrees to go to the tanker's heading. As the tanker continued straight and level, Chunks continued his right turn to arrive behind the KC-135 with enough closure to immediately scoot up into the starboard observation position. Chunks looked forty-five degrees to his left. There was his nemesis. Trailing behind the KC-135 was ten feet of rigid hose and a tiny, heavy basket. Chunks switched the stick from his left hand back to his right.

"Rocky 51, Easy 31, starboard observation, switches are safe, nose cold."

"Easy 31, Rocky 51, you're cleared to the pre-contact position."

Chunks maneuvered his jet down and left, arriving at the pre-contact position.

"Rocky 51, Easy 31 is pre-contact."

"Easy 31, Rocky 51, cleared in."

Chunks exhaled once. He relaxed his grip on the stick. He exhaled again. He wiggled his toes. He reached down by his left thigh and hit a switch to lower his seat just an inch or so for a better sight picture. Then he inched the throttles forward with just enough force to achieve the necessary three to four knots of closure on the basket. Closer, closer, closer - dink. The refueling probe nicked the basket at the eight o'clock position, and Chunks missed to the left.

Chunks immediately retarded the throttles to stop his downrange travel, and then exhaled again. He slid the throttles back a hair further, allowing the F-18D to slip back to the pre-contact position.

"Rocky 51, Easy 31, pre-contact."

"Easy 31, Rocky 51, cleared to plug."

Chunks goosed the throttles once more, and the Hornet smoothly inched forward. Closer, closer, closer – dink. The probe hit the basket at the nine o'clock position and Chunks barely tapped right rudder to penetrate the basket. He heard the familiar clunk, meaning that their probe was connected in the basket. Now flying formation on the tail of the KC-135, he slightly goosed the throttles forward to push the basket in and force the hose into a nice, comfortable, 'u' shape. Most pilots felt comfortable in that position. Suddenly, the KC-135 hit a tiny burble of turbulence, and dropped ever so slightly, causing Easy 31 to disconnect and fall out of the basket. Chunks instinctively throttled back to stop his downrange travel once more.

"Shit," exclaimed Chunks.

He exhaled again, and finessed the throttles back even further, causing his Hornet to fall back to the pre-contact position for a third attempt.

"Rocky 51, Easy 31, pre-contact position."

"Easy 31, Rocky 51, you're cleared in."

Chunks nudged the throttles again, commencing another attempt. Closer, closer, closer – there was no dink. Instead, Easy 31's probe had penetrated the basket dead center, and the only audible sound was the clunk. Chunks drove the jet forward a little further, and laid a 'u' shaped hose perfectly over on the F-18D's nose.

"Rocky 51, Easy 31, contact."

"Easy 31, Rocky 51, good fuel flow."

The KC-135's little green light came on to confirm Rocky 51's last radio call. Fig checked the fuel gauges down by his left knee, and he keyed the ICS.

"I concur, there, Chunks, ol' boy. I'm showing good flow back here. Nice job"

Chunks exhaled, and desperately tried not to squeeze the living shit out of the stick while flying formation on the KC-135's tail.

For the past ten minutes, from fifty feet to the right, FOD and Ninja had been watching Chunks' jousting with the basket. Although FOD was currently relaxed and enjoying a Twinkie with his Hootie concert, he couldn't help but empathize with Chunks. After taking a small sip of water, FOD set his water bottle down on the left console behind the throttles, but then accidentally knocked it over with his elbow. In the process of reaching to catch it, FOD accidentally hit the communications radio relay switch backward. Now Hootie and the Blowfish was being broadcast to the world over the number one radio on tanker primary. You could just see the question marks above the canopies of the two German Tornadoes.

0803 Wednesday
U. S. Air Force Hospital
Third Floor
"I wanted to remind you to lock the door."

After stuffing his rope into the left shin pocket of his flight suit, Booger stared at window 322A from across the lobby. He inhaled deeply, trying to muster the courage and walk the thirty steps there. Finally, he told himself that maybe Doc was right. After all, if he *did* have a problem down south of the border, then maybe it was something that could still be corrected. Booger took one baby step. I'm sure that there's a woman out there somewhere who could still love a man with small, squishy balls. Booger took a second baby step. Hey, if what Doc said is true, then I can always adopt. Booger took a third baby step. And so it went through the waiting area, past all the seated, white-haired, old farts reading their retirement magazines and sneakily ripping out the Rogaine ads. Booger took a thirtieth baby step. There he was. Seated behind window 322A was a Clairol blonde nurse, noisily chomping her gum during breaks in a thick, Boston accent.

Chomp, chomp, chomp.

"May I help you?"

Chomp, chomp, chomp.

"Yes, my squadron's flight Doc sent me down to . . .um . . .use a little paper cup."

Booger immediately became paranoid. He knew that she knew. She just *had* to know. Right now, she was probably thinking, "Oh, yeah, you're the guy with small, squishy balls who's shooting blanks."

Chomp, chomp, chomp.

Booger envisioned her coldly thinking, "you're like a Christmas tree – your balls are there just for decoration."

Chomp, chomp, chomp.

"Sure, just a minute," she said.

Chomp, chomp, chomp.

She spun around in her chair, and opened a cabinet above the sink. Just as quickly, she spun back around, and handed a tiny, white paper cup to Booger.

Geez, what am I doing? Booger thought. *Gettin' ketchup at Wendy's?* Surely she didn't expect him to fill it.

Chomp, chomp, chomp.

"The bathroom is the third door down on your right."

Chomp, chomp, chomp.

Booger started to turn in that direction when he was halted by a question.

Chomp, chomp, chomp.

"Would you like a magazine?"

Chomp, chomp, chomp.

"A magazine?" asked Booger.

Chomp, chomp, chomp.

"Yeah, you know, a *men's* magazine?"

Chomp, chomp, chomp.

Booger lost it.

"Nurse, I've got to masturbate into this tiny cup, and you ask me if I want a magazine? I've only got *two* hands."

About fifteen white-haired, old farts popped their heads up from their retirement magazines and locked their gaze onto Booger. The sound of their ripping out Rogaine ads was momentarily interrupted.

Booger froze. Regaining his composure, he suddenly realized that maybe he could prop the magazine up on the back of the toilet.

"Why, yes, thank you," said Booger, snatching it from her hands.

Booger immediately faced right, and marched down the hall - a million thoughts racing through his mind. Why do I have to be the one to do the deed? I should get Miss Clairol back there to help. She can just as easily spit into the cup as I can whack into it.

Booger entered the bathroom, and quickly shut the door. God, he'd done this a million times before, but never at the request of Navy medicine. He propped Miss July up on the back of the toilet, and fixed her in place with an extra roll of toilet paper.

Booger unzipped his flight suit and proceeded to do his duty. Suddenly, the door burst open. The sight wasn't pretty for either of the two participants.

Chomp, chomp, chomp.

"I wanted to remind you to lock the door."

0805 Wednesday
In the Ready Room
"The only big picture that I care about is the one of *ME*, hanging on the wall at Top Gun."

A gaggle of aviators gathered under SPEED IS LIFE, MORE IS BETTER., jockeying for position around a clipboard that was hanging on a nail. Spine Ripper had quit bitching long enough for the vein in his forehead to go back down, and he had joined his pilot, Tuna, in reading the board before a brief. Screech and Butt Munch were still bitching as they read, while Ghost silently perused today's required reading. Buick's oversize body took up enough space for two Easy aviators, and Bama was simply tall enough to peer over the top of the gaggle. N.D. silently pushed his cleaning cart out of the Ready Room.

FROM: COMMANDING GENERAL, ALLIED TACTICAL AIR FORCE
TO: DISTRIBUTION LIST
SUBJ: ROE UPDATE
REMARKS: THIS MESSAGE OVERRIDES ALL PREVIOUS INSTRUCTIONS.
1. THE LATEST UNCONFIRMED INTELLIGENCE FROM UNCONFIRMED SOURCES CONFIRMS POSSIBLE SUPPLY AND RESUPPLY ACTIVITY IN THE VICINITY OF HIGHWAY 55 NEAR GROBNEV. SOURCES INDICATE TRUCK CONVOYS AND RUSSIAN MI-8 HIP HELICOPTERS PARTICIPATING IN SAID SUPPLY MISSIONS, CODENAMED MI-55. DO NOT CONFUSE GROBNEV WITH KRABNEF, WHERE RUSSIAN MI-24 HIND HELICOPTERS WERE SPOTTED BY RECONNAISSANCE ELEMENTS OF MI-12, WHICH IS THE

12TH REGIMENT OF THE 55TH BRIGADE OF THE MICHIGAN NATIONAL GUARD. GENERAL CRAPNOV, COMMANDING GENERAL OF THE SERBIANS WHO ARE ROGUE TO THE ORIGINAL ROGUE SERBIANS, HAS REITERATED FROM HIS HEADQUARTERS IN GROPNAF, THAT HE DEEMS THE MI-12 TO BE NATO AGGRESSORS THAT ARE IMPEDING THE PROGRESS OF MI-55. FURTHERMORE, HE BELIEVES THAT THE MI-12 IS A THREAT TO THE FLIGHTS OF BOTH THE MI-24S FROM KRABNEF, WHO HAVE BEEN ASSIGNED TO PROTECT THE MI-8S NEAR GROBNEV, AND THE ACTUAL MI-8S THEMSELVES, AS THEY CONTINUE TO SUPPORT MI-55. LASTLY, CRAPNOV STATED FROM GROPNAF THAT GROBNEV AND KRABNEF ARE SOVEREIGN SERBIAN CITIES.

Tuna and Spine Ripper stepped back from the crowd, and merely looked at each other. They both shook their heads, and proceeded towards their briefing room.

"Hey Tuna."

"Yeah, Spine Ripper."

"We're about to do an air-to-air mission, right?"

"Yep."

"So what are you going to do if we intercept an Mi-8 Hip helicopter?"

"Shit my pants."

Screech, Butt Munch, and Ghost were the next three to depart the front of the Ready Room, proceeding to the coffee machine for the usual lukewarm mud.

"Well, Butt Munch, after reading that, how is Delta looking *now*?"

"Never better, Screech, never better," laughed Butt Munch. "And United?"

"Rock solid, man," returned Screech. "What could possibly happen in the future that would knock the airline industry to its knees?"

"What about you, Ghost?" asked Screech.

"What *about* me?"

"What's your two cents, after reading that shit? Doesn't it make you want to just throw in the towel?"

"On the contrary, Screech," returned Ghost, "it makes me want to stay in and become a General."

"*What*?" asked Butt Munch, in total disbelief. "I didn't know that you had aspirations for stars."

"I don't," returned Ghost. "I hate the brass. I always have. I always will."

"Well, then, you're going to have to paint me a picture," said Butt Munch.

"I'm tired of Generals being like the teacher in a Charlie Brown special," explained Ghost. "They're in charge, but absent, and when they finally do show up and talk, you can't understand 'em."

"Good call," nodded Screech.

"Why can't a low key, common sense, dude like me rise to wear stars?" asked Ghost. "I would totally unfuck things like that."

The trio of confused aviators shuffled out of the Ready Room, leaving only Bama and Buick under SPEED IS LIFE, MORE IS BETTER.

"What do you make of all this, Bama?"

"This bullshit has no effect on me," he said.

"So how do you figure?"

"Hip. Hind. Mig. I don't give a shit *what* it is." said Bama. "If it flies, it dies."

"That's fine and dandy, Bama, but what about the big picture?"

"The only big picture that I care about is the one of *ME,* hanging on the wall at Top Gun."

"You just don't get it, do you, Bama? This no-fly zone is an Air Force show, and they're just letting us play. But as long as there are Marines on the ground over there that need our support, *they're* number one - not shooting down Migs. Understand?"

Bama clenched his fist at his side.

"But there's more people in this operation who need you besides that Lance Corporal," continued Buick.

"What do you mean?"

"Join the team, Bama, and quit fighting me."

"I'm not fightin' you," said Bama, raising his voice.

"Bullshit, Bama," replied Buick, cool as ice, "you're in your own little world, fighting imaginary Migs."

Bama was speechless.

"We're all on this team," continued Buick, "and we don't even realize who we're *really* fighting."

Buick looked into Bama's eyes. Fat versus fit, there was a moment of silence.

"We're fighting more than just a potential enemy," explained Buick. "We spend more time fighting a bullshit system and fighting each other."

Bama and Buick wheeled about and went their separate ways, as a hunched N.D. struggled to push his cleaning cart out of the Ready Room.

* * *

If the F-18 goes out of control....

An F-18's departure from controlled flight during air combat maneuvering was not an uncommon experience. According to the F-18's big, blue bible on standard operating procedures, the aircraft had departed when it was not properly responding to control inputs. To pilots, that simply meant that the F-18 wasn't doing what it was being told to do. Most of the time, departures took place when the F-18 was in a fight and slowly going over the top of a loop on its back. For example, a pilot would be attempting to aggressively make a killing maneuver with insufficient airspeed against someone beneath him, only to suddenly find himself out-of-control and dropping like a rock.

In reality, departures were no big deal. The bible went on to say that releasing the controls, taking the feet off of the rudder pedals, and retracting the speed brake would recover the aircraft from most departures. Thus, if the pilot simply followed those immediate action procedures, the F-18 would fly itself out of the departure and the pilot could resume control. Those procedures were recited - verbatim and aloud - by a pilot at the end of *every* brief for *every* flight that involved fighting another aircraft. Pilots had recited those procedures a million times.

If the F-18 goes out-of-control, release the controls, feet off the rudders, speed brake in. If still out-of-control, throttles idle, check altitude, airspeed, angle of attack, and the yaw rate.

If you continued down the list of procedures, you eventually got to the immediate action that you didn't want to recite.

If still out-of-control passing ten thousand feet above the ground, then eject.

Starting abeam each other with sufficient lateral separation, Butt Munch was ready and eager to start the fight. Last night's pasta had given him energy to burn.

"Easy 61, speed and angels on the right," stated Butt Munch.

"Easy 62, speed and angels on the left," returned Ham Fist.

There was a moment's pause.

"Easy 61, tape's on, fight's on."

"Easy 62, tape's on, fight's on."

Immediately, both Hornets turned in towards each other. Having learned from yesterday's fiasco against Tuna, Ham Fist yanked the harder pull of the two pilots to get inside of Butt Munches turn; consequently, he was considerably slower. Butt Munch aided Ham Fist's cause by intentionally floating his left turn for just a moment, and then pulling hard left into the fight.

"Left-to-left," stated Butt Munch, calling the initial pass.

"Left-to-left," concurred Ham Fist.

No sooner had the direction of pass been established, then Ham Fist sucked up a simulated heat-seeking missile into his face once again.

"Fox two," called Butt Munch over the radio.

Damn it, thought Ham Fist, still fumbling, trying to obtain a radar lock. *How do they do that?*

"Chaff, flares, chaff, flares," returned Dago from Ham Fist's back seat, acknowledging Butt Munches shot, while simulating the ejection of decoy expendables.

Seconds later, both Hornets passed left-to-left with eight hundred feet of lateral separation and nine hundred knots of closure. Butt Munch immediately recognized that Ham Fist had mistakenly given him three hundred feet of extra turning room over the minimum five hundred feet allowed. Butt Munch cranked in an early turn to the left, across Ham Fist's tail in two-circle flow, digging nose low in an out-of-plane maneuver.

Ham Fist, stubbornly sticking to his game plan of going up into the sun, repeated the same initial move as yesterday. However, instead of having the excessive airspeed that caused his jet to inscribe such a big arc in the sky yesterday, Ham Fist went into the vertical at a much slower airspeed. At the top of his loop, Easy 62 was flat on its back at twenty-three thousand feet, and Ham Fist recognized a potential shot opportunity at Butt Munch below him. However, Ham Fist was out of airspeed. He failed to reef the stick back into his lap, which would've caused the nose to track back down through the horizon and the airspeed to increase. Consequently, the F-18's angle of attack feedback system commanded nose down stabilator, causing Easy 62 to be in a relatively steady, inverted, and nose high attitude. Suddenly, the jet began a rapidly increasing yaw to the right in an uncommanded nose slice departure. Ham Fist had dicked the dog.

Immediately, Ham Fist and Dago recognized the departure warning tone, meaning that their F-18D now had a yaw rate of twenty-five degrees per second.

"Beep............beep............beep."

The aircraft violently continued its yaw to the right as the nose fell, pointing towards the water below. The departure warning tone increased proportionately with the F-18D's yaw rate.

"Beep...beep.....beep.....beep.....beep."

In the back seat, Dago, who always flew with his straps too loose, was slammed into the side of the canopy and pinned there by the side forces. Ham Fist's body was thrown in the same direction, but he was still able to maintain his hands on the stick and throttle. As the F-18's yaw rate hit forty-five degrees per second, the departure warning tone became constant.

"Beeeeeeeeeeeeeeeeeeeeeeeep."

Ham Fist momentarily froze. Then nine months of filling out immediate action exams caused the procedures to pop into his brain.

If the F-18 goes out of control, release the controls, feet off the rudder, and check speed brake in.

Even though it was a totally unnatural act for a pilot to do, Ham Fist released the stick. Then he had to make a concentrated effort to remove both of his feet from the rudder pedals and place them on the floor.

Four feet behind Ham Fist, the experienced Dago wasn't rattled, realizing that at this point in time, he and Ham Fist were just along for the ride.

"Knock it off, knock it off, Easy 62 is ballistic," Dago declared over the radio.

Looking straight above him and seeing Ham Fist's F-18D flopping down through the sky, Butt Munch echoed the radio call, stating, "Roger, Easy 61 copies, knock it off."

Then Butt Munch jammed his stick full forward and selected afterburner in an effort to get out from under Ham Fist's falling jet. In the meantime, four feet behind Butt Munch, One Nut was now worthless.

Caught by surprise with the g forces that Butt Munch snapped on the jet for the early turn, One Nut's head had been bounced off the side of the canopy, and he had strained the muscles in his neck.

Meanwhile in Easy 62, the same emergency procedures filled Dago's helmet. He pushed himself off of the canopy, cocked his head, and peered around Ham Fist's head box into the front cockpit. He could see that Ham Fist had grabbed the handles on both sides of the front canopy bow, thus Dago knew that Ham Fist had released the stick. Shit hot. Then Dago quickly checked his rear view mirror. The rudders were perfectly centered, so Ham Fist must have his feet off the rudder pedals. Shit hot again. Lastly, Dago could see in the mirror that the speed brake was in. Shit hot one more time.

No sweat, thought Dago. *We'll be out of this in no time.*

Suddenly, the F-18 entered a momentary zero g condition, causing Dago's head to bounce off the top of the canopy. Then the aircraft brutally yawed to the left, where the side forces pinned Dago on the opposite side of the canopy. Easy 62's F-18D was falling out of the sky in random twists and turns - like a leaf.

"Beeeeeeeeeeeeeeeeeeeeeeeeep."

From out of nowhere, the next step leaped into Ham Fist's brain.

If still out of control, throttles idle, check altitude, airspeed, angle of attack, and yaw rate.

Ham Fist reached down with his left hand and brought both throttles back to idle, just as he heard Dago state their altitude over the ICS, "One seven thousand feet"

Then Ham Fist checked both the HUD and the other displays. The airspeed, angle of attack, and yaw rate all indicated that his F-18D was not yet in a spin.

In the back seat, Dago quickly glanced down at the engine and fuel indicator by his left knee. The two needles indicating engine nozzle position had swung in the proper direction, telling him that Ham Fist had selected idle. Shit hot again. Likewise, he diverted his gaze to verify the airspeed, angle of attack, and yaw rate. He knew that Ham Fist would have to demonstrate an incredible amount of patience in recovering the jet from this departure. Dago silently hoped that the youngster in his front seat would do so. There was certainly no need for Dago to pull the ejection handle - yet.

Just as quickly as the departure had started, the indications abruptly appeared that the jet was recovering. The tones were removed from both of their helmets, and the side forces disappeared, allowing Dago's body to return to his seat. Easy 62's jet was now very nose low and accelerating rapidly through two hundred knots.

In the front seat, Ham Fist recognized the same recovery parameters, and removed his right hand from the handle on the canopy bow and grabbed the stick. Simultaneously, he removed his left hand from the other handle, and captured the throttles. He recalled from the big, blue bible that the minimum altitude loss in a departure recovery was achieved by advancing the throttles to maximum afterburner and maintaining twenty-five to thirty-five units on the angle of attack until a positive rate of climb was established. Once again, rote memorization saved Ham Fist.

Dago felt the g forces on the jet as Easy 62 rolled wings level and commenced a positive climb.

"Whew," exhaled Dago, slumping in the rear seat.

Meanwhile, Ham Fist stared wide-eyed out the front windscreen.

"Nice job on the recovery, Ham Fist," said Dago on the ICS.

Easy 61, having witnessed the whole affair from a safe distance and altitude, still had sight of Ham Fist as he climbed in his recovery.

"Easy 62, Easy 61," stated Butt Munch.

"Easy 61, Easy 62, go ahead," returned Ham Fist, his voice an octave higher.

"I'm visual at your left eight. I'll join on you and lead us back home. We're done for the day."

"Roger that."

1017 Wednesday
Easy 41 and 42, Air-to-Air Mission, In-country
"Damn it. Damn it. Damn it."

When Spine Ripper was on the hand controllers, he was a god at working the radar; consequently, he was the first to break radio silence with Pierre.

"Pierre, Easy 42, radar contact, at your last call. Low and slow."

Pierre, the French AWACS, immediately confessed, "Pierre, now clean there."

Just as Spine Ripper had stated, his radar contact was probably flying too low and too slow for the AWACS radar to detect amongst the mountains. Since Spine Ripper's pick-up was a mere twenty miles away, action had to be taken immediately. Spine Ripper took charge of the section and Easy 42 assumed the lead.

"Easy 41, 42 is lead right. Snap one three zero, two zero miles, angels three. Offset right, sweep left," Spine Ripper declared over the number one radio, ensuring that Pierre was also aware of the game plan.

"Easy 41, copy," returned Booger from the other jet.

"Roger, Pierre copies."

After a moment of silence, the French AWACS chimed in, stating, "Pierre declares an 'unknown' there. Visual identification is required."

"Pierre, Easy 42 copy, VID required."

"Easy 41, VID."

Booger goosed the throttles, rolled Easy 41 right, and yanked his F-18D up and behind Easy 42 to arrive on the outside of the formation, now abeam Tuna and Spine Ripper. As soon as he rolled wings level and had his nose heading one three zero, Ping was on the radar. Spine Ripper continued the calls to get Easy 41's radar onto the bad guy, saying, "Easy 41, contact, one one zero, one seven miles, angels three."

"Easy 42, 41 is contact, your call," Ping replied, now seeing the same thing on his radar as Spine Ripper.

Now at fifteen miles, Easy 42 locked his radar onto the unidentified adversary, and both Tuna and Spine Ripper brought up the infrared display on the cockpit's left screen. Thus, Tuna and Spine Ripper simultaneously had an ID of their contact - it was a Russian-made Mi-8 Hip helicopter. Spine Ripper momentarily adjusted the magnification to be sure of the ID. Yep, it was a Hip. In anticipation of a clearance to fire from Pierre, Tuna armed up the selected missile, a radar-guided Sparrow. Spine Ripper quickly prodded Pierre for the clearance.

"Pierre, Easy 42, systems ID adversary as a Hip, repeat Hip."

"Roger Easy 42, standby."

Pierre's response was not what they wanted to hear.

"Damn it," shouted Tuna over the ICS. "Damn it."

They were now down to only twelve miles, and knew what Pierre was doing. He was just now beginning the lengthy process of obtaining instructions from the CAOC.

"Ten miles," stated Tuna, retarding the throttles back just a bit.

Booger did the same in his position on Tuna's right, and at an altitude that was seven thousand feet higher. Having obtained a visual identification with the infrared display, there was now no need to pass near the Hip and visually identify him with the naked eye. Thus, Tuna began a climbing right hand turn at eight miles, and Booger remained in the same position, high and on the right. Passing through twelve thousand feet, Tuna reversed his turn to the left, keeping the Hip on the radar and his infrared display. They would establish a left-hand orbit overhead the Hip, and match its down range travel, awaiting a clearance to fire from Pierre.

"Pierre, Easy 42, five miles," pimped Tuna.

He had an itchy trigger finger.

"Easy 42, Pierre, stand by."

"Damn it. Damn it. Damn it," yelled Tuna over the ICS.

Tuna's eyes suddenly picked up the low flying Hip. He deselected the air-to-air Sparrow missile, and selected air-to-ground. Tuna's weapon of choice was now a simple, dumb bomb that he would drop in front of the Hip and let the shrapnel rip into the helicopter's body. Tuna inaugurated a left-hand orbit above the Hip at an altitude commensurate with a roll-in for a thirty-degree dive delivery.

Suddenly, the tables reversed. The Hip slowed to a stationary hover, and then began a controlled descent to the earth. The Hip's pilots must've been alerted to the Hornet's presence by either a radio call from a sharp ground controller, or through a visual pick-up of their own. The Hip knew how to play the game. The complicated rules of engagement did not allow the killing of a helicopter if it was sitting on the ground.

"Pierre, Easy 42," prodded Tuna.

He saw his air medal quickly slipping away.

"Easy 42, Pierre, stand by."

"Damn it," shouted Tuna over the ICS. "Damn it."

The Hip settled down in a farmer's field amidst a cloud of dust and debris; after which, its rotors began to slowly wind down. Easy 41 and 42 continued their left-hand orbit for two hundred and seventy degrees, until the radio silence was broken.

"Easy 42, Pierre."

"Pierre, Easy 42, go," Tuna quickly replied.

He was ready to pounce.

"The CAOC passes that you are to remain overhead until Paris 21, two Mirage 2000s, relieves you, then proceed to Texaco."

"Damn it. Damn it. Damn it," yelled Tuna over the ICS.

1029 Wednesday
On the Flightline
"We could be floating in our life rafts right now."

Ham Fist slowly taxied aircraft 02 into its parking position, carefully following the visual hand signals from the plane captain. On the left side of the Hornet's nose, the plane captain slowly brought his fists together over his head, and Ham Fist tapped the brakes, bringing the jet to a halt.

As Ham Fist set the parking brake, Dago began his shutdown procedures in the rear seat. He quickly updated the inertial navigation system, and informed Ham Fist that his hands and arms were away from the canopy.

"Good update, clear of the canopy, and set for shutdown," Dago said on the ICS.

"Roger that," returned Ham Fist.

He reached to his right and hit the canopy control lever, raising the canopy.

After placing the chocks under the tires, the plane captain emerged from under the F-18D and repositioned himself on the left side of the nose. He quickly ripped through all the hand signals that told Ham Fist where to position the flaps and other flight control surfaces. Next, the plane captain held up his right index finger to Ham Fist, and made a slashing motion across his throat with his left hand. Ham Fist promptly chopped the left engine's throttle to the off position, and monitored the RPM and exhaust gas temperature as the left engine wound down. Ham Fist also ensured that the appropriate hydraulic switching valves worked properly, as the number one hydraulic needle swung clockwise around the gauge. The plane captain showed two fingers to Ham Fist with his right hand, and made the same slashing motion. Ham Fist shut down the right engine.

"See you outside," said Ham Fist.

"Roger that."

Dago was the first one down the boarding ladder, and he did it in the same crazy manner that he always did. Dago was the only aviator in the squadron - and probably the world - who descended the boarding ladder facing *out* from the jet, rather than towards it. In any case, as soon as Dago was on the tarmac, the plane captain intercepted him, asking, "How's the jet, Sir?"

"02 is a great jet, Corporal," answered Dago, removing his right protective bootie. "No gripes from the back seat."

The pilots and WSOs wore ridiculous looking white booties over their flight boots every time that they climbed onto the jet and walked on the leading edge extension to get into their respective seats. The aircrew hated looking liked dorks, but it kept the jets clean from black boot marks and dirt. Thus, the aircraft spent more time in the air and less time at the wash rack.

Dago removed his left bootie, and began his post flight inspection. The plane captain turned to Ham Fist, now descending the ladder, and asked, "How's the jet, Sir?"

"Shit hot," returned Ham Fist. "No gripes from the front seat."

The plane captain pumped his right fist and proudly declared, "Yessssss."

With nothing on the jet that needed immediate maintenance, the Hornet could be quickly inspected and turned around to fly another mission later today.

Ham Fist removed his booties, and commenced his post flight inspection of the jet, in a clockwise direction. Once he was on the right side of the Hornet, he received a good-natured jab from one of the enlisted ordnance men.

"Rough day at the office today, Sir?" the young Marine wryly grinned.

"Yes, as a matter of fact it was," returned Ham Fist. "Why do you ask?"

The young Devil Dog had removed the buckets from the jet's belly that contained all of the expendable chaff and flare decoys. Both buckets were empty, meaning that Ham Fist had been on the defensive all day.

"Sir, all your chaff and flares are gone," he snickered.

"Yeah," replied Ham Fist, "meet me at the back of the jet and help me pry those missiles out of its ass."

They both laughed, and Ham Fist continued his post flight inspection.

Back at the tail end of the jet, Ham Fist met Dago, and it was the first time that he had seen his face since the departure. He didn't quite know what to do or say, and he didn't know his WSO well enough to read his expressions. Was Dago pissed that Ham Fist's poor aviation skills had almost gotten their F-18D into a spin? Ham Fist fully expected the temperamental little Italian to rip him a new asshole. Ham Fist halted his inspection, and momentarily grabbed Dago's arm.

"Hey Dago," he said sheepishly, "about today. I'm sorry, man."

"Sorry? For *what*?"

"Thanks to me, we came this close to pulling the ejection handles. We could be floating in our life rafts right now, waiting for a helo to pick us up."

"Don't be sorry, Ham Fist," returned Dago. "It's because you did the recovery procedures perfectly that we *aren't* in our life rafts right now. Nice job, man."

"Thanks, Dago."

"There was never a need for me to pull the handle. That's a decision that a WSO has to make, and then live with - or not."

Dago slapped Ham Fist on the back and continued his post flight inspection.

"The next time I fly with you, Ham Fist, I'm going to tighten down my lap restraints. I have a *terrible* headache from my helmet hitting the canopy."

Ham Fist just watched Dago in a stunned silence, and came to a realization. Dago was just like every other aviator in the squadron - a totally different man in the cockpit than he was on the ground. There was Dago, joking about a headache, after experiencing a potentially deadly departure from controlled flight. Dago was a true professional, and Ham Fist made a promise to himself that he wanted to become a member of this elite team of "misfits who shine".

* * *

Dirty Laundry

Rumors abounded concerning the "Human Frailties Board". The dirty laundry that was aired at this monthly witch-hunt would've weighed heavily on the mind of ANY man struggling to take care of a wife and a family - not just an aviator - but with one very important difference. Mr. average Joe, nine-to-five, Cubicle wouldn't plow a forty million dollar jet into the ground if life's problems were temporarily distracting him.

If you stop and think about it, the Human Frailties Board was such a double-edged sword. You certainly didn't want your squadron mates openly discussing your personal life and its problems. But then again, if it saved your ass one day, who was to argue? Yet come to think of it, was the Human Frailties Board more interested in saving an aviator's life - or the jet?

1058 Wednesday
In the Commanding Officer's conference room - door shut
"Besides, we're *all* fucked in the head to be in this line of work anyway."

Pope briefly bent over a super secret notebook that was normally kept under lock and key somewhere in the Safety Department's office. He scrawled some chicken scratching that seemed to take forever.

"Ok, you guys," continued Pope, "we're almost done with this month's Human Frailties Board. Hang with me."

"Thank God," sighed Bama, leaning back in his chair.

"Bama, you think *you* have problems," said Buick, "man, I need a beer."

Ghost chuckled under his breath, Bama smiled, and Doc looked away. Spine Ripper laughed too, but it had to hurt his face.

"Ok, then," Pope continued, "this Human Frailties Board concludes that we will all keep a cautious eye on any aviators currently experiencing marital difficulties."

Everyone nodded in agreement.

Buick's eyes quickly scanned those of the Board's members seated around the table. None of them cast any askew glances or suspicious looks at Buick. Thank God. Nobody in the squadron knew, and it was going to stay that way if Buick had anything to say about it.

"Doc, any final comments from the Medical Department?"

"No, the only flight physical this week was Booger's," replied the Doc, "and everything went fine."

"Good," quipped Pope.

"I'm currently having him do a minor follow-up test, but it is insignificant."

"Roger that," returned Pope. "Anything else from the Board?"

Buick raised his hand.

"Yeah, Buick?"

"I think Spine Ripper is a psycho," said Buick. "Does that count for anything?"

Another round of laughter spilled over the table's scratched, oaken surface. Even Spine Ripper cracked a smile, and it still must've hurt.

"And the Board wholeheartedly agrees," returned Pope. "So *now*, anything else?"

The only sound heard was the familiar whine of an F-18D starting one of its engines about two hundred yards away.

"Well, that's it," said Pope.

Everyone sighed in relief, and began to arise from their chairs.

"Alright," said Bama, pushing himself away from the table. "I'm out of here."

"Wait a minute," interrupted Spine Ripper.

"Oh, shit," mumbled Bama under his breath, slumping back down in his chair.

"Has anybody noticed anything different about Jock lately?" asked Spine Ripper.

Pope and Ghost caught each other's eye.

"What do you mean?" asked Pope, feigning sincerity. He didn't want to ask, but he *had* to. After all, he was running the Board.

"Oh, I don't know," continued Spine Ripper. "He's just been acting a little funny lately, that's all."

Give it a rest, man, thought Ghost, clenching his fist under the table.

That would be just like 'Mr. Intensity' to have noticed Jock, thought Pope.

"Well, it's no big secret that he wants to get out and fly for TWA," said Bama. "That's all I know."

"Precisely," proclaimed Spine Ripper. "I think that desire may be having an impact on his performance in the jet."

"Well, wait a minute," said Ghost. "Screech wants to get out and fly for United, and you don't see anything wrong with him."

"And then there's Butt Munch," added Pope. "He wants to get out and fly for Delta, and he's perfectly fine."

"Yeah, yeah, I know," said Spine Ripper, "but I would expect such comments from the two of you. You're both pilots and so are they."

"What does that have to do with anything?" asked Pope.

"I'm a WSO," continued Spine Ripper. "There's no chance of a distracted Jock plowing a jet into the ground with *you* in his back seat."

"So what are saying?" demanded Ghost.

"I'm saying that this squadron has a strong 'Pilot's Protection Union', that's all."

"Bullshit," said Bama, bolting erect in his chair and pounding his fist on the table.

"Easy, Bama," soothed Pope, struggling to maintain control of the Board.

"Pope," continued Spine Ripper, "I think that you and Ghost just may be protecting ol' Jock."

"You're crazy, Spine Ripper," said Ghost.

"You two know something that we don't."

"What about *you*, Buick?" questioned Bama.

"So what *about* me?"

"You're like the president of the 'WSO Protection Union'," said Bama. "What do *you* have to say?"

Buick, gathering his thoughts for a moment, was just thankful that the squadron had a 'WSO-who-is-overweight-and-drinks-too-much Protection Union'.

"You could end up in Jock's back seat someday," said Bama, "so is Spine Ripper onto something?"

"Shit," began Buick, addressing the Board, "go ahead and put me in Jock's back seat. I don't give a rat's ass."

When Buick spoke, people listened. The Human Frailties Board was no different.

"If I end up in a smoking hole four feet behind Jock, then donate my liver to medical science."

Doc was mildly repulsed by Buick's liver statement, and not quite sure of what to make of these men who were his medical responsibility.

"Besides," continued Buick, "we're *all* fucked in the head to be in this line of work anyway."

Bama chuckled.

"On *any* given day, *any* given pilot could be whacked out enough to kill me."

Spine Ripper nodded in agreement, as Buick let the silence build for a moment.

"Personally, I haven't noticed anything wrong with Jock," he continued in a calmer tone, "but I say, shit, just leave him alone. Things will be ok."

Quickly, Pope and Ghost caught each other's eye. They knew that they had achieved a silent victory, unbeknownst to the other members of the Board.

Whew, sighed Pope inside.

Yesssssss, thought Ghost.

"I guess Buick's right," admitted Spine Ripper.

"So can we finally call it a day?" asked an impatient Bama.

"Anything else from the Board?" added Pope, regaining control.

That same F-18D in the distance started its second engine.

"Very well then," said Pope, "the Human Frailties Board is adjourned until next month. Thank you, Gentlemen."

* * *

The spoon wasn't the *only* thing that was greasy

The Marine Corps had erected the squadron's compound of work buildings right next to the air base's golf course. How convenient. On days like today, where an aviator didn't feel like dancing the sidestep for lunch - or didn't have time - it was a no-brainer to walk twenty yards across a gravel road and grab a bite to eat at the Golf Shack. It was your typical greasy spoon diner selling burgers, dogs, and sandwiches, but it was a change of pace nonetheless. The aviators would've eaten every meal there, if Uncle Sam only paid them enough money.

When these men got together over lunch at the Golf Shack, the subject of conversation was, more often than not, about women. When deployed overseas for six months, you never quit thinking about the fairer sex. When you weren't flying - and sometimes when you were - your mind would aimlessly wonder to thoughts and dreams and fantasies. It's funny, because even though you walked around in a constant state of horniness, these thoughts didn't consist of crude, all-out, acts of wild animal intercourse. No. Instead, these thoughts consisted of soft, quiet, mindless memories of all the great little things that you loved and missed about women. A blonde ponytail, a perfect cleavage, belly-button fuzz, painted toenails, maybe a seductive tattoo, or an arched back…the list was endless.

1132 Wednesday
Golf Shack Pro Shop and Luncheonette
"Why doesn't the Marine Corps have a Miss Buxley?"

Chunks, Fig, FOD, and Ninja decided to reward themselves with lunch at the Golf Shack after surviving another session with the KC-135. The foursome was seated at a booth in the back, receipts in hand, simultaneously listening to a crackly loudspeaker while they talked about - what else - women.

"I'll tell you what, boys," began Ninja. "I'm from L.A., and there's no better looking women in the world than those in California."

"So Brian Wilson was right, huh?" joked Chunks.

"Brian *who*?" asked Ninja, with a puzzled expression on his face.

"Brian Wilson, lead singer of the Beach Boys," returned Chunks, with a condescending tone.

Fig felt compelled to pile on with the assault upon Ninja's ignorance, stating, "You know, Brian Wilson. He sang "California Girls"."

"No way," returned FOD, defending his WSO. "I saw the video, and that was David Lee Roth."

"Number forty-two, Reuben on rye", crackled the loudspeaker over a jukebox in the corner playing the Dave Matthews Band.

"Ok, Mr. Geezer-rock with your stupid Beach Boys," said Ninja. "Where do *you* think the hottest women are from?"

Before Chunks could answer, Fig interrupted.

"Throttle back, dude," he said. "Before you fly into Chunks, you should know that, right now, he's the luckiest bastard in the squadron."

"Lucky? Why?" asked FOD.

Fig spilled the beans.

"Because while all you guys are pining for your women back in the real world, Chunks is chasing some of the local talent."

"What?" Ninja asked, eyes widening. "Are you dating a woman out in town?"

Chunks was almost embarrassed, muttering, "Yeah, I guess you could say that."

"Number forty-three, turkey and Swiss cheese on wheat."

"Details, dude, details," pleaded Ninja, making a beckoning motion.

"Ooooo, an Italian Catholic. How *hot* is that?" joked FOD, fanning himself.

"But Italian Catholic is a double-edged sword," stated Ninja. "First - the good edge - is that she has to be drop dead gorgeous. But secondly - the bad edge - you can kiss pre-marital sex good bye."

"Pre-marital sex?" asked Fig. "Is there any other kind?"

"Number forty-four, cheeseburger and fries."

"Whoa. That's my number," said Chunks, who seized the opportunity to escape the heat by grabbing his receipt and running to the counter.

In the ninety seconds that it took for Chunks to get his burger, refill his Coke, and slide back into the booth, the subject had changed. The spotlight was no longer on him and his local squeeze, but the topic had returned to - what else - women.

"Nope, you're wrong, Fig," stated Ninja. "It's a blonde pony-tail, hands down."

"You're crazy," said FOD. "Am I the only guy here who digs short, black hair?"

"Oh, no way, FOD," mumbled Chunks with a French fry hanging from the corner of his mouth. "There ought to be a law that women never cut their hair. Never. The longer, the better."

"Number forty-five, chili cheese dog, onion rings."

"Oh, that's me, dude," said Ninja. "Let me out."

FOD and Ninja slid to their left, and Ninja departed. In his absence, FOD picked up the torch, asking, "Since we can't all agree on hair length, then what about hair style?"

"I like it poofy and feathered back, like Farrah Fawcett Majors," cooed Chunks.

"Ok, I'm back. What did I miss?" asked Ninja.

"Instead of hair length, we're now on hair style," returned Chunks. "I just said that I like it feathered back, like Farrah Fawcett Majors."

"Dude," said Ninja, sliding into the booth. "First it was Brian what's-his-name, and now it's Farrah Fawcett Majors. You need to come into the nineties."

"Number forty-six, ham and Swiss cheese on wheat."

FOD never got the chance to slide back in. He grabbed his receipt and sauntered to the counter. By the time he returned, the conversation had gotten out of control.

"Ok," began Ninja. "Who's the hottest female cartoon?"

"No question," answered Chunks. "It's got to be Miss Buxley in Beetle Bailey."

"Good call," added Ninja. "Why doesn't the Marine Corps have a Miss Buxley?"

"It *does*," replied FOD. "Did you see the General's driver this morning?"

"Number forty-seven, fried bologna."

Before Fig could even grab his receipt, each member seated around the booth, in one form or another, simultaneously looked at Fig and asked, "Fried bologna?"

"Oh, eat me," declared Fig as he slid out of the booth.

Fig returned with his gourmet sandwich, and chili on corn chips to boot. He slid back into the booth, partially spilling his Mountain Dew.

Yeah, life was good when not struggling to get gas from a KC-135. This morning's Rocky 51 - short hose, stiff basket, and all - was a forgotten nightmare.

* * *

The speed of heat

Flying the squadron's flight surgeon was a necessary evil. As the squadron's doctor, he was required to get a minimum amount of annual flight time. This obligation allowed the Doc to comprehend the dynamic environment and physical stressors that his aviator's endured. The best way to fly the Doc was on a simple all-weather-intercept hop. A flight of two F-18s would break apart, with one as the fighter and one as the adversary. At thirty to forty miles of separation, the two would turn in against each other, and the fighter would conduct a simple intercept to arrive in the bad guy's rear quarter. However, this good deal for the Doc led to a bitter irony of ironies. Because he flew so rarely, the poor flight surgeon's body was often unable to handle the cockpit environment;

consequently, he would get sick and vomit. His sickness was compounded by the fact that the hapless flight surgeon was always the butt of some sick prank.

1321 Wednesday
Easy 51 and 52 in the Training Area south of the Airfield
"OK, Doc. Tighten down your straps. Here we go."

"Easy 51, ready in the west as the fighter," said Joisey.

"Easy 52, ready in the east as the bad guy," returned Screech.

"Roger, Easy 51, turning in, tape's on, fight's on."

"Easy 52, turning in, tapes on, fight's on."

Screech, as the bad guy, had Doc in his backseat, so he tried to make the one hundred and eighty degree turn as easy as possible. He maintained a constant two g's, in a level, left turn at twenty four thousand feet, to a heading of two seven zero. Screech had no sooner rolled wings level, when he heard a painful retch come from the back seat.

"Raaaaaallllppphhh."

God, thought Screech. *Already? That was only two g's.*

He keyed the ICS, asking, "Hey Doc. You ok?"

There was a moment of silence as Screech awaited an answer, and then the smell finally reached the front seat. Screech's body reacted with the obligatory gag reflex, and he returned his oxygen mask back over his face to deter the odor.

"Yeah," Doc lied over the ICS. "I'm fine."

Then Joisey and Shitscreen, in Easy 51, made the first radio call of the intercept.

"Easy 52, Easy 51 is radar contact."

Screech was momentarily overwhelmed in trying to simultaneously fly the plane, work the radar, and make sure that Doc was ok. Screech keyed the mike to play AWACS for his playmates, Joisey and Shitscreen, declaring, "Easy 51, that's your bad guy. Visual ID is required."

"Easy 51 copy, offset left, sweep right," returned Shitscreen, totally oblivious to the near emergency currently going on in the back seat of Easy 52.

Screech continued down range as the enemy toward Easy 51, maintaining as near wings level as he possibly could for the poor Doc. Screech envisioned vomit splattered all over the rear cockpit.

"Doc, were you able to get your sick bag out in time?"

A sheepish reply came back over the ICS, mumbling, "Um . . . no."

Shit, thought Screech. *I knew it. There's puke over all the displays, and I'm going to be the one to have to clean it up.*

"Hey Screech."

"Yeah, Doc."

"I threw up into one of my flight gloves. What should I do?"

Inside, Screech was jubilant.

Yessssss, he thought. *Score one for the flight Doc. There'll be no cleaning up puke for this kid.*

"Doc, just tie it shut at the wrist and set it aside on one of the consoles."

Typical of most pilots, Screech didn't have a clue as to what the back seat looked like or where anything was. But he felt like that was a good answer. The rear cockpit had consoles, right? It *had* to, right? Screech looked into his mirror, and could see the Doc's helmet buried in his chest trying to accomplish the task at hand.

"Easy 51, tally single F-18," said Joisey over the number one radio.

That radio call jerked Screech back into the game. He looked out the right side of his canopy, re-focused his eyes, and visually picked up Easy 51 as they turned behind 52.

"Easy 51, 52 is tally," pronounced Screech over the radio.

"Hey Doc. Look outside," Screech instructed over the ICS. "There he is. Do you see him? He's about seventy degrees right, four miles, swinging our wingline to turn behind us, just above that cloud."

There was no answer from the rear seat. Was Doc still alive?

Joisey and Shitscreen completed a near perfect stern intercept, with their range in perfect parameters and closure totally under control.

"Easy 52, Easy 51, knock it off. We're going west to set up another run as the fighter," said Joisey.

"Roger, Easy 51. Easy 52, knock it off. We're heading east as the adversary," returned Screech.

As the two F-18Ds gained separation for the second run, Screech decided to play a little prank on the squadron's flight surgeon.

"Hey, Doc," he inquired. "Have you ever flown at the 'speed of heat'?"

After a few seconds, Doc's reply came in the form of a question.

"The speed of heat? You mean the speed of sound, right?"

"Oh, Doc, no, no, no." replied Screech, biting his lip. "The speed of heat."

"Um, no, I can't say that I have."

"Well shit, then," said Screech. "Let's go for it."

Screech then began to give the Doc instructions, baiting him along.

"Doc, put the HUD on the left screen, ok?"

Doc complied, and then sat, nervously awaiting

"Doc, look down at the lower left corner of the HUD," instructed Screech. "Do you see the capitol 'M' with the number after it?"

Doc silently searched for a few seconds, then replied, "Ok, got it."

"Well, that number is our Mach number. It's telling us how fast we're flying with respect to the speed of sound."

"I understand," Doc sincerely continued, unaware that he was about to be duped.

"Doc, it's a little known fact that the same number also represents how fast we are flying with respect to the speed of heat. As you approach Mach 1.0, the aircraft actually gets warmer. You can *feel* it."

Doc was in awe.

They never mentioned anything about the speed of heat at the Armed Forces Medical College, he thought.

"So Doc, are you ready to fly the speed of heat?" asked Screech enthusiastically.

"Sure, Screech, go for it," returned Doc.

"Ok, Doc. Tighten down your straps. Here we go. Right now I'm showing Mach .72 in the HUD."

Screech jammed the stick full forward, and selected full afterburner, throwing their Hornet into a forty-five degree dive, screaming towards the surface of the water. With his eyes glued to the HUD display, Doc earnestly watched the Mach number rapidly begin to climb - M .75, M .78, M .80. In the front seat, unbeknownst to Doc, Screech reached down by his right thigh, and increased the flow of heat to the rear cockpit.

"Doc, can you feel anything yet?"

"Yeah, no shit. It's getting warmer," replied Doc.

His eyes were now affixed to the HUD - M .84, M .86, M .89.

At M .90, Screech cranked the heat to full hot. He also started to shake the stick back and forth ever so slightly, and to alternately tap the rudders with his feet. The F-18 began to shiver and quake and yaw in its dive.

"Oh my God," said Screech. "We're almost there."

"The heat, the heat, I can really feel the heat," shouted Doc. "Is the plane ok?"

At M .95, Screech reefed the stick back into his lap and deselected afterburner. He also cranked the heat back to the full cold position as the Hornet began a five g pull to a zoom climb. They had bottomed out at M .98.

Then came the same sound from the rear cockpit.

"Rrrraaaallllllpppphhh."

In the climb back to their original altitude, Screech looked into his mirror, asking, "Doc, are you ok?"

There was no immediate answer. In anticipation of possibly getting sick again, Doc had earlier removed a plastic puke bag from his flight suit's bicep pocket. However, in a cruel joke of the most heinous kind, the Marines that work in flight equipment had cut the bottom out of the bag, refolded it, and placed it back in Doc's sleeve. Consequently, the vomit was all over Doc's lap and splattered on the back seat displays.

As Screech leveled the F-18D at twenty-five thousand feet, he quickly replaced his oxygen mask back over his face to avoid the smell. He knew he would be wiping up puke as soon as they landed, but he still managed to laugh.

* * *

Red Rover, Red Rover...

The Russian made Mig-29 Fulcrum was the ultimate prize. When F-8Ds were scheduled to fly the in-country air-to-air patrols, their crews prayed to God for Mig-29s to challenge their presence. It was like that old childhood game played back in the school yard - "Red Rover, Red Rover, we dare Mig-29s to come over."

As the latest and greatest fighter to grace the Soviet inventory, the Mig-29 possessed a thrust-to-weight ratio and advanced avionics and weapons that rivaled America's best fighters. Mig-29s frequently tap danced along the northern border of the no-fly zone, thumbing their noses at the NATO aircraft - but they weren't stupid. If they wanted to pick a fight, it was going to be at the time and place of their choosing.

1340 Wednesday
Easy 43 and 44 on an in-country Air-to-Air Mission
"Picture is clean."

"Stonehenge 04, Easy 43," stated Bama, checking in with the AWACS.

There was no reply.

"Stonehenge 04, Easy 43," repeated Bama.

Again, there was no answer, but a weak, muffled transmission of some type was barely audible.

Man, thought Bama, *maybe there's something wrong with my number one radio.*

"Hick Boy, this is Bama on the number two."

"Bama, Hick Boy, go ahead."

"Give a shout to Stonehenge, and see if you can raise him."

"Wilco."

"I wonder what *that's* all about," Buick said to Hick Boy on the ICS.

"I don't know," returned Hick Boy, "but here goes."

"Stonehenge 04, Easy 44," stated Tennessee's finest.

Once again, a low, garbled radio transmission was heard, slightly louder now.

"Stonehenge 04, Easy 44," repeated Hick Boy.

The same weak reply barely crackled the number one radio.

"Hey Buick, can you make that out?" asked Hick Boy on the ICS.

"Nope, Hick Boy."

"Bama, Hick Boy on the number two radio. No luck. Back over to you."

"Bama copies."

The flight of two Hornets continued inbound towards point Bravo, having just completed another red-ass refueling from a KC-135. Easy 43, Bama and One Nut, and Easy 44, Hick Boy and Buick, drilled north on a heading to take them in-country with a full bag of gas. This was to be their second air-to-air station time under the control of Stonehenge 04, a British AWACS. They were able to talk to Stonehenge just fine on their way out to the KC-135 thirty minutes ago, but now there was no answer.

"Stonehenge 04, Easy 43," stated Bama, attempting to check in with the British AWACS again.

"Easy 43, Duster 01, has you loud and clear, go ahead," was the muffled reply.

"*Who* was that?" Bama muttered to himself.

Now Bama had a dilemma. He could totally grovel, and ask his WSO, One Nut, if he had heard the same weak transmission. Or Bama could go external to his jet and ask Easy 44. But then Hick Boy and Buick would know that God's gift to F-18 aviation was unsure of something. God forbid that Bama should seek help from *anyone*.

"Hey, One Nut," Bama said over the ICS, intentionally choosing his own young WSO over the more experienced Buick.

"Yeah, Bama?"

"Did you catch that last radio call?"

"It sounded like *Buster* 01 to me."

"Roger, copy Buster 01."

Bama resumed his dominance over the airwaves, stating, "Buster 01, Easy 43 is a flight of two fighters for your control. We're presently mission complete with Texaco and at point Bravo, proceeding inbound."

"Easy 43, Duster - repeat *Duster* - 01 has you loud and clear," was the reply, getting louder as the two Hornets got closer to land.

Duster? Not Buster? Bama thought. *Fuckin' WSO One Nut. Not only is he half blind, but he also can't hear.*

"Easy 43, Duster 01 has you radar contact. Proceed inbound. Picture is clean."

Duster? Who the hell is Duster? Bama thought. *What happened to Stonehenge?*

Again, Bama faced a dilemma. He just had to know who Duster was, but refused to let anyone know that he was clueless. God forbid that Bama ever look bad. Finally, he cracked, and reluctantly sought the aid of the most experienced aviator in the flight.

"Buick, Bama, on the number two radio."

"Bama, Buick, go."

"One Nut wants to know who Duster is," Bama lied.

In the rear cockpit, One Nut flipped the bird towards the front seat.

"Roger that," replied Buick. "Duster is a Marine radar controller on the ground. I don't know what happened to our AWACS."

"Buick, Bama, thanks."

"Easy 43, Duster 01," said the young Marine.

"Duster, Easy, go ahead," returned Bama, back on the number one radio.

"I show you on station. Picture is clean."

"Duster 01, Easy 43, copy picture clean."

Bama, One Nut, Hick Boy, and Buick settled in for what looked like a long afternoon of drilling holes in the sky with nothing on their radars. Then Bama's curiosity finally got the best of him.

"Duster 01, Easy 43, interrogative."

"Easy 43, Duster 01, go ahead with your question," returned the Marine.

"Duster, what happened to Stonehenge?"

"Easy 43, Stonehenge 04 developed a mechanical problem and had to return home," explained the young Marine Corporal. "The CAOC shifted control of all air-to-air missions to Duster's radar station down here on the ground."

"Easy 43 copies," replied Bama confidently.

"Easy 43, be advised," continued the Corporal "that a previous flight of German Tornadoes reported my radios to be weak and unreadable."

"Yeah, no shit," muttered Bama, confidence waning.

"Easy 43, *also* be advised," persisted the young Marine, "that our ground radar has weak coverage towards the northeast due to the mountains."

"That's just peachy," said Bama, confidence gone. "It just keeps getting better."

At that moment, Easy 43 and 44 reached the end of their oval racetrack, so Bama turned them around, ordering, "Easy 43, tac turn, ninety left, go."

Hick Boy, in Easy 44, and flying in a combat spread formation on the right, immediately cocked his F-18D onto a knife edge, and pulled his jet around in a ninety degree left turn. As soon as he passed behind Easy 43, Bama did the same, placing both jets on a heading towards the northwest with Easy 43 now on the right.

"Easy 43, tac turn, ninety left, go," commanded Bama once more.

Bama and Hick Boy executed the exact same turn, with Easy 43 going first this time. Now the flight of two Hornets was heading frigid towards the southwest with Easy 44 having returned to the right side and their tail pipes towards the threat.

"Duster 01, Easy 43 is frigid."

"Easy 43, Duster 01, picture clean."

The next ten minutes contained more of the same mundane radio communications as Easy 43 and 44 drilled around their oval racetrack in the sky.

"Easy 43, tac turn, ninety left, go."

"Easy 43, tac turn, ninety left, go."

"Duster 01, Easy 43, we're turning to burn now."

"Easy 43, Duster 01, picture clean."

If this had been a Western, then tumbleweed would've blown through the scene.

"Easy 43, tac turn, ninety left, go."

Suddenly, a Mig-29 appeared from nowhere two miles behind Easy 43 at his five o'clock position. It was Buick who first made the visual pickup of the Mig's undetected entry into weapon's firing parameters. He recognized the distinctive white nose cone and camouflage paint scheme, and immediately took charge of the flight.

"BAMA, BREAK RIGHT! BANDIT AT RIGHT FIVE LOW!"

Immediately, Bama had the stick into his lap with full afterburner selected. Bama simultaneously looked over his right shoulder, and then saw the Mig, saying, "I'm tally."

Their F-18D broke hard to the right in an effort to force the Mig to overshoot their flight path. Furthermore, Bama methodically dispensed the decoy expendables that would save their lives if the Mig took a shot. In the rear seat, One Nut was buried under the sudden application of g forces.

"Duster 01, Easy 43 is engaged, defensive," coolly stated Bama.

"Easy 43, Duster 01, say again. Your transmission was broken."

"Uuuuuuugh," grunted One Nut in an attempt to return blood to his brain.

"Chaff, flares. Chaff, flares."

Fuckin' WSOs, Bama thought, *why didn't One Nut see him?*

"Easy 43, Duster 01, picture is clean."

The Mig-29 must've had a sharp pilot, for he was able to maintain an offensive position on the inside of Bama's right turn.

"Shit!" muttered Bama.

Hick Boy didn't have to be told, for he immediately executed a hard right turn in an effort to shoot the Mig off of Bama's tail.

"Select Sidewinder," instructed Buick from the back seat.

Hick Boy immediately changed his air-to-air weapons system from radar-guided missile to heat-seeking missile, saying, "Good call. Thanks, Buick."

"Boop."

Easy 43 suddenly received indications in the cockpit that the Mig-29 had them locked on his radar.

"Fuck!"

"Easy 43, Duster 01, picture clean."

There was plenty of lateral separation between Easy 44 and the Mig-29, which equated to turning room for Hick Boy's potential shot. But as of yet, there had been no telltale corkscrew of white smoke emerging from beneath the Mig-29, indicating a missile shot of his own. Hick Boy was handcuffed.

"Can I shoot?" Hick Boy asked Buick.

The only thing the Mig-29 had done so far was roll in behind Easy 43. There was no crime in that.

"Not yet," replied Buick.

The Mig-29 tightened his right turn to maintain the offensive position on Easy 43.

What's he doing now? thought Tennessee's finest.

Hick Boy couldn't believe his eyes. He was now looking at the underside belly of the Mig-29, for it executed a right turn in *front* of Hick Boy and Buick in Easy 44.

"Easy 43, Duster 01, picture clean."

Evidently, the sharp pilot in the Mig-29 wasn't so sharp that he had picked up *both* of the Hornets when he commenced his offensive entry. He must've only seen Easy 43 on his initial roll-in; thus, he was prosecuting an attack simply on Bama and One Nut. The Mig-29 was totally oblivious to Easy 44's offensive position behind him.

"Easy 43, Duster 01 shows you maneuvering. Is everything alright?"

With ice water in his veins, Bama continued to methodically dispense decoys and successfully parry a shot, but he knew the decoys wouldn't last forever.

"Chaff, flares. Chaff, flares."

He continued to watch the Mig-29 over his right shoulder. Could it be that the Mig-29 pilot really *was* that sharp after all, and only waiting for Bama to run out of flares before he fired a heat-seeking missile? Bama ratcheted down his right turn just a hair tighter. The Mig-29 did the same, still maintaining an offensive position.

"This fuckin' pig of a jet," said Bama, his frustration growing.

There was still no Mig-29 overshoot of their flight path.

"Damn it."

The three fighters now formed a daisy chain in a descending death spiral, with a defensive Easy 43 in front, and an offensive Mig-29 in the middle that was unaware of Easy 44 behind him.

With a front windscreen containing the two tail pipes of a Mig-29, the cockpit indications in Easy 44 were screaming at Hick Boy and Buick to shoot.

"Remember to arm up."

"Good call, Buick. Thanks again."

However, so far, the Mig had done nothing "hostile".

"Hick Boy, get this fucker off of me," pleaded Bama.

The Mig-29 continued to nibble away at the range.

"Passing twelve thousand feet," cautioned One Nut from the rear.

"Bama, this is Buick on the number two radio. Ring the door bell."

"I can't," returned Bama, watching the Mig-29 inch closer over his right shoulder. "I'm not going to bring my head into the cockpit."

"Then, One Nut, do it for him," commanded Buick.

Immediately, One Nut brought his head inside, reached down by his left knee, and punched the Emergency Jettison Button, which resembled a door bell.

"Got it."

Instantly, everything on Easy 43's belly - pylons, racks, bombs, fuel tanks, *everything* - was jettisoned from the jet, and tumbled towards the earth. Now with increased maneuverability, Bama ratcheted his right turn down tighter once more.

"Easy 43, this is Duster, radio check."

The Mig-29 tightened down his turn too, still maintaining an offensive position and pecking away at the range.

"Shit."

There was still no flight path overshoot.

"Ugh . . . ugh . . . ugh," grunted One Nut.

The cockpit indications in Easy 44 were still howling at Hick Boy and Buick to shoot. Still, the Mig-29 had done nothing "hostile".

"Easy 43, Duster, how do you hear?"

Then the inevitable happened. Easy 43 ran out of decoy expendables. With the sudden disappearance of the stream of flares from Bama's F-18D, Hick Boy anticipated a shot at any second from the Mig-29.

"Passing ten thousand," warned One Nut.

Microseconds ticked away.

"C'mon, man, c'mon," whispered Hick Boy, as he applied an ever so slight pressure to the trigger.

"Damn it," mumbled Bama.

Now if the Mig actually shot, there was little that Hick Boy could do other than simply shoot the Mig.

"I can't save their lives," Hick Boy realized.

"Easy 43, Duster, radio check."

More precious microseconds ticked away.

Was that a fair trade - a Mig-29 for an F-18D?

The three fighters continued their death spiral to the right.

Was that a fair trade - a Mig-29 for Bama and One Nut?

"Passing eight thousand."

"Fuck."

Hick Boy squeezed the trigger ever so slightly some more, saying, "C'mon, man."

"Easy 43, Duster, radio check. Can you hear me?"

Microseconds clicked.

Suddenly, Hick Boy and Buick noticed the Mig-29 drop its right wing just slightly, and then instantly reverse hard to the left and dive for the earth. The pilot had finally looked over his right shoulder, and noticed Easy 44.

"Shit."

"Damn."

"Fuck."

"Uuuuuuugh."

In an instant, both of the Mig-29's afterburners were aglow as it accelerated from the scene of the crime, executing mild, thirty degree check turns to the left every few seconds to maintain sight of Easy 43 and 44. His camouflage paint scheme served him well, for he disappeared into the countryside below a moment later, making good on his escape to the northeast. Hick Boy took command of the flight.

"Bama, Hick Boy, safe southwest."

"Easy 43, copies safe southwest."

Bama immediately steadied his F-18D on a heading to the southwest, one hundred and eighty degrees out from the Mig-29. Likewise, he selected full afterburner and dove for the earth to execute his bug-out. Hick Boy adeptly maneuvered Easy 44 into a position of defensive combat spread, while Buick and One Nut executed the physical gymnastics required in the back seat to check that their sixes were clear.

"Duster 01, Easy 43, we're bugging out southwest," said Bama.

There was no answer.

"Duster 01, Easy 43," repeated Bama.

There was still no reply from their controller, due to Easy's low altitude egress and the mountains that had originally prevented the controller's radar from detecting the Mig-29. The two F-18Ds continued fleeing to the southwest, alone and unafraid.

1510 Wednesday
Tent City Bathroom Building
"How could this happen to *me*?"

Bama was sitting in the exact same position where a wily Mig-29 pilot had caught him just hours before - with his pants down around his ankles. Now he was pissed.

Bama had gone straight from the debrief to the bathroom, deeming it the only place where he could fume alone. He had immediately checked the urinals to ensure that he was by himself, and then slid the trashcan in front of the door. That way, anyone entering would knock it over and warn him. Then he hid in a stall.

Bama was livid, and he repeatedly punched the stall door. He was furiously engaged with an imaginary listener, and assigning blame.

WHAM.

"Damn it. How could this happen to *me*?"

WHAM.

"I'm invincible. I want to be an American hero."

WHAM.

"It wasn't my fault. It *couldn't* have been."

WHAM.

"That fuckin' lucky Mig pilot has no aviation skills."

WHAM.

"That fuckin' Duster with his bad radios, and mountains blocking his radar."

WHAM.

"That fuckin' Hick Boy, not squeezing the trigger."

WHAM.

"That fuckin' Buick for taking charge of the fight."

WHAM.

"That fuckin' One Nut. He was supposed to be checking our six."

WHAM.

"I'm going to see to it that One Nut is ostracized from this community. He will never set foot in an F-18D again."

WHAM.

"He's weak. He's not tactical. He's baggage. He's going to get someone killed."

WHAM.

Bama buried his head in his hands, and momentarily paused to catch his breath. Plus, his fist hurt. He used the last few squares of toilet paper on the roll, and rose from his throne. Bama pulled up his boxers, noting for the first time that there was a shit stain from this afternoon's incident.

"Damn it."

Bama pulled up his flight suit, and wrestled the arms of his massive frame into the sleeves. That was always a battle. He zipped the front, and opened the stall door. His big boots tromped to the door, where he slid the trashcan back to its original position. Bama inhaled deeply, exhaled, and regained his composure. Then he exited the bathroom as if he was Superman.

A few seconds of silence hung over the smell of urine, and then Ham Fist emerged from the closet in the corner. As one of the squadron's FNG's, he had been assigned to conduct a random urinalysis tomorrow; consequently, he was in the bathroom closet looking for paper towels when Bama had entered. Bama's sweep to check the urinals had failed to look in the closet. Ham Fist had heard every word.

1524 Wednesday
The Tent City Weight Tent
"Nil corborundum illigitime."

Jock, Ghost, and Ping were in the more popular of the two weight tents, trying to squeeze in a late afternoon workout. As far as gyms go, the Tent City weight tents were pretty damn humble. Actually consisting of two, huge Marine Corps general purpose tents – one with iron free weights, and one with various weight machines – they were barely tolerable. With a third of the machines broken at any given time, most Marines chose to lift free weights.

However, that particular tent was not without its shortcomings. It was dirty and dusty, with the only York bar bent like a banana. The tent contained two homemade supine benches, and a squat rack made out of welded metal pipes.

The five, ten, and twenty-five pound plates were a hodge-podge mixture from various companies, which used to drive Ping nuts. He was one of those guys who had to have matching weights on each side of his bar. Several dumbbells had no mate, which further frustrated Ping. Why would anyone walk out of the weight tent with a dumbbell?

The larger plates were in kilograms instead of pounds, which persistently frustrated Ghost. Was it 2.2 kilograms per pound, or 2.2 pounds per kilogram? He could never keep that straight. Higher math always kicked a Marine's ass.

Ghost was the obvious gym rat of the three aviators. Muscular and buff with a Gold's Gym tank top, he was determined to not let six months of a makeshift gym ruin his physique. Ghost wore stretchy, black, workout shorts because – well – because he could. He was also the only guy in the squadron who actually had weightlifting shoes. Yeah, that's right – shoes specifically made for lifting weights. He always wore padded gloves that were tainted yellow from years of sweat, and a thick, leather weightlifting belt that was discolored brown for the same reason.

On the other hand, Jock was the opposite. It was obvious why some cruel aviators in the past had tagged him with that callsign – because he obviously wasn't. In a desperate effort to stay one step ahead of the Marine Corps' weight control program, Jock had always busted his ass playing manly games like softball and golf, and his body showed the results. His loose fitting, Hard Rock Café, t-shirt failed to hide the small spare tire around his waist. As for the stretchy, black, workout shorts, thank God that Jock never wore them. That was one sight that nobody wanted to see. Obviously, Jock didn't have weightlifting shoes. Instead, he looked like a dork in his black Keds. Lastly, Jock had no gloves or belt or anything.

However, under Ghost's tutelage, Jock was determined to chisel his physique into something respectful. More importantly, he wanted to be like Teflon.

". . . eight, nine, ten," grunted Ghost as he completed a warm-up set.

Then he re-racked the bar upon the benches uprights and sat up from his supine position. Ghost exhaled forcibly.

"Thanks for the spot, Ping."

"No sweat, man."

Stretching in the corner and unconfident, Jock meekly joined the conversation.

"Hey, Ghost."

"Yeah, Jock?" panted Ghost, rising from his seat on the bench.

"Do you mind if I watch and try to learn something?"

"Think nothing of it, Jock. I've been in the Marine Corps for ten years on a weightlifting scholarship, so just ask if you have any questions."

Ghost walked over to the entrance, swinging his arms in wide circles to further loosen his shoulders. Ping put a twenty-five pound plate on each side of the banana.

"Hey, Jock, not to sound mean or anything, but have you ever done *anything* really physical?" asked Ghost rather bluntly.

"Well, I took Tai Chi in college."

"Is that the one where you do all the movements in slow motion?" asked Ghost.

"Yep," replied Jock.

"Geez," said Ping. "What good is *that*, unless you get attacked by an NFL highlights film?"

Ghost returned to the bench and assumed the supine position for his next set. He spent an eternity trying to find the perfect grip on the banana bar. While he was constantly adjusting his grip and gazing up at the canvas, Ghost inhaled and exhaled loudly, and arched his back. Between breaths, he continued to lecture Jock.

"I played college football for a small school, Nottingham State," reminisced Ghost, "and we had the ugliest blue 'N' on our helmets."

Lording over Ghost's head and awaiting his command, Ping stated, "The football team at Navy had an 'N' on their helmets too. It stood for knowledge."

Ghost immediately ceased his ritual, thanks to Ping ruining his concentration. He momentarily sat up to restart the whole process.

"Ping, are you *ever* serious?"

During Ghost's short break, Ping left his post as spotter in search of matching plates for his own upcoming set.

"Damn it," mumbled Ping. "Where are those York tens?"

"Jock, you really should consider getting serious about this gym shit," stated Ghost. "Between flying in the F-18D and lifting weights, I get two orgasms a day."

"For a deployed Marine Officer, that's pretty damn good," said Jock.

"You can call it *three* if the bathroom has toilet paper in the morning," added Ping.

"What about weightlifting gloves?" asked Jock. "Ghost, I notice that you wear them, but Ping, that you don't."

"That is strictly personal preference," answered Ghost.

"Yeah, I really should wear gloves," replied Ping, looking at the palms of his hands. "Calluses hurt my dick."

Half the time, Jock could never tell whether Ping was joking or not, and Ghost was certainly no road map. He merely ignored his lifting partner's silly comments.

"Aha." shouted Ping triumphantly. "Here they are."

Ping bent over by the lat pull-down machine, and tried to wrestle the two York, ten pound plates from under the base. He was unsuccessful. That particular machine was missing part of its pedestal; consequently, it rocked back and forth. Evidently some bonehead had crammed the plates under the one side to prevent the rocking.

"Damn." intoned a frustrated Ping. "Who's the idiot who used the good York tens like a doorstop?"

Ghost shrugged a reply, and Jock merely faked concern.

"Can you guys give me a hand over here?" asked Ping.

Ghost grudgingly arose from the bench and joined Jock. They assumed places opposite of each other on the pull-down machine, with their hands firmly positioned on the upper cross brace. Ping knelt down in front of them.

"Ok, you guys. Lift up on three," commanded Ping.

Ghost and Jock nodded.

"One, two, three."

Ghost and Jock pushed upward on the cross brace, and Ping yanked the two York tens from beneath the wobbly base.

Now having found matching plates, Ping returned to his position as Ghost's spotter. Ghost returned to the bench, and Jock retired to his observation post.

Ghost rubbed more chalk on his gloved hands and breathed deeply, staring at the two hundred and seventy-five pounds resting on the benches uprights. He sat on the end of the bench, wiggling his fingers, and loudly inhaling and exhaling. Yep, Ghost was definitely one of those "loud" guys. Ping stood behind the bar, awaiting Ghost.

Then the ritual began again. Ghost laid back upon the bench in a supine position. It must've taken him another three minutes to finally finish adjusting his grip. The whole time, he was inhaling and exhaling, inhaling and exhaling, inhaling and exhaling. Ping assumed a good spotter's position, and lightly grasped the bar. Ghost looked up at Ping.

"Are you ready?" asked Ping.

"Ready." said Ghost.

"Ok then. On three?"

"On three."

Ping nodded. Ghost violently arched his back one last time, and then fixed his gaze upon the green canvas over head.

"One. Two. Three," inhaled Ghost.

On the word 'three', it took the combined efforts of both Ghost and Ping – mostly Ghost - to lift the banana up and out of the benches uprights, and over Ghost's chest. Ghost gave a quick nod, and Ping released his grip. Jock stared in wide-eyed amazement as Ghost grunted out eight repetitions. Then Ping grabbed the bar and helped Ghost slam it back into the rack.

Ghost sprang up from the bench, making a pumping motion with his right fist.

"Yesssssssss."

"Nice job," said Ping.

Next came the arduous task of stripping down the banana to a lighter weight for Ping's set – much lighter. Ghost continued to lecture Jock while he aided Ping in removing the outer twenty-five and forty-five pound plates. Or were they twelve and twenty-two kilograms? Damn higher math.

"Jock, do you realize that weightlifting is probably the best exercise you can do as a fighter pilot?"

"Why is that?"

"Because when you lift weights, you're actually increasing your systolic blood pressure for an instant," instructed Ghost. "That's the same thing the human body must do to counter the g's in the F-18."

Jock was in awe.

Ghost and Ping simultaneously placed a twenty-five pound plate onto each end of the banana. After both of the smaller plates had clanged against the inner forty-five pound plates, the two lifters swapped roles. Ping sat on the end of the bench, rubbing chalk on his bare palms, and Ghost assumed the spotter's position.

Suddenly, the flap door of the tent lifted, and a high-n-tight, buzzed haircut poked through the entrance. It was the General's Aide.

"Hey, Marines," he said, trying to prove that he was still one of the guys. "The General is touring the camp, so anybody working out must be wearing 'green-on-green'."

Green-on-green meant a standard, green Marine Corps t-shirt and standard, green Marine Corps shorts. It was the standard uniform for the standard physical exercise back in the standard real world. Gold's Gym tank tops and Hard Rock Café' t-shirts just didn't cut it in the eyes of the Aide. Who knew if the General really gave a rat's ass?

Ghost wanted to just crush the Aide's head like a grape.

"Man, you've got to be shittin' me."

However, his calmer alter ego prevailed. Still disgusted with this morning's breakfast, he had sought refuge in the weight tent. He thought he would be safe in there.

"Nope," said the Aide. "Anybody working out has to be in green-on-green."

Ghost stepped down from his domineering spotter's position, as the General's Aide raised the flap and stepped into the tent, revealing the gold epaulet. Sensing trouble, Jock cowered down behind the lat pull-down machine.

"It probably wouldn't hurt to square away this gym a little too," added the Aide, glancing around the weight tent. "Pick up some of these weights. This place was cleaner when I was in here this morning."

"What were you doing in here this morning?" inquired Ghost.

"The General played a round of golf after breakfast," replied the Aide.

Typical General, thought Ghost.

"So I dropped in to lift," continued the Aide. "Did you guys know that the lat machine rocks back and forth?"

Ghost and Ping looked at each other. They saw this coming a mile away.

"I had to cram some ten pound plates under the base so it wouldn't wiggle."

At that instant, the flap to the weight tent arose again, and the General's driver slipped into the tent behind the Aide. Holy shit. She was definitely not wearing green-on-green. She had her hair back in one of those sexy ponytails that women athletes tie up with squiggies or squishies or squirellies or whatever they're called. Her spandex suit was painted onto her nubile, upper body, and you could just see the outlining traces of a sports bra that protected two perfect breasts. The spandex thong looked more like butt floss, and two very toned and tanned legs extended from a tight ass. Lastly, she wore those fat, sexy leggings around her ankles that were popularized by the movie "Flashdance." Who cares if they went out with the '80s? They looked good on her. The General's driver strutted into the gym, acting as if the three males weren't even there. But she knew that she had their full, undivided attention. She possessed the power that a hot woman has in *any* gym, no matter whether it's a Gold's Gym or a green canvas tent.

Without saying a word, she pulled the blue exercise mat from the corner, and spread it on the dirty floor by the squat rack. Ghost bit his lip again, and a tiny bead of sweat rolled down Ping's forehead. The married Jock had to look away.

Not wanting to appear confrontational in front of the young, female enlisted Marine, Ghost backed down from his aggressive posturing, and calmed his tone of voice to the Aide, stating, "We're not going back to our tent and get dressed in green-on-green."

"Fine by me," huffed the Aide, spinning about and stomping out of the tent. "I was just trying to help."

Ghost resumed his spotter's position, lording over the banana bar. Ping sat back down on the end of the bench, and rubbed more chalk on his palms. Jock stepped out from behind the lat pull-down machine.

Holy shit again. The General's driver was stretching on the blue exercise mat. She silently did those stretches that do nothing but force the male brain into overdrive. She did the splits, touching her nose to both knees. She arched her back while kneeling on all fours, the butt floss sticking high in the air. She sat on the mat and pulled each leg behind her head, one at time. Damn. She was so limber and flexible, that she just *had* to be the secret fantasy of every red-blooded male - a former gymnast.

In a sudden turnabout of events, Ghost unbuckled his belt.

"Well, thanks for the work-out, guys," he stated. "That's it for me."

Ghost grabbed his water bottle and towel, and then headed for the entrance flap. Ping and Jock just looked at each other, for they knew that Ghost was nowhere near finished. Ghost exited under the flap with a cursory good-bye thrown over his shoulder.

"See you guys."

Jock was dumbfounded. His hero had fallen. However, Ping knew better. Ping casually strolled to the flap, nonchalantly raising it above his head. He briefly turned to Jock, before ducking through.

"See you later, man."

As soon as Ping was safely outside of the tent, he sprinted down the sidewalk in an effort to catch Ghost. He purposely didn't yell after him, for he didn't want the driver to hear, thus knowing that she had knocked two grown men off their game.

That left the hapless Jock in the tent with the General's driver continuing to stretch. When she bent over in front of him and put the palms of her hands on the floor, Jock decided that it was time to exit. Thinking on his feet, he quickly poured a tiny bit of water from his bottle over his head to make it look like he had sweaty hair.

"Yeah, that was quite a work-out today," he intoned, twisting his torso. "Time for a protein shake."

Jock tried to exit with the same cool nonchalance, but his black Keds didn't allow it. He nervously bid good-bye to the driver, as if a secret camera in the corner was recording his every move in the government's fraternization case against him.

"Have a good day, Lance Corporal."

"You too, Sir."

As soon as Jock was outside the tent, he quickly glanced to the right and to the left. Aha. There they were. Jock ran down the sidewalk and caught up with Ghost and Ping, just as the conversation was starting.

"Ghost," queried Ping. "What's the matter, man?"

"This whole General thing just pisses me off," he replied.

"What do you mean?"

"It all started when I had breakfast this morning," he explained. "The mere sight of the General and all his lackeys in a dining tent that looked like it never really does just totally disgusted me."

"But Ghost, it – ", injected Jock.

"Stay out of this Jock," interrupted Ping in a rare display of seriousness. He then turned back to Ghost.

"I couldn't even eat my breakfast," continued Ghost. "I carried it back to my tent and ate it there."

"Well, Ghost, if that shit bothers you," stated Ping, "just ignore it, and stay as far away from as possible."

"That's what I was *doing*, man, with my daily lift," continued Ghost. "The weight tent is *my* turf."

Ping nodded.

"But then the General's Aide comes in and tells me that I'm supposed to be wearing green-on-green, and the General's driver comes in and begins her stretch fest."

"But Ghost," said Ping, "don't you see? By walking out of the dining tent and walking out of the weight tent, you let them win."

Ghost cast an inquisitive glance at Ping, while Jock stood idly by.

"Nil corborundum illigitime," stated Ping.

"What the hell is that?"

"It's Latin, Ghost."

"Latin? Latin for what"

"Never let the bastards get you down. Never let the bastards get you down."

1723 Wednesday
Tent City, Tent 08
"How could this happen to *me*?"

Dear Jenny,

Before I write another word, I want to tell you to save this letter. Put it in the shoebox containing all of my other letters and our Prom picture. Sure, I could *call* and tell you what I'm about to write, but words fade over the years. I want you to have this letter forever.

First of all, we had a little incident today against a very experienced Mig pilot with good aviation skills. Don't worry. It was no big deal. No one got hurt, other than a bruised ego. I'm ok, everyone else is ok, and life will go on. I can't tell you the details, but nobody is to blame.

However, what I *can* tell you is the realization that came to me. Honey, I am not invincible. I am not immortal. I am not a hero. Even though aviators may think they are modern day Supermen, it only takes a nickel's worth of bad luck to snuff them out. Jenny, I am expendable.

Life is short, Jenny - too short. It's certainly far too short to spend time away from you. Jenny, you're the best thing that has ever happened to me. I've been through both Marine Corps boot camp and Marine Corps Officer's Candidate School, and then spent twelve years in the Marine Corps, but it has taken a shy woman from Virginia to mold me into the kind of man that I always wanted to become.

Jenny, in response to your recent demand, a man shouldn't have to choose between two loves. Yet I find myself in that very predicament. How could this happen to *me*? I love you and I love flying. I don't want one or the other - I want *both*. So please don't ask me to choose.

Consider this, Snuggle Bunny. As soon as the squadron gets back to the real world, I will be up for Lieutenant Colonel. Why don't we wait and see what happens? Sweetheart, if I make Lieutenant Colonel, then I'll probably get sent off to some desk job in Quantico or the Pentagon. There won't be anymore flying, Babe. It'll just be you and me and the kids. I'll be home every night and every weekend. We can work things out, Pumpkin. Let's give it a try. Jenny, think about it, ok? I love you, Jenny.

Well, I've got to go. I'll drop this into the box so that it goes out tomorrow.

Your big love machine is still running on all eight cylinders,

Buick

* * *

Yep, they really did blow it

It really *was* a good thing that the bathroom wasn't bugged. More rumors and half-truths and bullshit flowed in there between men with flight suits down around their ankles than anywhere else in Tent City.

1838 Wednesday
Tent City Bathroom Building
"Tom-foolery?"

"Hey Screech."

"Yeah, Butt Munch."

"Would you believe that there's these huge holes in my stall door?"

"Really?"

"Yeah, I wonder how *that* happened?"

"God only knows, Butt Munch."

"I swear, there's never any toilet paper in here. You have any extra?"

"Yep, standby. I'm almost done."

"Good thing, Screech. We have to hurry if we're going to catch One Nut's Wednesday night follies in the Officers' Club."

"Roger that, Butt Munch."

"Hey, man, did you hear what happened today?"

"No, what."

"Bama got jumped by a Mig-29."

"No shit? Who was with him?"

"Easy 43 was Bama and One Nut. Easy 44 was Hick Boy and Buick."

"What happened, Butt Munch?"

"The Mig-29 ended up in the middle of a sandwich. He was hot on Bama's tail, not realizing that Hick Boy was right on his Russian ass. The three jets spiraled down until the Mig pilot finally saw Hick Boy. So then he got the hell out of Dodge."

"Wait a minute, Butt Munch. Say that again."

"The Mig-29 picked up Hick Boy at the last second and bugged out."

"No, not *that* part. The part where you said the Mig-29 was offensive on *Bama*?"

"Yep."

"Oh, my God."

"It turns out that Buick directed most of the fight from the back seat of Easy 44."

"Well, that's no surprise. Buick is the best."

"Yep."

"So did they learn anything about the Mig-29?"

"Well, Bama and Hick Boy got their eyes watered by the Mig's ability to turn."

"Wow."

"Plus, its engines put some serious thrust out the ass end."

"Man."

"Screech, that's nothin'. You'll never guess what happened when they got back."

"What happened?"

"The General shit all over Bama and One Nut for ringing the doorbell."

"No shit?"

"Yeah, no shit. He also shit on them for expending all of their chaff and flares."

"Unbelievable."

"His exact words were 'The Marine Corps doesn't have the money *or* the assets for such Tom-foolery'."

"Tom-foolery? He actually said the words Tom-foolery?"

"Yep."

"Un-fuckin'-believable."

"Speaking of the General, he wants to talk to all of us Officers tomorrow morning at 0900 in the Ready Room."

"Yeah, that's what I heard."

"So how are we looking for that toilet paper?"

"I'm done, so here you go."

"Thanks, Screech."

"FIRE IN THE HOLE."

"Vwooooooooooosh."

Various versions of "thank you" resounded from the shower building next door.

"See you down in the Officers' Club, Butt Munch."

"Roger that, see you there. I wouldn't miss it for the world."

1856 Wednesday
Officers' Club Tent
"Jenny is all that I've got in this world."

It was Wednesday night in the Officers' Club, and the usual emcee had center stage in front of a whooping gallery. One Nut stood in front of the TV and VCR with a VHS tape in one hand and a letter from his wife in the other. Only Buick and Tuna seemed disinterested, sitting on two stools at the bar and carrying on a very hushed and apparently serious conversation. Tuna really enjoyed Wednesday nights - especially "Friends" - but Buick could give a rat's ass. Tonight, for once, Tuna would forego One Nut's show to talk with Buick, one of the few WSOs that he actually liked. He admired Buick's tactical prowess in the jet. It reminded Tuna of himself.

"Ladies and Gentlemen - and Joisey," began One Nut. "I have in my right hand, last week's Thursday night escapades from back in the real world."

A raucous cheer erupted from the gallery.

"However," continued One Nut, "I have some bad news."

The Officers' Club grew silent. Waving the letter in his left hand, One Nut confessed his guilt, stating, "My wife regrets to inform you that the tape ran out, thus it only contains "Seinfeld" and "Friends" - and not "ER"."

A wave of boos spilled from the seats, and One Nut got pelted with empty beer cans and popcorn. Unfazed, One Nut proceeded to forge onward.

"However, the show must go on."

The Officers' Club roared.

"So, without further delay, are you ready to rock-n-roll?"

One Nut spun about, and slipped the tape into the VCR. Grabbing the remote control and wiping the beer from it on his flight suit, he pressed the play button. The Officers' Club fell silent again, save for the muffled whispers of Tuna and Buick.

As the tape began, Jerry, Elaine, Kramer, and George were sitting in their favorite booth at Monk's. George was being admonished by the others, because his mother had caught him in the bathroom with her copy of Glamour.

"So what's up, Buick?" asked Tuna. "I can tell when something's wrong with the Buick monster."

Tuna stirred his Gin and tonic. Buick gazed into his beer.

"Tuna," returned Buick, "How long have you been married?"

"Four years now," said Tuna, "But six if you count the wind chill factor."

Buick laughed and sipped his beer, shaking his head.

"Would you say that Lisa has been happy?" continued Buick.

"Well, I suppose that our marriage is no different than anybody else's. It has its ups and downs," returned Tuna. "But, yeah, I would say that Lisa has been happy."

"Does she like the Marine Corps?"

"Whoo, boy, now *there's* a loaded question," said Tuna. "Who's wife *does*?"

"Good call," chuckled Buick.

"I would say that Lisa *tolerates* the Marine Corps at best," continued Tuna, "because she knows that I love the flying."

Buick nodded as if he could relate, and Tuna knew that this was serious.

"Level with me, man," pressed Tuna. "What's with all the questions?"

"Tuna," stated Buick, looking solemnly into his eyes, "Jenny wants a divorce."

From his side of the booth, Jerry proclaimed to his three friends how doing such a thing was part of the male lifestyle.

That comment piqued Booger's attention.

My God, he thought. *Is this episode about masturbation?*

Meanwhile, every other officer in the club cheered - save Tuna and Buick at the bar. Then laughter rolled through the gallery, and One Nut cranked up the volume with the remote. Ping accidentally kicked over his beer, and Hollywood was the last to finally quit laughing.

Tuna sat in a stunned silence, before finally admitting, "Buick, I'm sorry, man."

"Oh, don't be sorry," returned Buick, shrugging his shoulders. "Shit happens."

"What went wrong?" Tuna asked his favorite WSO. "Did you see it coming, or was it a total blindside?"

"Well, Tuna," continued Buick. "Over the past year or so, I noticed Jenny growing slightly colder to me."

"No shit?"

"Yeah, every time she spread her legs," explained Buick, "a little light came on."

Tuna guffawed aloud, and then quickly muffled his laughter so as not to disrupt "Seinfeld". He patted Buick on the back. It was good to see that he still had his sense of humor. After a moment of silence, Buick sipped his beer, and then continued.

"Seriously, Tuna, it's funny that you ask if I saw it coming. You see, Jenny had this standard line that she always used whenever someone asked her how things were going with Buick."

"What was it?"

"She would tell our friends," Buick continued, "in all these years of marriage, I've never *once* thought of divorcing Buick. Murdering him, yes - but divorce, never."

Tuna tried to hide the smile, but couldn't. He covered his mouth with his napkin.

"What the hell, Tuna?" asked Buick, "Whose side are you on anyway?"

Tuna smacked Buick on the back again, and replied, "Yours, man, yours. But you've got to admit, that *is* funny."

Buick agreed, smiling and nodding his head, mumbling, "Yeah, it always was. Classic Jenny."

Kramer walked back into Jerry's apartment, slapped his money down on Jerry's counter, and promptly declared that he was out of the contest.

Booger squirmed in his chair and feigned a laughter that was muffled by the roar of the other Officers. One Nut turned up the volume again, and Shitscreen accidentally blew a beer bubble out of his nose from laughing so hard.

"So back to the question, Buick," said Tuna, "Did you see it coming?"

"I'm not sure," continued Buick. "We've been through so much together - the old F-4, a FAC tour, the transition to the F-18D, Desert Storm - and she never once complained. Jenny was always such a trooper."

"I hear you, Buick. A wife can make or break an Officer and his career."

Tuna stirred his gin and tonic, continuing to lend the obligatory ear.

"But things started to change about a year ago when we found out the squadron was going to Italy."

Buick polished off his beer, and grabbed the next cold soldier standing in line on the bar. There followed a number of silent minutes between the two.

"Jenny has had it with the Marine Corps, and gave me the classic ultimatum - it's the Marine Corps or her."

A sexually frustrated Jerry desperately explained to George how something had to happen - and happen quickly.

Ninja snorted while tittering like a child, and Hick Boy sniggered aloud. The Officers' Club gallery thought that it was hilarious that "Seinfeld" had tackled such a subject. Booger felt otherwise.

Man, I don't need this shit, he thought.

Booger then stood up, faking a tired stretch and a wide yawn.

"Guys, I'm bushed. I'm going to call it a night," he lied. "See you tomorrow."

Booger exited the Officers' Club, despite the hail of beer cans, popcorn, and insults that reigned down upon him.

Tuna and Buick momentarily halted their whispers as Booger walked by them to the tent's flap, and then they resumed their conversation.

"But I *love* the flying," continued Buick.

"Roger, that Buick. I can totally relate," returned Tuna. "Flying the F-18 is like taking a drug. It's an addiction that only we understand."

"That's it, exactly," said Buick.

"Besides," continued Tuna, "Flying the F-18 is the most fun you can have with your clothes on."

Both aviators laughed. Then there was more silence as they both drank. And more silence. And more sips.

"Yet at the same time, I also love Jenny," said Buick. "I told her that a man shouldn't have to choose between two loves."

Then Buick's voice quivered, and he got a tear in the corner of his eye.

Since every other set of eyes was glued to "Seinfeld", they never saw what happened next, a mere fifteen feet behind them. Tuna hugged Buick. They separated, and there was more silence.

"Tuna, you are one class dude," continued Buick. "Persian rugs in your tent, gin and tonics in the club, you've got it all. You are the shit, man. You are the cat's ass."

Tuna had to feign humility, for in reality, he agreed.

"Plus," continued Buick, "you've got it all back in the real world, man, with Lisa, a 'vette, a condo on the beach."

"What's your point, Buick? "

"My point is this," Buick solemnly reflected. "What am I? I'm just a broken down, alcoholic, old F-4 guy trying to hang onto his youth in the F-18D."

"Don't be so hard on yourself, Buick."

"And you know what?" continued Buick, ignoring Tuna's condolences. "Just look at my future - my life ain't shit. I won't be flying in the F-18D forever. I can't run anymore because of my knee. I'm an only child with two deceased parents. Jenny is all I've got in this world, Tuna. She's all I've got. I don't want to lose her."

1922 Wednesday
Easy 77 and 78 on an In-country air-to-air mission
"Pant….pant….pant."

Easy 77, a flight of two F-18Ds on a night air combat patrol, drilled through the darkness with their radars trained downrange. Easy 77, Ghost and Frap, were in a combat spread formation with Easy 78, Jock and Pope, inscribing an oval racetrack in the sky, and listening to the voice of AWACS drone on and on and on and on in their helmets.

"Easy 77, Pierre, picture clean."

"Easy 77, Pierre, picture clean."

"Easy 77, Pierre, picture clean."

It was not unusual for an aviator to fly twice in one twenty-four hour period, and today was no different. On a daily basis, the Operations Department took painstaking efforts to construct a flight schedule that didn't violate any of the required time constraints that were written in aviator's blood. Likewise, the Safety Department monitored the daily flight schedule for any oversights that could possibly lead to an accident due to crew fatigue. Despite their best efforts, inevitably, such days always involved long hours, missed meals, little sleep, and a disruption of circadian rhythms.

Pope's day had started with a 0030 brief and flight, which was followed by the daily F-15E Strike Eagle alarm clock at 0600. But he was able to sneak back to his tent after the morning sidestep to grab some REM, so he was fine. Thank God for foamy earplugs and what he called his "Lone Ranger Mask" - for lack of a better term. Pope's crutch for daytime sleeping was actually one of those black masks that flight attendants give the passengers in first class to wear. Pope always caught hell from his tent mates when he wore it, but the REM was worth it. Furthermore, Pope needed the sleep anyway, because he had to assume an alert later that night after Easy 77 landed.

For Ghost, this was his only flight of the day; consequently, he was on his game. But then again, Ghost was *always* on his game. Sharp, aggressive, and tactical, Ghost was certainly rock solid as a fighter pilot. The afternoon workout, despite the pain-in-the-ass General's Aide and the General's sexy driver, had invigorated and refreshed him.

"Hmmmmm," mumbled Ghost. "Nil corborundum illigitime. I'm going to have to remember that one."

However, for Jock, it was a different story. He was tired, dehydrated, pissed off, hungry, and frustrated. Yet he was fully engaged in the demanding, surreal world of flying on night vision goggles. His entire existence revolved around peering through two miniscule tunnels where objects were grainy and green. Furthermore, they provided no depth perception.

In an abreast formation with Easy 78 on the right, the two F-18Ds possessed a mile of lateral separation and Easy 78 had an altitude that was three thousand feet higher. The two F-18Ds drilled downrange with different conversations in each cockpit.

"Easy 77, Pierre, picture clean."

"Hey Frap," said Ghost over the ICS.

"Yeah, Ghost."

"Do you know the worst part about nights like tonight?" asked Ghost.

"Flying on the goggles?"

"Nope."

"Listening to a French AWACS?"

"Nope."

"Having to get gas from a KC-135?"

"Nope."

"Then what?" Frap laughed.

"The worst part about tonight," said Ghost, "is that we have to miss One Nut's weekly show in the Officers' Club."

"Yeah," sighed Frap, "I love that."

"Me too," concurred Ghost. "It's a little slice of the real world in a bullshit pie."

"Easy 77, Pierre, picture clean."

"So Pope, did my name come up at this morning's Human Frailties Board?" inquired Jock on the ICS, deadly serious.

"Yep," said Pope, hoping the conversation would end there. But he knew better.

"And?" pressed Jock.

"Don't worry about anything," said Pope. "We covered you."

"You mean you told the Board all about me?" panicked Jock. "That's just great."

"No, no, no," said Pope, "we didn't have to expose you."

"How is that?"

"Buick made an impromptu speech," explained Pope, "that totally saved the day. Ghost and I didn't have to say a word."

"Whew," sighed Jock.

"Yeah, no shit."

"So nobody knows about what happened last night in the Chapel tent."

"Nobody but Ghost and I," said Pope, "and we ain't talkin'."

"Thanks, man."

"No sweat, you're still cleared to fly."

"So Pope," asked Jock, "when did you become a dues paying member of the Pilot's Protection Union?"

"When I first read 'do unto others as you would have them do unto you'," laughed Pope. "I figure that we're all on the same team."

"Roger that."

"Easy 77, Pierre, picture clean."

"Hey Frap."

"Yeah, Ghost."

"I figure about one more lap and we'll be takin' it home."

"Roger that."

"Easy 77, Pierre, picture clean."

"Jock, Ghost," the pilot of Easy 77 stated on the number two radio.

"Ghost, Jock, go ahead," returned the pilot of Easy 78, now exuding more confidence.

"This will be our last time around," instructed Ghost. "I'm almost bingo fuel."

"Roger, copy."

"Easy 77, Pierre, picture clean."

"Pierre, Easy 77, same. Break. Break. Easy flight, in-place left turn, go."

In commanding an in-place turn to the left, Ghost desired both Hornets to execute a one hundred and eighty degree turn to the left in such a manner that they would roll out wings level on an opposite heading with Easy 78 then on the left side. Even wearing night vision goggles, an in-place turn was basic, flight school stuff. No sweat.

Jock looked to his left and ensured that he could see the green, glowing dot that was Easy 77, then he commenced his left turn. He slightly goosed the throttles and adeptly manipulated the stick and rudders in an attempt to roll out on the left side of Ghost in a perfect mirror image of his former position. Since Jock's left turn was being executed behind Ghost's left turn, it was Easy 78's responsibility to maintain visual contact with Easy 77, and prevent a midair collision.

"Jock, Ghost is blind", Easy 77's pilot said over the number two radio as soon as he had lost sight of Easy 78 turning left at his five o'clock.

"Ghost, Jock is visual," stated the pilot of Easy 78 to reassure Ghost.

Ghost rapidly shifted his body from looking over his right shoulder to looking over his left, in anticipation that Jock's left turn would soon make him reappear at Ghost's eight o'clock.

Confident that all was well in Easy 78, Pope brought his head back inside the rear cockpit and began retrieving his water bottle from the map case at his right hip.

Meanwhile, Jock brought his head back into the cockpit too, to check his altitude and airspeed on the HUD. To do so, Easy 78's pilot had to alter his scan in such a way to look *under* the night vision goggles. He momentarily froze his head's position, allowing his eyes to readjust to the cockpit lighting, while maintaining his left turn. It took Jock's eyes longer to refocus than he had anticipated.

"Man, I am tired," he admitted to himself.

Jock blinked his eyes a few times, and then attempted to refocus on the HUD once more. He squinted slightly.

"Altitude - good," he confirmed. "Airspeed - good."

Jock quickly shifted his vision back up so that he was looking through the goggles again, and moved his head to where he projected Ghost's aircraft should be. He blinked his eyes one more, and squinted again.

"There he is," he convinced himself. However, he had focused on the green, glowing dot of a low star on the horizon. Now attempting to fly formation on a star, Jock retarded the throttles just a smidgen and relaxed the g of his turn.

How did Ghost dick the dog on this one? thought Easy 78's pilot. *He shouldn't be over there.*

Things like this were always the *other* pilot's fault.

Unknowingly, Jock also began a slight descent.

In Easy 77, the hair was beginning to stand up on the back of Ghost's neck.

"Something ain't right," he mumbled to himself. "I should see him by now."

"You got 'im yet?" asked Ghost over the ICS.

"Nope. Not yet," replied Frap, straining his head and neck to the left. *Boy, Jock screwed the pooch this time,* thought Easy 77's pilot.

Presently, two F-18Ds were conducting a left, in-place turn within one half mile of each other in pitch darkness. Of the eight eyeballs in the flight, no pair had sight of the other aircraft.

Meanwhile, Jock continued to squint at the star, occasionally blinking his eyes and shaking his head. In his rear cockpit, Pope looked up when he felt the g forces slightly relax and the angle of bank decrease.

"What's going on?" his gut instincts asked.

He quickly glanced under his goggles at the HUD display on the left screen.

"Why are we descending?" he asked himself.

Then, no sooner had Pope transferred his vision outside to the left, and he visually picked up the green image of Easy 77 approaching their nose.

Simultaneously in Easy 77, Ghost suddenly spied the green, grainy nose of Easy 78 pointed directly at their aircraft.

"JOCK, PULL UP," Pope screamed over the ICS in Easy 78.

"SHIT," Ghost yelled aloud in Easy 77.

Jock immediately rolled his wings right and jerked back on the stick, causing Easy 78 to almost leap vertically in the sky. Ghost jammed his stick full forward and bunted the nose of Easy 77 into a full dive. Easy 78 passed over Easy 77 with scarcely fifty feet of vertical separation, barely avoiding a midair collision.

"Jock, you got it?" Pope asked over the ICS.

"Yeah, man, I got it."

In the rear of Easy 77, the sudden application of negative g forces had bounced Frap's helmet off of the canopy.

"Ouch," cried Frap. "Damn it."

Meanwhile, Ghost had kept sight of Easy 78 while in his dive, and immediately reefed the stick back into his lap and selected afterburner. He rolled his aircraft into a climbing right turn, and saw Jock's F-18D level off at Easy 77's five o'clock.

"Man, are you ok?" Pope asked Jock on the ICS.

There was no answer. All he could hear was Jock's heavy breathing.

"Pant…pant…pant."

"Jock, are you alright?"

"Pant…pant…pant."

"Jock, this is Ghost on the number two radio," interrupted Easy 77. There was nothing but silence.

"Jock, this is Ghost on the number two," repeated Easy 77.

"Easy 77, Pierre, picture clean."

"Pierre, Easy 77, standby one," commanded Ghost. "We've got a problem."

"Pierre copies. Standing by."

"Jock, Ghost. Can you hear me?"

"Jock," said Pope on the ICS, "Ghost is calling you on the number two radio."

"Pant…pant…pant."

"Pope, this is Ghost on the number two."

"Ghost, Pope, go ahead."

"Is everything alright? Why doesn't Jock answer?"

"I don't know. Jock isn't talking to me either."

"Ok," said Ghost, "I'm visual. I'm going to join on your left side."

"Roger that, Ghost."

Immediately, Ghost achieved a radar lock upon Easy 78 in order to maintain a safe distance and reliable rate of closure. Then he slowly maneuvered Easy 77 onto the appropriate bearing line at Easy 78's left, eight o'clock position, and began creeping his F-18D forward towards Jock's aircraft. In Easy 78, Pope continued his interrogation.

"Jock, can you hear me?"

"Pant…pant…pant."

Pope reached down to his left leg's flight suit pocket, and stroked the bulge formed by his rosary and the laminated card containing the prayer to Saint Jude. With no stick and throttle in the back seat of the F-18D, being in-country with a freaked out pilot was not a good place to be.

"Jock, are you ok?"

"Pant…pant…pant."

He must be ok, thought Pope, because Easy 78 was presently maintaining perfectly straight and level flight while Easy 77 crept in at their eight o'clock.

"Half mile," said Ghost, stating the range, with ice water in his veins.

"Jock, have you got it?" asked Pope.

"Pant…pant…pant."

"Four tenths of a mile," continued Ghost.

"Jock, everything's cool, man."

"Pant...pant...pant."

"Three tenths of a mile."

Then Jock erupted, screaming at the top of his lungs, "FUCK THIS SHIT. I'VE HAD IT. FUCK THIS SHIT."

"Jock, easy man, easy," continued Pope on the ICS.

"FUCK THESE DAMN THINGS."

Jock ripped the night vision goggles off of his helmet and threw them into the front windscreen.

"FUCK THIS NO-FLY ZONE."

Amazingly, Jock still maintained straight and level flight as he raged in the front seat of Easy 78.

"Two tenths of a mile," continued Ghost, unable to see the ranting in the front cockpit of his wingman's jet due to the darkness. Obviously, nor could he hear it.

"Stop there," injected Pope on the number two radio. "Jock is going postal in the front seat right now. Don't get any closer."

"Ghost copies."

He froze Easy 77 on a perfect bearing line at two tenths of a mile from Easy 78.

"What did Pope say?" Frap asked Ghost on the ICS.

Oh shit, thought Ghost, *the cat is out of the bag.*

"He didn't say anything, Frap."

"Didn't say anything?" asked Frap. "I distinctly heard Pope say that Jock was going postal."

"Don't worry about it, Frap."

"What's going on, Ghost?"

"Nothing, Frap. Let it rest."

"FUCK LIVING IN A TENT AT THE END OF A RUNWAY," continued Jock.

"Jock, be cool, man," instructed Pope.

"FUCK COLD SHOWERS."

"Jock, everything is going to be ok."

"FUCK THE KC-135."

"Jock, easy, man."

Then Jock just stopped.

"Pant...pant...pant."

"Jock?"

"Pant...pant...pant."

"Jock?"

"Yeah, Pope, what do you want?"

Pope couldn't believe his ears. Jock had finally answered, and he sounded perfectly composed and calm.

"Are you ok, man?"

"Yeah, I'm fine."

"Ghost is joining on us at our left eight o'clock, two tenths of a mile."

"Yeah, yeah, I know. I see him," Jock stated as a matter of fact. "He stopped at two tenths of a mile when you told him that I was going postal."

Pope was stunned.

"Jock, Ghost on the number two radio."

"Ghost, Jock, go ahead."

"Are you ok?"

"Yeah, I'm fine," returned Jock. "Just take me home."

"Roger that, Jock. I've got the lead on the left."

"Jock copies. Lead left."

With that, Ghost slowly maneuvered Easy 77 to a position in front of Easy 78 and to the left.

"Pierre, Easy 77," said Ghost.

"Easy 77, Pierre, go ahead."

"We've developed a minor problem," Ghost lied. "We've got to go home."

"Pierre copies. Picture clean."

2021 Wednesday
On the sidewalk outside of Maintenance Control
"Trust me. You *don't* want to defy that union."

Since Easy 77 had parked their F-18D first, Ghost and Frap would've normally been the first aviators to commence the long walk down the sidewalk from the flight line to Maintenance Control. However, Ghost was the master of manipulation. He intentionally meandered around his F-18D in slowly doing his post flight inspection, for he wanted himself and Pope to speak to Frap - alone. Thus, while Frap waited for Ghost at the nose of their jet, the delay purposely allowed Easy 78 to park, complete their own post flight inspection, and then beat Ghost and Frap to the sidewalk. Ghost noticed that Jock and Pope were walking together towards Maintenance Control, but they weren't speaking. Ghost and Frap quickly jumped onto the sidewalk about ten yards behind Jock and Pope. Just as the crew of Easy 78 arrived at the door of Maintenance Control, Ghost yelled ahead to them.

"Hey Pope. Wait up a minute."

Pope, sensing a ploy of some kind, was quick to aid Ghost's set-up. Pope was sharp, and a team player.

"Jock, you go ahead and get a jump on the paperwork," Pope insisted, opening the door for him. "I'll be right behind you as soon as I talk to Ghost."

Unaware of Ghost's trick, Jock just nodded and entered Maintenance Control, and then Pope shut the door and waited for Ghost and Frap.

Mentally drained and physically exhausted, Ghost and Frap still joked on their way down the sidewalk to do the necessary post flight paperwork. Frap mentioned nothing about the near midair collision, nor did he press Ghost about Pope's 'going postal' comment. They arrived at the door to Maintenance Control, to greet the waiting WSO from Easy 78.

"Hey there, Pope," said Ghost.

"Yeah, Ghost. What's up?" asked Pope, continuing to play the game.

Ghost abruptly froze on the sidewalk, and grabbed Frap's arm, spinning him to face the pilot of Easy 77. Taking his cue, Pope slid to his right and leaned back against the door of Maintenance Control, so that it couldn't be opened from the inside. He folded his arms across his chest.

"Frap, young man," began Ghost.

"Yeah, Ghost?"

"I'm going to tell you something that stays right here on this sidewalk. Do you understand me?"

Wide-eyed and scared, Frap looked at Ghost, then at Pope, and back at Ghost.

"Uh…yeah…sure. Go ahead."

"You didn't hear *anything* tonight, Frap."

"Nor did you *see* anything," added Pope.

"Do we need to repeat ourselves?" asked Ghost, rather sternly.

"No, Sir. I understand."

"Don't call me 'Sir'," instructed Easy 77's pilot. "I'm still Ghost."

"And I'm still Pope."

"We're not mad at you or anything," continued Ghost. "We're just taking you under our wings for a little counseling. Understand?"

"Yes, Sir," quivered a WSO who was obviously nervous and shaken.

"Listen to me, Frap," began Ghost.

"And listen hard," added Pope.

"Yes, Sir."

"Fighter pilots are a rare breed," began Ghost. "They live on an edge that people back in the real world don't understand. Ego is everything."

"Yes, Sir."

"Consequently, this life-on-the-edge is one that can severely stress an individual. Are you with me?"

"Yes, Sir."

"So us pilots tend to look out for each other," continued Ghost. "We joke about a Pilot's Protection Union, but believe you me, it is *real*. Understand?"

"Yes, Sir."

"It's a no-shitter, Frap. Trust me, you *don't* want to defy that union."

"Yes, Sir."

"So let's just say, that Jock has a tiny problem, but the union will take care of it."

"Yes, Sir."

"Now repeat after me. I didn't hear anything during tonight's flight."

"I didn't hear anything during tonight's flight."

"Good."

"And I didn't see anything during tonight's flight," added Pope.

"I didn't see anything during tonight's flight."

"Roger that," added Ghost.

"One final note," injected Pope, playing perfectly off of Ghost. "If you have any questions about the unions that exist in a squadron, then talk to Buick. Got it?"

"Got it."

"Great," returned Pope, "I'm glad that we have this little understanding."

"Now get in there and help your pilot with the paperwork," commanded Ghost.

"Roger that."

Pope stepped aside, and opened the door for Frap, who quickly slipped into Maintenance Control. After shutting the door, Pope leaned against it once more and folded his arms across his chest, asking, "So?"

"So what?" returned Ghost.

"Do you think he'll keep quiet?"

"Yeah," nodded Ghost, "Frap is like you. He's a good WSO and a team player. He can keep a secret."

"But you know what?" asked Pope.

"No, what?"

"I hope that he talks to Buick about unions," admitted Pope.

"Yep. Me too."

"So Ghost, would you care to join me in Maintenance Control?"

"I would love to, Pope, under one condition."

"And that would be?"

"That you share tonight's experience with me over a cold one at the club."

"Sure, man."

"Great," said Ghost. "Then I have just one question before we go in."

"Fire away."

"Were you scared?"

"Listen to me, Ghost," began Pope, "and listen hard."

"Yes, Sir," returned Ghost, picking up his cue.

"Fighter WSOs are a rare breed," commenced Pope. "They live on an edge that people back in the real world don't understand. Ego is everything."

"Yes, Sir," laughed Ghost.

"Consequently, this life-on-the-edge with no stick or throttle can severely stress an individual. Are you with me?"

"Yes, Sir."

"So us WSOs tend to look out for each other," continued Pope. "We joke about a WSO's Protection Union, but believe you me, it is *real*. Are you with me?"

"Yes, Sir."

"It's a no-shitter, Ghost. Trust me, you *don't* want to defy that union."

"Yes, Sir."

"So let it suffice to say, that WSOs are too crazy to be scared, but the union will take care of that."

"Yes, Sir," agreed Ghost.

With a slap on Ghost's back, Pope opened the door to Maintenance Control.

"Flying is just like taking a shit," stated Pope.

"How's that?"

"It ain't over until the paperwork is complete."

2132 Wednesday
At a Picnic Table Outside of the Officers' Club Tent
"...but a woman takes her time."

Hollywood and Shitscreen sat facing each other at a lone picnic table outside of the Officers' Club. Though it was dark, a single floodlight cast its white glow down upon them as they huddled over beers, notes, pens, and a yellow, legal pad with chicken scratching. Most everyone else had retired for the evening, or returned to the Ready Room to do some type of busy work for tomorrow. Only Hick Boy, Dago, Jock, and Buick were still in the Officers' Club tent, which explained why Hollywood and Shitscreen had moved outside to the picnic table. They had to plan their next gig without the prying ears of other aviators.

"Man. my side still hurts from laughing," said Hollywood, holding his ribs.

"Yeah," added Shitscreen. "That "Seinfeld" has to be the best show on TV."

"Oh, I concur. It's so well written."

"Speaking of writing," said Shitscreen, "we have to get cracking on this or we'll be up all night."

"Roger that," returned Hollywood, still rubbing his ribs.

"So how soon do we want to pull off the next skit?" asked Shitscreen.

"I don't know," replied Hollywood. "I'll yank the schedule writer aside tomorrow and see what he's got planned for next week."

"Joisey and Pope seemed to enjoy the show this morning."

"Yep, they sure did," agreed Hollywood.

"I like doing this," added Shitscreen.

"Well, by God," said Hollywood, "if I'm going to get up at oh-dark-thirty to brief a flight and fly, I'm at least going to have fun doing it."

"Roger that, Hollywood."

"I think that everyone else feels the same way," he concluded.

"It would probably be a good call to wait about a week or so," said Shitscreen. "That way, Joisey and Pope will quietly spread the word. Plus, we can feel out the Commanding Officer and the Safety Department to see if they're any the wiser."

"Concur, Shitscreen."

Hollywood continued to rub his side. It felt so good to laugh when you were overseas. Cold beer also helped.

"Plus, that One Nut puts on a good show, huh?" asked Shitscreen.

"Yep, ol' One Nut is going to make it," agreed Hollywood. "Thank God he has such a cool wife."

"Ok, let's get started," said Shitscreen, tapping his pen on the legal pad. "Do you have any particular ideas in mind?"

"How about if we ding the General and his 'unannounced inspection'?"

"Let's save that one for about a month from now," returned Shitscreen, "when they announce the results."

"Ok."

"Besides, that bit *might* not be too funny if the squadron really screwed the pooch on the inspection."

"Yeah, good call."

Hollywood tapped his pen and Shitscreen stared down the sidewalk.

"Hey, Shitscreen," said Hollywood, "Joisey and Pope seemed to like the laundry lists that we did this morning on the six steps of military program development and the seven rules to live by, so let's do another list like that."

"Good call," returned Shitscreen, springing back to life. "But on what?"

Easy's version of Abbot and Costello stared up into the night sky and scratched their respective chins.

"I've *got* it," said Shitscreen.

"Well, spill the beans, my man."

"Let's do a list," grinned Shitscreen, "on why F-18s are better than women."

Hollywood rolled his head back and laughed, then slammed his fist on the table.

"Cindy would kill me - but I like it," he returned. "Let's run with it."

"For example," beamed Shitscreen, "F-18s are better than women because F-18s don't mind if you look at *other* F-18s."

"Good one," said Hollywood.

"Here's another," said Shitscreen. "F-18s are better than women because, when you fly an F-18, both you and your F-18 always arrive at the same time."

Hollywood started rubbing his ribs again. "Don't do this to me, man."

"F-18s are better than women," continued Shitscreen, "because F-18s don't care how many other F-18s you have flown."

"These are good," said Hollywood. "Are you writing these down?"

Hollywood slid his tablet across the table to Shitscreen, and surrendered his pen. Shitscreen furiously scribbled, but then had a momentary brain fart. He stared up into the sky again, trying to think of more.

"F-18s don't come with in-laws," continued Hollywood.

"Wait a minute, man, let my pen catch up."

Both aviators suddenly realized that they had discovered gold. This list would surely have their next brief rolling in the aisles. Suddenly, Abbott and Costello clicked.

"You can fly an F-18 any time of the month," said Shitscreen.

"That's nothing. F-18s can be turned on by the flick of a switch."

Both aviators had to take a break - Hollywood to rub his aching ribs, and Shitscreen to relieve his cramped writing hand. Tears streamed down Hollywood's cheeks while his partner in crime chugged down his beer. The momentary silence allowed both aviators to peacefully notice the insects fluttering in the light. Then Shitscreen continued to write, but Hollywood had hit a wall. More silence followed.

"Bingo." proclaimed Shitscreen, sitting tall in his seat. "I have the number one reason why F-18s are better than women."

"And?"

"An F-18 will kill you quickly - but a woman takes her time."

2247 Wednesday
The darkened Ready Room
It sucks being four feet tall, made of teak, and unable to talk.

They call me Easy Eddie - and I call this the "dead zone". Man, this is the only time of the entire day that I don't enjoy being the squadron mascot. Why? Because I'm all by myself, that's why.

Don't get me wrong. During the day, it's a real hoot. There's never a dull moment, and I love it. The friction between Bama and Buick is worthy of a novel, while the bouts between Dago and Joisey are always good for a laugh. Spine Ripper is wound so tight, Ghost is like Teflon, and Pope is so Catholic. Jock is losing it. The FNGs are constantly under the gun. It's totally hilarious.

But then I also see the things that I don't understand. Every morning they walk the flight line looking for tiny bolts and screws. All day long superstitious aviators stroke the fish on my stringer because they think it will help them go home. Hollywood and Shitscreen are always off in a corner whispering, while Ping is always scribbling some notes in a little red book. N.D. silently pushes his cleaning cart around at all hours of the day and night.

So my days are good. But there's a small window of time at night where I'm alone, and I hate it. No aviators are briefing or flying, so there's no Duty Officer. The CAOC hasn't assigned the Alert Sixty to the boys from Easy, thus there's no tired aviators rolled up in blankets and sleeping in the Ready Room. The Air Force MP assigned to guard the safe always takes a fifteen minute smoke break at this time. Sigh. I'm all alone.

Click. Creeeaaaaaak.

Hey. What's that? Was that the Ready Room door?

Creeeaaaaaak. Click.

Somebody just came into the Ready Room.
Shuffle. Shuffle. Shuffle. Shuffle.
It's that guy with the flashlight again.
Shuffle. Shuffle. Shuffle. Shuffle.
Click-click-click-click-click-left.
Click-click-click-right.
Click-click-click-click-click-click-click-left.
Oh my God, he's opening the safe.
Clunk.
Bama. Buick. Somebody. ANYBODY. Help!
Eeeeeeeeeet.
Whoever that is, he certainly has a hard time pulling open the drawer.
Rustle. Rustle. Rustle.
He's rifling through the folders.
Shuffle. Shuffle. Shuffle. Shuffle.
What's he doing at the copy machine?
Zshing. Zshing. Zshing.
Oh, my God.
Zshing. Zshing. Zshing.
Shuffle. Shuffle. Shuffle. Shuffle.
Rustle. Rustle. Rustle.
Eeeeeeeeeet.
Clunk.
Click-click-click-click-click-click-right.
This can't be happening again.
Shuffle. Shuffle. Shuffle. Shuffle. Shuffle. Shuffle.
Click. Creeeaaaaaak.
Somebody stop him.
Creeeaaaaaak. Click.
He's gone. Who WAS that? Man, it sucks being four feet tall, made of teak, and unable to talk.

* * *

The FNGs didn't erect Masterbatoriums

If an aviator's tent mates happened to be on the same flying schedule, then it meant that they were all hitting the rack at roughly the same time. If that was the case, then day's end brought together four men who probably hadn't even seen each other all day. Consequently, it meant catching up with each other's experiences through a casual conversation. But this talking wasn't done face-to-face, where eye contact and facial expressions revealed feelings and emotions. Instead, it was conducted after the lights were out, when each participant was lying on his horizontal time accelerator, staring up at green canvas. They were just voices in the dark from separate masturbatoriums, sharing what they had done that day, and how they felt, using voice tones and inflections to convey feelings and emotions. Those moments in the dark, where they shot the shit right before falling asleep, were the male bonding experience that so many writers describe in their stories of war.

Eventually, the conversation would die as tired bodies succumbed to weariness, but there would be this quiet dead time right before they fell asleep. A lot of things run through a deployed aviator's mind in that dead time. For men back in the real world, it was things like the wife, the mortgage, and money for the kid's college. For deployed Marine Officers, it was things like the wife, the mortgage, and money for the kid's college, plus trivial matters like not getting shot down on tomorrow's mission.

It was during that quiet, dead time, where men became most pensive and reflective, most fearing and doubtful, most scared and worried. Staring up at green canvas in the dark tended to do that. They couldn't help but think, what kind of a life is this? Here they were, lying in a masturbatorium, just so they could get an ounce of privacy. Here they were, lying on a horizontal time accelerator, thinking all they wanted to do was go home.

This instinct for self-preservation had brought the squadron's four FNGs into one canvas sanctuary. Ham Fist, One Nut, FOD, and Ninja shared the same tent, and most likely the same experiences, during that summer. Ham Fist and One Nut were no shit, *real* FNGs, having just joined the squadron right before deploying to Italy. However, FOD and Ninja were a little more experienced, having been with the squadron through the entire build-up process. Besides, FOD was a "retread" - a former WSO who had transitioned to become a pilot - so he was actually the saltiest aviator in the FNG tent.

But here's where the FNG's tent differed from *every* other tent in the compound. The FNGs didn't erect Masterbatoriums. Whereas all the experienced aviators sought to escape from each other at the end of the day, the FNGs sought each other for comfort and consolation. The nightly conversation in the FNG tent was also different. FNGs didn't bitch, bitch, bitch.

It was pitch-black, and four tired FNGs were staring up at green canvas. Ham Fist, One Nut, FOD, and Ninja were trying to wind down, discussing the day's events. One Nut had painted the details of today's Mig-29 encounter for the millionth time, and the other three were in awe.

In the momentary silence, Ham Fist was lying flat on his back, hands interlocked behind his head. One Nut had a heating pad under his neck, for today's constant g's from the defensive turn had strained his Trapezius muscles. FOD was lying on his back, listening to The Cure with the volume just low enough to hear his tent mates' conversation. Ninja was already fading in and out of sleep.

"Shit," reflected Ham Fist. "Yesterday, I fought Tuna, and I got my doors blown off. The day before, Bama totally hammered my tits."

"Well only your pride got hurt," said One Nut, massaging his Trapezius. "With this neck, I may be crippled for life."

"Ham Fist, considering your experience level in the Hornet," stated FOD, "it certainly is no crime that you always get shot by the likes of Bama and Tuna."

"Yeah," added Ninja. "Tuna is damn good."

"He sure is," said FOD. "Just ask him, and he'll tell you."

Ninja decided to jump on the Tuna-bashing bandwagon.

"Yeah, do you know how Tuna changes a light bulb?"

Ham Fist, One Nut, and FOD, just laid there and silently waited, knowing that they were about to find out.

"He just grabs the light bulb," said Ninja, "and the world revolves around him."

The foursome laughed in the dark, and then a short silence fell over the tent.

"So here's a hypothetical question for you guys," stated One Nut. "If you could get out of the Marine Corps tomorrow and do your dream job, what would that be?"

"Oh, that's a no-brainer," answered Ham Fist. "I'd be a rock star."

Ninja rolled onto his side again, staring at Ham Fist's silhouette in the dark, and stating, "Dude, you're living the life of a rock star right now, in an F-18 squadron."

"Besides," said FOD, "They don't call you Ham Fist for nothin'. Having hands like that, and you think you can play a guitar?"

The FNG tent rocked with laughter, as One Nut's hypothetical question had triggered a whole new topic.

"I would be some kind of a Federal agent," stated FOD. "You know, FBI, CIA, DEA, I don't care."

"FOD, what about the ATF?" asked One Nut.

"The Bureau of Alcohol, Tobacco, and Firearms?" said Ninja. "Shit. That's not a government agency - that's my dad's bowling team."

After the laughter had died once again, there was more silence, with four FNGs staring up at the canvas.

"Hey One Nut," baited Ham Fist, "what do you think of Bama?"

"Oh, I think he's a damn good pilot. I like flying with him."

"No, I mean as a Marine Corps Officer and as a person."

"Whoa," interrupted Ninja. "Where is *that* coming from?"

"Yeah, Ham Fist," said FOD. "That's certainly out of left field."

"Hold on, you guys," insisted Ham Fist. "One Nut, just answer the question."

"Shit, I don't know," replied a confused One Nut. "Why do you ask?"

"Well," said Ham Fist, "I was in the bathroom closet today ensuring that we had paper towels for tomorrow's urinalysis."

"Yeah, so?"

"Bama came into the bathroom right after you two got jumped by the Mig-29."

"Really?"

"Yeah, man. He didn't know that I was in the closet."

"So what did he do, Ham Fist?"

"He went totally Richter, yelling at himself, and punching holes in the stall door."

"Wow."

"But that's nothin', One Nut."

"There's more?"

"Yep. Bama blames you for the entire Mig-29 incident."

"Oh, fuck."

"He thinks that you're just baggage, and he vowed that you will never fly again."

"Oh, fuck."

An eerie silence hung under the darkened canvas, until a panicky One Nut finally spoke, his voice cracking.

"Shit, you guys. What should I do?"

"The only thing that you *can* do," said FOD. "Be tactical in the jet."

"I agree," added Ninja. "That's *all* that matters in the F-18 community."

Then Ham Fist proposed a question, asking, "One Nut, have you ever heard what all the senior guys say about being a 'good bridge builder'?"

"I have," said Ninja.

"So have I," said FOD, "and it's true."

"What do they say? What do they say? Tell me. Tell me," begged One Nut.

"You can build a thousand bridges," began Ninja, "and nobody will know you as a good bridge builder."

"But suck one dick," said FOD, "and you're known as a dirty cock sucker."

"One Nut, be a good bridge builder," summarized Ham Fist, "because your tactical reputation means everything."

There was a moment of silence.

"Thanks, you guys," sighed Bama's WSO. "Good night, everybody."

"Sleep tight, One Nut."

"See you, tomorrow, One Nut."

"G'd night, One Nut," said Ham Fist. "Be tactical in the jet. That's all they want. That's all that matters."

One Nut silently stared up at the canvas, worried and wide-eyed. He certainly wouldn't get much sleep tonight.

Thursday

0021 in the Ready Room
Easy 44 and 45 Prior to a SEAD Mission Brief
"*Life* preys on the weak."

Easy 44 and 45 had coffee in hand and home-on-the-brain during the few remaining minutes before a 0030 SEAD brief. Bama, the lead pilot, was putting the finishing touches on the white board while his WSO, Shitscreen, was obtaining the weather data at the duty desk.

Shitscreen also retrieved the required "Notices to Airmen". There was a *new* Notice that could prove to be quite important to the boys from Easy, if not life threatening. The radar for ground controlled approaches at the emergency divert airfield just south of the tanker track was down. That would be bad news should an F-18D experience an aerial refueling emergency. An F-18D forced to divert there would be unable to get precise glide slope data and course information while doing a ground controlled approach.

Easy 45's pilot, Tuna, and his WSO, Spine Ripper, were already seated in the front row and feverishly writing information on their kneeboard cards. Meanwhile, N.D. hunched over his cleaning cart as he exited the Ready Room. Under the watchful eyes of Easy Eddie, Spine Ripper initiated the conversation.

"So if the shit hit the fan tonight," asked Spine Ripper, "and I mean the shit *really* hit the fan, how do you think America would do in a war?"

Tuna, the flashy, egotistical jet jock forced to languish in Bama's shadow, glanced at the dark, intense Spine Ripper, asking, "Don't you think that's pretty deep for one o'clock in the morning?"

"No, man," said Spine Ripper, passionate as ever. "Hear me out."

Bama momentarily quit writing on the board, and turned around to listen. Shitscreen hung up the phone at the duty desk.

"Damn weather guessers," Shitscreen muttered. "They put me on hold, anyway."

That was fine, though. Shitscreen would call them back again in a minute - he certainly didn't want to miss out on *this* one.

"I honestly believe," lectured Spine Ripper, "that if Uncle Sam goes toe-to-toe in the near future, he is going to get his ass kicked."

"Not a chance," said Shitscreen, shaking his head at the duty desk.

"You're an idiot," stated Tuna.

"No way, Spine Ripper," insisted Bama.

"*Yes*, way, I'm telling you," said Spine Ripper.

He scooted to the front of his chair and gazed intently around the circle.

"What makes you say that?" asked Tuna, defiantly folding his arms.

"It's because of the decay of American society," explained Spine Ripper. "It's the erosion of the family and the crumbling of morals. It's "MTV", "Jerry Springer", and video games. America is going to Hell in a hand basket."

"He's got a point, there, Tuna," said Bama. "I'm not agreeing with his prediction about America getting its ass kicked, but I *do* agree with his view of American society."

Bama put down his marker, hooked his thumbs in the waistband of his flight suit, and leaned back against his board, settling in for the long haul. The brief could wait. Shitscreen pulled the duty phone's jack out of the wall. The weather could wait. Tuna leaned forward and set his tepid mug of coffee on the floor. His need for caffeine could wait. Spine Ripper arose and assumed a position below SPEED IS LIFE, MORE IS BETTER. He *couldn't* wait.

"Two hundred, three hundred - shit, I don't know - maybe five hundred years from now," boldly lectured Spine Ripper, "I predict that the world's college students will be studying the demise of America like they now study the fall of the Roman Empire."

"Ok, then Spine Ripper," Tuna said, "explain to me how this social decay is going to cause us to lose the next war."

"I'll tell you how," Spine Ripper returned, as that vein started to pop out of his forehead again. "It's because today's kids are soft."

Shitscreen left the duty chair, and walked over to sit next to Tuna.

"Just look at our grandparents," said Spine Ripper. "They were some *hard* people. They struggled through the Depression, and then rose to the challenge of fighting World War Two. Today's kids would never do that. They'd quit."

Bama jumped into the fray, seeing Spine Ripper's point.

"That's because," said the former offensive tackle, "they'd rather stay inside and play video games, than go outside and play a physical sport."

"Bingo," stated Spine Ripper.

"They're wussies," mumbled Bama, rubbing his bruised knuckles.

Shitscreen set his coffee down, allowing both hands free to ask a question, "So, how does *our* generation compare? Are *we* as tough as our Grandparents?"

"Damn straight we are," said Tuna. "For example, remember when we were kids, and we'd play 'smear the queer'?"

A round of laughter arose from Easy 44 and 45, as the mere mention of those three words brought back schoolyard memories. That was America, by God - a gaggle of prepubescent boys running around like banshees and tackling whoever had the ball. It was all there - muddy jeans, a bloody nose, and a disdain for the bell to return to class.

"He's right," said Bama. "Kids today don't play 'smear the queer' anymore."

"Remember that?" continued Tuna. "Man, we beat the shit out of each other."

Everyone smiled and nodded with a distant look of reminiscing.

"That's why we're here today, by God," said Bama, "as Marine Officers and fighter aircrew. It's because we played 'smear the queer' as kids."

"Kids today are twats," stated Tuna, following Bama's logic.

"Ok, Tuna, let me play devil's advocate," said Shitscreen, preferring not to square off with Bama.

"Sure, go ahead."

"I agree. As kids, we may have played 'smear the queer', and played bicycle chicken, and played Army with real BB guns," reasoned Shitscreen, "but we also played sissy games like Red Rover and Freeze Tag."

"So?" asked Tuna.

"So how did *those* games make us tough like our grandparents?"

"I'll tell you how," replied Tuna.

"Wait a minute," said Shitscreen, "I'm not finished yet."

Tuna sighed and rolled his eyes, conceding the floor to Bama's WSO.

"We also grew up watching "Gilligan's Island", "Captain Kangaroo", and "the Monkees," continued Shitscreen. "How did *those* make us tough like our grandparents?"

"Well, they didn't," admitted Tuna.

"Correct. So don't you think that the guys who fought in Vietnam said the same thing about us?" asked Shitscreen. "That *we* were soft? That *we* were twats? That *we* would lose the next war?"

"Good point," said Spine Ripper. "Every generation of males looks down on the previous."

"Yeah, Tuna," stated Shitscreen. "What's the difference between you sitting in front of a black and white TV screen twenty-five years ago, and a kid sitting in front of a computer screen today?"

Shitscreen was on a roll, not allowing Tuna the time to answer.

"And Vietnam's vets grew up on "Howdy Doody", hula hoops, and malt shops," lectured Easy 44's WSO, "so I'm sure that the Korean War vets all thought *they* were soft, that *they* were twats, and that *they* would lose the next war."

"Is it ok if I talk now?" asked Tuna, growing impatient at a WSO's control.

Bama, Spine Ripper, and Shitscreen, all leaned slightly forward.

"I can name some examples right now," said Tuna, "that weren't around when we were kids. Furthermore, they weren't around when the Vietnam Vets were kids, or even the Korean vets, or *whenever*. And it's *these* things that are the cancer to today's American youth."

None of the four even noticed that they were eating into their brief time. None of them really cared.

"Right now, back in the real world," continued Tuna, "there are some high school districts that ban kick-offs in football games. School officials and parents say that kick-offs are 'too violent'. Do you believe that shit? 'Too violent'?"

"That's bullshit," said Bama. "Back in the real world, football is the closest thing we have to combat."

Tuna chuckled. He had heard this speech a million times before.

"The violence, the aggression, the pain, the overcoming of adversity, the never quitting, the trust in your teammates - they're all there in football," declared Bama.

He inflated his chest beneath SPEED IS LIFE, MORE IS BETTER.

"Well, those things are *combat*, too - the violence, the aggression, the pain, the overcoming of adversity, the never quitting, the trust in your teammates. You don't get that from a computer screen."

The other three nodded in agreement.

"Furthermore, that's *life*," summarized Bama.

There was an eerie stillness, until Spine Ripper broke the silence, stating, "That ban on kick-offs is nothing. Did you hear that *some* schools are even banning dodge ball? Do you believe that shit? Dodge ball, for Christ sakes."

"No way." said Tuna.

"Yep," continued Spine Ripper. "School administrators and parents are saying that dodge ball preys on the weak."

"I got news for today's kids," said Bama. "*Life* preys on the weak."

Spine Ripper nodded.

"God," laughed Bama, "I can remember taking one of those little red balls and smacking this kid so hard in the head that he lost his retainer."

Shitscreen laughed, not at the thought of the retainer flying across the gym floor, but at the memory of those dumb, red, dodge balls with the sandpaper surface that must've been used universally across the country.

Tuna chuckled at the thought of the weak that every school had, like the poor, fat kid who lacked the agility to successfully dodge anything, or the dorky little bookworm who threw like a girl.

Spine Ripper reminisced about how his gym teacher would yell "ALL OVER", meaning that there were no lines restricting where a player could run. Thus, it led to the weaker boys getting run down like rabbits and mercilessly pummeled by a red ball at point blank range.

Suddenly, Bama looked at his watch. It was 0051.

"Shit, you guys, we're late," said Bama "That's it, boys. Shitscreen, go back over and get our weather while I finish up my board."

Then Bama turned to the instigator.

"Spine Ripper, I honestly believe that the eleven o'clock news only shows the shit heads who make up one percent of the population. Station managers know what grabs the ratings. It's the shit heads who shoot their teachers, and the shit heads who drown their children, and the shit heads who have sex with their cousins."

Bama took a moment to inhale while Tuna worshiped, Spine Ripper nodded, and Shitscreen dialed.

"But, should the shit hit the fan, from the other ninety-nine percent of the population that you *don't* see on the news, will arise a new breed of kids just like our grandparents. They'll be just like the Korean War vets and the Vietnam vets. In fact, they'll be just like us. After America gets challenged in a way never before imagined, they will rise up to overcome that challenge. This country will possess a patriotic fervor never before seen. Suddenly, we won't be a country of Blacks and Jews and Spicks, but a united country of *one*. The American people will always bond together and rise to a challenge."

"For America's sake," summarized Spine Ripper, "I certainly hope so."

Snail Mail

When deployed overseas, Marines absolutely *lived* for mail. A letter, a card, a magazine - anything with a stamp on it - would bring a smile to their faces and warm them inside. A good, old-fashioned, hand written letter from a loved one was the cat's ass. It meant that someone back in the real world was thinking of them. Reading a hand written letter made a Marine look like the cover of a World War Two issue of *Life*.

Nothing made the heart skip a beat like a love letter, especially those that had some type of girly, smell-good stuff on the envelope. Girlfriends and wives never put a return address on the outside. Instead, they always just wrote something cute like "Me" in the upper left corner. They wrote in that sexy script that only women use, with all the curls and loopdy-loops and furls. Marines would tear right through the SWAK on the reverse side, and dive into the letter, smiling at the way women made those feminine script 'y's', and how they always dotted their 'i's' with a little smiley face or a flower.

Nothing will ever replace the intimacy of a hand written letter. Norman Rockwell would've *never* painted a woman at a computer keyboard, typing a letter to her Marine.

0551 Thursday
Tent City, Tent 08
"Hhhmmmph. Aaaaaaahhhh."

An exhausted Dago shuffled down the sidewalk. He had been unable to sleep, so he merely went for a walk. In his hands, Dago held yesterday's mail that he had retrieved from the Ready Room. He lifted the flap to his tent, and tip toed to his rack, which was immediately on the left. Thank God he had the rack closest to the entrance, and didn't have to risk stubbing his toes on junk that Tuna, Butt Munch, or Spine Ripper might've left lying around. He parted the curtains to his masturbatorium, and sat on the edge of his rack. Dago clicked on a tiny reading lamp that he had jury-rigged to his headboard, which cast just enough light to not disturb the others.

On top was a letter from Katrina, his loving wife. He set the rest of the mail between his feet, and held Katrina's letter in both hands, staring at the way she looped her 't's'. Then he closed his eyes, and brought the envelope to his nose, sniffing the front.

"Hhmmmph. Aaaaaaahhhh."

Yep, that was Katrina, right after stepping out of a shower. He turned to his left, and rubbed the envelope on his pillow, hoping to transfer the scent. Dago loved Katrina, and she was the only person on earth who ever saw this side of him. Since he wanted to save the best for last, the loving, caring, Italian husband set Katrina's envelope on his pillow and picked up the rest of the pile.

"*The New Yorker* - it can wait," and he dropped it on the floor between his feet.

"Credit card statement - screw that," and he flipped it onto *The New Yorker*.

"Sears' annual summer white sale - ditto."

The pile on the floor was growing.

"Alumni letter - ditto."

"What's this?" he whispered. "You may already be a winner. Yeah, right."

Another piece of mail dropped to the floor.

"A letter from mom," he grinned. "Alright. I'll read that right after Katrina's."

Dago set the letter from home on top of the pile.

That was it. He sighed and sat up straight. Even though he could barely hold his eyes open, nothing was going to come between him and Katrina's letter. He unlaced his boots, and kicked them off, away from the tent's main walkway, thus sparing the toes of Tuna, Butt Munch, and Spine Ripper. Dago stood up and unzipped his flight suit, letting it fall to the floor, and then pulled his stinky green t-shirt over his head. Now, Dago was only sporting dirty, green, regulation socks, and a pair of silk boxer shorts that were a gift from Katrina. This morning, they would serve as pajamas.

Dago fell backwards onto his rack. He just closed his eyes, and laid Katrina's letter on his face, resting it atop his eyebrows and the bridge of his big, Italian nose, where he could savor the aroma.

"Hhhmmmph. Aaaaaaahhhh."

Dago slowly started to drift into nirvana.

"Tower, Diamond 01, flight of four for take-off."

"Diamond 01, tower, you're cleared to position and hold. Awaiting release."

"Tower, Diamond 01, position and hold."

Three Air Force F-15E Strike Eagles moved forward and positioned themselves on the runway in an echelon formation to the right, and the fourth waited his turn in the hold short area to the left.

"Tower, Diamond 01, take-off four."

"Diamond 01, tower, you're cleared for take-off. Switch to departure control. Have a safe flight."

"Tower, Diamond 01, cleared and switching. Will do. Button four go."

"Two."

"Three."

"Four."

The sudden roar of four F-15E afterburners jolted Dago upright, and Katrina's letter flew across his masturbatorium to hit the mirror and drop to the floor. There, next to his Bible, was a box of stationery and a calligraphy pen. Katrina's soft, sensitive, lover used them both to write her every day.

Meanwhile, in Joisey's tent, a letter fell to the floor, which he had started the night before. It began "Dear *Penthouse* Forum".

0718 Thursday
Note on the Ready Room whiteboard,
beneath SPEED IS LIFE, MORE IS BETTER
"Unfuck yourselves, assholes."

Ok, you pigs. Every morning when I open the safe, I have to reorganize the material back into the appropriate folders. So let me say this again for the *last* time. If you slobs use shit from the classified safe, ensure that you put it back in the correct folder. Unfuck yourselves, assholes.

Love and kisses,
Your Easy Intelligence Officer

0733 Thursday
On the Flightline,
Morning FOD Walk
"This shit ain't worth it."

"DAMN IT," yelled Gunny Morris. "KEEP THE LINE STRAIGHT."

This morning's FOD walk representation from amongst the officers only included Hick Boy and Pope. Hick Boy was hoping the walk's fresh air would help to clear last night's Jack Daniels from his brain. As for Pope, he was very diligent about trying to make FOD walk every morning. They carried on a casual conversation while slowly taking baby steps across the tarmac's concrete.

"Hey, Pope," said Hick Boy, "you'll never guess what Cathy sent me."

"You're right, I won't."

"She sent me the latest *Victoria's Secrets* catalog."

"Man, you have one cool wife."

"Yep," said Hick Boy. "Cathy's cool in that way. I would much rather look at a catalog from Vicky S. than a *Playboy* or a *Penthouse*."

"Personally," said Pope, "I read *Cosmopolitan* when I'm in the check-out line."

Hmmmm, thought Tennessee's finest, *I've found another closet Cosmo reader.*

"Oh, wait a minute," stated Pope as he stopped and picked up a small bolt from beneath a dandelion that had worked its way up through a crack. He rejoined Hick Boy, taking baby steps across the concrete and allowing his eyes to continuously scan.

"Man, I can't wait to see Cathy again," sighed Hick Boy. "It's been so long that I'm only going to last about three strokes."

Both aviators laughed.

"Hick Boy," said Pope, "that's why you never have one of those clocks in your bedroom with those big, digital, glow-in-the-dark numbers."

"Why is that?"

"Because it's a little embarrassing," continued Pope, "to be all done with the act of sex, and three out of the four numbers haven't changed."

Hick Boy chuckled and shook his head.

"And that includes the time spent taking off your clothes," added Pope.

"Yeah, Cathy says that's why women enjoy real nice dinners with their men," said Hick Boy.

"Why is that?"

"Because," grinned Hick Boy, "a nice dinner is the only thing that they're both guaranteed to finish at the same time."

"I'll tell you what, Hick Boy," stated Pope. "Women give us shit about premature ejaculation, but every woman on this earth should - at *one* time in her life - experience what an impending male orgasm feels like, and then try to hold it back."

Hick Boy hooted aloud, then quickly muffled his mouth, hoping that Gunny Morris didn't hear. Pope distanced himself from the scene of the crime by bending over to pick up a tiny rock, and then he changed the subject upon rejoining the advancing line.

"So Hick Boy, tell me about that Mig-29."

"I'll tell you what, Pope, that thing is a turning machine."

"No shit?"

"Yeah, no shit," continued Hick Boy. "He got in Bama's knickers yesterday, and Bama couldn't shake him."

"Wow."

"It was like our old hound dog on the leg of the mail man."

Pope laughed at the visual image.

"One Nut even rang the doorbell from the rear seat, and it didn't help."

"Shhhhh," hushed Pope. "The taxpayers might hear."

"And you talk about fast. I was blown away."

"Really?"

"As soon as that Mig-29 saw me and made the decision to bug out, he was *gone*."

"So why didn't you shoot?" asked Pope.

"How could I?" replied Hick Boy. "According to ROE, he did nothing hostile."

"Fuckin' ROE," muttered Pope. "It's like they *know* what we can and can't do."

"What did you just say?" asked Hick Boy in wide-eyed amazement, while Pope suddenly realized his error.

"Nothing."

"Whoo whee, dawgs," exclaimed Hick Boy. "When my pappy was really pissed, he used to say that the cause was enough to make a preacher cuss."

"Yeah, yeah, yeah," mumbled Pope. He saw what was coming from a mile away.

"But now I can honestly say that this shit is enough to make the Pope cuss."

"Bless me, Father, for I have sinned," said Pope, making the sign of the cross.

"You want to know what else, Pope?" asked Hick Boy, turning serious again.

"What's that, Hick Boy?"

"Yesterday I came to a realization, that this shit ain't worth it."

"What?"

"This shit ain't worth it," repeated Hick Boy. "Yesterday we could've lost two shit hot aviators - Bama and One Nut - and for what? I shoot down a Russian Mig? Big deal. That's no trade."

Only a tiny screw on the tarmac was enough to halt Hick Boy's philosophizing. He bent over to retrieve it while Pope continued to baby step forward. Hick Boy placed the FOD in a plastic bag, and then slightly jogged to catch up with the line.

Pope glanced over upon Hick Boy's return, stating, "Hey, Hick Boy, did you get the word about the Commanding Officer wanting all of the officers in the Ready Room this morning?"

"Yeah," he returned, "at 0900, right? I wonder why."

"Yep, 0900. I guess the General is going to give us a little 'atta boy' speech."

"Oh, great," replied Hick Boy.

"Don't be late, my man," added Pope. "The Skipper wants us all in our seats by 0845. I even heard word through the grapevine that he's made a seating chart."

The long line of blue mechanic's uniforms, green flight suits, and camouflage utilities came to the far side of the flight line, as this morning's FOD was collected from waiting hands and placed into plastic bags.

"FALL OUT," bellowed Gunny Morris. "NICE JOB, MARINES."

0747 Thursday
In the Aircrew Van
Corner of Mendamucci Street and Ricci Avenue
"Did they teach *that* at the super-secret General's school, too?"

Ghost was in the aircrew van, weaving his way downtown to Rialto's pastry shop and bakery as the sun was just beginning to creep over the mountains to the east. On Thursday mornings at 0800, Rialto's unveiled fresh Tiramisu that was a real hit amongst the Easy aircrew. Dago said it reminded him of his boyhood days in Brooklyn. Frap enjoyed it with his daily Frappuccino. Hick Boy devoured it, having never seen such a dessert in Tennessee.

After Wednesday night's "Seinfeld" and "Friends", the short straw had ended up in Ghost's hands, thus designating him to make the usual Thursday morning Tiramisu run. That was ok. Ghost didn't mind - he liked Italian mornings. The cooler temperature forced an older Italian woman to wear a shawl as she swept her porch with a shoddy broom. Likewise, an older man had donned a sweater to walk his greyhound on the cobblestone. Or as Ghost jokingly noticed, the greyhound was walking *him*. Ghost thought to himself how Italy would never be a powerful country. The men were all too soft. With delicious pasta, bountiful wines, and gorgeous women, who wanted to fight?

Rialto's was just around the corner and a couple streets over, so Ghost would be back at the Ready Room in no time. It would be no sweat to make the mandatory meeting with the General at 0900. Ahead on the left was Stefano's Bed and Breakfast Inn. Ghost had heard nothing but rave reviews from his fellow officers about this place, so he thought he would swing by to check it out. Namely, Tuna and Spine Ripper both had their wives come over to Italy for a week, and they stayed at Stefano's. So if that place was good enough for the pretentious Tuna and Lisa, and the meticulous Spine Ripper and Susan, then Stefano's was definitely good enough for an athletic F-18D pilot and his down-to- earth Boston girlfriend.

Ghost pulled up to the Italian stop sign, glancing to his left. After easing the van to a halt, Ghost admired Stefano's. He hurriedly glanced into the rear view mirror to do a quick traffic check - nothing was coming - so that he could sit and appreciate such a beautiful Inn. Two story, red brick, ivy covered - it had all the little things that chicks dig. He would be a hero in his girlfriend's eyes. Ghost especially liked the balconies that were attached to each second story bedroom. The balconies had wrought iron railings around their perimeters with the same dark green ivy entangled within the iron's grasp. Italian patio furniture on the balcony beckoned Ghost to collapse on its foamy cushions. The balcony would be the perfect place to enjoy an early morning cappuccino after an all-night session of making love.

Suddenly, one of the second story balcony doors crept open, and the early morning breeze forced silk curtains to flap onto the patio furniture.

Whoa. What do we have here? Ghost thought.

A young, gorgeous, brunette stepped out onto the balcony wearing only a man's collared white shirt, barely buttoned at the waist. She glided to the wrought iron railing, placed both hands upon it, and closed her eyes, deeply inhaling the fresh morning air. Her tasseled hair glistened in the morning sun, and fell all the way down her back.

"Wait a minute," Ghost said, taking a closer look. *"That's the General's driver."*

Ghost checked the rear view mirror again for traffic - nothing was coming - and then slammed the van into park. The Tiramisu could wait, because this was a free peep show. Then he couldn't believe his eyes.

The General emerged from the room and onto the balcony wearing only a pair of boxer shorts, and one of those white, cotton, tank-top t-shirts that old guys wore. He gently stepped behind his satisfied playmate, placed his arms around her waist, and softly kissed her neck and hair. She removed her hands from the railing, and placed them upon his forearms, then nestled back into his grasp, cooing in delight.

"Holy shit." exclaimed Ghost. "Did they teach *that* at the super secret General's school, too?"

Ghost didn't know what to do. He frantically looked around to make sure that no one saw him. Then he glanced back up at the balcony to ensure that the two lovebirds hadn't seen him either. He put the van back into drive, but intentionally didn't remove his foot from the brake. Ghost could ill afford to squeal out, leading to the General spotting an Air Force van laying a patch of rubber in front of Stefano's. He slowly eased his foot from the brake, and immediately turned right, just to get away from the scene of the crime. Then he floored the gas pedal. As he sped down the street, his mind was racing a million miles an hour.

"How could this possibly be?" he asked himself out loud. "What could she possibly see in his gray, wrinkly, fat-ass, fifty-eight year old body? This May-October romance just couldn't be true. Wait a minute. May-October? Bullshit. She can't be a day past April, and I'll bet he's pushing November. The General certainly had no reason to be so cranky if he was sleeping with something like *that* every night."

Ghost wondered. Was the driver simply a nice girl who had been seduced by a lecherous, powerful, old man? Or was the General just a good man who had succumbed to the powers of the flesh?

0802 Thursday
In the Ready Room
"It just keeps getting better."

The daily ten pounds of shit stuffed into a five pound bag forced this morning's attendance at the Intell clipboard to be a mere four Officers. Hick Boy and Pope walked into the Ready Room after the morning's FOD walk, but did so only because the flight line was so close. They would've felt guilty if they hadn't. Joisey happened to be in the Ready Room putting up a briefing board for later that morning, and Dago wandered around the Ready Room with a cold cup of mud, just avoiding

Joisey. Flights and duties and briefs and whatever else would force the other aviators to complete their mandatory reading sometime later that day - and they would. They always did the right thing.

Hick Boy and Pope stood shoulder to shoulder, with Tennessee's finest holding the clipboard with his left hand and the Catholic's Catholic holding the clipboard with his right. As their four eyes did the typewriter scan of today's update, Joisey put down his white board markers long enough to saunter up next to them on Pope's right. The tiny Italian from Brooklyn filled his coffee mug one last time and then joined the threesome on Hick Boy's left - the opposite side from Joisey.

FROM: COMMANDING GENERAL, ALLIED TACTICAL AIR FORCE
TO: DISTRIBUTION LIST
SUBJ: ROE UPDATE
REMARKS: THIS MESSAGE OVERRIDES ALL PREVIOUS INSTRUCTIONS.
1. UNCONFIRMED INTELLIGENCE FROM UNCONFIRMED SOURCES CONFIRMS THAT THE HIGHWAY 55 SUPPLY MISSION NEAR GROBNEV, CODENAMED MI-55, CONTINUED OVERNIGHT WITH INCREASED VEHICULAR ACTIVITY AND MORE FLIGHTS OF MI-8S AND MI-24S. RECONNAISSANCE ELEMENTS OF THE FIRST BATTALION, THIRD MARINE REGIMENT REPORT THE INTRODUCTION OF RUSSIAN MADE T-62 AND T-72 TANKS INTO THE VICINITY OF GROBNEV. AIRCREW ARE ADVISED THAT GENERAL CRAPNOV, THE COMMANDING GENERAL OF THE SERBIANS WHO ARE ROGUE TO THE ORIGINAL ROGUE SERBIANS, POSSESSES ONLY T-62 TANKS IN HIS COMMAND. NATO AIRCREW ARE SPECIFICALLY INSTRUCTED TO VISUALLY IDENTIFY ANY TANK AS A T-62 BEFORE THE RELEASE OF ANY AIR TO GROUND ORDNANCE UPON SAID T-62.
2. THE FOLLOWING GUIDELINES APPLY:
    A. NATO AIRCREW MUST VISUALLY CONFIRM THAT THE DRIVER OF SAID T-62 TANK IS WEARING A BLACK SKULL CUP. THIS UNIFORM ITEM IS ONLY - REPEAT ONLY - WORN BY THE T-62 TANK DRIVERS OF GENERAL CRAPNOV'S SERBIAN FORCES.

B. IF SAID DRIVER OF T-62 TANK IS WEARING A HELMET SO AS TO DENY VISUAL CONFIRMATION OF A BLACK SKULL CAP, OR IF HE HAS CLOSED HIS HATCH, THEN NATO AIRCREW ARE TO VISUALLY CONFIRM THAT SAID T-62 TANK HAS A BLACK STAR PAINTED ON THE FORWARD (FRONT) STARBOARD (RIGHT) BOTTOM (UNDER) SIDE OF THE TURRENT BENEATH THE SMOKE LAUNCHERS.

"Man, you have *got* to be shittin' me," sighed Pope.

"Visually *see* a black skull cap on the driver of a tank?" asked Hick Boy. "How in hell are we supposed to do *that*?"

"It just keeps getting better," stated Joisey.

"Shit," said Hick Boy. "I still don't know if we're keeping the Serb-hating Muslim Croats from the Bosnian Croat-hating Serbs, or what."

"I think we're trying to protect the Serbian Muslims from the Bosnian Muslim-hating Croats," stated Pope.

"You're both wrong," said Dago, "we're keeping the peace between the Croatian Serbian-hating Bosnians and the Serbian Bosnian-hating Muslims."

"You know what, Dago?" interrupted Joisey. "You're an idiot."

"Oh, yeah?" countered Dago. "Well, who's going to protect you from an Italian Catholic, New Jersey-hating Brooklynite?"

"Oh yeah? Well, who's going to defend you from a Protestant, New Yorker-hating Jersey boy?"

The two quickly squared off against each other, collapsing the line of four aviators into the letter 'u'. Pope hastily stepped forward between Joisey and Dago, putting the palms of his hands into their chests.

"Hey, hey, hey, you two," Pope stated. "Does either of you know the words to the prayer of Saint Francis?"

"Who the hell is Saint Francis?" asked Joisey.

"The Catholic saint who was kind to animals," injected Dago with the air of a know-it-all. "Saint Francis the sissy."

"What did you just say?" asked Pope, staring at his fellow Catholic.

"Saint Francis the sissy."

Pope shook his head, still maintaining separation between the two.

"It was Saint Francis *of Assisi*," said Pope in disbelief.

"See? You *are* an idiot," said Joisey.

"Eat me," said Dago, with the only counter that he knew when cornered.

"In any case," continued Pope, "the prayer to Saint Francis simply states, 'Lord, make me an instrument of Thy peace. Where there is hatred, let me sow love'."

The two combatants were speechless. Dago wheeled about and departed the left side of the line to get another cup of coffee. Joisey spun about on the right to go finish his briefing board.

"Geeez," sighed Pope, "do you believe those two?"

"Nope," returned Hick Boy. "It reminds me of the feud between the Tennessee, Kentucky-hating Hill Jacks, and the Kentucky, Tennessee-hating Hillbillies."

0838 Thursday
In the Bathroom Building
"Sir, did you sleep well last night, Sir?"

Ghost checked his watch. Damn. If the Skipper wanted everyone seated by 0845, he would have to hurry. After dropping off the Tiramisu in the Officers' Club refrigerator, Ghost half-walked and half-ran down the sidewalk. Did he have time to take a piss? Ghost checked his watch again. Sure, why not? He did a quick detour to his left and jumped up the two steps, pushing open the bathroom door. He bounded past the stalls and froze in his tracks facing the urinals. There was the General - alone - at the center urinal, violating rule one of the code. It was too late to fake anything at the sink, so Ghost wheeled about and opened the stall door. There sat Buick on the toilet, fully clothed, with his knees tucked up into his chest so that nobody could see his flight boots. Buick silently rendered a Polish salute to Ghost, shrugging his shoulders and raising his outstretched palms. He smugly smiled.

Damn, thought Ghost. *Buick must've entered the bathroom right before me and executed the same maneuver when he saw the General.*

From inside the stall, Buick intentionally dropped an empty toilet paper tube onto the floor. The noise was just enough to cause the General to look over his right shoulder from the urinal. With the General gaining sight of Ghost, the F-18D pilot knew that he was trapped like a rat.

Ghost silently mouthed "You asshole" to Buick, and then shut the stall door.

"Sir, good morning, General, Sir," greeted Ghost.

Ghost was now forced to approach the General and the three porcelain urinals. The masking tape and sign had been removed from the broken left urinal, even though it hadn't been fixed yet. Thank God the General didn't decide to use that one, or his attempted flush would've backfired onto his uniform. Still, the General's choice of the center urinal was in direct violation of the code, and placed Ghost in an awkward position. Not to mention the fact that Ghost was fuming inside. Just like the dining tent, the tape removal from the left urinal was all part of polishing turds.

As Ghost stepped up to the urinal on the General's right, he noticed the fresh urinal cakes in the bottom, and the lack of cigarette butts clogging the drain. The urinal's porcelain was absolutely spotless, and there was also a solid air freshener sitting on top - country morning potpourri. Ghost stopped at the urinal, and commenced the slowest unzipping of his flight suit that he had ever done in his life, all in the hopes that the General would finish and walk away. In accordance with the code, Ghost stared straight ahead at the wall.

"Good morning, son," barked the General, looking directly at Ghost - another blatant violation of the code.

Inside, Ghost panicked. The General was now looking directly at the left side of Ghost's face - the same side that he would've seen from Stefano's balcony.

Does he recognize me? Ghost thought. *Surely, he doesn't want to carry on a conversation.*

Ghost continued to stare straight ahead at the wall. Gulp.

"Sir, Good morning, Sir."

"It looks like it's going to be another fine Marine Corps day, Devil Dog."

"Sir, yes, Sir," returned Ghost, still staring at the wall. "Sir, did you sleep well last night, Sir?"

The question was out of Ghost's mouth before he realized what he had just asked. He was only trying to make conversation, and that question was just the first thing that popped into his head. Idiot.

Did I have a sarcastic tone? Ghost feared.

Ghost wished he were in a cartoon, where he could reach up and grab the balloons that contained his words, then stuff them into the urinal before the General heard them.

"Yes I did sleep well, thank you, Marine," he returned. "The VIP tent here is quite comfortable."

VIP tent, my ass, thought Ghost.

The bubbling sound emanating from the General's urinal slowly died down. Shake, shake, shake. Ziiiiiiiip. The General was done. Inside, Ghost sighed in relief.

The General smartly wheeled about, washed his hands at the sink, and then strode out the door, saying, "Have a fine Marine Corps day there, Leatherneck."

"Sir, yes Sir."

The bathroom door had no sooner slammed shut, and then Ghost heard Buick's heavy flight boots hit the floor, and the stall door creaking open.

Buick danced like a fairy towards Ghost, sarcastically cooing, "Oh, General, Sir, did you sleep well last night, Sir?"

"Shut up, Buick."

"Ghost, you kiss ass, brown noser, suck-up."

"I said shut up, Buick."

Ghost zipped up and whirled about.

"C'mon, asshole," quipped Ghost. "We've got to run if we're going to make it to the Ready Room by 0845."

0856 Thursday
In the Ready Room
"Wah, wah, wah, wah, wah..."

Most of the officers were gathered in the Ready Room, awaiting the General's arrival. He had completed his 'unannounced inspection' yesterday, and wanted to pitch some motivational 'atta boy' speeches to both the squadron's aircrew and the enlisted Marines. The officers sat in seats assigned by the Commanding Officer, and killed the time with tested and proven methods. FOD listened to Toad the Wet Sprocket on a Walkman's headphones. Jock read a guide for prospective TWA employees. Hick Boy wrote a letter to Cathy. Ping scribbled in his little red book.

While time slowly dragged for the waiting aircrew, it stood at a complete standstill for the squadron's Commanding Officer. He nervously paced back and forth in the front of the Ready Room, periodically stopping and glancing out the window towards the parking lot. Then he would check his watch and begin pacing again. He was wearing a path into the tiled floor.

The Skipper must've worked at a roadside fruit stand in the days of his youth. A savvy fruit stand manager will always place the big, plump, juicy blackberries on top of the tinier, lesser quality ones. Likewise, he will display the larger, shinier apples on top of the smaller, bruised ones. Thus, it was the same in the Ready Room. In accordance with the Skipper's mandatory seating chart, Bama, Tuna, Hollywood, Ghost,

Spine Ripper, and Pope occupied the front row. By comparison, seated in the back row were Joisey, Dago, FOD, Ninja, Shitscreen, Jock, and Booger. Buick was supposed to be there too, but hadn't arrived yet.

After the fiasco in the bathroom, Ghost and Buick were late by the Skipper's 0845 demand. Ghost had run all the way from Tent City, and then sauntered into the Ready Room at 0847 like he owned the place, barely breathing. Buick had walked, and then stumbled into the Ready Room at 0851, panting heavily. The Commanding Officer merely cast a cold glance at both of them upon their entrance.

Ghost took a quick glance at the Skipper's seating chart, and assumed his mandatory position in the front row. Buick entered shortly thereafter, and he didn't even bother to look at the chart - he went straight to the back row without saying a word.

Ghost's eyes wandered about the Ready Room. It was different.

Buick's poster of the Heineken girl had been taken down from behind the coffee mess area, which was actually clean for once. In fact, the coffee mess area had no spilled coffee, no dusting of sugar, no stained mugs, and no broken stir sticks.

There were no used kneeboard cards lying around, and no charts or laminated maps spread across the table. There were no visible nav bags, no dirty helmet bags, and no old take-out sacks from the Golf Shack.

The white board had been cleansed of all the "so-and-so, call your wife" and "so-and-so, pay your mess bill" messages. There were no scrawled demands from the Safety Nazis to do immediate action exams. There was no spaghetti of blue and red arrows depicting a one-versus-one. The note stating, "Unfuck yourselves, assholes", was gone.

The duty desk, which was normally the epitome of clutter, now looked like the work center of some possessed receptionist. The jacks for both the phone and radio had been unplugged from the wall, and all of the F-18D publications were neatly arranged from largest to smallest.

Worst of all, the bra had been removed from Easy Eddie, and someone had taken down SPEED IS LIFE, MORE IS BETTER. Ghost sighed.

More polishing turds, he thought.

Ghost looked at his watch. It was 0912.

Why were Generals always late? Ghost pondered.

Suddenly, the Skipper, after casting a glance outside to the parking lot, froze in mid pace.

"Standby," he warned his audience, and then assumed a ramrod stiff position of Attention next to the door.

All of the officers casually stood up at their seats, sensing nowhere near the degree of urgency that the Skipper demonstrated. The aircrew assumed a more relaxed stance, awaiting the final word. The Ready Room was silent, save for the tick, tick, tick of the clock behind the duty desk. Hick Boy coughed. Buick cleared his throat. FOD turned off his Walkman and removed the headphones.

The typical blur of a busy General suddenly whisked by the Ready Room's front window from right to left, followed closely by a tightly packed entourage of Marine Corps Charlie uniforms. No sooner had the knob to the Ready Room's front door started to rotate, the Commanding Officer called the Ready Room to Attention.

"Attention on deck." said the Skipper.

The officers stiffened their relaxed stances to the correct position of Attention with eyes fixed straight ahead, chests out, and arms affixed rigidly to their sides. Spine Ripper even had his fingers properly curled and his feet at the proper forty-five degree angle.

"At ease, Gentlemen, at ease," returned the General, striding into the Ready Room. "Take your seats, please."

The General immediately peeled away from the front of his entourage, strutting to the front and center position of the Ready Room. The Commanding Officer humbly slithered to his seat in the front row, as the entire Ready Room sat down in their seats. Ghost slumped down in his seat to avoid the General's detection.

The entourage, led by his spit-n-polish Aide, assumed standing positions along the side of the Ready Room. The last person to enter was the General's driver. She quietly closed the door behind her, and then sat down in a chair specifically reserved for her in the front, left corner of the Ready Room. She crossed her legs at the ankles, and Ghost bit his lip again.

"Good morning, Leathernecks." greeted the General.

"Sir, good morning, General, Sir," returned the Easy aircrew, like first graders responding to their teacher.

"It's another glorious day to be in the Corps."

"Sir, yes, Sir."

Then the General began his motivational 'atta boy' speech. But Ghost didn't hear a single word. The General was talking like Charlie Brown's teacher.

"Wah, wah, wah, wah, wah."

Ghost checked the General's posturing left hand. Yep, he was wearing a wedding ring. Ghost slightly glanced around the seated aircrew. He was the only one who knew.

The General continued to ramble in front of the Ready Room, but only the words of bitter irony got etched into Ghost's brain.

"Wah, wah, wah, wah, wah . . . honor and integrity . . . wah, wah, wah, wah, wah . . . morality and self-discipline . . . wah, wah, wah, wah, wah . . . be true and faithful to your country and your God . . . wah, wah, wah, wah, wah."

That was all Ghost remembered. The next thing he heard was the C.O.'s voice, stating, "Attention on deck."

The officers jumped from their seats. Ghost intentionally timed his rise to blend in with the crowd. The General smartly turned to his right, and bounded out the door that had already been opened by the Skipper. The same blur flew by the Ready Room's front window from left to right as the entourage departed in reverse order - the driver, the lackeys, the Aide. As soon as the General was gone, the Commanding Officer took charge of the Ready Room.

"At ease," said the C.O., who then ran out of the Ready Room, chasing after the Genral's entourage.

Easy's Marines were already assembled in the hangar to hear the same speech.

0930 Thursday
Briefing Room Two
Easy 55 and 56 Brief an in-country CAS Mission,
Under FAC Control
"…even bigger than Godzilla versus Rodan."

The squadron's Operations department had committed the ultimate error. Maybe it was just a cruel joke perpetrated by the schedule writer, and the Operations Officer simply didn't catch it. Likewise, the Safety Department's Nazis didn't notice it either in their daily check of the flight schedule. They *should've* caught it, because this mistake had the potential to rival the Hindenburg disaster. The Commanding Officer didn't even catch it when he signed the final version of the flight schedule. Thus, the written word became gospel. It was going to happen. There was no stopping it now. Joisey and Dago were scheduled to fly in the same jet.

This would be bigger than Frankenstein meets the Werewolf. This promised to be even bigger than Godzilla versus Rodan. This would be the ultimate clash of the Titans - a crew coordination nightmare. There already existed a natural geographic rivalry between the two, with Dago being the tiny Italian from Brooklyn, New York, and Joisey being the horny pervert from Bayonne, New Jersey. However, this friction was bound to come to a head with the two of them trapped in the same jet for four to five hours.

Whispers ran rampant through the Ready Room as soon as the flight schedule came out. Now the Coffee Mess Officer was taking undercover bets on who would triumph over whom. Plus, Buick had created a secret pool to entertain guesses on how many minutes they would peacefully last together starting from the end of the brief. In the bitter irony of ironies, Joisey and Dago, in Easy 55, would be leading FOD and Ninja, the squadron's two laid back, stress free, surfer dudes, in Easy 56. Those two could give a rat's ass about who was in the other jet.

Joisey's brief went off without a hitch - but only because Dago refused to acknowledge Joisey's existence, and FOD and Ninja were too young and ignorant. The flight was scheduled to go in-country for a simulated CAS mission under FAC control.

Therein lied the rub. After the heightened tensions resulting from Jock's AAA incident on Tuesday, and yesterday's Mig-29 ambush, fighting could erupt between the warring factions on the ground at any moment. Thus, NATO's peace-keepers could get sucked into an ugly vortex of violence. If *any* Easy flight had the potential to suddenly be called upon to deliver the thousands of pounds of death and destruction that they carried, then it was the daily, close air support hop. It was a scary thought indeed - today, such a responsibility could fall upon the likes of Joisey, Dago, FOD, and Ninja.

After the brief, the clock began running on Buick's secret pool. The four aviators left the Ready Room with no major problems. They passed through the Intelligence shop to get the usual threat update - still no difficulties. The foursome walked from there to the maintenance hangar, where things began to unravel in the flight equipment shop.

Joisey unzipped his nylon flight jacket, and threw open the front to remove it. Dago's locker was fifteen feet away, but he immediately scrunched his nose and glared at Bayonne's best.

"Whew," said Dago. "Is that *you?*"

"What?" Joisey naively returned.

"When was the last time that you took a shower?" asked Dago.

"What's it to ya, pizza breath?"

"I have to fly with you," snapped Dago. "*That's* what it is to me."

"Oh, yeah," said Joisey. "*You're* one to talk about cleanliness. A bar of soap hasn't touched your skin in years since you grew that carpet of hair on your back."

"At least my body gets put under a stream of water every day."

"My shower frequency is *my* business," said Joisey.

"I see that it's time for Bama and Ghost to scrub your ass again."

"Hey, Dago, the human body secretes innate pheromones, and I prefer to remain in my more natural state. Chicks dig me."

"Well listen, asshole, you just keep those pheromones in the front cockpit."

Meanwhile, at the lockers displaced one row over towards the Maintenance Control counter, FOD was stuffing tapes into his helmet bag and inspecting the wiring of his latest splice job.

"Hey Ninja," he said. "Who do you want today? Soul Asylum or the Stone Temple Pilots?"

"I don't care, dude," answered Ninja. "You pick."

"That reminds me, did Scott Wyland ever get out of drug rehab?" returned FOD, referring to the lead singer of the Stone Temple Pilots.

"I don't know, dude," replied Ninja. "I've been out of the loop since we left the real world and Hick Boy cancelled my subscription to *Rolling Stone*."

"Did Hick Boy really *do* that?"

"Yep, dude, he sure did," continued Ninja. "He said he didn't want any of that subversive, communist crap laying around the squadron. But I got him back."

"What did you do?"

"I intercepted the big brown envelope containing his most recent copy of *Appalachia Monthly*. Then I removed it, and stuck in my latest *Guitar World*. That certainly rocked his backwoods Tennessee world."

The four aviators next walked to Maintenance Control, where they read the maintenance book for the jet that they had been assigned. Dago made a conscious effort to remain upwind of Joisey.

The tension only continued upon preflight inspection of their F-18D. The pilot and the WSO always met their plane captain at the boarding ladder on the left, front side of the F-18D. They handed their nav bags to the plane captain, who quickly climbed the ladder and prepared each cockpit for its occupant. The plane captain placed each nav bag in each cockpit, and readied the eight straps and fittings that the aircrew would use to strap the jet to their back. Meanwhile, the aircrew walked around the jet to conduct a preflight inspection. The pilot always went around clockwise, which Joisey commenced, while the WSO always walked around counter-clockwise, which Dago did. It was yet another unspoken ritual in a world of checklists and rules.

Dago's first stop was the left wheel well. When Dago ducked under the left wing and stood up in there to check its integrity, he suddenly felt the urge to urinate. But it was too late to run back into the hangar, so what was he to do? He then noticed that the left wing's external fuel tank blocked the hangar's view of his position in the left wheel well. Thus, nobody in the hangar could see him. Furthermore, the plane captain was still on top of the F-18D, preparing the front seat, and Joisey was on the right side of the aircraft inspecting the wing tip. Consequently, neither of them could see Dago either. So Dago decided to quickly urinate there on the left tire. He unzipped his flight suit from the bottom zipper, and let his urine silently run down the tire's rubber and form a puddle on the tarmac. As soon as he had completed, he quickly zipped up, and continued his preflight inspection. No one was any the wiser.

When doing their preflight inspection, the pilot and WSO always met at the rear of the jet. There, while checking the snubber pressure of the arresting hook, Dago cheerfully greeted Joisey, stating, "Hey, there, dickhead."

While inspecting the turkey feathers of the left exhaust, Joisey returned the same, declaring, "Good day, ass wipe."

Dago continued on his counter-clockwise trek to check the right flaps, and Joisey continued clockwise to check the left wing's downlock. When Joisey got to the left wheel well, he couldn't help but notice the strange puddle by the tire. What was this? Was it a leak of some kind? It definitely wasn't hydraulic fluid - it wasn't thick and red. It was too thin and clear to be oil. Joisey knelt down by the left tire and studied the odd puddle. It didn't smell or look like fuel. Finally, he dipped his right index finger into the fluid, and brought it to his nose, sniffing it. There was still no recognition of any possible F-18 fluid. So then he touched his index finger to his tongue.

"Damn it," screamed Joisey, in the sudden realization. "That *bastard*."

He bolted from beneath the jet and tackled Dago under the right wing tip. As the two rolled down the tarmac in a tangle of cursing and flight equipment, FOD and Ninja stood at the boarding ladder of their F-18D, having just completed their own preflight inspection. Each looked at his watch, and then at each other.

"Damn, dude," began Ninja. "In Bama's pool, I had fifty minutes."

"I had sixty-two," FOD calmly returned. "Shit."

"Oh well."

They shrugged at each other, and climbed the boarding ladder, as the two bodies tussled down the concrete in front of their jet.

Meanwhile, plane captains, grease monkeys, maintenance trouble-shooters, and enlisted Marines of every type sprinted down the tarmac to the scene of the crime. But did they try and separate the two feuding Officers? Noooooo. Instead, they formed a cheering gauntlet as the two Titans rolled and cursed and punched and gouged their way down its middle.

Buick and Screech, who were just returning to Maintenance Control, simultaneously spied the huge double line that had formed. Likewise, they heard the cheers and jeers that filled the flight line's air.

"Hmmmm," said Screech, "I wonder what's going on over there."

"I don't know," returned Buick, "but the air smells like Joisey."

"And the cussing sounds like Dago," added Screech.

The two aviators suddenly froze, realizing the possibility.

"Shit."

"Damn."

Buick and Screech immediately dropped their nav bags and sprinted towards the gauntlet. Well, Screech sprinted anyway. Buick never ran anywhere for anything at any time. Upon arriving at the gauntlet, Screech quickly parted two enlisted, blue coverall uniforms like the Red Sea, demanding, "Lemme through."

After spying the rolling tussle, Screech jumped on top to merely stop its motion. As luck would have it, the result placed him on the back of a pissed off Italian. Dago looked and sounded like that old cartoon, the Tasmanian devil, as he pummeled a bloody Jersey boy. Screech promptly reached around Dago's face to pull him off, and Dago bit his forearm.

"OUCH."

Buick arrived just in time to help Screech pull back on Dago's shoulders, revealing a fat Italian lip and a blackened eye. The two of them succeeded in getting Dago off of Joisey, who had a bloody nose and scratched forehead. Screech restrained Dago from behind, and Buick sat on the boy from Bayonne. Joisey certainly wasn't going anywhere *now*. The enlisted Marines erupted in a raucous cheer.

"Alright, Devil Dogs," commanded Buick, "the show's over. Get back to work."

The crowd quickly dispersed, exchanging dollar bills and laughing. Buick maintained his seat upon Joisey's sternum, and Screech pulled Dago further away from the former pile.

"Easy, Dago," said Screech. "Calm down, man."

"You sick Jersey bastard," fumed Dago, slowly winding down his wild flailing.

Joisey failed to reply because he couldn't breathe under Buick's weight. After an eventual moment of calm, Screech slowly released Dago, and Buick rolled off of Joisey's chest to establish a blocking position between the two panting gladiators.

"I don't believe you two," scolded Buick. "There's a potential *real* enemy in-country, and you guys are duking it out here on the flight line."

Joisey sat up to catch his breath, failing to make eye contact with Buick, while Dago stood with his hands on his hips, panting, and staring down at the concrete. They both knew that Buick was right.

"You two have a close air support mission to fly for Marines on the ground," continued Buick. "So get your asses to the jet and get out of here."

"Wait a minute, Buick," said Screech. "I have an idea."

"What's that?"

"Let's get Pope over here to make peace between them."

"Good idea," agreed Buick. "Where's Pope?"

"I don't know," said Screech, looking around. "He was here a second ago."

"Has anybody seen Pope?" asked Buick.

There was no reply. Pope was last seen happily skipping towards the hangar, and jubilantly shouting, "I won the pool. I won the pool. I won the pool."

* * *

More snail mail reflections

A simple box of chocolate chip cookies in the snail mail would bring tears to a Marine's eyes. More importantly, it was an unwritten rule that care packages were opened, and then set either upon the Ready Room's duty desk or the Officers' Club bar for open consumption. It didn't matter if that box of cookies was now a crushed package of crumbs - thanks to the trip across the pond through the military postal system. They were still a piece of the real world, and they were now to be shared with your brothers.

Care packages came in every size and shape, but they all looked the same. Every one had the same exterior - brown wrapping paper and so much postal tape that it looked like the sender feared the cookies might somehow escape. In the top, upper right hand corner was always such a conglomeration of stamps that the sender just *had* to have pissed off the entire line waiting behind him at the Post Office. In the top, center was always a butchered form of the squadron's military address; thus, it was a wonder that *any* care package ever made it to its intended addressee. Lastly, the sender never failed to write the word "FRAGILE" all over the brown paper - as if that fact warranted special handling. Most deployed aviators were convinced that those words only caused postal workers to shake the package even more, or kick it across the floor.

Once an aviator had clipped and cut and ripped and shredded his way through the brown paper and postal tape, the inside of every care package always looked the same too. Tissue paper lined the inside, and what were originally cookies was now a huge heap of crumbs. Some moms and wives and girlfriends knew the time-tested secret of placing a slice of bread in the box. Somehow, the slice of bread would get hard and stale, but the cookies wouldn't. Go figure. Nobody knew the physics behind that trick, or why it worked - it just did.

1011 Thursday
Officers' Club Tent
"Let's just say that they're in arbitration."

Frap strode down the sidewalk with a load of laundry flung over his right shoulder and a brown cardboard box under his left arm. Being on his way to throw in a load of whites, he intended to swing by the Officers' Club tent and stash a care package in the refrigerator. Frap's recently arrived box of chocolate chip cookies would certainly be the cat's ass later tonight. He planned to store them in the refrigerator and get them good and cold, for that was the *second* best way to eat chocolate chip cookies. Of course, number one was to have them still warm and gooey from the oven. After a couple of hours in the refrigerator, he would break them out tonight for everyone right after the evening sidestep

Frap detoured into the Officers' Club tent, only to see Buick in his seat at the end of the bar. The overweight WSO had a cold beer in one hand and a fly swatter in the other. Frap stopped and checked his watch, asking, "Buick, do you realize it's only ten o'clock in the morning?"

"Yeah," he replied, "but it's five o'clock *somewhere*."

Frap chuckled and continued his way into the club.

"Besides," reasoned Buick, "I'm not flying any more today. I just got back from a post maintenance check flight with Screech that never got airborne. I would say that warrants a cold beer."

"Roger that, Buick."

Frap stopped at the end of the bar, after noticing Buick's latest play toy.

"What are you doing with that fly swatter?" inquired Frap.

"What am I doing with this fly swatter?" returned Buick. "What do you *think* I'm doing with this fly swatter? I'm killing flies."

"Yeah, I guess that *was* a pretty stupid question," admitted Frap.

"So far I've killed three males and two females."

"What?" asked Frap. "How do you know *that*?"

"Three were sitting on that beer can, and two were on the phone."

Frap should've known better than to take Buick's bait.

"Care Package from home?" asked Buick, pointing to the cardboard box stuck under Frap's left arm.

"Yeah," replied Frap. "They're chocolate chip cookies from home. Want one?"

"Sure," said Buick. "That Ho-Ho didn't quite fill me up."

Ho-Hos and beer at ten in the morning? Frap thought. *Yikes.*

Instead of continuing behind the bar to the refrigerator, Frap dropped his bag of laundry, and paraded down the line of stools. H set the box on the bar next to Buick.

"I'm sorry that they're mostly crumbs," apologized Frap.

"No sweat," replied Buick, scooping his free hand down through the box to get a handful. He then dumped the crumbs on the bar in front of Frap, and pulled the entire box over in front of himself.

"Thanks," Buick said.

Frap's jaw hit the bar, and he just stared at Buick.

"I'm joking, man," stated Buick with a smile.

He slid the full box of crumbs back over in front of Frap, and then scraped the smaller pile of crumbs on the bar back to a spot in front of himself.

Frap picked up the box, and backed away from the bar. He returned to the other end, stepped over his laundry bag, and then turned right to the refrigerator. He opened the refrigerator door, and observed the cesspool that Hick Boy was supposed to keep clean. The inside was fully stocked with beer, but it was the odds and ends littered around the cold bottles that caught Frap's attention.

There was a box of cookies that Lisa had sent Tuna three weeks ago. They were crumbs too. However, they were now *hard* crumbs, for Tuna had just stuck them in the refrigerator without telling anybody. That was Tuna's idea of sharing. There was a half-eaten sub that Joisey had placed in there and then forgotten. Now the bun was like a brick, and mold was growing on the cheese. Lastly, Hollywood had bought a bottle of wine to mail to Cindy, but made the mistake of storing it in the refrigerator. Shitscreen and Buick simply left a "Thank You" note in the bottom, and then replaced the cork.

Since Frap wanted his chocolate chip crumbs to remain a secret until after the evening sidestep, he placed his box in the vegetable crisper on the bottom left. The vegetable drawer would be the *last* place that Marine aviators would look in a refrigerator. To be safe, Frap wished there was a drawer labeled "tofu". In any case, hopefully none of the pigs would find his cookies before he offered them up tonight.

While Frap was bent over in the refrigerator with the door open, Buick beckoned him from the end of the bar, asking, "Hey, while you're in there, can you grab me another barley pop?"

"Sure, Buick."

"Thanks, man."

"Carbo-loading for the marathon?" asked Frap, sarcastically.

Frap twisted off the top of another beer, and then walked it to Buick's end of the bar. Frap didn't know much about Buick, but he did know *one* thing for sure. Buick could switch gears faster than anybody when he had a few beers under his belt. One second he could be joking about killing male and female flies, and then the next he could be conversing seriously about the F-18D. So Frap figured that now was as good a time as any to ask.

"Hey, Buick?" began Frap, handing him the beer.

"Yeah, man."

"What can you tell me about the WSO Protection Union."

Buick froze in mid-sip, for Frap's question was certainly out of the blue. He then set the beer down on the bar.

"Who told you about the WSO Protection Union?" Buick cautiously asked.

"Oh, I just heard about it," was Frap's sheepish reply.

"So what do you want to know?"

"Does it exist?"

Buick returned the beer to his mouth for a swig. He was back on his game, boasting, "You're talkin' to the unofficial President."

Wow. The young WSO didn't quite know where to go next.

"So what does the WSO Protection Union do?"

"Simply stated, my young man," continued Buick, "we look out for each other. Older WSOs take the FNG WSOs under their wings and protect them."

"Protect them? From who?"

Buick hesitated for another swig, and then continued, saying, "Pull up a stool."

Frap pulled the one stool with the uneven legs away from the bar, and sat upon its wobbly seat. Safely maintaining the required one-body buffer between himself and Buick, he scooted it forward to place his elbows on the bar.

"This F-18D is a brand new, two-seat jet," instructed Buick. "Consequently, WSOs are trying to carve a tactical niche in a world of single seat F-18 pilots."

"That doesn't make sense," returned Frap. "Aren't we all on the same team?"

"You would think so, young man. You would think so."

"I mean, that sounds so…so…so…what's the word I'm looking for?" struggled Frap. "Territorial?" Jurisdictional?"

"Bingo," continued Buick, taking another sip of his barley pop. "You are mature beyond your years, young man."

Frap momentarily glanced down at the bar, then returned his gaze to Buick, asking, "So is there also a Pilot's Protection Union?"

"You better damn well believe there is," schooled the master. "It's a no-shitter."

"How's the relationship between the two unions?"

There was an awkward moment of silence.

"Let's just say that they're in arbitration," chuckled Buick.

Frap reached over to Buick's pile of cookie crumbs, and stopped short just above the top of the pile, inquiring, "May I?"

"Sure," returned Buick, then burping.

"Thanks."

Frap scooped some crumbs with his right hand, and ate them like a squirrel.

"Frap," said Buick, " a classic example was yesterday's flight with Easy 43."

"Why, what happened?"

"You heard that we got jumped by a Mig-29, right?"

"Yeah, I talked with One Nut about it over dinner."

"Well, Frap," said Buick very seriously, "the President of the Pilot's Protection Union is blaming that whole incident on One Nut."

"Would that be Bama?"

"I'm just saying the President of the Pilot's Protection Union, that's all."

"How could that have been One Nut's fault?" asked Frap, raising his voice. "One Nut gave me the whole scoop - the bad radios, the poor radar coverage – *everything*. I mean, shit happens, man. Shit happens. What do you expect?"'"

"Frap, I agree."

Then Buick looked into Frap's eyes, declaring, "Frap, I'm serious as a heart attack. If our union doesn't rise up right now to protect One Nut, then he will be forever relegated to a second class citizenship in the F-18D community."

"Well, what are you going to do?"

"Don't you worry about it," returned Buick. "I'll find their President and confront him this afternoon."

1105 Thursday
Easy 55 and 56 Airborne, on the Pasta Three Departure
"Well, he never met *you*."

As soon as Easy 55 was airborne, Dago reached up and flipped off his oxygen mask, so that it now dangled loosely from the left side of his helmet. In the front seat, Joisey did the same, more for comfort than anything else. However, in the rear, Dago had ulterior motives. He reached into the left sleeve pocket of his flight suit and pulled out his Marlboros and a Zippo.

"Hey Joisey," Dago said on the ICS. "Don't eject. In a moment, there's going to be smoke in the cockpit."

Joisey was puzzled. Smoke in the cockpit? What was Dago talking about? "Smoke in the cockpit" was an F-18D emergency with immediate action procedures that had to be performed. Moments later, Joisey sniffed the air. Was that cigarette smoke?

"Hey asshole," he said over the ICS. "Are you smoking in the cockpit?"

"So what if I am, stinky?" returned Dago.

"You idiot. What are you trying to do, get us killed?"

Smoking in the cockpit was strictly forbidden by the F-18's big, blue bible. Pure oxygen and fourteen thousand pounds of jet fuel was not a good environment for an open flame. Joisey quickly countered Dago's filthy habit, for the pilot controlled the flow of air in the F-18's cockpit, and it mainly blew from front to rear. He immediately selected the 'full cold' position and cranked the volume up to full blast. Within moments, not only was Dago freezing, but he was also wallowing in a noxious combination of cigarette smoke and Joisey's B.O. Dago quickly inhaled down to the filter, snuffed the butt out on the right console, and flicked it into the map case. He then put his oxygen mask back on, and pouted in the rear seat, realizing that he had lost the battle, but not the war. From the front cockpit, Joisey launched a verbal assault. In Easy 55, it was all-out war.

"Dago, I can't believe that, out of five million sperm, *you* were the winner."

"Oh eat me, Joisey, you stinkin' pervert."

"Dago, did your mom have any kids that lived?"

"Hey, stinky, I'll have you know that I was specially selected for the F-18D."

"Oh, is that right?" asked Joisey.

"Yep, I'm hand-picked," bragged Dago.

"Big deal. So are boogers."

"My, aren't we the comedian today?" returned Dago.

There was no comment from the front seat, as Joisey fumed in disgust.

"Hey you douche bag," baited Dago. "I'm talking to you."

"What do you want?"

"Have you ever heard of Will Rogers?" asked Dago.

"Yeah," said Joisey. "He's the guy who said 'I never met a man I didn't like'."

"Yeah, that's right," returned Dago. "Well he never met *you*."

A cold silence hung over the ICS in Easy 55.

Meanwhile, in a combat spread position on their right, Easy 56 was cruising along fat, dumb, and happy. With Scott Wyland crooning in the background, FOD and Ninja split a pack of Twinkies.

* * *

The Piss test

For time-strapped aviators, the occasional random urinalysis only served to make it now *eleven* pounds of shit in the five pound bag. It was crazy. No aviator would risk losing the orgasm of flying the F-18D by making a date with Mary Jane. As for other narcotics, it was the same deal. Heroin? LSD? Cocaine? No way. They were out of the question.

The momentary high just wasn't worth the risk of losing the Hornet, not to mention the fact that they were illegal.

Yet still, someone, somewhere up the chain of command always insisted on random piss tests.

1113 Thursday
Outside the Tent City Bathroom Building
"What did you do - eat a whole jar of Fred Flintstones?"

Buick was fuming. He strode from the Officers' Club tent and down the sidewalk with the purposeful steps of a man on a mission. Taking long strides, Buick leaned forward - no doubt aided by his gut - and glared straight ahead. He kept telling himself over and over and over and over that a cooler head would have to prevail once he finally found Bama, but for right now, he was livid. He slowed his pace as he passed by the bathroom building, noticing the long line of Marines that snaked from the door. It could only mean one thing - a random urinalysis test.

There sat poor Ham Fist and One Nut at a makeshift table by the bathroom door with hundreds of little, white plastic bottles. As the squadron's newest FNGs, they had been assigned to conduct the urinalysis. Not only was this a shitty little job, but a random urinalysis was also a major red-ass to complete.

"Hey, Ham Fist. Hi there, One Nut," greeted Buick, slowing to a normal pace.

"Hi Buick."

"What's up Buick?"

"I should be asking you that question, One Nut," returned Buick.

"Oh, it's a random urinalysis test," replied One Nut.

"Oh shit," joked Buick. "I didn't study."

"If your social security number ends in an even digit," explained Ham Fist, "then you have to grab a bottle and get in line."

"Damn," said Buick.

"Fork over the ID, Buick," demanded One Nut, holding out his hand.

Buick sighed. Bama would have to wait. Maybe this urinalysis would help him to calm down. It would certainly give him time to think. Buick reached into his flight suit and pulled out his wallet. He fumbled through an old photo of Jenny, a crumpled receipt for some Oreos, and a handy-dandy laminated card designed to determine one's blood alcohol content. He found his military ID and handed it to One Nut.

One Nut accepted Buick's ID, and then hunched over it with a little white plastic bottle in his left hand and a sheet of sticky white labels in his right. He was trying in vain to read the miniscule printing on both. The proper labeling of the bottles, to ensure an accurate and legal test, was the *real* red-ass of the whole affair; consequently, Ham Fist and One Nut had to pay particular attention to detail. Meanwhile, Buick decided to kill the administrative time with some conversation.

"Ham Fist, have you seen Bama?"

"He pissed for us about an hour ago," returned the FNG pilot. "I haven't seen him since, though."

"Ok, thanks."

"No sweat," returned Ham Fist.

"By the way," continued Buick, "Why do you have a WSO like One Nut trying to read those tiny labels?"

"What?" asked Ham Fist.

"A pilot like you with his 20/20 vision ought to be doing that," Buick joked.

By then, One Nut had finally completed the proper labeling of both the plastic bottle and the labels, in addition to the logbook. It was a paperwork nightmare. He returned Buick's ID to him, along with a white plastic bottle.

"Buick, can you verify that the number on the bottle is your social security number?" asked One Nut, abnormally serious, and droning like Dragnet's Joe Friday.

"Yep, that's my social security number."

One Nut handed a green logbook to Buick, droning, "Buick, can you verify that the number I've printed into the book is your social security number?"

"Correct again," stated Buick, returning the logbook back to One Nut.

"Ok, Buick, You're good to go," said One Nut. "Take your bottle and go get in line."

At that moment, Shitscreen walked up to the table, and handed a plastic bottle full of yellow urine to Ham Fist.

"Damn it." yelled Ham Fist, dropping the bottle on the table.

"What's the matter?" asked Shitscreen.

"Shitscreen, if you're going to get piss on the bottle," fumed Ham Fist, "then the *least* you could do is wipe it off before handing it to me."

"Now do you see why *I* do the labeling?" winked One Nut, as Buick chuckled.

Ham Fist grabbed a paper towel from the corner of the table and picked up Shitscreen's bottle. He dried the outside, trying carefully to not smudge the ink of Shitscreen's social security number. Ham Fist also noted for the millionth time today how gross it was to actually hold a warm plastic bottle of another man's urine.

Now Ham Fist was the one who sounded like Joe Friday, droning, "Shitscreen, can you verify that the number on this piece of tape is your social security number?"

"Yep, that's it."

"Fine. Now place this tape securely over the lid of the bottle and ensure that both ends stick to the sides," continued Ham Fist.

Ham Fist handed the bottle to Shitscreen, along with the tape, which he promptly affixed to the top. Accepting the bottle back from Shitscreen, Ham Fist slid the logbook across the table in front of him.

"Please sign your payroll signature next to your social security number to verify that you have put the tape across the lid and that no one else has tampered with your urine sample," droned Ham Fist.

"Roger that."

It was very uncharacteristic to see Ham Fist and One Nut so serious. It probably resulted from their fun meters being pegged in the handling of so many plastic bottles of warm urine.

God, how soon before the next FNGs check in? Ham Fist thought.

Obviously, it couldn't be soon enough.

"Damn, Shitscreen," stated Buick. "Look how yellow your piss is."

"So what of it?"

"Didn't your mom ever tell you that old wives tale," said Buick, "that yellow urine means you're pissing out vitamins?"

"Shitscreen," asked Ham Fist, "what did you do - eat a whole jar of Fred Flintstones?"

Shitscreen turned, and merely walked away to go get a Mountain Dew.

Meanwhile, Buick shuffled his way to the end of the long green snake that started at the door to the bathroom building and stretched down the sidewalk. He couldn't help but think how ludicrous it was for the Marine Corps to conduct a urinalysis on him. Sure, maybe Buick had a drinking problem - he had always joked that his blood type was a full 3.2 - but drugs had never entered his body. They never had, and they never would.

* * *

20/20 doesn't always see the same

Pilots were supposed to have 20/20 vision. After all, that was the major factor in the initial flight physical, which determined whether a young Second Lieutenant went to pilot training or WSO training. However, pilots with the same 20/20 vision could certainly see things differently.

1147 Thursday
Lunch at the Golf Shack
"I'd rather have the eight hundred pounds of gas, than carry a WSO."

Tuna and Bama sat by themselves in a corner booth at the Golf Shack. They already had their drinks, and were trying to discern the lunch orders over the crackle of the cashier on the loudspeaker and the Dave Matthews Band on the jukebox. Three booths down, Screech and Butt Munch already had their lunch. Due to the crowd, each pair of pilots didn't know that the other was there; furthermore, little did the four pilots know that their conversations consisted of differing opinions on the same topic.

"Tuna, just between you and me, man," confided Bama, stirring his iced tea, "how do you like the F-18D?"

"Brother, you know my feelings on that. Why do you ask?"

"The other night in the club," continued Bama, "I got a little liquored up, and started shooting my mouth off to Hick Boy and Screech about the F-18D. Buick promptly came in the club and shit all over me."

"What about?"

"Oh, he kicked Hick Boy and Screech out of the club, and then lectured me with all this bullshit on how a WSO's one mission in life is to keep me alive."

"No shit?"

"Yep. Buick was drunk off his ass, so I took it all with a grain of salt."

"Buick drunk? Well, what did you expect?" asked Tuna.

"Number fifty-six. Chicken salad with tomato and lettuce on wheat."

"Screech," began Butt Munch. "What was all the yelling that was coming from the Officers' Club on Tuesday night?"

"Oh, Bama got all hooted up," replied Screech, "and then started disparaging the F-18D in front of Hick Boy. I tried to play peacemaker and get Bama to the rack, but to no avail. Evidently, the yelling was keeping Buick awake, so he came over."

"Ouch. Do I smell a confrontation?"

"I don't know," returned Screech. "Buick booted both me and Hick Boy out of the club, so I don't know what was said."

"Standing up to a drunken Bama," said Butt Munch, "now *that* takes some balls."

"Or stupidity," replied Screech. "I'm not sure which one it was, because Buick was stone cold sober."

"Well, there's a first time for everything," chuckled Butt Munch.

"Number fifty-seven. Chili cheese dog with French fries."

"Tuna, I never should've accepted those orders to a 'D' squadron," confided Bama. "Man, I was fat, dumb, and happy flying the 'C', when Headquarters tried to slam dunk me with a FAC tour. "

"So what did you do?" asked Tuna.

"I volunteered to switch over to Easy and the 'D', figuring that they needed pilots because it was a brand new squadron with brand new jets."

"Shit," said Tuna, "I got my orders to the F-18D shoved down my throat. Headquarters believes that a Hornet pilot is a Hornet pilot is a Hornet pilot - it doesn't matter whether 'C' or 'D'."

"Oh, I totally disagree with that," countered Bama.

"Yep. I got back from my last cruise on the boat, and wham. The next thing I know, I'm flying a Hornet with some guy jabbering at me from the back seat."

"Well, in a nutshell," said Bama, "I think I'd rather be on a FAC tour."

"Yeah, and I'd rather be on the boat than fly with a WSO."

"Number fifty-eight. Ham salad on wheat."

"I don't know what Bama was all spooled up about," continued Screech. "Personally, I love it that I got orders to an F-18D squadron."

"Yeah, I love the 'D' too," said Butt Munch.

"Man, I remember what it was like to fly the single seat F-18C."

"Oh yeah?"

"I was in the same squadron as Tuna on the boat," explained Screech. "God, I hated it. All you ever did was constantly hawk your fuel so that you had enough gas to get back to the boat and then scare the shit out of yourself trying to catch a wire."

Butt Munch had to laugh. He had been in land-based F-18D squadrons from the very beginning, and had loved every minute.

"And you can have that boat shit at night," added Screech. "Fuck that."

"I hear that," stated Butt Munch.

"Do you believe that shit?" continued Screech. "I went into the Marine Corps because I didn't want to go to sea, and I end up in a Marine F-18C squadron that was chopped to the Navy."

"Classic."

"Anyway," continued Screech, " I got my orders to a 'D' squadron handed to me like a gift from Heaven, because Headquarters believes that a Hornet pilot is a Hornet pilot is a Hornet pilot."

"And I totally agree with that," nodded Butt Munch. "It doesn't matter whether he's in a 'C' or a 'D'."

"So they played musical chairs with a bunch of us pilots," continued Screech, "and I got moved to an F-18D squadron."

"Consider yourself blessed, my friend," added Butt Munch.

"Yeah, I got back from the last cruise, and boom - the next thing I know, I'm flying a two-seat Hornet with some guy helping me from the back seat."

"I love WSOs."

"Flying the F-18D beats the shit out of landing on the back of the boat at night."

"Number fifty-nine. Cheeseburger and fries with slaw."

"The thing that I hate about the F-18D," explained Bama, "is that you just don't feel like you're in a fighter."

"Concur, my man," said Tuna. "The last thing I need is some idiot coaching me from the rear seat."

"Damn straight," agreed Bama. "I don't need a WSO telling me to do *anything*."

"The F-18 was originally designed to be a single-seat fighter, and that's the way it should've stayed," professed Bama.

"Concur again, my man."

"I'd rather have the eight hundred pounds of gas, than carry a WSO."

"Number sixty. Ham and cheese with chips. Extra mayo."

"The thing that I love about the F-18D," explained Butt Munch, "is that you're in a two-seat fighter."

"Oh, big time concur," added Screech. "Have you ever been in a fight, and the WSO gave you a perfectly timed airspeed or altitude call? What a great help."

"I wish I had a nickel for every time that I lost sight of the guy in a fight," stated Butt Munch, "and the WSO talked my eyes back onto him."

"Who needs the eight hundred pounds of gas?" asked Screech.

"Number sixty-one. Vegetarian Pita to go."

"Oooo, that's me. Are you ready to leave?" asked Tuna.

"Number sixty-two. Philly Cheese Steak to go."

"Oh, I am *now*. That one is me," answered Bama.

Tuna and Bama grabbed their drinks and whisked by the counter, plucking two brown paper bags from its greasy top, and leaving their receipts.

"Hey Butt Munch."

"Hey Screech."

"What's shaking, Tuna?"

"How ya hanging, Bama?"

* * *

Panel checks.

Do you want to know what was the worst part about a FAC tour? It wasn't sleeping in the mud and the rain. It wasn't humping those heavy radios or constantly being wet and cold. No, it wasn't even eating the scrambled eggs in those pre-packaged meals. The worst part about a FAC tour was controlling aviators who were your squadron mates just a few short months before.

As soon as the aviators checked in on the frequency, the FAC always recognized their voices. Then, the pain for *each* participant became apparent in the *other's* reactions. The FAC would answer their check-in with a painful wince, wishing that he was still up there, going five hundred miles an hour, and setting his hair on fire. The aircrew would reply with a painful wince, thinking, "Oooo, you poor bastard. Better him than me."

Consequently, the F-18 jet jocks would try to lift the spirits of their former comrade with a "panel check". With tongue placed firmly in cheek, the F-18D aircrew would ask the FAC if they could fly low and fast over his position. That way, he could visually check the bottom of the jet and ensure that no panels were loose or missing. Upon getting the FAC's approval, then the F-18Ds would scream over top of the FAC at close to five hundred knots before going back home. The grunts loved it. The aircrew loved it. The FAC loved it. The safety Nazis lost sleep over it. Besides motivating the hell out of the infantry Marines, a panel check served to put a smile on the FAC's face. He would sarcastically reply, "All of your panels look fine."

1212 Thursday
Mission Complete with Aerial Refueling
Easy 55 and 56, Inbound for a CAS Mission
Under FAC Control
"…we've got some potential trouble down here."

"Pierre 33, Easy 55," began Joisey.

"Easy 55, Pierre 33, go ahead."

Oh this is just great, thought Joisey. *As if having Dago in my back seat isn't bad enough, and two young rock-n-rollers in the other jet, I have to suffer having the French AWACS too.*

"Pierre 33, Easy 55, flight of two Hornets, two one miles south of Point Charlie. Complete with Texaco," said Joisey.

"Easy 55, Pierre 33, looking."

During the silence while Pierre searched his radar's scope, Joisey glanced into the rear view mirror to check on Dago. The Brooklynite was flipping him the bird.

"Easy 55, Pierre 33 has you radar contact, one eight miles south of Point Charlie. Proceed inbound."

"Pierre 33, Easy 55, wilco, continued Joisey. "We're supposed to work with Gunner 14 on Indigo."

"Easy 55, Pierre 33 copies all. Cleared to switch Indigo at Charlie."

Joisey keyed the ICS as their F-18D droned inbound to the entry point, saying, "Hey, penis face, would it be too much trouble for me to ensure that you've done all your combat checklists?"

"Don't you worry, ass wipe," returned Dago. "You just do your pilot shit."

Joisey decided to not pursue the issue any further.

"Pierre 33, Easy 55," stated Joisey.

"Easy 55, Pierre 33, go ahead."

"Pierre 33, Easy 55 flight is presently at Charlie, request switch Indigo."

"Easy 55, Pierre, cleared to switch Indigo."

"Pierre 33, Easy 55, switching Indigo."

Joisey waited an obligatory five seconds, hoping that his surfer dude wingmen had followed, and then keyed the number one radio.

"Gunner 14, Easy 55."

"Two," interjected FOD, to let Joisey know that he was up on the same frequency.

But there was no reply from Gunner 14.

"Gunner 14, Easy 55," stated Joisey once again.

"Easy 55, Gunner 14," finally came the reply, sounding more stressed than usual.

"Gunner 14, Easy 55, is a flight of two Hornets for your control."

"Easy 55, this is Yeti," returned the former Easy Pilot, still sounding a little tense, but glad to hear the voices of his former squadron mates. "Is that *you*, Joisey?"

"Yep, Yeti, it's me. But standby one."

"Gunner 14, standing by."

"Dago, work your magic," said Joisey on the ICS.

"Will do."

Dago quickly grabbed his nav bag from the left console and rifled through its contents for a certain classified card.

"Gunner 14, Easy 55," said Dago, "request you validate Phoenix Cleveland."

Yeti instantly responded, stating, "I validate Phoenix Cleveland as Miami."

"Bingo," said Dago on the ICS. "Miami is correct."

"Give him the failsafe to be sure," instructed Joisey.

"Will do."

"Gunner 14, Easy 55," said Dago on the number one radio, "what's the *worst* part about deployments to Twenty-nine Palms, California?"

"Easy 55, Gunner 14, that's *easy*. It's sitting on those tightly spaced shitters with no dividers, and feeling the hairy thighs of the guy next to you touching your own legs."

Yep. This Gunner 14 was the real Yeti.

It seemed like just yesterday. Way back when, it was Joisey who had taken Yeti under his wing and taught him how to bomb at Twenty-nine Palms. After that, Yeti was crewed up with Dago for a fantastic air-to-air deployment to Nellis Air Force Base. Yeah, those were the days. Now Yeti was in-country with the infantry, sleeping in a poncho liner, and eating cold, prepackaged ham loaf.

"So Yeti, how are you doin', man?" asked Joisey.

"Great. Who else do I have up there?"

"Easy 55 is Joisey and Dago. Easy 56 is FOD and Ninja."

"Shit hot, Joisey," returned Yeti, a little more relieved. "I can't believe that they put you and Dago in the same jet."

"It's a long story, Yeti," sighed Joisey.

"Roger that. So long time no see. How are you guys doing?"

"Good, Yeti," returned Joisey. "How can we be of service today?"

"Listen, fellows, we've got some potential trouble down here. We won't be doing any panel checks today."

Yeti's tone was now serious - serious as a heart attack.

1215 Thursday
Tent City Bathroom Building
"Damn it. You're as bad as Shitscreen."

Finally, thought Buick, reaching the front of the urinalysis line.

His prediction was correct. The wait had calmed him down a little. However, *now* he was pissed off at the whole urinalysis process.

Whenever a urinalysis was conducted, it was a total violation of urinal etiquette. Packed like sardines, shoulder-to-shoulder, at the two urinals, each Marine concentrated on filling his little white plastic bottle while a proctor stood behind him with arms folded across his chest. The proctor's mission in life was to ensure that each Marine filled his *own* bottle with his *own* urine. If it looked like Ham Fist and One Nut had pissed off expressions over the handling of warm, wet bottles of urine, then imagine the look on each of the *proctor's* faces.

The entire bathroom stunk. The floor beneath the two operable urinals was wet and slippery with the urine of attempts to fill a bottle that had missed. Next to the sink was the "penalty box", where Marines were sent who had been unable to fill their bottle. The proctor forced the humiliated Devil Dog to drink water from the sink's faucet, and then stand there and wait for Mother Nature to work. It certainly didn't help matters that the urinal on the left side was *still* broken. It was now fully clogged with cigarette butts and brown paper towels in murky, brownish-yellow water.

Buick, with his little white bottle in hand, waited for the next available urinal.

"Next," yelled one of the proctors.

Buick promptly stepped up to the center urinal, with the bottle in his left hand, while unzipping his flight suit with his right. He then removed the cap from the top of the bottle, and set it atop the dirty porcelain. Buick slowly began the task at hand. He rapidly filled his bottle, thanks to the beers he had downed earlier while talking to Frap. Buick momentarily closed his body's internal piss valves to stop the flow, removed the bottle from within the urinal, and then let fly with a stream of urine that sounded like someone had turned on a hose.

"Aaaaaaaahhhh," sighed Buick in relief.

Buick retreated from the urinal after placing the cap on the bottle and zipping up his flight suit. Then he momentarily stepped into the penalty box, and ran warm water over his plastic bottle. Buick stuffed a paper towel into his flight suit's pocket, and proceeded towards the door. He exited the bathroom building, and walked over to the makeshift table, noting that the line down the sidewalk was now even longer than before. He handed the warm, wet bottle to Ham Fist.

"Aaaauuugghh." screamed Ham Fist, dropping the bottle on the table. "Damn it, Buick. You're as bad as Shitscreen."

Buick busted up laughing, and then stated, "Relax, man. It's only warm water."

Buick snatched up the rolling bottle of urine before it got to the edge of the table, and retrieved the paper towel from his pocket. He thoroughly dried the bottle, and then held it, awaiting instructions.

"Ok, ok. That makes Buick - one, Ham Fist - zero," conceded a smiling Ham Fist, handing the correct sticky label to Buick.

Then the Joe Friday monotone returned, droning, "Buick, verify that the number on this tape is your social security number."

"Yes Sirree, that's my social."

"Good. Please place this tape securely over the cap of the bottle and ensure that both ends stick to the sides."

Buick followed the instructions to the letter and handed the bottle back to Ham Fist. Upon taking the warm bottle, Ham Fist slid the green logbook across the table.

"Buick, please sign your payroll signature next to your social security number to verify that you have put the tape across the lid and that no one else has tampered with your urine sample," droned Ham Fist.

"Roger that."

Buick and Ham Fist shook hands, and then Easy's overweight WSO continued on his trek to find Bama.

* * *

By God, bayonets on the wing tips

For all its quirks and hardships, the most important detail about a FAC tour was that the system worked. The arrangement was a success because of a very unique training syllabus that the Marine Corps employed.

First of all, the Marine Corps was the *only* military service that sent its brand new, Second Lieutenant, potential aviators to the same, initial, six month school as the infantry Officers. Thus, before ever setting foot in a cockpit, the aviators did what the grunts did, ate what the grunts ate, and slept where the grunts slept.

Secondly, the Marine Corps was the *only* military service that later pulled those very same aviators out of the cockpit as Captains, and made them FACs with those very same infantry Officers. There was a bonding between aviation and infantry, albeit a forced one.

Thus, Marine aviators would go through the very gates of Hell to support an infantry Officer and his boys on the ground. If close air support meant taping bayonets onto the wing tips, then by God, Marine F-18 aviators would do it.

1217 Thursday
Easy 55 and 56, In-country Close Air Support Mission, Under Yeti Control
"I miss you guys."

"Yeti, Joisey"

"Joisey, Yeti, go ahead."

"Can you paint us a picture?"

"Yeah, sure 55. Reconnaissance elements are 'eyes on' to three Russian T-62 tanks that have moved forward to hill eight seven zero. Nobody has fired a shot yet, but the Battalion Commander views it as aggressive posturing with potential hostile intent. We just need you to locate the tanks' position in case the shit hits the fan. Have your bombs ready to go."

"Yeti, Easy 55, copy all. Interrogative?"

"Easy 55, Yeti, go ahead with your question."

"Can you see if the tank drivers are wearing black skull caps?" stated Joisey.

There was an awkward moment of silence on the radio, and Easy 55 and 56 could see giant question marks above the FAC's position.

"Say again?" requested Yeti.

"Yeti, never mind," said Joisey, realizing the stupidity.

"So then, are you ready to take down a modified brief?" asked the FAC.

"Yeti, Easy 55, sure, go ahead."

Yeti proceeded to give an abbreviated version of the standard target brief that was normally given to close air support aircraft. He still appeared to be a bit harried and concerned, despite Easy 55 and 56 being on station.

"At grid 976347, elevation eight seven zero feet, three T-62 tanks. Friendly troops two thousand meters southeast."

Dago and Ninja, the WSOs, were already entering the target grid and elevation into their aircraft systems, and designating them as targets. Likewise, they plotted the grid's location on a 1:50,000 map of the area. In the front seat of Easy 55, Joisey double-checked the position of his armament switch as 'safe', and also brought up the ordnance page on the left display to run through each of his bombing programs. FOD did the same in the front seat of Easy 56, in addition to turning down the volume of his tape player.

"Proceed inbound and establish an orbit overhead the FAC's position, grid 953364," Yeti continued. "Stay at a safe altitude. The threat is possible man-portable, surface-to-air missiles in the area. Weather is good."

"Yeti, Easy 55, copy all."

"Easy 55, Are you laser capable?" inquired Yeti.

"Yeti, Easy 55 is laser capable," answered Joisey, knowing that every Easy aircraft that was assigned to do CAS carried a laser pod for designating targets.

"Roger," returned Yeti, breathing a little easier. "I'm unable to mark any targets because my laser is busted."

Easy 55 and 56 continued inbound, with both pilots unconsciously goosing the throttles a little forward. SPEED IS LIFE, MORE IS BETTER.

Yeti returned to Indigo once more to brief his plan, stating, "Once established overhead, I'm going to talk your eyes onto the tank's position. If shit hits the fan, I will pass control to Easy 55, who will laser-mark the targets for Easy 56 to drop his bombs."

"Break. Easy 55, this is Pierre 22. How copy?" suddenly interrupted AWACS.

"Pierre 22, this is Easy 55," replied Joisey, "We've got you loud and clear."

"Roger, 55. Be advised that Pierre 22 is monitoring Indigo with you, and will pass you the clearance to drop from the CAOC. How copy?"

"Yeti, Easy 55, copy all."

This sounded serious. Over Ninja's objections, FOD turned his tape player completely off.

Finally, the F-18Ds established a left-hand orbit over the FAC's position, and gazed down at the countryside below. Easy 55 would be focused on trying to digest the FAC's talk-on. Easy 56 would fly in a position that was higher and on the right, allowing FOD and Ninja to look down through their lead to the target area below. Easy 56's job was to alert 55 to any white, smoke trails that suddenly corkscrewed up from the countryside below. Such a warning would allow Easy 55 to execute defensive maneuvers. From their altitude sanctuary, the countryside looked like a patched quilt of green mountains and hills. It would be next to impossible to find three tanks with the naked eye.

"Yeti, Easy 55 is established overhead, ready for the talk-on," said Joisey.

"Roger," returned Yeti. "I hear you but I can't see you. Do you see the bridge over the river?"

"Copy cat," answered Joisey, meaning that he saw the bridge.

Meanwhile, Dago's head was buried in the cockpit on the infrared display. Manipulating its field of view, contrast, and background, he was attempting to see the same picture on the infrared display as Joisey was seeing with his eyes. Dago easily found the bridge, as its warm metallic construction made a great contrasting picture over the river's cool water.

"Roger," continued Yeti. "Do you see the obvious factory to the north of the bridge with two giant smokestacks?"

After a moment's hesitation in scouring the countryside for the factory, Joisey answered, "Copy cat."

In the rear seat, working the infrared display, Dago quickly found that the factory's warmer smokestacks easily stood out against the cooler green vegetation. Finding the factory was a piece of cake.

"The distance from the bridge to the factory is your 'unit of measure'," instructed Yeti. "How copy?"

"Yeti, Easy 55, copy, unit of measure is bridge to factory," said Joisey.

Meanwhile, Dago expanded the infrared display's field of view in an attempt to obtain the longer distance.

Bridge to factory, bridge to factory, bridge to factory, thought Dago, making a mental note. *Got it. Damn, that Yeti was good.*

"Easy 55, do you see the road that comes off the north side of the same bridge?"

"Copy cat," returned Joisey.

"Roger," continued Yeti. "That is Highway 55, the Grobnev Highway."

"Got it," said Joisey.

"Then look three units of measure north on that road until you get to an obvious 'x' intersection," instructed Yeti. "Report copy cat on the 'x'."

Joisey's eyes followed the road off the north side of the bridge, and looked north a distance that he perceived to be three units of measure. There the 'x' intersection was, barely visible. That Yeti was a damn good FAC.

"Copy cat," returned Joisey.

Dago narrowed the infrared field of view, and walked the display's symbology north on the road with his left hand-controller until the hotter pavement of the 'x' showed nicely amongst the cooler trees.

"Easy 55," continued Yeti, "move one fourth unit of measure northwest from the intersection, and there's your tanks on hill 870."

"Yeti, Easy 55, looking."

It was just as Joisey and Dago had suspected. From their altitude, as soon as Joisey moved his eyes from the obvious man-made objects into the vegetated hillsides, it was impossible to break out any tanks. However, the infrared display turned out to be a Godsend. Dago had moved the symbology approximately one fourth unit of measure to the northwest, and bingo. The hot engines of the T-62 tanks showed up as three little white dots on a cool, grassy black clearing.

"Got 'em," stated Dago on the ICS.

"Shit hot," replied Joisey. "Nice job."

Immediately, Joisey took charge of the situation, declaring, "Yeti, Easy 55, standby for five minutes and we'll be right back."

"Easy 55, Yeti, standing by."

Yeti's prior F-18D experience told him to simply shut up and stay off the radios while Easy 55 was attempting to solve their current dilemma.

"FOD, Joisey, on the number two radio."

"Joisey, FOD, go ahead."

"We've got the tanks with an infrared designation. I'm going to roll in from this altitude and take a look through the HUD so I can get an exact visual location."

"Joisey, FOD copies. I'm at your high right three."

Joisey may not have been a disciplined bather, but by God, Joisey was a very disciplined bomber. He always flew a good pattern at the correct altitude and the precise airspeed. From his left turn, Joisey hit the numbers for his turn-in point, closely followed by the numbers for his roll-in point. There, he rolled the jet inverted, and pulled Dago's symbology into the HUD's field of view. He rolled wings level, and bunted the stick slightly forward. In the dive, he could just barely make out three specks on a knoll - but that was all he needed. Joisey immediately commenced a four g pull to a climb, confident that he now had the exact location of the tanks.

Suddenly, FOD's voice pierced the silence from overhead, yelling, "JOISEY, BREAK RIGHT. SMOKE IN THE AIR, RIGHT FOUR LOW."

Joisey broke his F-18D hard right in a defensive turn as Dago ejected the defensive expendables. Sure as shit, at their low right four o'clock, a white corkscrew of smoke was ascending into the sky and attempting to pull lead on their jet. Easy 55 continued his defensive break turn, and then noted the corkscrew fall off to a lagging position on the canopy. The missile had been unable to hack their maneuver. It missed their F-18D and tumbled harmlessly into the greenery below. Joisey selected afterburner and commenced a climb back to a higher altitude. SPEED IS LIFE, MORE IS BETTER.

"FOD, Joisey on the number two."

"Joisey, FOD, go."

"Thanks, man. I owe you one. Let's climb back up and establish the same orbit."

"Easy 56, wilco."

Joisey decided to quickly brief Yeti on what had just occurred, stating, "Yeti, Easy."

"Easy 55, Yeti has you loud and clear, go ahead."

"Yeti, Easy 55 is tally the three tanks. Nice talk-on. Be advised, defensive maneuvers were taken to evade a SAM. We're going back to Pierre, and then return."

"Easy 55, Yeti copies."

Again, Yeti knew to shut up and let Joisey work his magic on the radios.

"Pierre, Easy 55."

"Easy 55, Pierre has you loud and clear, go ahead."

"Pierre, Easy 55, two Hornets working under Gunner 14 control. Be advised, three tanks have moved to within two thousand meters of 14's position. Furthermore, Easy 55 was forced to perform defensive maneuvers against a SAM. State instructions."

"Easy 55, Pierre, copy all, standby."

Ah yes, the infamous 'standby'. Easy flight had heard it all before. The AWACS was now talking to the CAOC, and attempting to obtain Easy 55's next move. Seconds turned into minutes. Minutes turned into wasted gas.

"Pierre, Easy 55," pimped Joisey.

"Easy 55, Pierre, standby."

More seconds turned into minutes. More minutes turned into wasted gas.

While waiting for the CAOC's instructions, Dago decided to return to the infrared display and confirm the position of the three T-62s. He couldn't believe what he saw. The middle tank of the three suddenly produced a wispy, white puff of smoke from its main battle gun.

Immediately, Yeti's panicked voice pierced Indigo, yelling, "Joisey, they're shootin' at us."

Joisey yanked Easy 55 around the sky towards the tank's position, and selected afterburner. Simultaneously, Dago witnessed two more white puffs of smoke from the other two tanks. In Easy 56, FOD and Ninja maintained the same position of high cover.

"Easy 55, Pierre," said the AWACS.

Joisey jumped on the radio, anticipating their instructions, "Pierre, Easy 55, go."

"The CAOC passes, you are cleared to drop."

It was sweet music to Joisey's ears, not to mention Yeti's. The clearance could not have come a second sooner. Joisey's maintenance of a disciplined bombing pattern had placed him at a perfect roll-in point.

"Easy 55 is in, from the south," said Joisey.

With precise parameters, he rolled his F-18D inverted and pulled the bombing symbology into the HUD. Joisey rolled wings level, and the F-18D's systems indicated a good laser designation.

"You're cleared to drop," exclaimed Yeti.

Joisey mashed down on the pickle button, sending a two thousand pound, laser-guided bomb plummeting towards the earth.

"Easy 55 is off, switches safe. One away," declared Joisey in the same rigid, disciplined communications that had been pounded into his head years ago. He then commenced a smooth four g climb to the safe haven provided by his previous altitude.

Meanwhile, Dago scoured the green patchwork for any more white corkscrews, and then returned his head back inside the cockpit to the infrared display. Seconds later, the middle T-62 was obliterated in a gray explosion. Better yet, hot shrapnel and metal fragments from the middle T-62 pierced the second tank that was positioned to the north.

"You shacked it, Joisey," exclaimed Dago over the ICS.

"Direct hit," confirmed Yeti.

Then the second tank also exploded from the shrapnel and metal.

"Secondary explosions observed," stated an ecstatic Yeti.

Joisey climbed back to his previous altitude, and got on his numbers again.

"Six is clear," stated the vigilant FOD from overhead.

Easy 55 continued around the circle, at the precise altitude and airspeed, until reaching his roll-in point again. It was like shooting fish in a barrel.

"Easy 55 is in again from the south," said Joisey.

With the same defined parameters, he rolled his F-18D inverted and again pulled the bombing symbology into the HUD. Again, the F-18Ds laser designation system worked flawlessly.

"Youy're cleared to drop," declared Yeti.

Joisey pressed the pickle button again, sending another two thousand pound, laser-guided bomb towards the third and final T-62.

"Easy 55 is off, switches safe. One away," said Joisey over Indigo, commencing the same four g climb to his altitude sanctuary. "Easy 56, say your position."

"We're at your high, right three," returned FOD. "Six is clear."

"Visual."

In a left turn, over the smoking hulks of three T-62 tanks and one empty missile launcher, Bitchin' Betty suddenly spoke for the first time today.

"Bingo, bingo," she blandly stated.

Easy 55 had reached bingo fuel - it was time to return home.

"Yeti, Easy 55."

"Easy 55, Yeti, go."

"Yeti, Easy 55 is bingo fuel. We're out of here. Thanks for the work, Yeti."

"Easy 55, Yeti copies all. No, thank *you*. Nice job."

"Yeti, I hope you understand that this ain't no Twenty-nine Palms. We can't do a panel check."

"Roger that, Easy 55," returned Yeti, laughing. "Joisey, I'll be back to the squadron in no time to kick your ass in the bombing derby."

"Oh, yeah," returned Joisey. "In your dreams."

"Joisey, Dago, FOD, Ninja, you all take care and fly safe. I miss you guys."

"Roger that, Yeti. See ya."

Easy 55 and 56 flew silently out of the country, until turning to go over the water at Point Charlie. There, Dago keyed the ICS, saying, "Hey dickhead. Nice job today with that stick and rudder shit."

"Good work finding those tanks on the Infrared display, you ass wipe."

1223 Thursday
The Ready Room
"You asshole."
"You fucker."
"You bastard."

Buick arrived at the Ready Room door, grabbed the knob, and froze. He didn't want to appear offensive or combative, so he inhaled once, and relaxed. Then he opened the door and entered.

Jock was on the duty desk, simultaneously sipping coffee and talking on the radio. Hick Boy was back at the coffee mess table, dropping coins into the can for a cup of Joe and a candy bar. Next to him, Ping was pilfering something from the refrigerator. Beneath SPEED IS LIFE, MORE IS BETTER., Hollywood and Booger were drawing blue and red arrows that depicted some past merge of F-18s and F-16s. Booger seemed disinterested, like his mind was elsewhere. His piece of rope was draped over his thigh.

However, there was no sign of Bama. Buick didn't want to appear as if he was intentionally looking for him. Likewise, he didn't want to seem confrontational, so he asked a dummy question.

"Jock, how is the weather looking for this afternoon's flights?"

"Great," snapped Jock. "It's clear and free of clouds. Winds are out of the Southeast, and the altimeter is steady at 30.10."

"Thanks," replied Buick, who then nonchalantly directed his question to the general crowd, asking, "By the way, has anybody seen Bama?"

Under Booger's empty stare, Hollywood momentarily interrupted his right hand from shooting down the Rolex on his left wrist, saying, "He's over at the Golf Shack, eating lunch with Tuna."

"Thanks, Hollywood."

Buick exited the Ready Room, shutting the door behind him. He stopped and momentarily thought on the sidewalk.

Oh great, contemplated Buick. *Right now, Bama is eating lunch with the only other single-seat ego as big as his own. I can't approach him now.*

To his distant left, Ham Fist and One Nut were cutting across the corn flakes rocks, each carrying a cardboard box containing numerous bottles of piss. Buick politely waved, and pondered his next move with Bama.

Just then, Tuna and Bama rounded the corner at the end of the sidewalk, coming from the Golf Shack. Like Hollywood and Booger, they were engaged in a conversation that involved one hand shooting down the other, despite a brown bag lunch in one hand. With the distance between them and Buick at twenty yards and rapidly shrinking, Buick mentally scrambled for a verbal entry.

To say 'Bama, can I talk to you alone?' would only put him on the defensive, thought Buick, *and would trigger Tuna that something was amiss.*

The distance was ten yards and decreasing.

To say 'Bama, we need to talk' would only accomplish the same thing, thought Buick. *Think, man, think.*

It was too late.

"Howdy, Buick," stated Tuna.

"What's shaking down, Buick?" asked Bama.

"Hey you guys," returned Buick. "How was the Golf Shack? Crowded?"

"Nah. Not bad," shrugged Tuna.

"Had a good conversation, though," replied Bama, winking at Tuna.

Tuna chuckled.

"So Buick, how's the union?" asked Bama, rather coldly.

"Fine. And yours?"

"Good," nodded a very terse Bama. "About to get better."

Unexpectedly, a trio of WSOs rounded the corner, coming from Maintenance Control. Pope, Spine Ripper, and Shitscreen were on their way to the midday sidestep.

Then Bama unknowingly gave Buick the entry opportunity that he desired, albeit an awkward one.

"Tuna, I'll catch you later," said Bama. "I need to talk to Buick alone."

So much for avoiding the offensive and triggering Tuna, thought Buick.

Then Bama made the opening remark between the two icons. He was still none the wiser that Buick had intended to corner him about One Nut and yesterday's Mig-29 ambush.

"Buick, now that the General is gone, can I get Easy Eddie's hat back from you?"

"Uh. Yeah, sure," replied Buick.

Inside, Buick was taken aback, for Bama's simple request only revealed that Bama and he were on totally different wavelengths. So what else was new?

"Thanks," added Bama, turning away to follow Tuna into the Ready Room.

"Bama?" blurted Buick, not wanting to let him slip away.

"Yeah?" replied Bama.

Out of the blue, Hick Boy and Ping exited the Ready Room. They squeezed by the trio of pilots who partially blocked the door, with Hick Boy on his way to a dental appointment, and Ping going to the gym. Lastly, N.D. departed the Ready Room, silently hunched over his cleaning cart.

"Remember our flight yesterday?" asked Buick.

"Sure," returned Bama. "What about it?"

Screech and Butt Munch rounded the corner, coming from the Golf Shack.

"Well," declared Buick, hardly the master of tact, "you can't blame One Nut for yesterday's incident."

"The hell, I can't," returned Bama, raising his voice. "It's the WSO's job to check six, and he failed miserably."

"Bama, there were extenuating circumstances."

"You sound like a fuckin' lawyer."

"No," countered Buick, "I sound like someone who understands tactical aviation."

Jock stuck his head out of the Ready Room, having abandoned his post at the duty desk to investigate the raised voices. Meanwhile, Ham Fist and One Nut entered the opposite end of the sidewalk with their boxes of piss, and the trio of WSOs from Maintenance Control arrived at the threesome of pilots.

"If we were really at war," ranted Bama, ignoring Buick, "then I could've been killed yesterday."

"You? Well, what about One Nut?" questioned Buick. "What about *his* life?"

"He'd *deserve* to die for failing in his job."

The six aviators clogging the Ready Room doorway suddenly ceased their conversations, noting the escalation between Bama and Buick. Hick Boy and Ping both halted on the sidewalk, and looked back over their shoulders. N.D. ignorantly shuffled down the sidewalk, approaching the two behemoths.

"Did you properly task him in the crew coordination brief?" continued Buick. "Or did you just tell him to get in the backseat and shut up?"

"I hate flying with WSOs," returned Bama, "let alone some FNG."

"Bama, at one time, we were *all* FNGs."

Screech and Butt Munch arrived at N.D., and stepped around him, noting the face off between Bama and Buick.

"I'm going to see to it," Bama raved, "that our young, worthless WSO never straps into an F-18D again."

Ham Fist and One Nut froze on the sidewalk, having heard Bama's declaration.

"And I don't care if you think you *are* so shit hot," countered Buick, "I'm going to see to it that One Nut is *assigned* to your back seat."

Bama inflated his chest and stepped closer to Buick, clenching a fist. He poked that same old broken finger into Buick's sternum, stating, "I've had it, you fat, drunken piece of FOD."

Bama cocked back his right arm to unleash a punch, but Screech saved the day. He physically grabbed Bama's massive arm, and Bama's attempted follow through swung Screech around like a gate. Simultaneously, Butt Munch aggressively pushed Buick out of harm's way.

The six aviators at the doorway couldn't believe their eyes. Tuna ran and tackled Buick, taking Butt Munch down with him. Hollywood jumped on Bama's back, and Pope attempted to bearhug the former offensive tackle. Shitscreen leaped upon the Buick pile like a referee at a hockey fight, while Spine Ripper secured Bama from the opposite side of Pope. Ham Fist and One Nut dropped the boxes of piss and joined the scuffle, with One Nut sitting on Buick's legs and Ham Fist helping Screech subdue Buick's right arm. Hick Boy and Ping sprinted down the sidewalk, and Hick Boy jumped on top of Shitscreen while Ping grabbed Bama's left arm. Booger merely watched as Jock bolted from the Ready Room doorway to help push Bama away.

The ensuing melee wasn't a clash between the two unions, with the pilots versus the WSOs. Nor was it a dispute between the old guys and the FNGs. Instead, it involved every available aviator - save for an indifferent Booger - attempting to establish peace.

Bama momentarily quivered under the weight. With Hollywood on his back, being in a sandwich between Pope and Spine Ripper, having Screech and Ham Fist hanging on his right arm, Ping on his left, and with Jock pushing from the front, he only *slightly* faltered.

Then the entire mass of bodies fell backwards, knocking over N.D. and his cleaning cart. A false bottom fell from the underside of N.D.'s cart, revealing a copy of this morning's ROE update. There was a copy of tomorrow's flight schedule. There was a copy of tomorrow's ordnance. There was a copy of tomorrow's callsigns and frequencies for AWACS. There was a copy of tomorrow's data for the FACs. Buick's worst nightmare was true.

The two unions combined as one. Immediately, fifteen Easy aviators, including Bama and Buick, piled onto the hapless N.D.

"You asshole."

"You fucker."

"You bastard."

Meanwhile, Booger silently shuffled down the sidewalk towards Tent City.

The collective unions would've pummeled the mole to death, if not for one thing. Suddenly, the Commanding Officer stepped out of his office. Like a good Skipper, he immediately took charge, demanding, "What the fuck is going on here?"

Fifteen heads turned and froze.

"Bama. Buick. *All* of you, get *off* of that man."

"Sir, you don't understand," pleaded Bama, arising from the pile.

"N.D. has been funneling shit to the enemy," explained Buick.

The Skipper silently looked into thirty eyes. He trusted his boys from
    Easy.

"Pope, take charge of this goat rope and call the MPs," commanded the Skipper. "Bama. Buick. I want to see the two of you in my office *now*."

1241 Thursday
The Skipper's Office
"I swear I don't know how *that* one slipped by me."

Bama and Buick were locked at Attention in front of the Commanding Officer's desk, still panting from the fracas. The Skipper was on the edge of his chair, and wagging a very stern finger at his two loyal subordinates.

"You two better listen to what I have to say, and listen good."

"Sir, yes, Sir."

"I will not - repeat *not* - tolerate fighting amongst my Officers."

"Sir, yes, Sir."

"Such a lack of discipline is a cancer, and it will destroy a squadron in a New York minute."

"Sir, yes, Sir."

"I don't even know how it happened, and I don't *want* to know."

"Sir, yes, Sir."

"All I heard was one voice call the other a piece of FOD, and the next thing I know, I look out my window to see a total melee amongst my commissioned Officers."

"Sir, yes, Sir."

"Worse yet, the fight was between the *two* Officers in the squadron that are most respected and revered by my youngsters."

"But, Sir," injected Bama.

"No *buts*, Bama. If this happens again, I'll have your request for orders to Top Gun revoked so fast your head will spin."

"Sir, yes, Sir."

"As for *you*, Buick."

"Yes, Sir?"

"I've tolerated your little secret for waaaaaaay too long. If this happens again, I'll send your ass back to the states for alcohol detox in a heartbeat."

"Sir, yes, Sir."

"Do you both understand?"

"Sir, yes, Sir."

"Am I clear on this?"

"Sir, yes, Sir."

"Very well, then. What's done is done."

The Commanding Officer sat back in his chair, and clasped his hands across his stomach. He exhaled and then briefly paused, before stating, "Now, concerning the issue with N.D."

"Sir?" asked Buick.

"Buick, *I'm* still doing the talking."

"Sir, yes, Sir."

"Concerning N.D., in the time it took me to go from my window to the door, the scuffle had evolved from two piles centered on Bama and Buick to one pile atop N.D. Again, I'm not sure what happened."

"Sir, yes, Sir."

"But I believe what you told me. I trust you. There *has* to be that two-way trust between a Commanding Officer and his subordinates. Agree?"

"Sir, yes, Sir."

"Ok then."

The Skipper paused.

"Gentlemen, there's been an obvious breach of security in the squadron."

"Sir, yes, Sir."

"That *also* reeks of a potential cancer, so I'm going to nip it in the bud."

"Sir, yes, Sir."

"Bama, you're the hard-charging bull in this squadron, so this is *your* baby now. By tomorrow morning, have a detailed plan on my desk that beefs up the squadron's security procedures."

"Sir, yes, Sir."

"Buick, you're the go-to-guy in this squadron, so you're not off the hook either. By tomorrow morning, have a thorough damage assessment on my desk."

"Sir, yes, Sir."

"You two will - repeat *will* - work closely together on these projects."

"Sir, yes, Sir."

"Do you both understand?"

"Sir, yes, Sir."

"Am I clear on *this* issue?"

"Sir, yes, Sir."

"Very well again."

"Sir, yes, Sir."

"Lastly, relax, and hear me out on a third item."

"What's up, Sir?" asked Bama and Buick simultaneously, as they relaxed their positions of Attention.

"Before all hell broke loose out there on the sidewalk, I was talking with the Intelligence Officer," stated the Skipper. "Things are heating up near Grobnev."

"Yes, Sir."

"Shortly thereafter, I was called by the Commanding General of the Allied Tactical Air Force," continued the C.O. "Easy 55 was cleared to drop only minutes ago."

"Who's in Easy 55, Sir?" asked Bama.

"Easy 55 is Joisey and Dago," replied the Commanding Officer, "and I swear I don't know how *that* one slipped by me."

"Yes, Sir."

"That's *good*, Sir," added Buick, giving a thumbs up. "Joisey is one of the squadron's most shit hot bombers."

"Yeah, Buick, I'm sure that he totally kicked ass, but I'm still waiting to hear."

"Yes, Sir."

"If shit hits the fan, do we have anybody in-country right now?" asked the C.O.

"Sir, Easy 31 and 32 just got airborne a minute ago," injected Bama, the expert on hardware and numbers and widgets, still striving to outdo Buick.

"And who is that?"

"Sir, I don't know," returned Bama.

"Sir, Easy 31 is Chunks and Fig. Easy 32 is Ghost and Frap," returned Buick, the consummate software and people person.

"Good," stated the Skipper, nodding his approval.

"So Sir, what do you need us to do?" implored Bama.

"Make sure that *all* the Officers are advised of the escalation in-country," instructed the Commanding Officer, "and pass the word that I want to see *all* Officers in the Ready Room at 1600."

"Yes, Sir," replied the two former presidents of unions that were now dissolved.

"Right now, I have to return a call to the Commanding General concerning future operations. Good day, gentlemen. That is all."

"Sir, yes, Sir."

1303 Thursday
Easy 31 and 32, SEAD Mission, on the Tanker Track
"Aviate, navigate, communicate."

"Fortress 04, Easy 32, is starboard observation, switches safe, and nose cold."

"Easy 32, Fortress 04, you can proceed to the pre-contact position."

Chunks effortlessly maneuvered his F-18D Hornet down and to the left from the starboard observation position. In the process, a sudden realization came over him.

"Hey, Fig," said Chunks. "You'll never guess what."

"What."

"I forgot to stroke Easy Eddie's fish on my way out of the Ready Room."

"How did *that* happen," asked Fig, trying to sound like it was no big deal.

"I guess I just got busy or something."

"Well, did you remember to touch SPEED IS LIFE, MORE IS BETTER.?"

"Yep," returned Chunks.

"Oh, you'll be ok then," consoled Fig. "Don't worry about it."

By that time, Easy 32 had arrived at the pre-contact position, which Chunks declared, "Fortress 04, Easy 32, now pre-contact."

"Easy 32, Fortress 04, cleared to plug."

Chunks exhaled once. This was going to be a piece of cake. It was a perfect day to be flying, and Fortress 04 was a KC-10 from the Kansas

Air National Guard. Easy 31, Ghost and Frap, had already gotten their gas - no sweat - and had climbed up and to the left. Chunks, the master of attention to detail, performed his same pre-tanking ritual. He relaxed his right hand's grip on the stick. He exhaled again and wiggled his toes. He reached down by his left thigh and flipped the switch to lower his seat. Then he massaged the throttles forward with just enough force to get three to four knots of closure. Actually, Chunks was slightly faster than that, but that was ok. It didn't matter. The KC-10 had a very forgiving refueling system. This was going to be duck soup. Closer, closer, closer - dink. The refueling probe rimmed the KC-10's soft basket at the four o'clock position. With just a touch of left rudder, Chunks was in and connected. Clunk. Yep, the KC-10's entire refueling system was very easy and forgiving.

"Fortress 04, Easy 32, contact," said Chunks.

"Easy 32, Fortress 04, good fuel flow."

The KC-10's little green light on the belly illuminated, and Fig backed up the call with the fuel flow indicator at his left knee, saying, "I concur, Chunks, good flow."

One hundred feet to the left, Frap had just passed his spare Power Bar up to Ghost in the front seat. Easy 31 was fat, dumb, and happy with a full bag of gas, and mindlessly watching Easy 32 about to become the same. Then they couldn't believe their eyes.

Upon plugging into the basket, Chunks' slightly excessive closure had caused a sine wave in the refueling hose to resonate from the basket up to the KC-10. However, the take-up reel in the KC-10 failed to respond. The sine wave bounced off of the take-up reel's housing and traveled back down the hose to the basket. Chunks couldn't retard the throttles in time to back out, and the force of the sine wave severed the lower portion of the refueling hose behind the basket. Immediately, fuel spewed all over Chunks' canopy, momentarily blocking his vision. Easy 32 now had the KC-10's basket impaled on its refueling probe, with approximately six feet of hose trailing from the back of the basket. Fuel streamed down the right side of Chunks' F-18D and into the intake. Then flames shot out of Easy 32's right exhaust, and Chunks slammed the right throttle off. Simultaneously he pulled left, cutting under Easy 31.

"Engine right, engine right," cooed Bitchin' Betty.

"I hear ya, Betty," yelled Chunks. "Stand the fuck by."

"Holy shit," exclaimed a wide-eyed Frap in Easy 31.

Ghost threw down his Power Bar and pulled up slightly to avoid a midair collision as Chunks cut underneath him. Then Ghost also pulled hard left to snap his F-18D around one hundred and eighty degrees. He selected afterburner to catch up with Chunks' rapidly descending aircraft.

Simultaneously, the KC-10 performed its emergency breakaway procedures from within, cutting the upper portion of the hose at the take-up reel's housing. The twenty feet or so of rubber and metal coil fell harmlessly to the sea.

"Fortress 04, Easy 32," said Chunks, amazingly calm.

"Easy 32, Fortress 04, go."

"It looks like we're taking a little memento with us back home. Sorry 'bout that."

"Shit happens, Easy 32. Can we be of any assistance?"

"Negative, Fortress. We're out of here. See you tomorrow."

"Roger, Easy 32, see you tomorrow. Fly safe."

"Easy 32 flight, switch Sky Eye, number one radio, go," commanded Chunks.

"Easy 32, 31 is switching," returned the very disciplined Ghost.

Because Easy 32 was the emergency aircraft, Chunks automatically assumed the lead. Easy 31 positioned itself high and on the right of Easy 32, where they could safely observe the right side of Chunks' aircraft.

Meanwhile, Chunks and Fig were falling back upon the very basics they had learned in flight school concerning the priority of actions to take when everything went to shit in an airplane - aviate, navigate, communicate. Aviate, navigate, communicate. Aviate, navigate, communicate.

Fig keyed the ICS, saying, "Hey Chunks, we don't have the gas to make it home. I think our best bet is to head to the tanker track's emergency divert airfield."

Chunks was on his game, declaring, "I'm one step ahead of you, my man. I'm coming around to a heading of one seven zero and putting the divert airfield on the nose."

"You da man," encouraged Fig. "You da man."

"It's waypoint seven, right Fig?" asked Chunks, commencing a climb.

"Waypoint eight," returned Fig, selecting both that waypoint and navigational steering to it on the moving map display.

They only had fifty miles to go. No sweat.

"Fig, I'm all assholes-and-elbows up here," continued Chunks. "Can you break out your pocket checklist? I can't do mine and fly this crippled jet at the same time."

"I'm on it like ugly on an ape," returned Fig.

He fumbled through his nav bag for his PCL, and immediately opened it to the appropriate emergency.

"Chunks, I'm on page 103, single engine procedures, and ready when you are."

"Roger, Fig, standby one, I'll be with you in a minute. I've got the comm."

"Roger, Chunks, you've got the comm."

Chunks and Fig were meshing perfectly. Confident now that everything was under control and that they had done everything they could possibly do, Chunks returned to the basics. Aviate, navigate, communicate. Aviate, navigate, communicate. Aviate, navigate, communicate.

"Sky Eye, Easy 32," stated Chunks.

"Two," injected Frap, letting Easy 32 know that Easy 31 had successfully followed them through the frequency switch.

"Easy 32, Sky Eye has you loud and clear, go ahead."

"Sky Eye, Easy 32, declaring an emergency, presently single engine on a heading of one seven zero, proceeding to tanker track emergency divert airfield."

"Easy 32, Sky Eye copies all, looking."

As the AWACS scrambled to find Easy 32 on his scope, Easy 31 took advantage of the radio silence.

"Chunks, Ghost," inquired Easy 31's pilot on the number two radio.

"Ghost, Chunks, go."

"How can we help?" asked Ghost.

Chunks painted them the best picture he could, saying, "Right now I've got the right engine shut down, and Fig is on page 103 of the PCL to talk me through single engine procedures. If you could, have Frap go to the same page to back us up."

"Wilco," replied Ghost, knowing that Frap was already there.

"Also, stay high on our right side and escort us down to a safe landing. Pay attention to the number one radio and you'll get everything else that you need to know."

"Roger, copy all," returned Ghost from the front seat.

"I'm on page 103 and ready to go," echoed Frap over the number two radio.

"Thanks, guys. I owe you each a beer," joked Chunks.

"What? Chunks is *buying*?" returned Ghost. "Down in Hell right now, the Devil is putting on his winter overcoat."

"Easy 32, Sky Eye," said the AWACS.

"Sky Eye, Easy 32, go ahead," returned Chunks.

"Sky Eye has you on radar, four five miles north of divert. Continue inbound."

"Sky Eye, Easy 32, thank you."

"Ok, Fig," said Chunks on the ICS. "I'm ready for that checklist."

"Roger that," returned Fig. "Under 'Single Engine Landing'. *Step one. Reduce gross weight.*"

"Copy that, Fig," Chunks calmly stated. "However, we're going to skip that one. Since we barely got plugged in to the KC-10, we hardly got any gas. We don't need to dump any fuel to get down to landing weight."

"Roger that. Next is step two. *Shut off all unnecessary electrical equipment.*"

In the front seat, Chunks reached down by his right hip and rotated the radar knob to the 'off' position. That was the only unnecessary electrical item to worry about right now. Everything else was small potatoes that could be gotten later.

"Next?" implored Chunks on the ICS.

"*Step three. When practical, maintain the operating engine RPM at or above eighty-five percent. If the failed engine's core is rotating freely, then crossbleed to retain the hydraulic system.*"

Both pilot and WSO immediately checked the parameters of both engines using the digital displays in front of their left knees, and the engine page on the left display. Chunks and Fig agreed that the core of the right engine was still freely rotating.

Chunks followed the procedures to the letter. He slightly goosed the left throttle until the display showed eighty-seven percent, and then crossbled the Hornet's systems so that the left engine's hydraulic system number one would keep the right engine's hydraulic system number two flowing. Then Chunks thumbed in some left rudder trim towards the good engine that he would remove on final approach. He also made a mental note to himself that once the landing gear was down, he would intentionally fly a slightly faster approach speed, placing the F-18's velocity vector at the bottom of the staple in the HUD. Chunks was a good pilot.

"Next?" asked Chunks on the ICS.

"*Step four. Put down the landing gear.*"

"Roger that," returned Chunks. "We're still a little too far out for that, so we'll hold off on the landing gear until around ten miles."

"I'm standing by, Chunks."

"Hey, Fig, I need to give you a heads up on some pilot shit."

"Go ahead."

"I'm going to fly a slightly faster approach. I'll try not to use afterburner on the good engine, because that's only going to aggravate our directional control problems. Plus, afterburner will only cause us to have a higher minimum control airspeed."

Chunks was a good pilot - a damn good pilot.

"Copy that," returned Fig. "You won't hear any complaints from me about a few extra knots for mom and apple pie."

"Secondly, to avoid any loss of directional control, I can't exceed fifteen degrees angle of attack with full flaps, or seventeen degrees angle of attack with the flaps at half. Back me up on that during the approach, ok?"

"Will do, my man."

Easy 32 had this emergency suit-cased. There was no way that they could dick the dog. It would only be a matter of time before the jet was safely on the ground.

Aviate, navigate, communicate. Aviate, navigate, communicate. Aviate, navigate, communicate.

* * *

Little Shop of Horrors

The famous Broadway play entitled *Little Shop of Horrors* ain't got nothing on the office of a Navy Dentist. F-18D pilots and WSOs would face a thousand SAMs and Mig-29s, before they would accept an appointment at Navy Dental. Never mind the obvioously painful evolutions of having a cavity filled or getting a root canal - F-18D aviators turned into the biggest babies for a simple, routine cleaning.

Marine Corps aviators were required to complete an annual dental examination in conjunction with their annual flight physical. Consequently, not only was a pilot or WSO annually poked and prodded by a Navy flight surgeon, he was also pricked and pruned by a Navy dentist.

The average aviator maintained a program of good oral hygiene, except for the occasional rebel who chewed tobacco or smoked cigarettes. Consequently, most annual check-ups merely resulted in the requirement for an innocent cleaning. That was all. It was no big deal. That is, unless your appointment was with Cruella DeVille.

All of the Navy dental hygienists who conducted these routine cleanings were truly compassionate - save for one. She was known as

Cruella DeVille, affectionately named after the sadistic female villain from Walt Disney's, *101 Dalmatians*. Professionally, Cruella DeVille knew her shit. But it was Cruella's domineering attitude and condescending approach to treating patients that gained her fame. That was second only to her callous ability to inflict pain with a needle or a drill. To Cruella DeVille, every mangy molar or basal bicuspid was a personal affront to her profession. She detested tartar. She deplored plaque. She hated halitosis. She jammed on gingivitis.

Cruella DeVille had the same long, bony fingers as her Disney namesake, and the equally disgusting long, sharp nails. Varicose veins and ugly age spots dominated the back of her bony hands, which were attached to match stick arms. She looked twice her age, having a body covered in that tanned, testicle skin so prevalent around swimming pools in Phoenix and Miami. With gray hair like Phyllis Diller and baggage beneath her evil eyes, she was simultaneously demanding and bitter and sarcastic, all the while relentless in her pursuit of plaque.

Pity poor Hick Boy. His annual flight physical was next week, so he had already completed his annual dental check-up. The result was - as expected - the requirement for a cleaning at the hands of Cruella DeVille.

Hick Boy had never even been to a dentist until he was a twenty-one year old, potential Second Lieutenant at Officer's Candidate School. There, the Navy dental personnel refused to believe that Hick Boy's mouth was cavity free from twenty-one years of brushing with his Grandma's baking soda. In flight school, a Navy dental hygienist introduced Hick Boy to Listerine; after which, he promptly drank it. He never did quite get the knack of flossing, failing to see what good it would do to run perfectly good fishing line between his teeth. Now as a Captain in a Marine F-18D squadron, Hick Boy still possessed an impeccably clean array of teeth.

However, today was not his day, and circumstances beyond his control put him on a collision course with Cruella DeVille. Unscheduled meetings and other bullshit had caused his morning to scream out of control, thus he didn't have time to eat a normal lunch and brush his teeth. So Hick Boy had grabbed a cup of coffee and a candy bar, and then proceeded unknowingly to his dental cleaning after the Officer's fracas outside of the Ready Room.

1308 Thursday
Navy Dental Office
"This won't hurt a bit, but you may feel a slight sting."

Hick Boy sat in Cruella's chair, affixing the protective white bib around his neck with the tiny chain and the little clip.

"What's this for?" grinned Hick Boy. "Are we having lobster?"

Not only did Cruella lack any semblance of a sense of humor, she was also brutally honest. She answered Hick Boy without batting an eye, coldly stating, "That's to keep blood and tiny chunks of tooth and tartar from splattering onto your pretty boy pajamas or zoot suit or speed jeans or whatever you call that thing you wear."

My, how pleasant, thought Hick Boy. *That's certainly nice to know.*

Cruella sat on her wheeled stool by the sink, examining Hick Boy's dental X-rays. Meanwhile, he scanned around her office, noting the grotesque pictures that Cruella used to motivate her patients towards good oral hygiene. There was a photograph of some poor sap's rotten and decaying teeth, with black holes and brown stains. His teeth were barely hanging onto inflamed and bleeding gums. Next to that was a picture of the bloody, infected, receding gums of some Marine who chewed tobacco.

Cruella finished with the X-rays, and rolled her stool next to Hick Boy, hitting a hidden switch that lowered Hick Boy's head below the height of his feet. From her domineering position, she placed a pair of clear, plastic glasses into his hands.

"Here," she said gruffly. "Put these on."

Out of fear, Hick Boy obeyed her every command. He put on the dorky plastic glasses, which looked like the kind of eyewear that fat, old men in Florida sported. No, wait. They looked more like a clear, plastic version of the glasses that Ray Charles wore.

Cruella donned a protective mask too, pulling down a clear plastic shield over her face that made her look like a riot cop. She also pulled a white mask over her mouth and nose from its former position around her neck. This mask offended Hick Boy.

"Ma'am," he stated in his most gentlemanly southern drawl, "I don't take too highly to your insinuation that I have bad breath."

Hick Boy's words hit the plastic face shield of Cruella's riot helmet, and fell to the floor of her office, sounding like dropped silverware. Cruella slightly growled.

Then, she grabbed some latex from the front pocket of her lab coat. Hick Boy couldn't help but notice that they were the same generic brand of medical gloves that Doc used to check his patients' prostate glands. The mental image of the same gloves being used to examine two different orifices was a little too much for Hick Boy to handle.

Cruella snapped on the latex gloves, one at a time, pulling down on them so hard at the wrists that her nails poked through the fingertips.

What kind of a macabre torture chamber is this? Hick Boy thought.

Then she reached over Hick Boy's head, and clicked on a spotlight that must've been bought at a prison yard sale. Blinded by the light, Hick Boy felt like he was on "Hogan's Heroes".

"Ok, ok, I'll talk," joked Hick Boy. "The radio is in the coffee pot."

This time, Hick Boy's attempt at humor zinged right over Cruella's riot helmet and stuck harmlessly into the sectional ceiling.

Cruella adjusted the angle of the lamp, directing the light into Hick Boy's mouth. Then she pulled a tray over next to her body that was physically attached to a mechanical, octopus arm. This tray contained the wicked tools that Cruella DeVille applied in her craft - sadistic, sharp, silver picks bent at all kinds of obtuse angles, and electrical drills with various grinder and wheel attachments.

"Open wide," ordered Cruella.

Hick Boy followed her orders precisely, and could see the wince on Cruella's face as the mixture of coffee and candy bar penetrated her white mask. She instinctively flinched backward.

Oh, oh, thought Hick Boy. *Now I've done it. I've pissed her off.*

Without saying a word, Cruella flipped the hidden switch again, lowering Hick Boy's head even further so that she could be even more domineering.

She adjusted the spotlight slightly to accommodate Hick Boy's lower elevation, and then grabbed a pick from her tray. The poor lighting in her office still managed to glisten off of the sharp tip, like it was Jack the Ripper's knife. She hunkered down over Tennessee's finest, demanding, "Open wide."

Hick Boy obeyed, but noticed a new development that was going to pose psychological problems for him. In this new position, he could see the reflection of his own mouth and teeth in the plastic face guard of Cruella's riot helmet. Cruella began picking and poking with her silver instrument of pain, and Hick Boy could see every move in the reflection. It was more than he could take - he tensed his entire body.

"Relax your jaw," she demanded. "Your lower lip is fighting me."

"I tham relassed," said Hick Boy, unable to talk with an open mouth.

Cruella forced Hick Boy's bottom lip down towards his chin with her left thumb, simultaneously pushing down on his chin to open his jaw.

She continued to prick his teeth with the silver instrument of pain for an eternity.

In an attempt to ease the pain, Hick Boy affixed his gaze to the left, away from the reflection, and upon the clock on the wall. That was a mistake. Time stood still, and Hick Boy swore that he even saw the second hand ticking *backwards*. Cruella eventually pulled the silver pick from his mouth, and retrieved another sadistic tool from the tray. It was the dreaded 'sucker thing'. Cruella strategically placed it into Hick Boy's mouth.

"Close your mouth."

The sucker thing proceeded to remove the saliva that had collected in Hick Boy's mouth. The sound alone was enough to gross out Hick Boy - not to mention the saliva collection tank that Hick Boy imagined at the other end of the hose. Cruella removed the sucker thing, and proceeded to humiliate the easy going F-18 pilot, or at least try.

"You had a candy bar before coming over here, didn't you?"

"Yes, Ma'am."

"I can tell. Chocolate is Satan's favorite tool of seduction."

"What?"

"Do you chew?"

"No, Ma'am."

"Do you dip?"

"Only when I go fishing with my Uncle Ned."

"Why? There is absolutely no reason to engage in such a filthy, disgusting habit."

"We smear some dip on our worms to cover our scent."

Not to be knocked off her game by Hick Boy's earthy, country clamor, Cruella let Hick Boy's words bounce off of her riot helmet again and fall harmlessly to the floor. She jumped right back onto her humiliation freight train.

"Do you smoke?"

"Cigars or cigarettes, ma'am?"

"It doesn't matter."

"Ma'am, I do cigars when I go home because Nelly likes to smell the smoke."

"Nelly?"

"Yes, Ma'am. Nelly is our mule."

Again, Cruella refused to get rattled by some homespun Tennessee tales.

"Do you drink a lot of soda?"

"Well, Ma'am, I'm partial to an occasional Mountain Dew."

"Don't you know that soda is the nectar of the devil?"

Hick Boy thought it best to not even mention the sugary, sweetened tea that his mother adorned their table with every night of the summer. It was like drinking syrup.

"I *knew* all of the above. I could tell," said Cruella. "Captain, your mouth is *gross*. We're going to have to do this cleaning in four different sessions, starting with the lower left quadrant."

Oh no, thought Hick Boy. *Not three more visits.*

Cruella wasted no time in preparing the lamb for the slaughter. She dabbed a cotton swab on Hick Boy's lower left gums. The gooey substance on it tasted like bubble gum to Hick Boy.

She's setting me up like a bowling pin, thought Hick Boy.

"This gel that I'm applying will dull the pain of the Novocain shot. Now I need you to relax."

Hick Boy hated shots.

Relax? Hick Boy thought. *How can I relax?*

Hick Boy diverted his gaze to the clock again. He didn't want to see the needle pierce his gums in the mask's reflection. Things would've been fine, too, if Cruella hadn't reached up with her right hand to slightly adjust the angle of the POW spotlight. She did so while holding the needle between her right thumb and forefinger, and it automatically caught Hick Boy's attention. Holy shit. The last time Hick Boy saw a needle that big, the Veterinarian had used it to sedate Nelly so that Hick Boy and his Pa could clip her hooves. A tiny drop of Novocain hung for its life from the tip of the needle, and then dropped in slow motion down to splatter on Hick Boy's nose.

"Open wide. This won't hurt a bit, but you may feel a slight sting."

The word 'feel' wasn't even off of Cruella's tongue when Hick Boy felt the needle jab into his inner gum on the lower left side. He clenched the armrests of Cruella's chair, and again diverted his gaze to the clock. Damn it. The second hand was ticking backwards again. Cruella held the first shot for an eternity as she slowly squeezed the Novocain into her victim. Then she removed the needle and pricked Hick Boy again along his inner left gum. Then she moved the needle to the outer left gum. She slowly pricked and squeezed again, and again.

"That should do it," stated Cruella. "In a couple of minutes, your lower left gum and cheek should feel numb, and your nose will feel like it is running."

While Hick Boy waited for the Novocain to take effect, he gazed around the office again at the pictures. There was Tommy Tooth, holding a brush and basking in the fun that was brushing your teeth. Next to that poster was Tommy Tooth again, now using a piece of dental floss across his backside like he was drying his butt with a towel.

"How does your mouth feel?" inquired Cruella. "Numb?"

"Yup, ib feelth mum."

"Open wide."

Then the true hell commenced. It was pick and scrape, pick and scrape, pick and scrape with Jack the Ripper's knife. It was suck and slurp, suck and slurp, suck and slurp with the sucker thing. It was grind and sand, grind and sand, grind and sand with the wheel on the octopus arm. It was tick backwards, tick backwards, tick backwards for the clock's second hand.

The pain was no problem for Hick Boy, thanks to the Novocain. It was just the cacophony of painfully sounding noises that tensed his entire body. The absolute worst part was the grinding of the wheeled attachment. It sounded as if Cruella was working a Black and Decker sander on Hick Boy's molars. Cruella's choice of office music - Burt Bacharach - did little to cover the sound of her removing layer after layer of tartar. Furthermore, it didn't help to notice the tiny chips of plaque and tartar that constantly spewed from Hick Boy's mouth, landing on the lobster bib. Cruella's only breaks in her assault came when she stopped and wiped the blood from Hick Boy's chin.

Finally, the torture ended.

Thank God, thought Hick Boy. *I only have three more sessions to go.*

"There. That wasn't so bad, was it?"

"Mo, ba'am, ib dibn't thurt at awh."

Cruella hit the secret switch, and it began elevating Hick Boys' head back to a normal level. She moved the tray on the octopus arm out of Hick Boy's way, and removed the lobster bib. Cruella lifted the plastic visor to her riot helmet, and took the plastic Ray Charles glasses from Hick Boy's nose. The second hand on the clock started ticking in the correct direction again.

Hick Boy's mind wandered in the few seconds that his head was being elevated. When he was in college, it was one of his secret fantasies to have sex in a dental chair. He envisioned a hot, blonde dental hygienist, fresh out of school and oh, so eager to please. In the fantasy, she lifted her lab coat to reveal a pair of crotchless panties. Then she climbed atop the chair and straddled Hick Boy. To heighten his pleasure, she placed a mask over Hick Boy's nose and mouth, and then turned on the Nitrous Oxide. She then proceeded to ride Hick Boy like a rented mule, while a gleeful Tennessee boy giggled like a child. That was then, this was now. Hick Boy looked at Cruella and shuddered.

Cruella handed a plastic cup to Hick Boy that contained some kind of evil liquid.

"Take this over to the sink and rinse for thirty seconds."

"Yeth, ba'am."

Hick Boy struggled to get out of the cushy chair while holding the tiny cup, because he didn't want to spill a single drop in front of Cruella. He walked over to the sink, which was spotless, and looked into the mirror. He had aged five years. There were bags under his eyes. His forehead was still sweating. There was a spot of blood on his chin. The bridge of his nose was red from the dorky, plastic, Ray Charles glasses. He was drooling from the left corner of his mouth. But by God, the lower left quadrant of Hick Boy's mouth was free of tartar and plaque.

Hick Boy slammed the white cup to his lips, and began rinsing and swishing and swirling, intentionally being noisy so that Cruella would hear.

God, winced Hick Boy, *this shit tastes terrible.*

He rinsed and swished and swirled until he couldn't take it anymore, and immediately bent over the sink, spewing the liquid all over Cruella's clean porcelain.

"That was only twenty-three seconds," said Cruella.

"Ba,am?"

"That was only twenty-three seconds," she coldly stated. "Here. Do it again."

"But ba'am, dith thtuff dathe awfuww."

"Ok, fine, young man. Then don't rinse. We can do this in *six* more appointments instead of three."

Hick Boy *immediately* slam dunked the second white cup, and began rinsing and swishing and swirling like you read about. Hick Boy didn't take any chances. At exactly thirty seconds, he spit the fowl green liquid into Cruella's sink once more. If there were any germs down that drain, they died a hideous and painful death, not to mention those still hiding in Hick Boy's mouth.

Cruella signed the appropriate page in Hick Boy's dental records, and then handed the humble red folder to him, saying, "On your way out, stop by the front desk and make an appointment for your next cleaning."

"Yeth, ba'am."

Then she gave Hick Boy a lollipop.

1315 Thursday
Easy 31 and 32, Aborted SEAD Mission,
Proceeding to the Tanker Track's
Emergency Divert Airfield
"The Devil is gettin' frostbite."

Now feeling very confident that everything was under control, Chunks asked for the assistance of his former lead.

"Ghost, Chunks," stated Easy 32's pilot on the number two radio.

"Chunks, Ghost, go ahead."

"Two things. First of all, have Frap jump off of the number one radio and get the ATIS information for our divert airfield."

"Wilco."

"Secondly, can you come in a little closer and visually check us out?"

"You got it," returned Ghost.

Frap changed the number one radio from Sky Eye's frequency to the Air Traffic Information Service, or ATIS, for the divert airfield. Immediately, the twenty-four hour, continuously broadcast, ATIS information played into their helmets.

". . . advise upon initial contact that you have ATIS information Delta. This is ATIS information Delta, time 1500 Zulu, the field has a ceiling measured at one zero thousand feet overcast, one four thousand feet broken, one nine thousand feet scattered, visibility is unrestricted, winds are calm, altimeter is 30.12. Currently landing runway one four zero. All aviators, be advised that the radar used for ground controlled approaches is inoperable until further notice. Taxiway bravo is closed for construction. Advise upon initial contact that you have ATIS information Delta. This is ATIS information Delta, time 1500 Zulu, the field has a ceiling measured at . . . "

As soon as Frap changed the number one radio back to Sky Eye, Ghost began easing his F-18D into a closer parade position on Easy 32. Flying within mere feet of Chunks' aircraft on the right side, Ghost keyed the number two radio, asking, "Ok, Chunks, what have you got for me?"

"Ghost, what's left of this hose up here on the basket is starting to unravel. I'm worried about that cable going down my intake. The last thing I need right now is to FOD my right engine and lose it completely."

"Ghost copies."

"I'm also afraid of some cable getting wrapped up in my flaps or rudders. Can you check *that* out?"

"Wilco."

"Lastly, see if there's any fire damage."

"Chunks, Ghost, copy all."

Ghost delicately adjusted his throttles, and deftly manipulated the rudder pedals and stick, to maneuver his F-18D up and down the entire length of Chunk's aircraft on the right side. Ghost and Frap scored Easy 32's F-18D, but couldn't see any dangling pieces of cable or wire that could possibly FOD the engine, or cause fouling of the flight control surfaces. Furthermore, they saw no other signs of damage. It all looked good.

"Chunks, Ghost, on the number two."

"Ghost, Chunks, go."

"Chunks, we don't see a damn thing wrong with your jet. Other than that big, ugly basket on your probe, I think you're good to go."

"Roger, Chunks copies. Thanks. I really do owe you a beer."

"Wow. The Devil is gettin' frostbite."

Then Frap chimed in on the number two radio, stating "ATIS information is Delta, weather's fine, ceiling is one zero thousand feet, runway one four zero, 30.12."

Frap had completely missed the information about the inoperable radar.

Chunks echoed Frap's call, repeating, "Copy information Delta, weather's good, one zero thousand on the ceiling, runway one four zero, 30.12."

Things were starting to really look up for Chunks and Fig. They only had twenty miles to go in a jet that had no major problems, to a field where the weather was good.

"Easy 32, Sky Eye."

"Sky Eye, Easy 32, go ahead," replied Chunks.

"Contact approach control on three five six decimal two. I've given them a heads-up on your emergency."

"Easy 32, switching approach control, three five six decimal two. Flight switch, number one, go."

"Two."

The final leg of the journey was about to begin.

"Approach control, Easy 32 with ATIS information Delta," said Chunks.

"Easy 32, this is approach control. I have you loud and clear. Thank you for obtaining information Delta. State your intentions."

"Easy 32 is a flight of two Hornets, two zero miles north, declaring an emergency. Easy 32 is requesting a ground-controlled approach to an arrested landing, runway one four zero. Easy 31 will escort 32 until short final, and then detach from us, and fly in front to land first on a visual straight-in to a normal rollout."

"Easy 32, approach control. Copy all. Be advised that our ground controlled approach radar is down. The best we can give you is a surveillance approach."

Chunks bit his lip. He didn't like the idea of trying to wrestle a crippled jet in to an arrested landing using only a surveillance approach, which consisted of non-precision glide slope, heading, and altitude data from the ground controller. Still, it was all he had.

"Approach control, Easy 32, we'll take the surveillance approach."

"Roger that, Easy 32. The cable is up and in battery, ready for your use. State your landing weight and speed."

"Approach, Easy 32, we'll be two nine thousand pounds and one four zero knots."

Everything was going just fine - almost *too* good. For the first time since departing from the KC-10, Chunks breathed a sigh of relief. In Easy 31, Ghost had resumed eating his Power Bar, and Frap had closed his pocket checklist and put it away. Fig dug into his nav bag again, and pulled out the field diagram for the divert airfield. Over the ICS, he gave Chunks a quick brief to familiarize him with the field.

"Chunks, we have ten thousand feet of runway to play with, and the field elevation is two hundred and ten feet. Our arresting cable is an E-28 located twelve hundred feet down the runway. If our hook skips over the cable, I recommend that we just keep this injured bird on the deck and use all ten thousand feet to roll to a stop."

"I concur, Fig," returned Chunks on the ICS. "Good call on the hook skip."

"Easy 32, Approach Control."

"Approach, Easy 32, go ahead," answered Chunks.

"Turn left to one six zero, descend and maintain four thousand. You're on vectors to intercept the final approach course for an arrested landing, runway one four."

"Easy 32, left one six zero, down to four, wilco."

Yep. Everything was going just fine.

1319 Thursday
The Officers' Club tent
"Do you guys mind if I take a chair from the Officers' Club?"

Spine Ripper, Pope, and Shitscreen stopped into the Officers' Club tent to relax a bit after the midday sidestep. They had some time to kill before they had to be back down to the squadron spaces, so why not? Pope flopped onto the big, cushy loveseat in the first row, groaning as his tired body fell prostrate on the leather with his legs dangling over the end. Shitscreen plopped onto the barstool that had a woman's long legs beneath the seat, and fiddled with the remote for the CD player. Spine Ripper strode to the TV, and shuffled through the stack of magazines sitting on top that aircrew donated to read.

"Damn it," stated Spine Ripper, "there's nothing new to read here."

"How does Buick manage to work this thing," Shitscreen asked the crowd, while thumbing various buttons on the remote, "especially when he's half looped?"

"Oh, my poor, aching body," complained Pope. "I need some serious rack time."

"Hick Boy's *Appalachia Monthly*?" Spine Ripper asked. "Nope. Too red neck."

"FOD's *Guitar World*?" he continued. "Nope. Too radical."

Then Spine Ripper cocked his head and glanced askew with a puzzled look on his face. He momentarily scratched his chin.

"Or is this Ninja's *Guitar World*?" he asked himself aloud.

"I can never keep that straight," Pope said, with eyes shut and hands clasped across his chest. "One of them gets *Guitar World* and the other gets *Rolling Stone*."

"Typical California radical surfer dudes," muttered Spine Ripper, as he continued to rifle his way through the magazines.

"Dago's *Penthouse*? Nope. It's too predictable. Besides, I've seen it."

"Joisey's *Hustler*? Nope. Too filthy gross."

Spine Ripper tried to toss Joisey's *Hustler* onto the VCR, but it partially adhered to his hand. Thus, it's trajectory fell short, hitting the VCR's face, and it dropped to the floor. It landed and still retained its form, with the pages stuck together. There was no doubt what Joisey had been using his *Hustler* to accomplish.

"Ghost's *Playboy*? Nope. Too hard to take the frustration."

Back at the bar, mad and annoyed, Shitscreen slammed the remote down onto the stool next to him, declaring, "You can put me in the backseat of a forty million dollar jet, and I'll be fine. Just don't give me a ten dollar remote from Radio Shack."

Pope laughed while in his partial stupor.

From totally out of the blue, Shitscreen offered a dilemma to the crowd, asking, "Hey guys, do you think draft dodgers have reunions?"

Spine Ripper and Pope just looked at each other.

"If they do," continued Shitscreen, "then what do they talk about?"

Spine Ripper resumed his search for something to read, shaking his head, and Pope put his head back down on the loveseat, closing his eyes.

"*Southern Living?*" asked Spine Ripper. "Bama gets *Southern Living?*"

"Yep," said Shitscreen, leaning his elbow on the bar. "And his wife, Linda, gets *Football Weekly*. Go figure."

"*Reader's Digest?* Who in the hell gets *Reader's Digest?*"

Again, a fading Pope proffered a reply, stating, "The Commanding Officer does."

"Why should that surprise you?" asked Shitscreen. "It's for old farts anyway."

"The funny part is," continued Pope, "that the Skipper gets the version with the extra large print."

"No shit?" asked Shitscreen, popping up from his elbow.

Spine Ripper wheeled about and flipped the tiny periodical to Shitscreen, saying, "Here. Check for yourself."

Meanwhile, Pope unclasped his hands, and grabbed the cushion from the end of the loveseat. He placed it over his eyes to block the light, and then scratched his crotch.

Taking note, Spine Ripper asked the gallery "Why do guys do that?"

"Do what?" asked Shitscreen, with his head buried in the Skipper's *Reader's Digest*, trying to find the 'Humor in Uniform' page.

"Guys scratch their balls right before they fall asleep and right when they wake up. *That's* what," answered Spine Ripper.

"Because there's nobody else here to do it for me," returned Pope.

"Spine Ripper, you are just too intense," said Shitscreen. "There are *some* things in life that you just can't get down to a gnat's ass."

Shitscreen's comment went into Spine Ripper's one ear and right out the other.

"Hollywood's *Entertainment Tonight?*" he continued. "Nope. Too glitzy."

"Would you guys mind holding it down?" asked Pope. "I'm trying to nab a little shut-eye here."

"You know what?" asked Shitscreen. "This 'Humor in Uniform' ain't got shit over the escapades that go on around here."

"Concur," stated a sleepy Pope.

"Screeches *Flying* magazine?" continued Spine Ripper. "No. Too professional."

"Pope's *Catholic Digest*? Nope. Too saintly and goody-two-shoes."

"I heard that, you asshole," said Pope.

"Tuna's *GQ*? Nope. Too Tuna."

Just then, the entrance flap to the Officers' Club tent was raised, and Booger peered inside. Dick and Screw darted through the entrance, playfully frolicking and nipping at each other. Dick ran straight to Shitscreen, and placed his front paws upon his thighs, with a wet tongue slobbering on his flight suit and a wagging tail that fanned the dirt on the floor. Screw bounded over to Pope's loveseat, and jumped upon his stomach, causing Pope to exhale with a grunt.

"Hi, boy," greeted Shitscreen, scratching behind the ears of Dick the dog.

"Hey there, Screw," stated Pope, sitting up and patting him on the head.

"Hey Booger," said Spine Ripper, ignoring the dogs. "What's the deal, man?"

"What do you mean?"

"Why didn't you help us separate Bama and Buick a little while ago?"

"Lay off, Spine Ripper," said Pope. "Let him amongst us who is without sin cast the first stone."

A disgruntled Spine Ripper returned to his magazine search.

Booger sheepishly entered the Officers' Club and closed the tent flap behind him. He could barely make eye contact, but asked, "What's up, you guys?"

"Hi Booger," returned Pope and Shitscreen.

"What are you guys doing?" asked Booger, feeling more relaxed. "Holding a WSO convention?"

Pope and Shitscreen chuckled.

"Man, you can't swing a dead cat in here without hitting a WSO," he declared.

"Yeah, Booger," returned Shitscreen, "in reality, we're petitioning Marine Corps Headquarters for a stick and throttles in the back seat."

"Don't hold your breath," joked Booger.

Then Spine Ripper threw a wet blanket on the party, stating, "How can you guys poke fun at yourselves and the WSO profession like that?"

"Oh, lighten up," stated Shitscreen, rolling his eyes.

Spine Ripper returned to his hunt for something to read, while Pope proceeded to rub Screw's belly.

"Well, I only meant to stop by for a minute," said Booger. "Do you guys mind if I take a chair from the Officers' Club?"

"What?" returned Pope, still rubbing Screw's belly.

"Do you guys mind if I take a chair?"

The three WSOs looked at each other with puzzled expressions.

"Shit no," answered Spine Ripper. "We don't give a rat's ass."

"What do you need it for?" quizzed Pope, now rubbing the attempted sleep from his eyes, while Screw pawed at his stomach,

"Oh, nothing," replied Booger, grabbing one of the chairs at the game table. "I just need a chair."

Booger placed the chair atop his head, and turned around towards the flap, calling over his shoulder, "C'mon, Dick. Come here, Screw."

Booger whistled and snapped his fingers, then lifted the flap with his free hand. He stooped to duck under the flap, as Dick and Screw bolted outside between his legs.

"Well, I guess it's time that we got back to work," Shitscreen sighed.

"Yep," agreed Pope.

"Damn," groaned Spine Ripper, holding Frap's *Sports Illustrated*. "Here's a magazine that I haven't seen yet."

After Pope arose from the love seat and stretched his gangly body, Spine Ripper hid the *Sports Illustrated* under one of its cushions, guaranteeing that it would be his tonight. Shitscreen hopped down from his stool.

The three WSOs left the Club for the walk to the Ready Room.

1320 Thursday
Easy 31 and 32, Aborted SEAD Mission
Proceeding to the Tanker Track's
Emergency Divert Airfield
"Fig, you up?"

There was only twelve miles to go. All Chunks had to do was simply put down the landing gear and the arresting hook, and then snag the cable. No sweat. Easy 32 was good-to-go.

"Easy 32, Approach Control, turn left heading one four zero, stand by for your final controller."

"Approach, Easy 32, left one four zero, standing by," returned Chunks.

"Easy 32, this is your final controller, how do you hear? Gear should be down."

"Approach, Easy 32, loud and clear. Standby, gear is coming."

"Ok, Fig," declared Chunks on the ICS. "I'm ready for the rest of that checklist."

"Roger that. *Step four. Put the landing gear down.*"

"Gear's coming down," echoed the front seat.

Chunks reached down by his left knee, and threw the landing gear handle to the down position. Both pilot and WSO breathed a sigh of relief as they heard the familiar clunk of the landing gear, and observed three green lights, indicating that all three gear were down and locked.

"*Step five. Put the hydraulic isolate switch to override for ten seconds.*"

"Hydraulic isolate switch is going to override."

Chunks moved his left hand back to the console by his left thigh, and found the hydraulic isolate switch. He flipped it to the 'override' position and held it there.

"*Step six. APU start.*"

"Starting the APU."

Chunks kept his left hand in the same locale, and kicked on the APU, which was an auxiliary power unit located in the belly of the F-18 used to start each engine.

"*Step seven. Put the engine crank switch to the right.*"

"Cranking the right engine."

"*Step eight. Recharge the APU accumulator.*"

"Recharging the APU accumulator."

Chunks already knew what to do. He immediately looked down by his right knee, and noted that the "APU Accum" caution light was on, meaning that the hydraulic pressure in the APU's accumulator was low. He waited for the caution light to go out, and then he held the hydraulic isolate switch to 'overrride' for ten seconds again.

"*Step nine. Flaps to half.*"

Chunks removed his left hand from the throttles once more, reached down by his left knee, and put the flap switch to the one half position. Then he made a mental note to not exceed seventeen degrees angle of attack.

"*Step ten. Make an arrested landing - *"

Fig's recital was abruptly interrupted.

"Flight controls, flight controls," Bitchin' Betty injected.

Suddenly, the aircraft yawed violently to the right and rolled left wing up.

"Chunks, you got it?" implored Fig from the rear cockpit, pinned against the canopy from the sudden forces.

"Beep............beep............beep."

Chunks countered the surprise yaw and roll with full left stick and a boot full of left rudder. There was no response as the crippled F-18D continued to yaw right, roll inverted, and pitch nose down.

"Beep...beep.....beep.....beep.....beep."

Chunks jammed the ICS switch, yelling, "EJECT. EJECT. EJECT."

Simultaneously, Chunks and Fig both grabbed for the black and yellow ejection handle between their legs.

"Beeeeeeeeeeeeeeeeeeeeeeeeep."

From overhead at five thousand feet, Easy 31 witnessed their wingman's violent departure. Ghost instinctively keyed the mike on the throttle, screaming, "EJECT. EJECT. EJECT."

To Ghost and Frap, the following seconds were a surreal world where everything happened in slow motion. As they watched the aircraft violently roll inverted and pitch nose down - booooomp - there went the canopy from Easy 32's crippled Hornet.

"C'mon, Chunks, c'mon Fig. Get out."

Four tenths of a second after the canopy's departure - zoooosh – Fig's rear seat shot from the jet.

"Alright," yelled Frap.

The rocket-propelled seat blew from the rear of the plummeting Hornet, trailing white smoke in a spiral corkscrew. A tiny drogue parachute from the top of Fig's head box pulled out a larger, white and orange parachute that blossomed in the wind. The opening shock of the parachute ripped Fig's body out of the seat, which then tumbled end-over-end into the ocean. Fig barely got one swing in the parachute before violently smacking the water.

From overhead, Ghost and Frap knew that the pilot's seat would follow a mere four tenths of a second later.

"C'mon, Chunks. Get out."

Only four tenths of a second to go before the front seat would follow.

"C'mon, Chunks, c'mon."

He only needed four tenths of a second.

"C'mon, Chunks."

The aircraft impacted the water.

In a stunned silence from above, Ghost and Frap watched as the jet shattered and the ocean swallowed the F-18's tail pipes.

"Stay calm. Stay focused. Compartmentalize. Prioritize," Ghost told himself, his hands shaking on the stick and throttle.

Easy 31 began a climbing right hand turn over Fig's parachute in the water and the orange dye from his sea marker. With the emergency beacon from Fig's seat pinging in their ears, Ghost and Frap assumed the role of search and rescue on-scene commander.

Ghost changed the number two radio to the international emergency frequency, praying to God that Fig was safely in his raft, with survival radio in hand.

"Fig, you up?" Ghost asked.

There was no response.

"Fig, you up?"

Again, there was no response.

Ghost bit his lip and exhaled.

"Approach control, Easy 31."

"Easy 31, this is approach control, I've lost Easy 32 on radar."

"Mayday, mayday," alerted Ghost. "Easy 32 is down in the water. Launch the search and rescue bird ASAP."

* * *

Un - fuckin' – believable

Tinsel Town's best writers couldn't come up with some of the shit that I've seen.

1420 Thursday
Out in the Ville, Corner of Bruno and Delgado Streets
"Stick with me, Babe."

Angela Giancarlo had just stepped out of her obstetrician's office onto the shaded, cobblestone street. It had been a long wait in the doctor's office - punctuated by a mysterious, unexplained chill around 1:20 - but she had finally gotten the news. Now her head was spinning. She was pregnant

At first, Angela was scared. What would her parents say? Having been raised in a strict Catholic household as the youngest of seven, premarital sex was an unforgivable sin. Yet, at the same time, her parents absolutely adored the dashing young Marine pilot that she had met at a downtown café. Surely they would understand, and be happy for the two of them. Besides, she had remained a virgin for twenty-seven years, so certainly the Pope and God would have some compassion.

Then her religious fears turned to ecstasy. She was in love, and carrying his child. She joyfully skipped down the street, thinking of all that they had said and done in their short time together.

They had talked of marriage. Bill had always told her "Stick with me, Babe." He had promised to take her back to the states, and get a real job with the airlines. They would have a boy and a girl, and live forever in a huge, suburban house with a fireplace and a finished basement and a two-car garage. One of their vehicles would be a classic, soccer mom SUV. Yes, she was happy. She couldn't wait to tell Chunks.

* * *

The theme from M*A*S*H said that suicide was painless.

What does it take to make a man just quit? How much can a despairing man take before he finally just throws in the towel? If you want to strike at the very heart of a fighter pilot, then tell him that there's something wrong with his balls.

1532 Thursday
On the Sidewalk to The Air Force Showers
"I've been dealt an unfair blow..."

Ping checked his watch again. Damn. Word was just passed that the Commanding Officer wanted all of the Officers in the Ready Room at 1600.

What for? Ping thought. *We were just there this morning for the General.*

Ping had just enough time to catch a quick shower, but the Marine Corps showers weren't open for another three and a half hours. No sweat. Ping decided to sneak over to the Air Force showers. He grabbed his towel and shower kit, shoving them into his black backpack, and bolted out of his tent. He would have to hurry.

It was a gorgeous Italian summer day, and Ping sang Bruce Springsteen's "Thunder Road" as he strolled down the sidewalk. That was Ping's song.

As he passed the laundry tent, he suddenly heard loud expletives with a New Jersey accent coming from within. Ping laughed, peeking inside to see Joisey pounding his fist on a washer.

"Joisey, what's the matter?"

"This damn washing machine just quit working right in the middle of the cycle," explained Joisey. "All my clothes are in it."

"Hey, Joisey, you don't have time to do laundry anyway," returned Ping. "Didn't you hear? The Skipper wants to see all the Officers at 1600 in the Ready Room."

"Yeah, yeah, I know," answered Joisey, kicking the washer. "You piece of shit."

Ping just withdrew from the laundry tent, shaking his head. On his way out, he noticed the two, missing, twenty pound dumbbells on the floor of the laundry tent, holding down a corner. Ping was under too much of a time crunch to get pissed, so he continued on his way. He could still hear the cursing when he got to the end of the sidewalk and turned right to enter Air Force country. Still singing "Thunder Road", nothing was going to ruin Ping's Thursday.

As Ping turned right on the sidewalk, Dick the Dog and Screw the Pooch suddenly came running to greet him. They were both yelping and bouncing about, with an exaggerated energy that Ping had never before seen.

"What's the matter, you guys?" asked Ping, scratching them both. Ping was second only to Booger in his love for dogs.

They continued to frantically yelp and jump.

Ooooo, this is like an episode of "Lassie", thought Ping.

"What's the matter, boys?" he joked. "Has Timmy fallen into the well?"

Ping continued down the sidewalk to the Air Force shower tent, with Dick and Screw leading the way.

"Take me to Timmy, boys."

Ping stopped and lifted the flap to the Air Force shower tent. Dick and Screw halted in their tracks, and looked up at Ping. He stooped over to enter, but halted because a chair was in his path, lying on its side.

That's weird, thought Ping. *What's a chair doing in the Air Force showers?*

He kept his head down to avoid tripping over the obstacle, and pushed the chair to the side with his free hand. When he raised his head and stood erect to continue into the shower tent, Ping instantly froze.

"Oh my God. No, God, no, please, no," he frantically cried.

Before him was Booger's limp body, hanging from an overhead bar. There was a simple, hand written poem pinned to his chest.

In this crazy, hectic world,
it matters not if you're a star.
A mansion is for naught,
So is your type of car.

Despite what many men may think,
A million dollars in a pile
Cannot surpass the simple joy,
In a tiny child's smile.

I've been dealt an unfair blow.
I have no more to give.
If I can't be a daddy,
Then I don't want to live.

* * *

Simply 1604

As the Officers slowly filed their way into the Ready Room, the Commanding Officer sat at the duty desk. He had his arms folded across his chest and his feet propped upon the desk. With his body language portraying no sense of urgency or tension or anger, the Skipper merely looked pensive and reflective. He sipped coffee from a porcelain mug that bore the brown stains of twenty-two years in the Marine Corps.

"Buick, let me know when everybody is here."

"Yes, Sir," replied Buick, positioning himself near the door. He began counting the bodies as they meandered into the Ready Room.

Joisey entered, wearing a wet flight suit, and reliving this morning's SAM shot and ordnance delivery with FOD. Dago walked in still massaging the welts on his back from yesterday morning's towel assault. Ninja strode in, singing along with the Smashing Pumpkins in his headphones. Tuna strutted in like Tuna, and Bama followed shortly there after, looking for any missing members of his union. Screech and Butt Munch entered, still pleasantly stuffed from their Golf Shack lunch. Ham Fist and One Nut came through the door almost simultaneously, FNGs protecting each other to the very end. Hollywood turned his entrance into a production by stopping, glancing about the Ready Room, and primping his locks. Hick Boy stumbled over the door jam because he had his head down, reading *Appalachia Monthly*. Pope walked in, still laughing about Dago's shower incident, followed by Spine Ripper mumbling something to his psychotic self. Jock shuffled in alone with today's issue of *Stars-n-Stripes*, followed by Shitscreen with a letter from home. Shitscreen shut the door behind him.

"We got 'em?" the C.O. asked.

"Sir, by my math, we've got four people missing," answered Buick, who then turned his attention to a captive audience.

"Has anybody seen Booger and Ping?" asked Buick.

All of the boys from Easy merely shrugged and looked at each other, before Joisey spoke up in his damp flight suit.

"I saw Ping just a few minutes ago in the laundry tent. I think he was on his way to the Air Force showers," stated Joisey. "But I haven't seen Booger."

"Did Ping know the Skipper wanted to see the Officers at 1600?" inquired Buick.

"Yep," answered Joisey. "He was the one who told *me* about it."

Buick continued his interrogation.

"What about Chunks and Fig? Has anybody seen them?"

Again, Easy's aviators looked at each other with puzzled, unknowing expressions.

But in the last row, Ghost and Frap sat next to the Doc. They had been instructed to remain silent by the Commanding Officer, so they didn't want to draw attention to themselves. Ghost didn't want anyone to see that he had been crying, so he buried his forehead into his hands. Frap simply sat with the stare of a deer frozen in oncoming headlights. Doc tried to quietly comfort both of them with whispers and pats on the back. The problem is, Bama noticed. He turned around in his seat.

"Hey Ghost," said Bama.

Ghost merely looked up from his hunched position.

"Where is Easy 32?"

"Bama, that's enough," interrupted the C.O. "I will explain in a moment."

"Yes, Sir," stated Bama, spinning back around in his seat, while Ghost buried his head again.

Buick turned to the Skipper, and gave his informal report, stating, "Sir, everybody is here except Booger, Ping, Chunks, and Fig."

Buick awaited the Commanding Officer's response, not knowing if he was pissed or aggravated or what.

"Roger that, Buick," the Skipper said. "No matter."

"Roger that, Sir," intoned Buick, taking a seat in the front row.

The Skipper reached down and completely turned down the volume of the duty radio. Then, he reached below the aircraft status board, and pulled the phone jack out of the receptacle, declaring, "We certainly don't need that damn thing ringing."

He slowly stood up from the duty chair, groaning slightly, as forty three year old men are apt to do. Then he even went so far as to bend over and unplug the clock. The constant tick-tick-ticking that went unnoticed by every aviator - save the Skipper - was suddenly halted, and time for the boys from Easy was frozen at 1604. The C.O. took another sip of coffee, sighed, and shuffled to the front of the Ready Room. He faced his audience. The Skipper wrung his hands under SPEED IS LIFE, MORE IS BETTER. Easy Eddie still looked happy.

Once Ninja shut off his CD player, the Ready Room was totally silent. There was no muffled Smashing Pumpkins. You couldn't hear Tuna's gargantuan fighter pilot watch. Ghost muted his sniffles. There was no tick-tick-ticking.

"Gentlemen, I have two things that I have to tell you."

The Ready Room was utter silence.

"First, we lost a jet this afternoon."

There wasn't a sound. The boys from Easy were stunned.

"Easy 32 had a minor emergency on the tanker track, and subsequently crashed trying to make it to the divert airfield."

The Skipper's morbid announcement was followed by still more silence.

"A search and rescue helicopter picked up Fig, but he's got a broken back."

The Skipper paused to regain his composure. He exhaled.

"Chunks didn't make it out of the jet."

Every Easy Officer sat in a bewildered, speechless daze.

But for Bama, the stupor turned to bitter anger. That was such bullshit. For a pilot to have survived SAM shots and AAA and night vision goggles and Italian drivers, only to die from such a mundane thing as a tanking emergency, was bullshit.

Buick simply hung his head. How many was that now? Eight? Ten? Twelve? How many of his friends had died? Years ago, he quit counting the number who had violated the most basic rule of aviator math – their total number of take-offs was one more than their total number of landings.

Pope was dumbfounded. He realized that, if not but for the grace of God, that accidental death could just as easily have been him. However, at the same time, his faith in God faltered. How could a loving God have allowed such a thing to happen? Pope reached down to his left shin pocket, and felt the outline of his laminated card containing the prayer to Saint Jude. He also stroked the lump that was his rosary.

In a coldly morbid way, Tuna blamed Fig. Was he late in pulling the ejection handle? Damn Fig.

Hollywood was pissed. There was a great American like Chunks, and his life had been snuffed out like a candle. Yet all those shitheads from "Jerry Springer" would go on, living their sick, pathetic lives. They would get to marry and hear the laughter of their children, unlike Chunks, who so deserved the best of everything.

Joisey reminisced about the cross-country he had taken such a long time ago with a young First Lieutenant Chunks. He fought back the tears and bit his lip, remembering a drunken Chunks, passed out on the floor of a strip club. Man, those were the days.

Ham Fist and One Nut only looked at each other. This was the first death that they had ever experienced, so they didn't know how to act. Innocence and naiveté were the perfect traits for just such a condition, and ones to be dearly cherished and tightly held. That is, until the tragic events of life in the Marine Corps ripped them from your soul, and hardened you into a callous lump.

Dago only blessed himself in silence over and over and over. The constant rendering of the Sign of the Cross was the first outward expression of his Italian Catholicism that anyone had ever witnessed. It exposed a slight chink in the armor of his gruff exterior. He wished he could be with Katrina.

FOD started to cry. It wasn't so much for Chunks, as it was for Angela. FOD and Fig were the only other Officers who knew that she might be pregnant.

The Skipper continued, stating, "The Safety Department has taken care of all the necessary messages and paperwork. I've already called Chunks' next-of-kin."

The C.O. halted and sighed, almost sounding relieved to have the administrative bullshit out of the way so that he could get on to more important things.

"Gentlemen, the second thing that I have to tell you is that we have been authorized to conduct offensive operations by the Commanding General of the Allied Tactical Air Force."

Easy's aviators sat in a stunned silence.

"Earlier this afternoon, Easy 55, Joisey and Dago, and Easy 56, FOD and Ninja, were cleared to drop ordnance on three Russian T-62s."

Joisey sat up erect and tall, so that every one could see him, while Dago showed some compassion, thinking of poor old Yeti, sleeping in the mud. FOD thought of his home and family in beautiful San Francisco, and Ninja wondered if the escalated conflict would have an effect on Soul Asylum's world tour.

"Those tanks had just fired upon our Marine Corps brethren in the First Battalion, Third Marine Regiment," explained the Skipper.

That's why we're here, thought Buick. *Not to shoot down Migs.*

"The President has authorized offensive operations," continued Easy's C.O., "thus, we are currently waiting to be assigned tomorrow's missions from the CAOC."

"It's finally here," muttered Bama, "my once-in-a-lifetime chance to bag a Mig."

"So with the tragic loss of Chunks' life, the injury to Fig, and Easy being on the tip-of-the-spear," stated the Skipper, his voice cracking, "I just want to take a moment and tell you guys what I honestly think of you, and what I expect from you."

Shitscreen looked down at his boots as tears welled up in his eyes. For his entire military career, he had been wrongly perceived to be a turd by the Marine Corps; consequently, he had been prosecuted as such. All his life he had been told he was a screw-up. Maybe on this one day, the Skipper would convince him otherwise.

"To start with," philosophized the C.O., "I love you guys. People back in the real world are so ignorant of the United States Marine Corps, let alone an F-18D fighter squadron. They have no concept of what we do, or what our lives are like."

The Skipper momentarily halted to regain his composure.

"I was once sitting at a bar, and the bartender asked me what I did. I simply told him that I was in the Marine Corps, to which he replied, 'what? No tattoos?'"

The C.O. paused for effect, and let that ignorant bartender's question sink in.

"That was it. Tattoos. That was the extent of that bartender's knowledge of the United States Marine Corps."

The Skipper's eyes panned across the Ready Room.

"One other time, when I told someone that I was in the Marine Corps, that person asked me, 'so who did you *yell* at today?'"

Again, Easy's leader briefly halted.

"That was it. Yelling. His only impression of the United States Marine Corps was grown men yelling at each other."

Easy's Commanding Officer exhaled.

"Another time, a person asked me what my rank was. After telling him I was a Lieutenant Colonel, he asked, 'is that higher than a Sergeant?'"

The Commanding Officer paused.

"Ignorance – it was pure and simple ignorance. People back in the real world just don't know about the United States Marine Corps."

Hick Boy shuddered. He felt that truer words had never been spoken. Back in the Tennessee hills, Hick Boy was the country version of "the kid who made it off the block." He was a hero whenever he returned home, in much the same manner as Alvin York. However, Hick Boy was forever sentenced to silence. The only thing that his kin knew about him was that he flew a jet. They just wouldn't understand heat-seeking missiles and laser-guided bombs. Thus, Hick Boy never bothered to explain, leaving them blissfully uninformed.

"Yet despite America's ignorance, you guys never quit or give up. You guys, as F-18D aviators, are the epitome of Marine."

The Skipper temporarily ceased his speech, and let his gaze scan across the Ready Room once more. He confidently continued.

"Every day, I see you guys lay your life on the line for those same ignorant people. For a country in which an ex-football player can murder his former wife and walk away scot-free, you still maintain standards of personal integrity and honor. For a country gone soft with video games and "MTV", you still uphold standards of physical fitness and mental toughness. Despite it all, you never quit or give up. You, as F-18D pilots and WSOs, are the archetype of Marine."

In the last row of the Ready Room, Ghost buried his forehead further into the palms of his hands. Where were the men of honor and integrity?

A former pro running back and a General - men who were supposed to be revered as heroes, but instead, failed to live by the requisite standards. They get to live while a man like Chunks dies. Where was the justice?

The Skipper continued.

"I don't see how you pull off the transformation that I witness on a daily basis. I don't know what it is about that F-18D cockpit, but somehow it is responsible for a metamorphosis that cannot be explained."

The confused looks on the Skipper's audience belied the eagerness to hear where the C.O. was going now.

"You see, people back in the real world," explained the Skipper, "have a perception of F-18 aviators. To them, you are spoiled, undisciplined, pretty boys who only fly by day and hit the club by night. You are perceived - I repeat, *perceived* - to be slackers with no leadership ability or military bearing."

Again, the Skipper halted for effect.

"Yet, you take that same aviator, and put him into the cockpit of an F-18D, and he is transmogrified. He becomes the most self-disciplined, the most dedicated, and the hardest working individual on the face of the earth. He becomes the most demanding perfectionist, and the consummate professional."

Bama and Buick caught each other's eye.

"The only problem is that those people - our civilian friends in the real world - never see that. They only see you on the ground with your longer hair, sexy flight suit, dirty boots, and a beer in your hand. They don't see you in the cockpit. They don't live in our world. They never get to see the men that I do. You, as F-18D aircrew, are the prototype Marine."

The Commanding officer's transformation comment meant nothing to Bama, Tuna, Hollywood, Pope, Butt Munch, and Spine Ripper. They all had the Midas touch in everything that they had ever attempted in their lives. However, the comment rang true to Joisey, FOD, Ninja, Dago, Shitscreen, and Buick.

"Trust me, I know what you are enduring here in Tent City. The showers, the laundry, the food, the bathroom, the tents, the mail - the very lifestyle itself - I'm in it with you, brother, I'm in it with you."

Joisey and Dago exchanged glances.

"Furthermore, I realize what you've been tolerating in-country. The bad weather, the KC-135, Russian SAMs, Russian Migs, French FACs, AAA, the bullshit rules of engagement - the very no-fly operation itself - I'm flying it with you too, brother. I'm flying it with you too."

The C.O. halted to wipe something from the corner of his eye.

"Lastly, I understand what you are suffering as deployed Marine Officers and aviators. The loneliness and the boredom, the sexual tension and frustration, the low pay, the time away from your families and loved ones - the very existence itself - I've been there for twenty-two years. Yet you continue to put your head down and plow through it all. You, as F-18D pilots and WSOs, are the ideal Marine."

Jock removed his glasses, and raised his gaze from the floor. He stared at the Skipper. He couldn't help but feel guilty for his Tuesday night breakdown. Maybe he wasn't alone after all, in the temporary misery that the Marine Corps called a six-month deployment. If the C.O. could weather the storm, then certainly, Jock could too.

Spine Ripper was just the opposite. To him, with his kick-ass-and-take-names outlook on six-month deployments, all of the obstacles and adversities and bullshit just came with the turf. Most of the boys from Easy thought that he actually enjoyed the pain, suffering, and discomfort.

"Second to my love of you guys, is my love for the F-18D. If it is actually possible for a man to love a jet, then I can only hope and pray that you love the Hornet *half* as much as I do. For the past twelve years or so, I have placed the F-18 Hornet above everything else in my life. I absolutely live to snap those eight fittings around my body, and propel myself skyward. The F-18 is the best fighter in the world, Gentlemen, and don't ever forget it."

Bama and Tuna caught each other's eye. These two former F-18C pilots related more to the Skipper's love of the Hornet than any other "stick wigglers" in the Ready Room. Only the love of a jet could've forced them to do all those landings on the back of a pitching, tossing deck in the black darkness of a moonless night. Only the powerful love of the F-18 could've caused them to unwillingly accept orders to an F-18D squadron, as a chance to simply continue flying that machine.

"Now I have reached the pinnacle of success - Commanding Officer of a Marine Corps fighter squadron - but at what price? I no longer have a wife and family. I don't have the worldly possessions that my friends from school have. I don't have the stability and peace of a normal life."

The Commanding Officer scanned the Ready Room.

"But you know what I *do* have? I have you guys. And I have the F-18. And I wouldn't trade either of them for anything in the world."

In the second row, Screech and Butt Munch caught each other's eye. They too, absolutely lived to get airborne in the F-18D Hornet, but didn't want to pay the ultimate price like the Skipper. Though both were still single, they secretly longed for the love of a wife and a family and a normal lifestyle. With Screech bound for United, and Butt Munch headed for Delta, neither wanted to end up as a grizzled, old man, alone in the world, and standing in front of some other men, professing his love for a jet.

The Commanding Officer halted once more to wring his hands, then continued.

"Now with the escalation and subsequent clearance for offensive operations, I expect nothing less than perfection from the aviators in Easy. This is the big dance, gentlemen, but we have always trained like we intended to fight. We are ready."

There was a knock at the Ready Room door, which the Skipper ignored.

"I want all of you to call your family tonight and tell them that you love them. Then get a good night's sleep."

The knocking on the Ready Room door persisted, which visually perturbed the Commanding Officer.

"I'll get it," said Buick, but the door opened as he started to arise from his seat.

It was an Air Force Military Policeman, followed by Ping, who looked like he had been crying. A junior Air Force MP followed in trail, but he remained outside on the sidewalk.

"That's him," whispered Ping to the senior MP, pointing to the Skipper.

"Sir, I'm Tech Sergeant Patrovski, Air Force Military Police."

"Yes, Tech Sergeant, how can I help you?" replied the C.O.

"Sir, can we have a word with you outside?"

Sensing the urgency, the Commanding Officer politely nodded.

"Stand by, gentlemen," he said to the Ready Room. "I'll be right back."

Ping stepped out onto the sidewalk first, followed by Tech Sergeant Patrovski. The Skipper followed in trail, and shut the Ready Room door behind him.

Immediately, the Ready Room erupted in a cacophony of primal exultations. For every war-mongering, chest-thumping proclamation, there was also an equally humble, pensive reflection.

"By God, I'm gonna get me a Mig."

"God, deliver us from this potential Hell," whispered Pope.

"That SA-2 can kiss his ass good-bye."

"Man, I hope that Yeti and his buds are ok."

"Another decision," said Ghost, "made by some Charlie Brown teacher."

"I guess I'm really in the shit now," reflected Jock.

The Ready Room door reopened, and the Skipper entered, leaving Ping and the two Air Force MPs outside. He purposefully strode to front and center, beneath SPEED IS LIFE, MORE IS BETTER., and faced the silenced crowd.

"Gentlemen, this meeting is over," he said. "I have an urgent matter to attend to back in Tent City."

1711 Thursday
Tent City Bathroom Building
"I've got a war to fight."

By now, the news of Booger had ripped through Tent City. Bama was again sitting in the exact same position where he had been only twenty-four hours before. Only this time, the bathroom building reflected the flashing lights of a nearby Air Force ambulance. Bama was pissed again.

WHAM.

"Damn it. How could Booger have done such a thing?"

WHAM.

"He's a quitter – a fuckin' quitter. He had no reason to do that."

WHAM.

"That fuckin' loser."

WHAM.

"Not only did he fuck his squadron, he fucked his country."

WHAM.

"He doesn't deserve to be called Marine."

WHAM.

Bama buried his head in his hands just like yesterday, and paused to breathe. Now, his *other* fist hurt, and Bama muttered, "Damn it."

Bama pulled up his flight suit, and stuffed his huge arms into the tiny sleeves. He zipped the front of his flight suit, and opened the stall door. Bama tromped to the door, but momentarily halted with his hand on the knob. He inhaled deeply, exhaled, and recollected his poise. Then he exited the bathroom and strutted onto the sidewalk.

"I've got a war to fight."

1719 Thursday
Tent City, Tent 08
"I've got a war to fight."

Dear Jenny,

You'll never guess what. I've got to ask you to save *this* letter, too. Honey, if this keeps up, we're going to have to get a bigger shoebox. Anyway, shit is happening fast over here, so I've got to keep this brief.

First of all, I'm no idiot. I realize that by the time this letter reaches you, the wives' network will have completely dissected what Booger did today. The rumor mill will be out of control, so let me begin by setting things straight.

Booger was a great American, and a superlative Marine Corps Officer. We will probably never know why he chose to end his life. There is any number of reasons. Perhaps the boys from Easy are partially to blame, for failing to notice the indicators.

Jenny, this lifestyle is stressful and tough. Men cope in different ways. I drink, Bama gets pissed, Ghost lifts weights, Pope prays, and Joisey masturbates. Whatever a man does, he can *still* only be pushed so far. Every man has his limits. When the stressor finally overcomes the man's coping mechanisms, a despairing man turns to hopeless measures. Booger wasn't a loser. Booger wasn't a quitter. He was just a man who failed to cope.

Secondly, I'm sure that, by now, the wives' network knows that the boys from Easy have been cleared for offensive operations. Most likely, we will be up most of tonight planning missions for tomorrow. Babe, you may not hear much from me for the next few days, weeks, months – whatever – until this thing is resolved. But please don't worry about me. I'm flying in the best fighter in the world, with the best pilots in the world. Everything will be fine. I am confident that I will survive.

Lastly, Jenny, I just want to tell you that I love you. Mere words cannot express my heart's desire to be with you forever. Babe, you're my reason for living.

I'll try and write again tomorrow. Right now, I've got a war to fight.

Your big love cruiser could stand to get a lube job,

Buick

Friday

0718
Easy 53 and 54 on an in-country Air-to-Air Mission, Easy 21 on the Suppression of Enemy Air Defenses
"That one's for Booger, you asshole."

"Stonehenge 02, Easy 53," stated Bama, checking in with the AWACS.

"Easy 53, Stonehenge 02, has you loud and clear, go ahead."

"Stonehenge 02, Easy 53 is a flight of three fighters for your control. Presently complete with Texaco and at point Delta, inbound."

"Easy 53, Stonehenge copies, looking."

This is going to be a great day, thought Bama. *I can just feel it.*

Now that the damn KC-135 red-ass was behind them, it would be smooth sailing. Easy 53 was in the lead, with Bama having One Nut in his rear seat – Buick had achieved a political victory. Their wingman was Easy 54, with Hick Boy and Buick. They were heading in-country for an air-to-air mission under the control of Stonehenge 02, a British AWACS. Their playmates included Dover 11, two British Tornadoes.

This was going to be great. The only glitch in the morning so far had occurred with their two Easy playmates that were scheduled to provide the SEAD. Easy 21 consisted of Hollywood and Spine Ripper; however, Easy 22 had developed a hydraulic leak upon start-up. Thus, Easy 21 would be alone and unafraid

"Easy 53, Stonehenge 02 has you radar contact. Proceed inbound. Picture clean."

"Stonehenge 02, Easy 53, wilco," returned Bama.

Bama keyed the number two radio, jokingly stating, "Hick Boy, don't you just love a British accent?"

"Roger that, bloke," answered Hick Boy in a Cockney accent with a Tennessee twang. It was as bad as it was corny.

The fact that Bama had asked Hick Boy - and not Buick - about the British accent didn't bother Easy's overweight WSO. Conversations conducted between F-18s normally used the pilot's personal callsigns anyway. Furthermore, such conversations were usually pilot-to-pilot. However, Buick was unsure of what to make of the morning's events. Bama had not said a word to him through the brief. Had he forgotten the drunken incident on Tuesday night? Was he ignoring their confrontation from yesterday? Still, being the masters of compartmentalization, both Bama and Buick had left their squabble back at the airfield. An air-to-air mission was at hand.

Buick could tell by the radio communications that Bama was working everything in his jet – radar, radios, infrared display – everything. It was as if he was still flying in the F-18C. God only knew what he had told One Nut in their crew coordination brief. In any case, One Nut was now just sitting on his thumbs. What a waste of an asset.

Like clockwork, Easy 53 and 54, with Easy 21 oddly attached, had a very wide, right-to-right pass with Dover 11 and 12 as the two Tornadoes headed outbound to their own British L-1011 for gas. It was like the changing of the guard as Dover 11 passed the baton to Easy 53.

Upon going over land, Bama and Hick Boy assumed a perfect spread formation with Hick Boy on the left. At Point Delta, the flight of three F-18Ds split, with Hollywood and Spine Ripper proceeding to their SEAD station, and Easy 53 and 54 continuing on their combat air patrol. Sounding relaxed, Bama pimped AWACS, asking, "Stonehenge, Easy 53, picture?"

"Easy 53, Stonehenge, picture's clean."

Easy 53 and 54 turned forty-five degrees to the right and pointed their radars downrange into the anticipated threat sector. Just as Stonehenge had stated, Bama and Hick Boy were clean on their radars too. At a pre-briefed point, Easy 53 and 54 conducted a one hundred and eighty degree left turn to frigid, maintaining mutual support throughout the turn. Now with their tailpipes pointed towards the threat sector, they paid particular attention to Stonehenge.

"Easy 53, Stonehenge 02, picture still clean."

"Stonehenge, Easy 53, copy all."

That was comforting – yet disappointing – to hear. Bama wiggled his toes and relaxed his grip on the stick to get the blood flowing. In his back seat, One Nut took a quick swig of water, and then he returned his plastic water bottle back to the map case by his right hip. Hick Boy adjusted the throttles slightly to maintain the proper position on Easy 53. Buick selected the radar parameters that *he* liked to use, instead of employing the squadron's standard sets.

Moments later, Easy 53 and 54 completed the same left turn back to burn, with their radars sweeping the distant sky.

"Easy 53, Stonehenge," pimped the AWACS.

"Stonehenge, Easy 53, go."

"Easy 53, sources confirm, two Fulcrums airborne three minutes ago," alerted the AWACS. "However, Stonehenge is clean."

"Stonehenge, Easy 53, copy all."

The hair stood up on the back of Bama's neck. What perfect timing for two Mig-29s to get airborne. Easy 53 and 54 had just completed their left turn back to burn, towards the northeast, and they had their radars trained into the threat sector. There was absolutely no way they could possibly screw the pooch.

Bama was the only pilot in the squadron whose trigger finger itched more than Tuna's. Being the fiercely competitive rivals that Bama and Tuna were, the former Alabama football player now chuckled at a thought. For Bama to shoot down a Mig – let alone a Mig-29 – would be the ultimate triumph to shove up Tuna's ass. In Easy 53, Bama's fangs came out.

In Easy 54, it was a different story. Buick's state of mind was more of a controlled aggression, accepting the fact that his limited knowledge of the Mig-29 consisted of only playing the role for Air Force training flights. Buick thirsted for a beer, figuring that nothing would come of the two Mig-29s being airborne.

Hick Boy, on the other hand, was "book smart" on the Mig-29. He had immersed himself into anything and everything that he could read on the Fulcrum's capabilities and systems. His pilot skills were sharp, and he was definitely one of the squadron's young front-runners in line to pick up the next Top Gun quota. Shooting down a real Mig-29 would certainly enhance his resume'.

Lastly, there was One Nut. The squadron's FNG WSO, not yet tactically proficient, was the consummate team player. He decided to support Bama in whatever way he could, and if that meant being a mere piece of luggage, then so be it. Maybe his visual lookout would pick up the second Mig-29 in a dogfight - or even a third or a fourth Mig-29 for that matter - and save the day for Easy 53. He'd be a hero.

Meanwhile, twenty miles to the northwest, Easy 21 was drilling oval holes in the sky. Hollywood's mind drifted back and forth between the SEAD mission presently at hand, and his next production with

Shitscreen. Meanwhile, Spine Ripper aggressively manipulated the buttons and controls and knobs for the HARM missile system.

"Hey Hollywood."

"Yeah, Spine Ripper?"

"I'm seeing some SA-2 radar activity."

"Yeah, yeah, yeah, that's nice," droned Hollywood.

"Today could be the day that we nail Mr. SA-2."

"I'll tell you what," said Hollywood.

"What, man?"

"You take care of all that magic shit with the HARM from the back seat," instructed Hollywood, "and then just tell me when to shoot the damn thing."

"Roger that," said Spine Ripper, intently burying his head even further into the HARM display.

For the air-to-air players, Stonehenge was eerily silent, with no further updates on the Mig-29s. Easy 53 and 54 droned down range for what seemed like an eternity.

"Easy 53, clean."

"Easy 54, clean."

They reached the end of their track with no radar contacts.

"Shit. Shit. Shit," exclaimed Bama in Easy 53.

He hated to do it, but he turned the flight frigid, placing their tailpipes towards the threat sector again. Bama goosed his throttles, forcing Hick Boy to jockey his own throttles even more to maintain position. Buick and One Nut both expended a program of chaff to help cloak their aircraft to the Mig-29's radars.

"Stonehenge, Easy 53, picture?" asked Bama.

"Easy 53, Stonehenge, clean. But sources confirm bad guys airborne."

Shit. Shit. Shit, thought Bama again.

Then came the call from an excited AWACS, suddenly stating, "Easy 53, Stonehenge 02. Hostiles bearing zero four three, four one miles, two one thousand feet."

"Stonehenge, Easy 53, committing to your call."

A shiver ran up Bama's spine. This was better than the Sugar Bowl. This was better than Top Gun. This was better than sex. This was the shit, man. This was the cat's ass.

"Easy 53 flight, in-place left turn, go," commanded Bama.

"Easy 54," returned Hick Boy.

The in-place turn was executed flawlessly, turning the F-18Ds around one hundred and eighty degrees towards the last call from Stonehenge. Hick Boy and Buick were higher and on Bama's right side.

In each front cockpit, Bama and Hick Boy executed the procedures that they had only simulated a million times before. Their left arms locked out straight as they jammed the throttles forward into full afterburner.

SPEED IS LIFE, MORE IS BETTER.

They also punched the selective jettison button, discarding the external fuel tanks from beneath their jets, thus increasing their F-18D's maneuverability. Six fuel tanks tumbled end over end to the earth below. Lastly, they flipped the missile armament switch to the 'arm' position.

"Easy 53, Stonehenge. Hostiles bearing zero four five, four zero miles, two one thousand feet."

"Easy 53."

The two F-18Ds leveled their wings. Bama masterfully manipulated the radar's cursors, while One Nut's head was on a swivel, ensuring that they didn't get jumped from behind like yesterday. Hick Boy struggled to maintain position on Easy 53, while listening for any wisdom to come from Buick, who was running the radar. Bama won the race to find the Migs.

"Stonehenge, Easy 53, contact, zero four zero, three eight miles."

"Easy 53, Stonehenge. Those are your hostiles. CAOC passes cleared to fire."

"Stonehenge, Easy 53, copies cleared to fire."

"Easy 54 copies cleared to fire."

Holy shit, thought Bama. *We've been cleared to fire. This really is the shit.*

With a single Mig-29 now on his radar, Bama turned the flight thirty degrees to the right to obtain some offset. He frantically worked the radar's cursors in an attempt to find the second Mig-29. Hick Boy climbed another two thousand feet, just as the familiar blip suddenly appeared under Buick's radar cursors.

"Easy 53, 54 has contacts your call," calmly said Buick on the number two.

"Easy 54, 53 copies. Offset right, sweep left."

"Easy 54, offset right, sweep left," repeated Hick Boy.

Up until now, the radar work and communications between the two F-18Ds had been perfect. All Easy 53 and 54 had to do *now* was find each Mig-29, and lock their respective radars onto their briefed adversary. In Easy 53, Bama stared at the radar presentation, while in

Easy 54, Buick slightly adjusted his radar's search parameters. Bama and Buick demonstrated extraordinary patience and skill in manipulating the radar.

"Easy 53, 54 is locked right," said Buick

Damn, that Buick could work a radar. He had found the second Mig-29 and locked Easy 54's radar onto him. Seconds passed that seemed like an eternity.

"C'mon, baby," stated Bama, with a bead of sweat on his brow as he scanned the radar display. "Bingo."

Bama also found the second Mig-29, declaring, "Easy 54, 53 is locked left."

The tactical range was now down to twenty-seven miles, and the four adversaries were closing towards each other at twelve hundred knots. One Nut was ensuring that the flight's six o'clock was clear, and Buick expended more chaff. Hick Boy was constantly trying to gain a more offensive position, and another drop of sweat fell from Bama's brow. This vector was the whole reason why he had cut the fingertips off of his flight gloves – so that he could have that extra sensitive feel of direct skin contact on the radar controls, the stick, and the trigger.

"Boop"

"Easy 54 is barbed, eleven o'clock," stated Hick Boy.

Damn, thought Bama. *The Mig-29s have Hick Boy on their radar.*

"Easy 53, nothing," returned Bama, getting no such indications in his own jet.

It's hero time, Bama thought. *They don't have me.*

Then the surprise call came from Stonehenge that nobody expected.

"Easy 53, Stonehenge shows the hostiles maneuvering at two five miles."

Amongst Easy flight, three out of four heads immediately affixed their gaze upon the radar display. Only One Nut kept his head out of the cockpit, scanning the skies for the unseen Mig-29 that could possibly swoop down upon them. Bama, Hick Boy, and Buick simply *had* to confirm what the British AWACS had just told them.

"Shit. Shit. Shit," screamed Bama, as he pounded his left fist on the canopy.

True to Stonehenge's call, each Mig-29 had executed a one hundred and eighty degree turn, and was now rapidly descending towards the earth. They were running away. Bama saw his name on the Mig killer plaque at Top Gun quickly fading away.

"You bastards."

Bama instinctively matched his right hand with his left, jamming the stick full forward and screaming his Hornet towards the earth, gaining airspeed. He refused to let this once-in-a-lifetime chance slip away. Hick Boy did the same, having more altitude to play with than Bama, in his trade for airspeed. Both of the Easy radars had followed the Mig-29s through their maneuver. Now the boys from Easy were faced with the Fulcrums having full tail aspect and opening airspeed on the pursuing Hornets. The Mig-29s were more than just running away – they were making good on their escape.

"Boop."

The tone caught Bama by surprise, and he had a momentary brain fart. Bama had to stop and question himself, while his F-18D continued to scream down range at over five hundred knots. That was not good.

How can a radar have me targeted when the Mig-29s were tail-on and thirty miles in front of me? Bama thought.

He was confused. However, it wasn't a *Mig-29* radar that had targeted Easy 53.

Meanwhile, a few miles to the northwest, Spine Ripper screamed into the ICS, stating, "Hollywood, shoot, man. SHOOT."

Instinctively trusting his WSO, Hollywood immediately fired a HARM missile, sending a smoking fence post toward the SA-2 site that had just targeted Bama.

Still unclear of the present indications in his cockpit, Bama made the appropriate radio call to inform his wingman anyway.

"Easy 53 is barbed at eight o'clock."

Wait a minute. Eight o'clock? Buick thought in the other jet. *That doesn't make any sense.*

"Easy 54 is nothing," returned Hick Boy, for his jet was not receiving the same indications of being targeted.

"BAMA, BREAK LEFT. SAM AT LEFT EIGHT LOW," screamed One Nut into the ICS, simultaneously ejecting decoy expendables.

The Mig-29s had successfully dragged Easy 53 and 54 into a surface-to-air missile trap. Now Bama was in for the fight of his life against an SA-2.

Bama immediately executed a defensive break turn to the left in an effort to defeat the SAM, simultaneously spitting out more decoy expendables. As Easy 53 pulled down and to the left in a very nose low attitude, the SA-2's smoke trail adjusted its flight path down and to the north. That only meant one thing - the SA-2 had followed the Hornet through the break turn and was still pulling lead on Easy 53.

Previously, Hick Boy and Buick were higher and on the right of Bama and One Nut as they tried to catch the fleeing Mig-29s. Hick Boy had only brought his head into the cockpit momentarily to check his fuel, and then he looked back outside, when suddenly - Bama was gone. Easy 53 had maneuvered just when Hick Boy looked inside.

"Shit," panicked Hick Boy. "Where did he go?"

Hick Boy immediately began scanning around Easy 53's last observed position in the sky, when he noticed the white smoke trail climbing from the green vegetation below.

"Easy 54, 53 is defending to the north," Bama calmly stated over the number one.

That radio call told Hick Boy and Buick everything they needed to know, even though they presently didn't see Easy 53. First of all, Easy 53 was still alive. Thank God. Secondly, it meant that Bama's defensive break turn had been to the left, which helped Hick Boy and Buick to narrow their visual search. Hick Boy mentally projected the smoke trail's flight path ahead of its tip. Bingo. There was a very defensive Easy 53 in a nose low, left turn.

"Easy 53, 54 is visual," said Hick Boy.

Fleeing Mig-29s, be damned. Hick Boy had to rejoin his lead and get back into a position of mutual support. He executed a hard left turn and maintained his present altitude, with him and Buick keeping sight of Easy 53. God forbid they should suddenly see an explosion, followed by two parachutes.

Considering the duress of their present situation, none of the four Easy aviators noticed the white trail of smoke in the northwestern sky from Easy 21's HARM

"Easy 53, 54 is visual," reaffirmed Hick Boy.

"Easy 54, 53 is blind, still defensive," returned Bama, telling Hick Boy that he did not have sight of him. No shit. He had his hands full battling an SA-2.

Just seconds from impact, the SA-2 continued to fly its intercept course.

"Hang on, One Nut," Bama coolly stated over the ICS. "Here it comes."

"Four feet behind you," returned One Nut, indicating that there was little else that he could do.

"Three, two, one – here we go," said Bama.

Bama rolled their descending aircraft to the left, and placed the front of the smoke trail on their F-18D's lift vector, simultaneously pulling the stick back into his lap. Bama executed a flawless barrel roll around the front of the smoke trail, and the SA-2 attempted to follow him.

"Ugh . . . ugh . . . ugh," grunted One Nut. Some things never change.

One Nut continued to strain, and both aviators could now see the actual missile itself. Suddenly, the missile lagged off of its course and overshot the flight path of the defending Hornet. It couldn't hack the turn. The SA-2 exploded harmlessly behind Easy 53, but the concussion from the shock wave rattled the Hornet.

Meanwhile, now overhead Bama in a left turn, Hick Boy attempted to take charge of the faltering pair of Hornets.

"Boop."

"Shit," said Hick Boy.

Damn, thought Buick.

The same SA-2 radar had now targeted Easy 54.

"Easy 53, 54 is barbed at right four," said Hick Boy.

Unbeknownst to Easy 53 and 54, the HARM from Hollywood and Spine Ripper suddenly impacted into the SA-2 site. Metal and Shrapnel spewed skyward with a reddish-orange ball of flame and debris.

"Boop."

The locked indications in Easy 54's cockpit disappeared, thanks to Hollywood and Spine Ripper.

"Easy 53, we ain't barbed anymore," stated Hick Boy. It may have been a poor radio transmission in the format department, but Bama and One Nut still got the idea.

There is a God, thought Buick.

"Easy 53, 54 shows clear to the southwest," said Hick Boy.

Without even questioning Hick Boy's radio call that it was safe to escape to the southwest, Bama selected afterburner, jammed the stick full forward, and ran for his life. Overhead, Hick Boy quickly traded his altitude for airspeed, and was instantly back in formation on Bama's right side. It was definitely time to go home, with both jets approaching bingo fuel, and Easy 53 out of decoy expendables. Both F-18Ds pushed the nose forward, achieving mach airspeeds. In the back seats, Buick and One Nut strained to check their six o'clock positions.

"Easy 53, Stonehenge," called AWACS.

"Stonehenge, Easy 53, go ahead."

"Easy 53, THREAT, zero five zero, *two zero* miles."

Shit, thought Bama, realizing what the Mig-29s had done.

Those bastards, thought Buick, knowing the same.

Assholes, thought Hick Boy.

What does that mean? One Nut questioned.

When Easy 53 had executed his defensive break turn against the SA-2, the escaping Mig-29s had done a one hundred and eighty degree turn back to the southwest. They were *now* in hot pursuit of the fleeing Hornets. The tables had been reversed.

SPEED IS LIFE, MORE IS BETTER.

"Easy 53, Stonehenge, threat, now zero five zero, *one eight* miles."

"Stonehenge, Easy 53 copies," replied Bama, realizing that the Mig-29s were gaining on them.

Buick was practically turned all the way around in the rear seat, and he expended what little chaff Easy 54 had left. In Easy 53, One Nut was also executing the same gymnastics, and hitting the expendable switch, even though nothing was coming out. In the front seat of both jets, the pilots selected the appropriate radar parameters to clear the airspace before them as they ran to the southwest. The pilots also executed a pre-briefed lookout doctrine to ensure their survival, and were whipping the ponies as best they could

"Easy 53, Stonehenge, threat, now zero five zero, *one six* miles."

The Mig-29s were still gaining.

"Stonehenge, Easy 53 copies."

"Boop."

Hick Boy and Buick heard the tone that they didn't want to hear.

"Easy 53, 54 is barbed at six o'clock," fretted Hick Boy, realizing that the Mig-29's now had him on radar.

"Easy 53, nothing," returned Bama.

He had spoken too soon.

"Boop."

"Shit," said Bama. "Easy 54, 53 is now barbed, six o'clock."

Damn. The Mig-29s had both Hornets and were rapidly closing. One Nut and Buick continued to contort themselves in the back seat in an attempt to visually find the Mig-29s. Bama and Hick Boy tried to shove the throttles through the cockpit's front console. Then came the unthinkable.

"Engine left, engine left," bitched Betty in Easy 54.

"Shit," yelled Buick on the ICS, without bringing his head into the cockpit to check the displays. "Betty, not NOW."

Hick Boy executed the immediate action procedure, *Throttle affected engine – Idle*, which caused Easy 53 to spit out in front. No longer mutually supportive, Easy 54 began falling behind 53. Having one engine at idle was no place to be with Mig-29s in hot pursuit.

"Bama, Hick Boy," said the struggling pilot of Easy 54 on the number two radio. His voice was an octave higher.

"Hick Boy, Bama, go."

"I've got a problem with my left engine. Standby. I'm working it."

Bama instinctively retarded both of his throttles ever so slightly. He couldn't leave Hick Boy behind. But the huge difference in throttle positions between the two Hornets continued to drive Bama further in front.

"Easy 53, Stonehenge, threat, now zero five zero, *one two* miles."

"Stonehenge, Easy 53 copies."

Bama was straining to look over his right shoulder and maintain visual contact with Hick Boy. Finally, he just couldn't take it anymore.

"Easy 54, 53 is comin' back around."

Bama shoved both of his throttles back into afterburner, and executed a one hundred and eighty degree, right turn towards Hick Boy's position.

"Hick Boy, I'm tally two at six o'clock," stated Buick on the ICS, visually spying the Migs at ten miles. Damn, Buick was one good WSO. Of course, the black smoke trails in the sky behind the two Mig-29s aided Buick's ability to find them. His WSO vision certainly wasn't *that* good.

"Easy 53, Stonehenge, threat, now zero five zero, *eight* miles."

"Easy 53, copies. Tally two smoke trails," returned Bama.

In his haste to turn the jet and talk to Stonehenge and find the Migs and keep sight of Hick Boy and *also* complete a million other tasks, Bama had neglected to change his radar's search parameters. Thank God for an FNG WSO seated four feet behind him.

"Good lock, on the nose, six miles. SHOOT. SHOOT," said One Nut.

Still not trusting his WSO, Bama brought his head into the cockpit to check both the radar and HUD displays. Precious seconds went screaming by.

"Shit," said Bama, "everything looks good."

Bama squeezed the trigger.

A Sparrow missile departed their F-18D from the right fuselage station and accelerated in front, sounding as if a freight train had just gone beneath them.

"Vwoooooosh."

Bama chuckled at how much the Sparrow *also* sounded like a Tent City toilet.

"One Nut, which one did you lock?" Bama frantically asked on the ICS.

Bama needed to know immediately, for it would drive his tactics to the Migs.

"The right."

Sure as shit, the Sparrow's white smoke trail was guiding towards the right black smoke trail. That Mig-29 was now was four miles away.

"Shit hot," said Bama, instinctively selecting his Sidewinder missile.

Meanwhile, Easy 53 had a wide left-to-left pass with the crippled Easy 54, as Hick Boy and Buick struggled to regain their left engine.

"One Nut, keep sight of Hick Boy for me."

"Gotcha, Bama."

Suddenly, the sky at Easy 53's one o'clock position exploded in a blazing orange fireball. There was no ejection or parachute observed.

"Stonehenge, splash one bad guy," stated Bama.

"Whoo whee dawgs," yelled Hick Boy in the front of Easy 54, pounding his fists on the canopy in glee.

"Shit hot," screamed Buick.

Bama jerked the stick slightly to the left to avoid the Mig's debris, and then quickly resumed his attack course for the other Mig-29. No sooner had he done so, his cockpit indicated that the second Mig-29 was within shot parameters.

"Fox two," Bama declared over the number one radio as he squeezed the trigger.

"Vwoooooosh."

A Sidewinder departed Easy 54's left wing tip and cork-screwed towards the second black smoke trail.

"Fox two again," said Bama, squeezing the trigger once more.

"Vwooooosh."

A second Sidewinder departed the right wing tip.

"*That* one's for Booger, you asshole," he said to himself.

Seconds later, the sky at Easy 53's left eleven o'clock position erupted in a conflagration of fire and smoke. Again, no ejection seat or parachute was observed.

"Stonehenge, splash the second."

"Yeehah," whooped Hick Boy, still nursing his left engine.

Easy 53's second Sidewinder harmlessly guided onto the first explosion, and then flew into the fireball for good measure.

"One Nut, where's Easy 54?" asked Bama on the ICS.

Without missing a beat, the young Lieutenant quickly replied, "Left eight o'clock, long, the speck above the bridge."

"Got 'im," Bama said, looking over his left shoulder. "Thanks One Nut."

Having found Easy 54 immediately, Bama whipped Easy 53 around in an aggressive one hundred and eighty turn to the left.

"Easy 54, 53 is visual at your six o'clock, three miles. Joining."

"Easy 53, 54 is looking," stated Hick Boy, straining as he looked over his left shoulder to find Bama.

Suddenly, a British accent other than AWACS pierced the number one radio, saying, "Stonehenge 02, Dover 11."

"Dover 11, Stonehenge 02, standby. I'm up to my ass with Easy 53 and 54."

"Stonehenge, Dover, we know. We've been listening since completing Texaco."

"Dover, Stonehenge copies. Stand by."

As Easy 53 joined his crippled partner on the left side, Bama passed the lead to Hick Boy so that he could safely handle the emergency. The poor pilot from Tennessee had been all assholes and elbows in trying to fly his disabled Hornet with Mig-29s in hot pursuit. After initially completing the immediate action procedures, both Hick Boy and Buick checked the left screen for any other warnings or cautions to be displayed. Sure as shit, there was the culprit – an "L OIL PR" caution. For some reason, the oil pressure of the left engine was out of limits. Buick quickly reached into his nav bag and retrieved the pocket checklist.

"I'm breaking out the book," he coolly stated over the ICS.

"Roger that," returned Hick Boy. "The immediate action step is complete. I've already got the left engine at idle."

"Copy," continued Buick. "The book says that if the caution stays on, *step two, throttle off the affected engine, if practical.*"

"Well, the caution is still on," said Hick Boy.

"Yep," concurred Buick.

"Hmmmm. Now let me think," joked Hick Boy, feeling a little safer. "We're still in-country, after getting chased by Mig-29s, and shot at by a SAM. I don't think that it would be too practical right now to shut down the left engine."

"I concur," chuckled Buick from the back seat.

"Bama, Hick Boy on the number two radio."

"Hick Boy, Bama, go ahead."

"Here's the skinny," explained Tennessee's finest. "We've got an 'L OIL PR' caution, and we've done all the appropriate procedures. The caution is still on, but we think it's best to not shut down the engine just yet."

"Concur," agreed Bama. "Good call."

"We'll rethink it once we get safely over the water."

"Easy 53 agrees."

"Bama, take me home," whimpered Hick Boy. "I've had enough for one day."

"Roger that, Hick Boy. Easy 53 has the lead on the left."

Bama momentarily relaxed in his seat and exhaled. Then he continued with the task at hand. There was no rest for the weary.

"Stonehenge 02, Easy 53."

"Easy 53, Stonehenge 02 has you loud and clear, go ahead."

"I understand that our relief, Dover 11, is presently on station," stated Bama. "Easy flight is out of here and going home."

"Stonehenge copies. Have a safe flight."

"Roger that. Thank you," returned Bama. "Easy 54, let's start climbing back up and put point Delta on the nose."

"Easy 54, wilco."

There was a moment of silence as all four members of Easy 53 and 54 breathed a sigh of relief. Meanwhile, the British Tornadoes assumed the same combat air patrol that Easy 53 and 54 had just vacated on their original commit to the Mig-29s.

"Easy 53, Dover 11."

"Dover 11, Easy 53, go ahead," returned an exhausted Bama.

"Well, it looks like you bloody Yanks pulled another one out of your ass, just like at Yorktown."

"Roger that," laughed Bama, "I'd rather be lucky than good."

"Concur, Easy 53. You have a safe flight home."

"Easy 53, wilco."

"Cheerio, bloke," said Hick Boy in the same bad Cockney accent with a Tennessee twang.

Buick just shook his head and laughed.

0813 Friday
Easy 53, 54, and 21 immediately after landing back at Base
SPEED IS LIFE, MORE IS BETTER.

"Ground Control, Easy 53," confidently stated One Nut.

Yes, that was *really* One Nut's voice on the radio - and not Bama's.

"Easy 53, Ground Control, go ahead."

"Ground Control, Easy 53, single F-18D, clear of the active runway, taxi to my line," declared One Nut. By God, he wasn't requesting permission to taxi; but instead, One Nut was *telling* Ground Control that he was going to taxi.

"Easy 53, Ground Control, you're cleared to taxi back to your line."

Having exited the runway, Bama and One Nut proceeded onto taxiway alpha, and then executed an immediate right turn onto the parallel taxiway that would take them back to Easy's parking ramp. Bama reached down by his right thigh and grabbed the handle that would open the canopy.

"Clear of the canopy?" Bama asked on the ICS.

It was a courtesy call from pilots to always ask the WSO if his hands and arms were clear of the canopy to avoid any possible injuries. This was the first time in Bama's three-year career of flying the F-18D that he had ever asked the WSO such a question.

"I'm clear of the canopy," returned One Nut.

Bama activated the handle by squeezing it backwards, and the canopy popped open and slowly buzzed upward. The breeze felt cool and refreshing upon their flight suits, which were soaked with sweat.

What an orgasm this is, thought Bama, *to be taxing back to the line with empty missile stations. I am going to shove this soooooo far up Tuna's ass.*

Bama smugly gazed ahead to Easy's parking ramp.

Is that people? Bama thought, squinting to get a better look at all of the activity.

Sure as shit, there were hundreds of military personnel – both Marine and Air Force - milling about the flight line. Furthermore, there were even some civilians.

"Hey One Nut," Bama stated on the ICS.

"Yeah, Bama?"

"Look's like we've got a welcoming committee."

"Why?"

"I guess word travels fast."

"Roger that."

"One Nut, call your folks as soon as you get in," added Bama. "You're a hero."

Then Bama just happened to look in the distance beyond Easy's ramp. He noticed a monstrous Air Force C-5 transport aircraft, with engines turning in the hold short area, awaiting clearance to take-off. Bama felt a lump in his throat. That was the C-5 taking Booger's flag-draped coffin to Ramstein, Germany. From there, it would make the follow-on trip across the pond to Dover Air Force Base and the real world.

Bama slipped into a momentary trance - then shook himself out of it.

"Hey One Nut," stated Bama on the ICS.

"Yeah, Bama."

"Remember to call base and let them know we're back," pimped Bama. His young WSO had forgotten to complete that transmission, but that was ok. He would learn, smiled Bama.

"Oh, shit. Good call, Bama."

One Nut mashed his right boot down on the foot pedal for the number two radio.

"Base, Easy 53."

"Easy 53, Base, go ahead," returned Screech, the duty officer manning the desk in the Ready Room. What a shitty place to be on the first day of hostilities.

"Easy 53, Bama and One Nut, safe on deck," stated One Nut. "Our jet is up."

"Roger, copy, up jet," mimicked Screech. The F-18D's 'up' status told Screech that there were no maintenance problems; consequently, the jet could be turned around and used again on today's flight schedule.

There was a brief silence, and then a different voice cut the base radio frequency, saying, "Easy 53, this is the Skipper."

One Nut froze in the back seat.

"Easy 53, I say again, this is the Skipper."

"Bama, what do I *say*?" panicked One Nut on the ICS.

"Just talk to him," laughed Bama.

"Sir….um….uh," fumbled One Nut.

Bama quickly pushed his left thumb down on the throttle's microphone switch, jumping onto the number two radio.

"Sir, this is Bama, sorry 'bout that."

"No problem, Bama," joked the Commanding Officer. "I guess that even young WSO war heroes aren't immune from the weight-on-seat switch."

"Roger that," laughed Bama.

"The CAOC tells us that you're taxiing back to the line with one less Sparrow and two less Sidewinders."

"Yes Sir," aggressively injected One Nut, eager to resume control of the radios. Normally, Bama would've castrated any WSO who pulled such a stunt, but Bama smiled.

"That's shit hot," applauded the Skipper.

"Thank you, Sir."

"Bama, Skipper."

"Yes, Sir?"

"Your Siamese twin, Tuna, will meet you at the jet with some important news."

"Roger that, Sir."

"Ok, then. I'll see you two in the Ready Room."

"Yes Sir."

Bama and One Nut continued to arrogantly taxi in silence, until One Nut keyed the ICS with a standard call to the pilot, stating, "I'm 'safe' and un-strapping in the rear."

One Nut had placed the handle that controlled his seat's ejection into the 'safe' position, making an ejection impossible. Then he commenced to unbuckle the eight harness attachments that strapped him into the rear seat.

"I'm 'safe' and un-strapping in the front," echoed Bama, meaning he had done the same as his WSO.

This is going to be cool, he thought. *Tuna has some news? What news?*

Bama silently pondered what it could possibly be.

"Ground Control, Easy 54," said Buick.

"Easy 54, Ground Control, go."

"Ground, Easy 54 is a single F-18, clear of the duty runway, taxi to my line."

"Easy 54, Ground Control, taxi to your line."

Hick Boy and Buick quickly rolled through taxiway alpha, then executed the same right turn onto the parallel taxiway to follow one thousand feet behind Easy 53.

With two experienced aviators in Easy 54, the crew coordination of their return process went much smoother.

"Buick, are you clear of the canopy?"

"I'm clear."

The canopy slowly cranked open.

"Ahhhh man, just feel that breeze," purred Hick Boy.

"Base, Easy 54," said Buick.

"Easy 54, Base, go ahead," mumbled an obviously frustrated Screech.

"Easy 54, Hick Boy and Bama, safe on deck, our jet is down."

"Down?" questioned Screech. "Why are you down?"

"Let's just say," sarcastically stated Buick, "that Bitchin' Betty gave us a Left Engine Caution at a very inopportune moment."

Hick Boy shook his head and grinned in the front seat.

"We'll tell you all about it in the Ready Room," continued Buick.

"Roger that," returned Screech. "Break, break. Maintenance? You copy? Easy 54's jet is down for a Left Engine Caution?"

The squadron's Maintenance Department monitored the same radio frequency that the aircraft used to contact the Duty Officers. Thus, the Gunny's voice immediately responded to Screech's interrogation.

"Sir, Maintenance copies. We're on it like stink on shit."

"The duty copies," returned Screech.

"Hick Boy, I'm 'safe' and un-strapped in the rear."

"Buick, I already beat you to it in the front."

"Roger that."

Once more in the Ready Room, Screech was forced to relinquish the duty desk radio to the Commanding Officer.

"Easy 54, this is the Skipper."

"Sir, go ahead," returned Buick.

"Congratulations you two. Nice job."

"Thank you, Sir."

"The safe and expeditious handling of that emergency under such dire straits is a testament to your aviation capabilities."

"Jeez, Skipper," laughed Buick, "with a golden tongue like that, I can see how you made Lieutenant Colonel."

"Put it in terms that a good ol' boy from Tennessee can handle," requested Hick Boy.

"You two kicked *ass*," returned the Commanding Officer. "I've got some Jack Daniels and a beer with your names on the bottles, right here in the Ready Room."

Hick Boy and Buick smiled at the thought.

"Ground Control, Easy 21," said Spine Ripper, trying to sound cool and laid back. He still sounded stiff and uptight.

"Easy 21, Ground Control."

"Ground, Easy 21, single Hornet, clear of the runway, taxi to my line."

"Easy 21, Ground, you're cleared to taxi as requested."

Hollywood followed in trail of Bama and Hick Boy, blowing through alpha and turning right on the parallel taxiway. In the rear cockpit, Spine Ripper removed his hands and arms from the canopy railing, and waited for the courtesy call from Hollywood. It didn't come. Spine Ripper waited a few more seconds. There was still no courtesy call.

"Hey Hollywood," he pimped on the ICS. "I'm clear of the canopy."

There was no answer.

"Hey Hollywood."

There was still no answer.

Spine Ripper leaned to his left in order to see around the huge, black head box on top of the pilot's front seat. He did so to check and see if

Hollywood was ok - and he couldn't believe what he saw. Hollywood was taxiing back to the line with no helmet.

"HEY HOLLYWOOD," screamed Spine Ripper, trying to overcome the thunderous whir of two jet engines beneath him. "PUT ON YOUR HELMET."

His showboat pilot must've heard him, for Spine Ripper grudgingly watched, peering around the head box, as Hollywood obliged him. Spine Ripper gave Hollywood a second or two to get all plugged in, and then he keyed the ICS, asking, "Hollywood, what are you doing?"

"What do you mean?"

"Why the hell are you taxiing without your helmet?"

"You never know," explained the pretty boy. "There might be some cameras awaiting our arrival."

Spine Ripper buried his helmeted forehead into both of his palms, shaking his head. Between Bama, Tuna, and Hollywood, he didn't know who had the biggest ego.

"Well how about popping the canopy open anyway?" asked Spine Ripper. "I'm hot back here."

"I don't want the breeze to mess up my hair."

Spine Ripper couldn't believe his ears. He was about to go totally Richter on Hollywood - in true Spine Ripper fashion - when the number two radio crackled.

"Easy 21, Base," stated Screech.

"Get that radio call," said Hollywood. "I'm taking my helmet off again."

"Aaaaauuugggghhh." screamed Spine Ripper, before complying with Hollywood's request.

"Easy 21, this is Base. How do you read?"

"Base, Easy 21, loud and clear, go ahead," replied Spine Ripper.

"Easy 21, Base. Say your status," requested Screech.

"Easy 21, safe on deck, our jet is up," said Spine Ripper.

Again, the Commanding Officer grabbed the microphone from the duty officer to congratulate his returning warriors.

"Easy 21, this is the Skipper."

"Go ahead, Sir."

"Who is this? Spine Ripper?"

"Yes, Sir."

"Congratulations, Spine Ripper," said the Commanding Officer. "The CAOC Intelligence folks tell me that a certain SA-2 site has been completely destroyed."

"It's all in a day's work, Sir," boasted Spine Ripper.

"Well, there's a crew here from "CNN" that wants to talk to the six of you."

"Roger that, Sir."

"I'll see you and Hollywood in the Ready Room, Spine Ripper."

"Yes Sir."

Hmmmmm, pondered Spine Ripper, scratching his chin. *A crew from "CNN" is in the Ready Room?*

Once again, Spine Ripper leaned to his left and peered around the pilot's head box. Hollywood's golden locks were perfectly in place. Spine Ripper removed his helmet, too.

By this time, Easy 53, Bama and One Nut, were parking back in the line. No sooner had both engines been shut down, then the throng of people raced across the tarmac to greet them. Tuna outraced everyone but Ham Fist to Easy 53. As usual, the WSO was first down the boarding ladder, and One Nut was immediately greeted with a slap on the back from Ham Fist.

"Congratulations, you *former* FNG, you," said Ham Fist.

"Thanks man,"

"Now that you've made the grade," continued Ham Fist, "I suppose that you'll be erecting a masterbatorium tonight, huh?"

"Nyah," replied One Nut, without missing a beat. "I want to stay in touch with my future rock star."

Tuna assumed a position next to the jet, immediately below the front cockpit. He reached up to take Bama's helmet bag as he handed it over the side. Then Bama wrestled his massive frame out of the front seat and down the boarding ladder.

"Hey asshole," greeted Tuna. "Nice job."

"Thanks, dickhead."

"It's not enough that you bag two – count 'em – *two* Migs on the same flight," stroked Tuna.

Bama laughed, inflating his chest.

"And it's not enough that those two Migs just happen to be brand, spankin' *new* Mig-29s," continued Tuna.

Bama grinned from ear to ear.

"But your dreams have come true," baited Tuna.

"Dreams? What dreams?"

"You've got orders to be an instructor at Top Gun."

Easy 54 slowly rolled to a stop at its designated parking spot, as Hick Boy eased off of the brakes. As usual for Tennessee's finest, the nose wheel tire was precisely on the painted marker. After the engines spun down to a complete stop, Buick threw his nav bag down to Pope, and

Hick Boy tossed his helmet bag over the side to Ghost. Buick jockeyed his overweight body down the boarding ladder, and then turned to get a hug from Pope. As soon as their bodies parted, Pope handed a beer and a cell phone to Buick.

"It's your wife," Pope stated.

Buick immediately took the phone and ducked under the left wing, kneeling by the landing gear, in an attempt to get away from the noise and people.

Ghost and FOD greeted Hick Boy's descent of the boarding ladder with a bottle of Jack Daniels.

"Congratulations, Hick Boy," smiled Ghost, "not bad for a coon-ass."

"Thanks, man," returned Hick Boy, after downing a gulp of whiskey.

"We heard about the Left Engine Caution," said FOD, "so tell us about it."

Hick Boy obliged FOD's request, but only after another swig.

"As soon as Betty bitched," he laughed, "I thought that we were goners."

Ghost and FOD put their arms around Hick Boy, and were all ears on the way back in to the Ready Room.

Meanwhile, Pope intentionally walked to the nose of the jet, so that he couldn't hear Buick's phone conversation under the wing. He didn't want to know. It was none of his business, but he certainly hoped for the best.

"Sure, Babe," whispered Buick, with a tear in his eye. "I'm so glad to hear that you're willing to make it work."

"I love you too, honey. Good bye."

Lastly, Easy 21 rolled into the line to its designated parking spot. Both aviators – sans helmets - smiled and waved to the horde of enthusiastic well-wishers that ran towards their jet. The first were Joisey and Dago, who had the misfortune to be in Easy 22 earlier that morning, and had developed the hydraulic leak. Dago didn't even wait for Spine Ripper to completely descend the boarding ladder. He grabbed the back of Spine Ripper's torso harness, and yanked him off of the ladder and down to the tarmac. Then he planted himself upon Spine Ripper's chest, seated upon his sternum and poking a finger into his face.

"You lucky bastard."

"Get off of me, you crazy Italian."

"You got your SA-2, you lucky bastard."

"Somebody, help me."

But the follow-on WSOs seized the perfect opportunity to celebrate with their successful back seat brother.

"Pile onnnnnnnn." yelled Ping, who immediately jumped on Dago's back.

Doc and Ninja joined Ping shortly thereafter, crushing Spine Ripper beneath six hundred pounds of WSOs and a Doctor. True to form to the very end, Spine Ripper failed to see the humor, groaning, "Get off of me, you assholes."

Meanwhile, Joisey greeted Hollywood as he stepped down from the ladder.

"Hollywood, man, this is like a solid gold guarantee to get you laid."

"Where are the cameras?" asked Hollywood, ignoring Joisey's comment.

"Cindy is going to totally bone your brains out."

"Where are the "CNN" cameras?"

"Cindy? Forget Cindy, man. Hell, now you can nail *any* broad you want."

"The Skipper said that there were "CNN" cameras," stated Hollywood, brushing Joisey aside and scanning the crowd. "Where *are* they?"

Amidst all the hoopla and celebrating and back-slapping, none of the Boys from Easy noticed the flashing siren of an Air Force MP van. It sped down Perimeter Road, transferring N.D. to the Naval Investigative Service.

Furthermore, not all of the Boys from Easy made the celebration that day on the tarmac. Because life goes on, Easy 71, Butt Munch and Shitscreen, with Easy 72, Jock and Frap, were dropping bombs at that very moment. Yeti had spent another night sleeping in the mud. In his hospital bed, Fig was completely sedated. Easy Eddie was fated to forever be silent in the Ready Room. And a lone C-5 lumbered down the runway on its way to Germany.

SPEED IS LIFE, MORE IS BETTER.

Epilogue

Yeah, I remember it like it was yesterday. I was a young WSO in the back seat of the F-18D Hornet for a Marine fighter squadron. We were sent overseas to Italy for six months in the mid '90s to enforce a NATO no-fly zone over Bosnia-Herzegovinia. Man, those were some days.

I don't know why, but I particularly remember that one-versus-one training hop on Monday afternoon. Maybe because that flight marked the beginning of a week in my life that I will never forget. Or maybe it's because that flight contained two of the greatest men that I have ever met in my life - Bama and Buick. They were shit hot.

You couldn't find two Marine Officers who were more opposite, yet still equally revered by those men whose lives they touched. Bama was a hulk of a man, a true physical specimen. In fact, he played offensive tackle for Bear Bryant. However, he shunned the NFL and decided to serve his country by becoming a Marine Corps fighter pilot. His only objective in life was to bag one of those mysterious new Russian fighters, the Mig-29, and then become an instructor at Top Gun. He used to lay awake at night and envision himself climbing those stairs to the Top Gun academic classrooms, and seeing his name on one of those Mig-killer plaques that adorned the wall.

Bama had graduated from Top Gun as a student the previous summer, and he was certainly eager to apply the latest air-to-air tactics that he had studied. Still fresh in his mind were the lessons learned over the Nevada desert against simulated Mig-29 Fulcrums. He had already practiced locking horns with the Soviet's best fighters and their advanced weaponry - now all he wanted was the payoff.

Buick was just the opposite. He was an overweight slob of a WSO who was an alcoholic. Or at least, it's *my* opinion that he couldn't handle his liquor. Some aviators might think otherwise. In any case, Buick was just a big, fat, loveable teddy bear who wouldn't hurt a flea. His only objective in Marine Corps aviation was to have fun. I think that other aviators ignored his drunken slovenliness for one reason. He was good -

damn good - in the back seat of that jet. He could work magic with that radar, and was always thinking one step ahead of the pilot. Or maybe he was just eager to end every flight so that he could land and have a beer.

The more experienced aviator of the two, Buick, had also graduated from Top Gun. However, he did so as a dinosaur in the F-4S, way back in the dark ages. There, he had practiced fighting against simulated Mig-21s and Mig-23s. With those aircraft now relegated to being the antiquated jets of most third world countries, Buick felt behind the power curve in his knowledge of tactics against newer Russian fighters like the Mig-29.

The funny thing is, those two icons never quite saw eye to eye on how best to employ the F-18D. Bama was a hard core, single-seat, "I fly alone - I die alone", fighter pilot. Buick was an old school, two-seat, "do it for the team", fighter WSO. Yeah, I guess that those two juggernauts were just destined to bump heads.

James A. Michener's classic novel, *The Bridges of Toko Ri*, about aircraft carriers and Navy pilots, contains a timeless line that I will never forget. Admiral Frederick March, exhausted from the Battle of Midway, mutters in sheer amazement, "where do we get such men?" Well, I'm here to tell Admiral March that the Naval aviators who launch themselves off of the pointy end of a carrier ain't got nothin' on the cast of characters - from shit hots to FNGs - that I met while flying Marine F-18Ds. Where do we get such men? Men like Bama and Buick? A more perplexing question has never been asked.

Thus, I used to ponder over a similar question that I suppose was a lot like the chicken or the egg thing. Did the kind of men who became Marine F-18 aviators do so because the job required a certain personality? Or did those crazy bastards already have a personality that seemed to migrate to Marine F-18 aviation? I tend to accept the latter. I refuse to believe that an IBM board meeting had the same crazies as a Marine F-18 squadron's all-Officer's-meeting. I refuse to believe that the coffee break banter at AT&T even remotely compared to any conversation that was held in a Marine F-18 squadron's Ready Room.

Marine F-18 aviators were just different, that's all. For starters, where else but in an F-18 squadron would fully grown men call each other by silly, childish callsigns? You could tell a lot about a Marine aviator just by hearing the label placed upon him by his fellow squadron mates. Without ever having met the man, just knowing his squadron moniker was the greatest insight into his personality, capabilities, and quirks - whether perceived or real. Branded for life - good or bad - a Marine aviator was his callsign.

Over the years, I heard some fantastic callsigns. Some were simply based upon where the aviator was from, with obvious examples being Tex or Buckeye or Bayou.

Other callsigns were an acronym for some type of a funny trait. These included SHOE - slowest human on earth, MOTO - master of the obvious, and NOAH - number one asshole.

The majority of callsigns were awarded based upon an aviator's looks, or physical attributes, and the best ones I've ever heard demonstrated just how jokingly cruel Marine aviators could be to each other. These included Mutant, Frog, Grinch, Kramer, Huge, Jason, Meat, Pig, Gumby, Big Bird, Mule, Stool, and Rodent.

Other aviators earned their callsign by doing a particular act in the jet. There was Assassin, shortened from the Comm Assassin, for the way in which he butchered radio communications. I knew a Tube, who once landed his F-4S too fast and too hard, thus blowing the tires and skidding off the side of the runway. Also, Hoover was on a low-level route in southern Nevada, using the most famous dam in the world as a turn point. However, the funniest all-time, performance-related callsign just had to be Speed Bump.

Lastly, other callsigns were creatively derived from an aviator's last name. I knew Tinker Toy, Cookie Crum, LC Greenwood, Popeye Doyle, Dorsal Finn, Wadd Holmes, Pinch Penny, Blue Jean, Rip Van Winkle, Buck Rogers, Loni Anderson, and Dire Strates, to name a few. The most ingenious callsign in this category was given to a guy with the last name of Lengyel - they called him Cunna.

Yet the laundry list of wackos and crazies that I just mentioned doesn't even hold a candle to the cast of characters and events that I remember from that one week in July. Sure, Bama and Buick were the cast's Oscar winners, but they had a supporting cast of unsung heroes that were equally as strong.

It's funny that I should compare those aviators to actors. Because the sad thing is, F-18 aviators were susceptible to the same type of up-n-down careers and emotional distress as singers and actors.

So every now and then, I'll be flipping through the remote, and I'll stumble across some kind of a "where are they now" special. You know the type - they're always about some "one-hit-wonder" singer from a rock band, or some "one-famous-line" actor from a sitcom. I would like to think that most people, after hearing my story about that week in July, would like to know what ever happened to so-and-so and what's-his-name. Sure, some of the Boys from Easy turned out to be one-hit-wonders, but for the most part, they all turned out ok.

"What the hell was THAT?"

Our Commanding Officer did just what he said he was going to do. He ran out the clock on the General's staff, and then retired from the Marine Corps. There was no reason for him to stay in. The General slammed him for Booger's suicide and Chunks' death. Once you had bad paperwork in your past, then you had no chance for promotion. Most civilians never understood that. To them, a letter of reprimand, and then still being allowed to retire at one's present rank, seemed like a slap on the wrist. But it was more than that. Forced retirement from the Marine Corps was more like a slap in the *face*. The organization that you had poured your youth into was bluntly stating that you had let them down. You were ostracized from the band of brothers. To most Marine Officers, that was worse than a knife in the heart.

But you know what? The skipper couldn't have given a rat's ass. He had lived a full, dream-come-true life as a Marine Corps aviator. He had accumulated over two thousand hours in the F-4, over three thousand hours in the F-18, and held command of an F-18D squadron. He was a Top Gun graduate, and had lived in such fun places as Florida and Hawaii and southern California.

Contrary to popular belief, there *were* some Officers in the Marine Corps who didn't aspire to wear stars. They merely desired to serve their country, fly, and have fun. Our Commanding Officer was just such a man. He became the president of a major college in the southeast, and lived happily ever after, just like a fairy tale.

* * *

Doc resigned his commission as a Lieutenant in the Navy, and opened his own practice in the real world as a gynecologist. Money was not the reason that he got out, nor was it the promise of a normal life with normal hours in a normal world. He didn't get out because of the second-rate facilities with which Navy medicine was forced to function, nor did he resign his commission because of sagging morale.

No, Doc got out because of the good-natured, but condescending, manner with which aviators treated him. For all the times that Doc got sick in the airplane, or didn't quite get the joke, or failed to fit in, I'm sure that he is *now* getting the last laugh. For all the times that Doc followed medical procedures by the book, thus grounding an aviator, and then received the squadron's cold shoulder for doing so, he is *now* doing the right thing - guilt free.

Years later, I asked Doc why he became an overworked, underpaid, and unappreciated Navy flight surgeon in the first place. Certainly, life as a doctor in the real world would've been far better than anything the Navy could offer in terms of money and lifestyle. Doc just looked me in the eyes and simply stated, "Because I wanted to serve my country." It was as simple as that, and I respected Doc for it. The Marine Corps could never function without the dedicated professionals of Navy Medicine.

* * *

Jock forsook the job with TWA that he constantly professed was his life's blood, and stayed in the Marine Corps for twenty-two years. He never became a squadron Commanding Officer, but he *did* become an Executive Officer. That's the number two man, which is still respectful in its own right. More importantly, Jock became deadly serious about fitness as a tool to combat depression. He placed himself on a disciplined regimen of lifting weights that eventually led his competing in the Mr. Atlantic Coast bodybuilding contest. He also wrote a book on overcoming depression.

Nobody else ever found out about the pathetic breakdown that Pope and Ghost witnessed on that Tuesday evening. Furthermore, Frap did as he was told and never exposed the airborne breakdown from Wednesday night. The Pilot's Protection Union really went out on a limb for Jock, because if he had failed to properly compartmentalize one day, and plowed an F-18D into the ground, then there would've been two deaths that would've haunted Pope, Ghost, and Frap forever.

* * *

Frap became a seagull - sad but true. A seagull is an aviator who, for whatever reason, one day becomes scared to fly. The standard joke is that you have to throw a rock at a seagull just to get him airborne. In any case, it's usually caused by a near fatal experience. With Frap, it happened during his second tour in the F-18D. While flying low over the Arizona desert, he and his pilot survived an ejection resulting from a bird strike. Frap actually came through the ejection without a scratch. You know what the funny thing was? He and his pilot walked about a mile from the crash site to a sheep farmer's house, and called the rescue helicopter's squadron with Frap's AT&T credit card.

But Frap was never the same after the ejection. The internal fire to fly and the aggression in the cockpit were gone. As corny as it may sound, he needed to get right back in the cockpit immediately after the ejection, just as if he had fallen off of a horse. But Frap chose not to do so. Thus, he rode out a twenty-year career in the Marine Corps bouncing from one desk to another, doing shitty little jobs related to aviation, and never seeing the F-18D again. I hated to see such a young, hard-charging WSO atrophy into a grounded desk jockey, but it happened. Maybe it was just as well. No aviator was more worthless in the jet than a Major or Lieutenant Colonel who was scared to fly. On a positive note, though, after Frap retired from the Marine Corps, I heard that he became the president of some union somewhere.

* * *

Butt Munch got out of the Marine Corps, sadly with a bad taste in his mouth. Butt Munch was just one of those quiet, unassuming, rock solid performers who became disillusioned with the Marine Corps. When aviators were FNGs, all of the older guys always said that Captain was the *best* rank in the Marine Corps - so enjoy it. But for young, shit hot, invincible, know-it-alls, those were meaningless words. Butt Munch was that way, for he simply loved being a Captain, where he had nothing better to do but be tactical in the jet and set his hair on fire.

Then he made Major, and his world came crashing down. He was suddenly thrust into the upper echelons of the Marine Corps, where he was now supposed to be responsible and serious. Butt Munch didn't like being the adult leadership, for he still wanted to be "one of the boys". He was a Major trapped in a Captain's body. At those upper echelons, he saw aviators who were formerly aggressive warriors now sadly relegated to some bigwig's staff, and making conservative decisions about things like safety awareness, risk management, and saving money. Butt Munch also saw the limited number of flying jobs that actually existed for Majors and Lieutenant Colonels, and he could find no reason to stay in.

Most importantly, Butt Munch wasn't willing to make the perceived personality change that was required to be a good Major. It used to be a running joke amongst the Captains and Lieutenants that a Marine Officer underwent three operations when he became a Major. He first had a lobotomy, removing his brain. Secondly, he had his spine removed. Lastly, he had a hinge installed on the back of his neck, so that his head could constantly nod up and down in agreement with his seniors. Not wanting to be a "hinge head", Butt Munch put in his letter of resignation, and became a high school teacher. There, he could stay young forever.

* * *

Screech was in the same category as Butt Munch - he just didn't want to become a Major. Thus, he got out of the Marine Corps and was hired by United Airlines. Again, the Marine Corps lost another solid performer. Screech went down in the annals of Marine Corps aviation history with the "speed of heat" stunt that he pulled on Doc.

Word on the street was that he kept the same sense of humor as a pilot for United. He wasn't one of those boring "look out the left and you'll see the Grand Canyon" kind of pilots, but instead he kept the crew and passengers in constant stitches with imaginative gags from take-off to landing. His all-time classic bit was the still-on-deck introduction of his crew, where he guaranteed a "very *interesting*" flight to his passengers. One, because the senior flight attendant was his ex-wife, and two, because the junior flight attendant was his twenty-two year old fiancé.

Screech continued to fly the Hornet with the Marine Corps reserves until he failed his annual flight physical when the Doc discovered prostate cancer on the finger wave. Screech beat the cancer, thanks to Doc's early detection, but he gave up the F-18 forever. Screech continued to fly for United Airlines, however, until retiring to become a flight instructor at Embry Riddle.

* * *

Hick Boy stayed in the Marine Corps for a career, assuming command of a squadron for his last eighteen months. Beneath that Tennessee boy exterior, boiled the acid ambition of a pure genius. Most men with such acid ambition end up destroying themselves, but Hick Boy was too intelligent to allow that to happen.

In reality, he was a far cry from the country bumpkin that resembled Woody from "Cheers". From his perspective behind the bar, he poured Jack Daniels, simply kept his mouth shut, and listened. It was in the unassuming roles of a shoulder-to-cry-on, a release-valve-to-vent-on, and a confidant-to-rely-upon, that Hick Boy learned about the Marine Corps' most valuable asset - its people. He listened and learned.

After retiring from the Marine Corps, Hick Boy returned to his home to serve the people that he loved - those from the eastern hills of the

Volunteer State - by representing them in the Tennessee House of Representatives. I'm sure that he was a laid back, common sense, man-of-reason during his legislative tenure, and a refreshing breath of fresh air in politics.

* * *

Then you had Fig. After he broke his back in the ejection, Doctors said he'd never walk again. Fig proved them wrong three years later by finishing the Marine Corps marathon. Running twenty-six miles is no small feat, but it pales in comparison with the *other* marathon that Fig annually completes. Every year, on the anniversary of their ejection, Fig visits Chunks' grave in Arlington National Cemetery. He cries a little, and just stares at Chunks' headstone, realizing what a difference four tenths of a second can make. To this day, he is tortured by the thought that Chunks might still be alive if his WSO had only pulled the ejection handle just tenths of a second earlier.

Fig also completes another annual marathon. On that same anniversary, he sends a single white rose to Angela. The lovely Miss Giancarlo, being the strong Catholic woman that she was, decided to keep Chunks' baby. She ended up having a strapping, nine pound boy, with Chunks' eyes, nose, and - unfortunately for Angela - his scrappy attention to detail. However, raising a child as a single mother in northern Italy labels you as damaged goods; consequently, Angela never got married again.

* * *

FOD got out of the Marine Corps for the simple reason that guys like him just weren't meant to be Marine Corps Officers. Aviators who read *Rolling Stone* magazine, play the guitar, and listen to alternative rock are destined to forever butt heads with the conservative machinery of the Eagle, Globe, and Anchor. FOD, after completing Naval flight school once to become an F-18D WSO, and then *again* three years later to become an F-18D pilot, simply left the Marine Corps feeling as if there was nothing left for him to accomplish.

Thus, he became a D. J. back in his native San Francisco. FOD was totally in his element as an alternative rock, on-air personality, because he felt that the Marine Corps had always had its thumb down on his creativity. Behind the microphone, he could finally be himself. With hair down to his shoulders, and surrounded by hundreds of CDs, FOD was in paradise. He did the mid-day shift from ten to two, which allowed him to cook the "electric lunch", an eclectic menu of alternative rock nuggets dredged up from the 1980s. Every day, FOD dined with DePeche Mode, U2, the Cure, and REM, while northern California brown-bagged it with him. The mid-day shift also allowed FOD to work out in the morning, and have a fantastic social life in the evening. FOD had a great life.

* * *

Years later, I found out that Ninja was partially blind in his left eye. Who would've ever guessed? Ninja was a good WSO, rock solid in the jet, and a damn fine Officer. When I heard how he slipped past his eye exam every year, I busted a gut laughing. He did so through some slick physical gymnastics that no Doc ever caught. When he was told to read the chart with his right eye, Ninja would raise his left hand and cover his left eye. Then, when told to read it again with his left eye, Ninja would drop his left hand and raise his right hand - but cover his left eye again. Pretty slick, huh?

In any case, Ninja got out of the Marine Corps and moved to Savannah, Georgia. There, he waited tables until he could gain admittance to the Savannah College of Art and Design. Nobody had a clue that Ninja was so talented. Once at SCAD, Ninja fit right into the arsty-fartsy, underground scene that was Savannah's nightlife. Like his pilot FOD, Ninja became a D. J. too, if only temporarily to work his way through school, playing alternative rock for coastal Georgia and South Carolina. The last I heard, Ninja was very happy as a graphic design instructor at his alma mater.

* * *

By the end of that six-month deployment, Ham Fist had honed his skills in aerial combat maneuvering to the point where he could at least remain neutral with Screech or Butt Munch. However, forget about Bama and Tuna, for they still continued to shoot the shit out of him. Upon our return to the real world, he continued to hit the books until he gradually forged his way to the front of the squadron's pack of hungry Captains. Ham Fist eventually got selected for a quota to attend Top Gun, and returned to the squadron to become the Pilot Training Officer.

Therein lied his greatest strength. As he took each new generation of Ham Fists under his wing - those who couldn't keep sight in a fight, or always failed to select the appropriate weapon, or never went over the top without departing the jet - he became a God to them. He had been there, done that, got the t-shirt. Ham Fist stayed in the Marine Corps to eventually become a squadron Commanding Officer.

* * *

One Nut didn't remain in constant lockstep with Ham Fist, his fellow FNG. Two years after that summer, the Marine Corps tried to give One Nut a FAC tour; after which, he would've returned to the F-18D cockpit for another three years. However, in a very nearsighted decision, One Nut opted for a civilian coat and tie instead of the infantry's camouflage utilities uniform. He resigned his commission, and went to work in the real world as a mechanical engineer.

A lot of junior officers were that way - unwilling to pay the price in the short term for a better life in the long term. Maybe those four aviators from the 0030 brief on Thursday morning - Bama, Shitscreen, Tuna, and Spine Ripper - were *right* about America's kids.

In any case, I ran into One Nut years later at a reunion while I was still in the Marine Corps. He was obviously doing well, and making money hand over fist at his engineering firm. He wore a slick, double-breasted Armani suit, and had the kind of Fabio hair that chicks dig.

However, it's funny how the grass is always greener on the other side of the fence. There I was, in my tattered jeans, tennis shoes, and favorite old sweater. I had no date, and was jealous of the suit and the hair and the gorgeous blonde hanging on his arm. I wanted to be in One Nut's shoes. However, there he was, making an admission to me that I will never forget. After he rattled off the laundry list of the impressive, materialistic, worldly things that he now owned, I confided how happy I was for him. He simply replied, "Yeah, but I'm not flying Hornets."

* * *

Tuna and his ego got out of the Marine Corps at the twelve-year mark, tired of living in Bama's shadow. Plus, the Marine Corps told him that his next assignment would be out of the cockpit. Plain and simple, the Marine Corps lost one of the best pure fighter pilots in the world.

Tuna became a pilot for some airline - I'm not sure which one - and proceeded to live the life that most men only see in their dreams. Married to a gorgeous woman like Lisa, living in southern California, driving his restored '69 Corvette, flying F-18s in the reserves, and skiing every weekend, Tuna had it all.

Over all my years in that green gun club, I saw a constant exodus of Tunas get out of the Marine Corps. No amount of money or medals or pay bonuses could keep them in, and it was sad. But I am happy for them. Obviously, Tuna is happy too, confident in that he made the right decision.

* * *

Spine Ripper got out of the Marine Corps too, and America's 911 Force lost another good man; albeit, one that was wound up just a little too tightly. Hopefully, his finally nailing that SA-2 on Friday lowered his blood pressure.

In any case, if Spine Ripper pursued his chosen civilian profession with *half* of the aggressive intensity with which he was a WSO, then I feel sorry for every thug and criminal and ne'er-do-well in southern California. You see, Spine Ripper became a lawyer in sunny Huntington Beach, just south of Los Angeles. But he was more than just a lawyer - he became a federal prosecutor. I pity every poor defense lawyer and the helpless bastard that he defended, for they faced off against a man who wasn't called Spine Ripper for nothing.

* * *

Hollywood got out of the Marine Corps to take a one-in-a-million shot at an acting career. There's a shocking news flash. However, he bounced around his namesake city, not as the stereotypical waiter, but as a writer for several sitcoms. Yet alas, Hollywood just wasn't really a comedy writer. In Italy, he just happened to click with Shitscreen, that's all. Furthermore, a captive audience attended their secret shows, and their comedy covered only military topics. Such material may have been hilarious at 0100 to Jarheads that were half-awake, but it didn't transition well to the real world. So Hollywood gave it up.

Tinsel town just never gave Hollywood the break that he labored so hard to obtain. Father time is a cruel parent, and Mother Nature shows no favorites. The cobalt blue eyes that cut through steel, and the dashing fighter pilot hair that never got messed up, gave way to farsighted cobalt peering through bifocals, and a creeping forehead that no producer wished to hire. Even the six-pack abs seceded to become a soft, white belly, so Hollywood returned to his first love. No, it wasn't Cindy. Being even more shallow and materialistic than Hollywood, she dumped his ass years before at the first sign of flab and a forehead.

Instead, Hollywood returned to aviation. He became a pilot for one of those companies that cater to plump, balding men having a mid-life crisis. Hollywood's company flew vintage World War One and World War Two fighters, and charged their customers thousands of dollars to fly them in mock dogfights.

In a way, that was probably Hollywood's destiny, for he was born about eighty years too late. He belonged in a Sopwith Camel, with a scarf fluttering around his neck, and one of those goofy leather caps with the goggles, all the while flashing a smile that glistened. I'll bet that flying biplanes *still* doesn't mess up his hair - what little that he has left.

* * *

God bless all of the Shitscreens in the world. Never in my life have I seen a man who simply didn't give a rat's ass about what the Marine Corps - or anybody else for that matter - thought of him. All he cared about was having fun. He didn't care about medals. He didn't care about ribbons. He didn't care about fitness reports. He honestly never read a single fitness report that was written on him during his entire stint in the Marine Corps. Save for one. As a First Lieutenant, a squadron Executive Officer wrote a fitness report on Shitscreen that was certainly less than flattering. In it, he mentioned the trait that Shitscreen didn't think was so obvious - he needed constant direction. Furthermore, the Executive Officer wrote that Shitscreen was talented, but unfocused. Shitscreen's career was fucked.

Most aviators would've gotten out after receiving such bad paper, but not Shitscreen. He absolutely loved flying, the other aviators, and the fun lifestyle. So he stayed in as long as he could, surprisingly making Lieutenant Colonel, until that fitness report caught up with him. Shitscreen never got command of a squadron, and it was a shame. If that had happened, the squadron's Captains would've loved him, the troops would've adored him, and his squadron would've been a total blast. Shitscreen retired from the Marine Corps and wrote children's books.

* * *

Joisey never did change his filthy, disgusting, horny, nasty way of life, and it was sad. He got out of the Marine Corps at the twelve-year mark as a Major, after being offered a three-year desk job at the Pentagon. Joisey turned it down, and returned back to his native New

Jersey to seek employment. It's just as well. Can you imagine Joisey in the Pentagon?

Once back in the Garden State, he bounced from job to job to job, tarnishing the hallowed image of Marine Corps Officers. He went through his third wife after developing a drinking problem, and burned his studio apartment to the ground when he fell asleep with a cigarette. Joisey never got involved with drugs - thank God - however, he *did* get busted for beating a prostitute. Maybe if just one of Easy's Officers, out of all those who simply shook their heads and laughed at Joisey's disgusting antics, had looked beneath the dirt and offered to help, then things might have been different.

* * *

Dago retired from the Marine Corps as a Major, and returned to Brooklyn to open a sports bar. Dago got passed over for Lieutenant Colonel on three different looks, which is something that I will never understand. I saw it so many times - an aviator who was one tactical dude *in* the jet failing to get promoted because he didn't complete some trivial, administrative requirement *outside* of the jet. So what was the big deal if Dago failed to complete his professional reading? So what if Dago was not politically correct? Who cares if Dago was a little rough around the edges? He was damn good in the jet.

However, failing promotion, Dago just punched the clock until he hit twenty years, and then pulled chocks to enter the real world. The last I heard, Dago's bar was really kicking ass, and did especially well for "Monday Night Football". Dago, the owner and proprietor, worked the bar himself every day from lunch until closing, and was happy as a pig in shit. I also heard the Joisey used to stop by for a cold one whenever he was in town.

* * *

Ghost went on to become a huge success in the United States Marine Corps. But then again, you knew he would excel at whatever profession he chose. It was ironic, too, because of all the Officers in Easy, I certainly didn't expect Ghost to become the Two Star General that he did.

It's hard to say what motivated him to pursue such a lofty rank, for he never mentioned such aspirations to anyone. During that summer, he simply detested the pomp and pageantry associated with wearing stars.

Personally, I can't picture Ghost in the super secret General's School. There was no way that they would *ever* teach him to frown or scowl, let alone play golf.

However, I *can* picture the squadron's former preacher of honor and integrity as the *different* kind of General that I heard he became. First, Ghost never picked up a golf club in his entire career. Instead, on any given day, he could hang with the biggest studs in the weight room, and most were *half* his age. Secondly, Ghost was not above telling his horde of lackeys to get their nose out of his ass and go find gainful employment elsewhere. Lastly, Ghost forsook the standard General's perk of having a personal driver. Instead, he drove himself everywhere he went. I don't know why.

Nil corborundum illigitime.

* * *

Pope probably pulled off the biggest surprise of any of the Boys from Easy. That is, it would only be considered a surprise unless you really knew Pope. He retired from the Marine Corps as a Lieutenant Colonel, and became a Catholic Priest. Transitioning from an F-18D WSO to a Catholic priest hardly seems like a logical progression. To go from a stereotypical jet jock, running around with his hair on fire, to a stereotypical Priest, running around trying to *avoid* the fire, just doesn't make sense to average men. However, Pope wasn't average, nor was he stereotypical - at either profession.

For as long as I knew Pope, he had always wanted to get married, and he was just as horny as the rest of us. Pope absolutely loved women, and he probably could've married any *one* of a parade of girlfriends through his life. However, he kept holding out and searching and waiting that someday he would meet the perfect Mrs. Pope - his Catholic, soul mate. But he just never did. Do you see the irony? In the end, it was Pope's rock solid Catholic faith that screwed him. You see, Pope didn't believe in divorce. He was committed to taking only one trip down that aisle. Consequently, in his quest for the perfect Catholic woman, he ended up alone.

But when you stop and think about it, going from jet jock to Catholic priest makes perfect sense. The qualities that make a good Marine Corps Officer - discipline, dedication, and devotion - are the same qualities that make a good Catholic Priest. When Pope retired from the Marine Corps, all he wanted to do was continue his life of service. He had just served his country for twenty years, and he simply looked around and asked himself how he could continue to serve his fellow man. Pope accepted the priesthood as God's will.

* * *

Good ol' Bama became the Top Gun Instructor that he always desired. He was probably happier there, as the lone Marine pilot on Top Gun's Navy staff, than he ever was in any squadron. Strapping on the F-18 and fighting every day was the ultimate ego trip. This adrenaline rush made him a self-perceived, all-American hero with wavy scarf and glistening teeth.

However, the glamorous Top Gun lifestyle turned out to have a dark underside. You see, for all those years when he was flying the single-seat F-18C, and then for three more years while he was enduring the two-seat F-18D, he constantly promised Linda that life would be better once he became a Top Gun instructor. He told her that the long workdays and constant deployments would be a thing of the past   So being the trooper that she was, Linda quietly hung on, and waited, and waited, and waited.

Once Bama finally did get to Top Gun, he ended up being deployed more than he was as an F-18 pilot. It took a terrible toll on his marriage. Thus, Bama decided to forsake the Hornet and get out of the Marine Corps for Linda. The last I heard, he was living happily ever after in Tuscaloosa, still married to Linda, and coaching high school football. I guess that he became an American hero after all.

* * *

The saddest story resulting from that summer just has to belong to Buick. To start with, the squadron's tactical guru in the back seat of the F-18D got passed over for Lieutenant Colonel. He just couldn't hide that gut in the full-length photograph that all Marines are required to submit to the promotion board. Despite a stellar record with glowing fitness reports and combat experience, Buick didn't make Lieutenant Colonel for the simple reason that he didn't look good in the Summer Service Charlie uniform. When Buick found out about his failure to get promoted, he went on one of his classic benders. Two hours later, Buick failed to negotiate a curve and plowed his car into a telephone pole.

Poor Jenny. Her decision to work things out with Buick only left her with a mortgage, three kids, and a folded flag.

Buick's funeral will go down in the annals of Marine Corps history as one of the most emotional ever. He was buried at Arlington on one of those rainy, gray, cloudy September days that make you feel pensive and lonely. Dago hired a cop friend of his from New York who played the bagpipes, and the Irish flatfoot solemnly played "Eternal Savior" on a knoll fifty yards away.

A properly played set of bagpipes will rip your heart out, let alone one playing "Eternal Savior" at a funeral in the rain. Consequently, you've never seen so many grown men cry. Meanwhile, everyone huddled in the cold around Buick's coffin under a cheap, tawdry cemetery tent. The pallbearers at Buick's funeral consisted of Tuna, Dago, Hick Boy, Ghost, Pope, Shitscreen - and Bama.

* * *

And then there was me. From the moment that I walked into that Air Force shower and found Booger's body, my life was never the same. I just didn't give a fuck anymore. I didn't want to be funny anymore. I got out of the Marine Corps.

For those of us who have lost a comrade and friend to suicide, it's difficult to comprehend the inconsistency of someone who is full of life, love, energy, and ambition, and at the same time besieged by bitterness, anger, depression, and low self-esteem. Such a phenomena really *can* coexist.

Years later, friends asked me how did I ever recall all of the details of that summer deployment, right down to the tiniest minutia of Dago's sweater, Hick Boy's towel, and Dick the dog. How was I able to remember masturbatoriums, the horizontal time accelerator, and Ho Hos? How could I possibly recollect trivia like Wednesday night tapes, the corn flakes rocks, and SPEED IS LIFE, MORE IS BETTER.?

Well, it wasn't so much my memory as it was some little red books. You see. I kept a diary. I realize that the term "journal" is a more masculine designation - real men don't keep diaries. However, I consider a journal to be something that was only kept for a short period of time, like on a trip or an adventure.

But that's *not* what I did. Instead, during my time in the Marine Corps, I kept a daily record in my diaries. In a tiny, four inch by eight inch, red, hardbound book with nothing but the current year embossed on the cover, I kept a daily archive of my emotions and feelings, triumphs and tragedies, victories and defeats.

Those little red books went *everywhere* with me, and I refused to go to sleep at night until I had written in my diary. Thus, I've written entries by flashlight in a tent in the California high desert. I've written entries by candlelight in a Quonset hut buried in the coastal, North Carolina pine forests. I've written entries flying at thirty thousand feet, driving eighty miles an hour, and sitting on the toilet.

These diaries became intensely personal. I completed my nightly ritual alone, sharing only the contents with my God. So you see, it was through no great memory that I reminisced about the summer of Easy. Thanks to some little red diaries, I remembered it all like it was yesterday, because I was Ping.

* * *

I suddenly awoke, and bolted upright in my bed.
"What the hell was THAT? Was it *all* a dream?"